MATHEMATICAL AND COMPUTATIONAL ANALYSIS OF NATURAL LANGUAGE

STUDIES IN FUNCTIONAL AND STRUCTURAL LINGUISTICS (SFSL)

Formerly

LINGUISTIC & LITERARY STUDIES IN EASTERN EUROPE (LLSEE)

The emphasis of this scholarly series is on recent developments in structural and functional linguistics practiced all over the world. It presents monographs and edited volumes on current empirical and theoretical issues, including the use of formal and computational methods.

Volume 45

Carlos Martín-Vide (ed.)

Mathematical and Computational Analysis of Natural Language. Selected papers from the 2nd International Conference on Mathematical Linguistics (ICML '96), Tarragona, 2-4 May 1996.

MATHEMATICAL AND COMPUTATIONAL ANALYSIS OF NATURAL LANGUAGE

SELECTED PAPERS FROM THE 2ND INTERNATIONAL CONFERENCE ON MATHEMATICAL LINGUISTICS, TARRAGONA (ICML '96), 2-4 MAY 1996

Edited by

CARLOS MARTÍN-VIDE
Rovira i Virgili University

JOHN BENJAMINS PUBLISHING COMPANY
AMSTERDAM/PHILADELPHIA

The paper used in this publication meets the minimum requirements of American National Standard for Information Sciences — Permanence of Paper for Printed Library Materials, ANSI Z39.48-1984.

Library of Congress Cataloging-in-Publication Data

International Conference on Mathematical Linguistics (2nd : 1996 : Tarragona, Spain)
Mathematical and computational analysis of natural language : selected papers from the 2nd International Conference on Mathematical Linguistics, Tarragona. 2-4 May 1996 / edited by Carlos Martín-Vide.
p. cm. -- (Studies in functional and structural linguistics; ISSN 0165-7712; v. 45)
Includes bibliographical references and indexes.
1. Mathematical linguistics--Congresses. I. Martín Vide, Carlos. II. Title. III. Series.
P138.I58 1998
410'.1'51--dc21 98-26169
ISBN 90 272 1554 5 (Eur.) / 1 55619 896 5 (US) (alk. paper) CIP

John Benjamins Publishing Co. • P.O.Box 75577 • 1070 AN Amsterdam • The Netherlands
John Benjamins North America • P.O.Box 27519 • Philadelphia, PA 19118 • USA

Foreword

This volume contains a selection of 24 papers (from a total of 43) presented at the II International Conference on Mathematical Linguistics (ICML'96), held in Tarragona, Spain, on May 2–4, 1996, and organized by the Research Group on Mathematical Linguistics and Language Engineering (GRLMC) of Rovira i Virgili University.

The meeting was funded by the Dirección General de Investigación Científica y Técnica (Spanish Government, grant n. CO94–0503), the Direcció General de Recerca (Catalan Autonomous Government, grant n. 1995AR-CS00100) and the Fundació Catalana per a la Recerca. It was attended by 54 people from 14 countries: Brazil, France, Germany, Italy, the Netherlands, Poland, Portugal, Romania, Russia, Spain, Turkey, the United Kingdom, the United States and the Ukraine.

The ICML'96 continues a series initiated by the ICML'93, from which a volume similar to this has been published (C. Martín–Vide, ed., *Current issues in mathematical linguistics.* North–Holland, Amsterdam, 1994).

The papers included here have been grouped into four sections according to their main content: Syntax, Semantics, Natural Language Processing, and Varia.

We hope this volume will reflect some current trends in the mathematical study of natural language and their applications or extensions. It will be of interest for people working in the broad intersection between linguistics and computer science.

In addition to our colleagues Rosa M. Hidalgo, M. Dolores Jiménez, Joan Miquel and Rosa M. Pérez, our assistants Lluís Fondevila and Gemma Bel deserve a special mention for having been capable of technically managing the process of publishing the book. We would also like to express our gratitude to John Bates, who checked the wording, to the editors of the series, who showed interest in the book, and to the technical staff of John Benjamins for their help.

Caldes de Montbui, May 1997

Table of Contents

Part II: Semantics

Part III: Natural Language Processing

Part IV: Varia

List of Contributors

Lourdes Aguilar Cuevas
Departament de Filologia Espanyola
Facultat de Lletres, Edifici B
Universitat Autònoma de Barcelona
08193 Bellaterra, Spain
lourdes@liceu.uab.es

Varol Akman
Department of Computer Engineering and Information Science
Faculty of Engineering
Bilkent University
Bilkent, Ankara 06533, Turkey
akman@cs.bilkent.edu.tr

Miguel Á. Alonso Pardo
Department of Computer Science
University of Corunna
Campus de Elviña s/n
15071 La Coruña, Spain
alonso@dc.fi.udc.es

J. Gabriel Amores
Universidad de Sevilla
Palos de la Frontera s/n
41004 Sevilla, Spain
gaby@fing.us.es

Jose Luis Caramés Casal
Facultad de Ciencias Matemáticas
Universidad Complutense de Madrid
Ciudad Universitaria, s/n
28040 Madrid, Spain

David Casacuberta Sevilla
Departament de Filosofia
Facultat de Lletres, Edifici B
Universitat Autònoma de Barcelona
08193 Bellaterra, Spain
david@liceu.uab.es

Jürgen Dassow
Fakultät für Informatik
Otto-von-Guericke-Universität Magdeburg
PF 4120
D-39016 Magdeburg, Germany
dassow@irb.cs.uni-magdeburg.de

Zygmunt Frajzyngier
Department of Linguistics
University of Colorado at Boulder
Campus Box 295
Boulder, Colorado 80309–0395, U.S.A.
zygmunt.frajzyngier@colorado.edu

Gianina Georgescu
Faculty of Mathematics
University of Bucharest
Str. Academiei 14
70109 Bucureşti, Romania
gianina@math.math.unibuc.ro

Lucian Ilie
Turku Centre for Computer Science
Lemminkäisenkatu 14 A, 4th floor
FIN-20520 Turku, Finland
& Faculty of Mathematics
University of Bucharest
Str. Academiei 14
70109 Bucureşti, Romania
lucili@utu.fi

Maciej Kandulski
Faculty of Mathematics and Computer Science
Adam Mickiewicz University
ul. Matejki 48/49
60-769 Poznań, Poland
mkandu@math.amu.edu.pl

Manfred Kudlek
Fachbereich Informatik
Universität Hamburg
Vogt-Kölln-Straße 30
D-22527 Hamburg, Germany
kudlek@informatik.uni-hamburg.de

Alain Lecomte
UFR Sciences de l'Homme et de la Société
Université Pierre Mendès-France
1251 Avenue Centrale, Domaine Universitaire de St Martin d'Heres
BP 47 X
38040 Grenoble cedex 9, France
& Projet Calligramme, INRIA-Lorraine
lecomte@shm.upmf-grenoble.fr

Vincenzo Manca
Dipartimento di Informatica
Università di Pisa
Corso Ttalia, 40
56125 Pisa, Italy
mancav@di.unipi.it

Solomon Marcus
University of Bucharest
Faculty of Mathematics
Str. Academiei 14
70109-Bucureşti, Romania
solomon@imar.ro

Rafael Marín Gálvez
Departament de Filologia Espanyola
Facultat de Lletres, Edifici B
Universitat Autònoma de Barcelona
08193 Bellaterra, Spain
rafa@liceu.uab.es

Carlos Martín-Vide
Research Group on Mathematical Linguistics and Language Engineering (GRLMC)
Rovira i Virgili University
Pl. Imperial Tàrraco 1
43005 Tarragona, Spain
cmv@astor.urv.es

Shinya Matsunami
Ph.D. Candidate
The Department of Linguistics (Student)
University of Hawaii
1890 East-West Road
Honolulu, Hawaii 96822, U.S.A.
matsunam@hawaii.edu

Valeria Mihalache
Turku Centre for Computer Science
Lemminkäisenkatu 14 A, 4th Floor
20520, Turku, Finland
& Faculty of Mathematics
University of Bucharest
Str. Academiei 14
70109 Bucureşti, Romania
valmih@utu.fi

Joan Miquel-Vergés
Research Group on Mathematical Linguistics and Language Engineering (GRLMC)
Rovira i Virgili University
Pl. Imperial Tàrraco 1
43005 Tarragona, Spain
jmv@astor.urv.es
& Department of Translation
Vigo University
Facultade de Humanidades
As Lagoas, Marcosende
36200 Vigo, Spain
jmv@uvigo.es

Ruslan Mitkov
University of Wolverhampton
School of Languages and European Studies
Wolverhampton WV1 1SB, United Kingdom
r.mitkov@wlv.ac.uk

Victor Mitrana
Faculty of Mathematics
University of Bucharest
Str. Academiei 14
70109 Bucharest, Romania
mitrana@moisil.math.ro

Juan Pablo Mora
Universidad de Huelva
Facultad de Humanidades
Av. Fuerzas Armadas, s/n
21071 Huelva, Spain
jmora@cica.es

Jan Mycielski
Department of Mathematics
University of Colorado at Boulder
Campus Box 395
Boulder, Colorado 80309–0295, U.S.A.
jmyciel@euclid.Colorado.EDU

Ángel Nepomuceno Fernández
Research Group in Logic
Facultad de Filosofía
Universidad de Sevilla
Avenida de San Francisco Javier s/n
41005 Sevilla, Spain
nepomuce@cica.es

Gheorghe Păun
Institute of Mathematics of the Romanian Academy
PO Box 1 – 764
70700 Bucureşti, Romania
gpaun@imar.ro

José Gabriel Pereira Lopes
Departamento de Informática
Faculdade de Ciência e Tecnologia da UNL
Quinta da Torre
28250 Monte da Capoarica Portugal
gpl@di.fct.unl.pt

Irene Pimenta Rodrigues
Departamento de Matemática
Universidade de Évora
Largo dos Colegeais
7000 Évora Portugal
ipr@dmat.uevora.pt

Lech T. Polkowski
Warsaw University of Technology
Institute of Mathematics
Warsaw, Poland
polk@mimuw.edu.pl

José F. Quesada
Centro de Informática Científica de Andalucía
Avda. Reina Mercedes s/n
41012 Sevilla, Spain
josefran@cica.es

Lisa A. Reed
Department of French & Center for Linguistics
The Pennsylvania State University
University Park, PA 16802, U.S.A.
lar13@psu.edu

Christian Retoré
Projet Calligramme
INRIA-Lorraine & CRIN-C.N.R.S.
B.P. 101
54602 Villers lès Nancy Cedex, France
retore@loria.fr

Francisco J. Salguero Lamillar
Research Unit in General and Applied Linguistics
Facultad de Filología
Universidad de Sevilla
Palos de la Frontera s/n
41004 Sevilla, Spain
salguero@cica.es

Arto Salomaa
Turku University
Department of Mathematics
20014 Turku, Finland
asalomaa@sara.utu.fi

Francisco Javier Sánchez González
Laboratorio de Lenguaje y Musicología.
Centro de Tecnologías Físicas
C.S.I.C.
Serrano, 144
28006 Madrid, Spain
javier@iec.csic.es

Bilge Say
Department of Computer Engineering and Information Science
Faculty of Engineering
Bilkent University
Bilkent, Ankara 06533, Turkey
say@cs.bilkent.edu.tr

Paul Schmidt
IAI
Martin-Luther-St. 14
66111 Saarbrücken, Germany
paul@iai.uni-sb.de

Maria Semeniuk–Polkowska
Warsaw University
Chair of Formal Linguistics
Warsaw, Poland
polk@mimuw.edu.pl

Manuel Vilares Ferro
Department of Computer Science
University of Corunna
Campus de Elviña s/n
15071 La Coruña, Spain
vilares@dc.fi.udc.es

PART I
SYNTAX

The Degree of Parallelism in Contextual Grammars with the Minimal Competence Strategy

Jürgen Dassow[a]
Victor Mitrana[b1]

[a]) *Otto-von-Guericke University, Magdeburg*
[b]) *University of Bucharest*

Abstract

A quite natural and dynamical measure of descriptional complexity, *the degree of parallelism*, is defined for contextual grammars working in the minimal competence strategy and for their generated languages. We relate this measure to the *index* of context-free languages which is analogously defined. Some properties of the degree of parallelism such as connectivity and computability are discussed.

Introduction

Contextual grammars were introduced in (Marcus 1969a) as a generative mechanism that does not use auxiliary symbols and that is based on a fundamental linguistic operation, namely the acceptance of a context by

[1]Research supported by the Alexander von Humboldt Foundation.

a word. Motivations can be found in (Marcus 1967) and (Marcus 1969b). A contextual grammar produces a language by starting from a given finite set of strings and iteratively adding pairs of strings (called *contexts*), which are associated with sets of words (called *selectors*), to the strings already obtained.

Many ways of adjoining contexts were considered: for instance, in the interior of a string (cf. (Păun and Nguyen 1980)), and only at the end of the string, with contexts selected by a mapping (cf. (Istrail 1967)). Moreover, the selectors can be used in maximal/minimal, local/global mode (cf. (Martín-Vide et al. 1995)). In (Marcus et al. 1995) it was shown that three of the usual restrictions appearing in natural languages as well as in artificial languages and outrunning the context-free barrier can be described by maximal use of selectors. On the other hand, the contexts can be added sequentially or in parallel (cf. (Mitrana 1994) (Păun et al. 1997)). A survey can be found in (Păun 1982); (Păun 1994) also presents a summary which includes the recent developments.

The present paper is devoted to the study of a descriptional complexity measure introduced for the class of contextual grammars defined in (Mitrana 1994), namely contextual grammars with choice (the contexts are selected in a regular way: the selectors which accept the same contexts form a language of a given type) in a derivation mode called *the strategy of minimal competence* (the name of this derivation mode was suggested by a similar derivation mode in grammar systems). The whole current string is split into subwords in such a way that some subwords appear in the selectors of the grammar (and contexts are adjoined to them) and the other subwords contain no subword in these sets (the maximal number of contexts with respect to a given decomposition of the current string are adjoined).

We shall provide some connections between the degree of parallelism and the well-known *index* measure for context-free languages.

As far as the relevance of this type of grammars in mathematical linguistics is concerned, they are able to cover two features of natural and artificial languages such as long distance dependence and agreements (cf. (Pullum and Gazdar 1982), (Shieber 1985)). Both of them can be modelled in a surprisingly simple way by contextual grammars working in the strategy of minimal competence and having the degree of parallelism equal to 2.

Basic definitions

We start with some formal language prerequisites. If V is a finite alphabet, we denote by V^* the free monoid generated by V under catenation. For a word $x \in V^*$, we write $lg(x)$ for the length of x and $lg(x)_U$ for the length of the string obtained from x by erasing all symbols not in U. We denote the empty word by λ and set $lg(\lambda) = 0$ and $V^+ = V^* - \{\lambda\}$. The set of subwords of a string x is denoted by $Sub(x)$. For supplementary details see (Salomaa 1973).

Let F be a family of languages over an alphabet V. A contextual grammar of degree n with F choice is a construct

$$G = (V, B, (R_1, C_1), \ldots, (R_n, C_n))$$

where

B is a finite subset of V^*,
R_i are languages in F, $1 \leq i \leq n$,,
C_i are finite subsets of $V^\times V^*$ of contexts, $1 \leq i \leq n$.

For a grammar G and two strings $x, y \in V^*$, we define the following derivation, and we call it the *strategy of minimal competence*

$$\begin{aligned} x \Longrightarrow^{mc} y \quad \text{iff} \quad & x = x_1 z_1 x_2 z_2 \ldots x_m z_m x_{m+1}, \\ & y = x_1 u_1 z_1 v_1 x_2 \ldots x_m u_m z_m v_m x_{m+1}, \\ & z_j \in R_{i_j},\ (u_j, v_j) \in C_{i_j},\ i_j \in \{1, 2, \ldots, n\},\ 1 \leq j \leq m, \\ & x_t \in V^*,\ Sub(x_t) \cap \bigcup_{k=1}^{n} R_k = \emptyset,\ 1 \leq t \leq m+1. \end{aligned}$$

The language generated by G in the strategy of minimal competence is

$$L_{mc}(G) = B \cup \{y \in V^* \mid x \Longrightarrow^{mc} y_1 \Longrightarrow^{mc} \cdots \Longrightarrow^{mc} y_p = y,\ x \in B,\ p \geq 1\}.$$

The family of languages generated by contextual grammars with F choice, using the strategy of minimal competence, is denoted by $C(F, mc)$. In this paper we shall consider only finite and regular choice; the families of finite and regular languages are denoted by FIN and REG, respectively.

Let us consider some examples

Example 1 If

$$G_1 = (\{a\}, \{a\}, (\{a\}, \{(\lambda, a)\})),$$

so we obtain

$$L_{mc}(G_1) = \{a^{2^n} \mid n \geq 0\}$$

because only derivations of the form

$$a \Longrightarrow^{mc} aa \Longrightarrow^{mc} a^4 \Longrightarrow^{mc} a^8 \Longrightarrow^{mc} a^{16} \Longrightarrow \cdots$$

are possible in G_1. Consequently

$$\{a^{2^n} \mid n \geq 0\} \in C(FIN, mc).$$

Example 2 We consider

$$G_2 = (\{a, b, c\}, \{abc, a^2b^2c^2\}, (R_1, C_1), (R_2, C_2))$$

with

$$\begin{aligned} R_1 &= \{a^2b\},\ C_1 = \{(a, b)\}; \\ R_2 &= \{bc^2\},\ C_2 = \{(\lambda, c)\}. \end{aligned}$$

We obtain

$$L_{mc}(G_2) = \{a^n b^n c^n \mid n \geq 1\}$$

since every string $a^n b^n c^n$ with $n \geq 2$ can uniquely be decomposed into $a^{n-2}a^2bb^{n-2}bc^2c^{n-2}$. Therefore

$$\{a^n b^n c^n \mid n \geq 1\} \in C(FIN; mc).$$

Restrictions leading to the second language can be identified in semiotics of folklore (cf. (Marcus 1978)) and Algol-like languages.

Note that both these grammars have finite choice; however, the languages generated by them are non-context-free, and the first one is even a one-letter non-context-free language.

Example 3 Let

$$G_3 = (\{a, b, c, d\}, \{abcd\}, (R_1, C_1), (R_2, C_2))$$

with

$$\begin{aligned} R_1 &= \{ab^+c\},\ C_1 = \{(a, c)\}; \\ R_2 &= \{bc^+d\},\ C_2 = \{(b, d)\}. \end{aligned}$$

The language generated by G_3 is

$$\{a^n b^m c^n d^m | n, m \geq 1\}$$

and can be identified in a dialect of German spoken around Zurich, Switzerland (cf. (Pullum 1985), (Shieber 1985)) which allows constructions of the form $NP_a^m\ NP_d^n\ V_a^{m'}\ V_d^{n'}$, where NP_a are accusative noun phrases, NP_d are dative noun phrases, V_a are accusative-demanding verbs, V_d are dative-demanding verbs, and the numbers have to match up. That is, $m = m'$ and $n = n'$.

If $x \in L_{mc}(G)$, then we have either $x \in B$ or x can be obtained from a finite number of words in $L_{mc}(G)$ by a derivation step.

A natural measure of the syntactical complexity of a word x is the smallest number of subwords in which a string in $L_{mc}(G)$ has to be split in order to obtain x. This number will be called *the degree of parallelism* associated to x.

Formally, for a contextual grammar $G = (V, B, (R_1, C_1), \ldots, (R_n, C_n))$ and $x \in L_{mc}(G)$, we define the degree of parallelism as follows

$$\begin{aligned} pd(x, G) &= min\{k \mid \text{ there exists } y \in L_{mc}(G) \text{ such that} \\ &\qquad y \Longrightarrow^{mc} x \text{ by adjoining } k \text{ contexts}\}. \end{aligned}$$

By definition, for any $x \in B$, we have $pd(x, G) = 0$.
Furthermore, for $F \in \{FIN, REG\}$, we set

$$\begin{aligned} pd(G) &= sup\{pd(x, G) \mid x \in L_{mc}(G)\}, \\ pd_F(L) &= inf\{pd(G) \mid L = L_{mc}(G),\ G \text{ with } F \text{ choice}\}. \end{aligned}$$

We recall now the definition of the index measure for context-free grammars and languages. Let $G = (N, T, S, P)$ be a context-free grammar. For a derivation

$$D : S \Longrightarrow w_1 \Longrightarrow w_2 \Longrightarrow \ldots \Longrightarrow w_n = x \in T^*,$$

we set

$$\begin{aligned} Ind(D) &= max\{lg(w_i)_N \mid 1 \leq i \leq n\}, \\ Ind(x, G) &= min\{Ind(D) \mid D : S \Longrightarrow^* x\}, \\ Ind(G) &= sup\{Ind(x, G) \mid x \in L(G)\}, \end{aligned}$$

and for a context-free language L,

$$Ind(L) = inf\{Ind(G) \mid L = L(G)\}.$$

A comparison with the index measure

Directly from definitions, we have

Lemma 1. *For any language L, $pd_{REG}(L) \leq pd_{FIN}(L)$ holds.*

In the sequel, we shall assume that whenever a measure is involved for a language L, the language L belongs to the corresponding class of languages.

The next result is obvious.

Theorem 1. *For any family of languages F, we have*

$$pd_F(L) = 0 \text{ iff } Ind(L) = 0 \text{ iff } L \text{ is finite.}$$

Theorem 2. *1. For any language L, $pd_{FIN}(L) = 1$ implies $Ind(L) = 1$.*
2. There are non-context-free languages L with $pd_{REG}(L) = 1$.

Proof. Let $G = (V, B, (R_1, C_1), \ldots, (R_n, C_n))$ be a contextual grammar such that $pd(G) = 1$, $R_i \in FIN$, $1 \leq i \leq n$. Further let k be the maximal length of the words in $\cup_{i=1}^{n} R_i$.

We construct the linear grammar

$$G' = (N, V, S, P)$$

where

$$N = \{S\} \cup \{[x] | x \in V^+,\ 1 \leq |x| \leq 2k - 1\}$$

and P consists of the following rules

1. $S \longrightarrow w$ for any $w \in B$,
2. $S \longrightarrow x[w]y$ where
   (i) $xwy \in B$,

(ii) $Sub(w) \cap \bigcup_{k=1}^{n} R_k \neq \emptyset$,

(iii) $1 \leq |w| \leq 2k-1$,

3. $[xwy] \longrightarrow z_1[z]z_2$ where

(i) $z_1 z z_2 = xuwvy, \ (u,v) \in C_i, \ w \in R_i, \ 1 \leq i \leq n$,

(ii) $Sub(z) \cap \bigcup_{k=1}^{n} R_k \neq \emptyset$,

(iii) $1 \leq |z| \leq 2k-1$,

4. $[w] \longrightarrow w$ for all $w \in V^+$ with $1 \leq |w| \leq 2k-1$.

Clearly, the rules (1) are used for generating all initial words.

The rules (2) and (3) are used in order to simulate the minimal competence strategy in G. This is possible because $pd(G) = 1$. Hence at each step just one pair of contexts is adjoined.

The second assertion follows from Example 3. □

On the other hand,

Theorem 3. *There are regular languages L with $pd_{FIN}(L) = \infty$.*

Proof. Consider the regular language $L = \{a\}^+$. Obviously, L can be generated by the contextual grammar with finite selectors

$$G' = (\{a\}, \{a\}, (\{a\}, \{(a, \lambda), (\lambda, \lambda)\}))$$

Let us assume that L is generated by a contextual grammar

$$G = (V, B, (R_1, C_1), \ldots, (R_n, C_n))$$

with finite choice. Let k be an arbitrary given integer and

$$p = max\{lg(xy) \mid (x,y) \in \bigcup_{i=1}^{n} C_i\},$$

$$s = max\{lg(w) \mid w \in \bigcup_{i=1}^{n} R_i\}.$$

Clearly, $x = a^{(k+1)(s-1)+k(s+p)} \in L$ holds. Assume, against all reason, that $pd_G(x) < k$. Because x is generated by adjoining at most $k-1$ contexts we infer that there exists $y \in L$ such that

$$lg(y) \geq (k+1)(s-1) + ks + p,$$

and

$$y \Longrightarrow^{mc} x.$$

Hence, for any k, there exists $x \in L$ with $pd_G(x) \geq k$ which concludes the proof. □

Furthermore,

Theorem 4. *For $F \in \{FIN, REG\}$, there are linear languages (i.e. of index 1) which are not in the family $C(F, mc)$.*

Proof. We consider the linear language

$$L = a^+ \cup b^+ \cup \{a^n b^n \mid n \geq 1\}$$

and assume that $L = L_{mc}(G)$ for some $G = (\{a, b\}, B, (R_1, C_1), \ldots, (R_n, C_n))$ with arbitrary R_i, $1 \leq i \leq n$.

In order to generate the infinite sets a^+ and b^+ we need some pairs (R, C) with $R \subseteq a^+$ and $C \subseteq a^+$ and some pairs (R', C') with $R' \subseteq b^+$ and $C' \subseteq b^+$.

If a context (a^{i_1}, a^{i_2}) appears in C, then we can replace it by $(\lambda, a^{i_1+i_2})$ without changing the generated language. Thus, without loss of generality we may assume that all contexts in the set C are of the form (λ, a^t) with $t \geq 1$. Analogously, any context in C' is of the form (λ, b^k) with $k \leq 1$.

Let $a^k \in R$ and $b^r \in B'$. Then, using the contexts $(\lambda, a^t) \in C$ and $(\lambda, b^s) \in C'$, the derivation

$$a^{kr} b^{kr} \Longrightarrow a^{r(k+t)} b^{k(r+s)}$$

exists. Therefore, $rt = ks$ is valid.

If C also contains also another context (λ, a^q), we conclude that $rq = ks$ and thus $q = t$. In conclusion, C contains only one context of the form (λ, a^t), $t \geq 1$. The same argument is valid also for C' and the context (λ, b^s), $s \geq 1$.

If R contains a word a^p different from a^k, then we obtain $ps = rt$, and it follows that $p = k$. Hence, a^k is the only string of this form which belongs to R. Again, the same is also true also for the string b^r and R'.

Let $(a^{k_q}, (\lambda, a^{t_q}))$, $1 \leq q \leq m$, and $(b^{r_u}, (\lambda, b^{s_u}))$, $1 \leq u \leq p$, all be pairs of the form above. Let us further assume that

$$k_1 < k_2 < \ldots < k_m \quad \text{and} \quad r_1 < r_2 < \ldots < r_p.$$

By induction we shall prove that $m = p$ and $k_q = r_q$ and $t_q = s_q$, for $1 \leq q \leq m$.

If $k_1 < r_1$ then

$$a^{k_1} b^{k_1} \Longrightarrow^{mc} a^{k_1+t_1} b^{k_1}$$

which contradicts $a^{k_1+t_1} b^{k_1} \notin L$. Hence $k_1 = r_1$ which implies $t_1 = s_1$.

We further assume that $k_1 = r_1, k_2 = r_2, \ldots, k_q = r_q$ and $t_1 = s_1, t_2 = s_2, \ldots, t_q = s_q$. If $k_{q+1} < r_{q+1}$,

$$a^{k_1+\cdots+k_{q+1}} b^{k_1+\cdots+k_{q+1}} \Longrightarrow^{mc} a^{k_1+\cdots+k_{q+1}+t_1+t_2+\cdots+t_{q+1}} b^{k_1+\cdots+k_{q+1}+s_1+s_2+\cdots+s_q}$$

holds. By the induction assumption, $t_i = s_i$ for $1 \leq i \leq q$, and so the obtained string is not in L, which is a contradiction again. Therefore, $k_{q+1} = r_{q+1}$, which implies $t_{q+1} = s_{q+1}$. The induction argument is complete.

Hence $m = p$ and $k_q = r_q$ and $t_q = s_q$ for $1 \leq q \leq m$. If $k_q = k_1 \cdot c_q + d_q$ for some $c_q \geq 1$, $0 \leq d_q < k_1$, then

$$a^{k_q} b^{k_q} \Longrightarrow^{mc} a^{c_q(k_1+t_1)+d_q} b^{k_q+t_q}$$

which implies $c_q(k_1 + t_1) + d_q = k_1 \cdot c_q + d_q + t_q$ and therefore $t_q = c_q t_1$. Since $k_q \cdot s_1 = t_q \cdot r_1$ we obtain $d_q = 0$.

In conclusion, $k_q = c_q \cdot k_1$ and $t_q = c_q \cdot t_1$ for $2 \leq q \leq m$. In this case, the effect of all pairs $(a^{k_q}, (\lambda, a^{t_q}))$ can be simulated by the pair $(a^{k_1}, (\lambda, a^{t_1}))$. Therefore, we may assume that (R, C) is the only pair involving only occurences of the symbol a. Now it is clear that G cannot produce all strings a^n, $n \geq 1$ (and b^n, $n \geq 1$, respectively). This contradicts $a^+ \subset L$. Thus, the equality $L = L(G, mc)$ is impossible. □

Note that the family of languages to which $R_1, R_2, \ldots, R_n$ belong plays no role in our proof.

Theorem 5. *1. There are non-context-free languages L with $pd_{FIN}(L) = 2$.*
2. There are context-free languages L with $Ind(L) = \infty$ and $pd_{REG}(L) \leq 2$.

Proof. The first statement is proved by Example 2.

For the second example, we consider the Dyck language D_{ab} which is of infinite index. The contextual grammar

$$G = (\{a, b\}, \{\lambda, ab\}, (\{a, b\}^+, \{(a, b), (ab, \lambda), (\lambda, \lambda)\}$$

with regular choice generates D_{ab}. Indeed, if $x \in D_{ab}$ and $x \Longrightarrow^{mc} y$, then one can easily check that $y \in D_{ab}$. Therefore, $L_{mc}(G) \subseteq D_{ab}$.

Let us now assume that, for some $n \geq 1$, all strings of length $2n$ which are in D_{ab} are also in $L_{mc}(G)$. Then we take a string $y \in D_{ab}$ with $lg(y) = 2n+2$ and consider the decomposition

$$y = x_1 x_2 \ldots x_k$$

of y where $k \geq 1$ and all x_i, $1 \leq i \leq k$, are non-empty words in D_{ab} which cannot be expressed as a catenation of two Dyck strings over $\{a, b\}$.

If $k = 1$, then y can also be written as $y = axb$, for some $x \in D_{ab}$. Hence $x \Longrightarrow^{mc} y$. Moreover, $pd(y, G) = 1$. If $lg(x_1) = 2$, that is $x = ab$, then we have the derivation $x_2 x_3 \ldots x_k \Longrightarrow^{mc} y$, and $pd(y, G) = 1$.

If $lg(x_1) \geq 4$, then $x_1 = axb$, for some $x \in D_{ab}$. Therefore, we infer that $x x_2 \ldots x_k \Longrightarrow^{mc} y$ and $pd(y, G) \leq 2$.

Consequently, $L_{mc}(G) = D_{ab}$ and $pd(G) \leq 2$. □

We finish this section by pointing out some *open problems* concerning the relation between the degree of parallelism and index.

1. What can be said, more exactly, about the index of the context-free languages L with $pd_{REG}(L)$ equal to 1 ?

2. Is it true that $Ind(L) = \infty$ implies $pd_{FIN}(L) = \infty$?

Some properties of the degree of parallelism

Obviously, for any language L, $pd_{REG}(L) \leq pd_{FIN}(L)$. The following problem naturally arises: Are there languages L such that $pd_{REG}(L) < pd_{FIN}(L)$ holds? We show that the answer is affirmative. As a matter of fact, the following theorem gives a more precise statement on the relation between the two measures.

Theorem 6. *There is a sequence of languages L_n, $n \geq 1$, such that*

$$pd_{FIN}(L_n) = n \text{ and } pd_{REG}(L_n) = 1.$$

Proof. Let $n \geq 1$ be a given integer. We set

$$L_n = \{a_0^{k_0} b_1 a_1^{k_1} b_2 \ldots a_{n-1}^{k_{n-1}} b_n a_n^{k_n} \mid k_i \geq 1,\ 0 \leq i \leq n\}$$

and claim that $pd_{FIN}(L_n) = n$. A detailed proof of this claim is left to the reader.

On the other hand, the contextual grammar

$$G = (V, \{a_0b_1a_1b_2\dots b_na_n\}, (R_1, C_1), (R_2, C_2), \dots, (R_n, C_n))$$

where

$$\begin{aligned} V &= \{a_0, b_1, a_1, b_2, \dots, b_n, a_n\} \\ R_i &= a_{i-1}^+b_ia_i^+b_{i+1}\dots a_{n-1}^+b_na_n^+ \quad \text{for } 1 \leq i \leq n, \\ C_i &= \begin{cases} \{(a_{i-1}, \lambda)\} & \text{if } i < n \\ \{(a_{n-1}, \lambda), (\lambda, a_n)\} & \text{if } i = n \end{cases} \end{aligned}$$

with regular choice generates the language L_n and its degree of parallelism is equal to 1. □

The measure pd_F is said to be *connected* if, for any $n \geq 0$, there exists a language L_n in F such that $pd_F(L_n) = n$.

Lemma 2. *For any family of languages F and any language L with $pd_F(L) = k$, there exist two constants $p, q > 0$ such that for each $z \in L, lg(z) > p$, the following conditions hold*

$$\begin{aligned} &(i) && z = z_1u_1x_1v_1z_2u_2x_2v_2\dots z_tu_tx_tv_tz_{t+1} \quad \textit{for some } 1 \leq t \leq k, \\ &(ii) && z_1x_1z_2x_2\dots z_tx_tz_{t+1} \in L, \\ &(iii) && 0 \leq lg(u_iv_i) \leq q, \quad 1 \leq i \leq t, \\ &(iv) && lg(u_1v_1u_2v_2\dots u_tv_t) > 0. \end{aligned}$$

Proof. Let $G = (V, B, (R_1, C_1), (R_2, C_2), \dots, (R_n, C_n))$ be a contextual grammar with $L_{mc}(G) = L$ and $pd(G) = k$. We set

$$\begin{aligned} p &= max\{lg(x) \mid x \in B\}, \\ q &= max\{lg(uv) \mid (u, v) \in C_i, 1 \leq i \leq n\}. \end{aligned}$$

If $z \in L$ and $lg(z) > p$ then there exists $y \in L$ such that $y \Longrightarrow^{mc} z$ by adjoining at most k contexts. If

$$y = z_1x_1z_2x_2\dots z_tx_tz_{t+1}, \quad t \leq k$$

and

$$z = z_1u_1x_1v_1z_2u_2x_2v_2 \dots z_tu_tx_tv_tz_{t+1},$$
$$x_j \in R_{i_j}, \ (u_j, v_j) \in C_{i_j}, \ 1 \le j \le t, 1 \le i_j \le n,$$

then $(u_j, v_j) \neq (\lambda, \lambda)$ for some $1 \le j \le t$.

Thus, all conditions of our lemma are satisfied. □

Theorem 7. *1. The measures pd_{FIN}, pd_{REG} are connected.*
2. There exists a language L with $pd_F(L) = \infty$ for $F \in \{FIN, REG\}$.

Proof. For the first assertion let us consider the language

$$L_n = \{a_1^k a_2^k \dots a_{2n-1}^k a_{2n}^k \mid k \ge 1\}.$$

By Lemma 2, $pd_F(L_n) < n$ with $F \in \{FIN, REG\}$ does not hold. On the other hand, the contextual grammar

$$G = (V, B, (R_1, C_1), \dots, (R_n, C_n))$$

with

$$\begin{aligned} V &= \{a_1, a_2, \dots, a_{2n}\}, \\ B &= \{a_1a_2 \dots a_{2n}\}, \\ R_i &= \{a_{2i-1}a_{2i}\}, \qquad i = 1, 2, \dots, n, \\ C_i &= \{(a_{2i-1}, a_{2i})\}, \ i = 1, 2, \dots, n, \end{aligned}$$

with finite choice generates L_n. As one can easily see $pd(G) = n$. Therefore $pd_{FIN}(L_n) = n$. Moreover, by Lemma 1, $pd_{REG}(L_n) = n$ follows.

If we consider the homomorphism $h : \{a_1, a_2, \dots a_{2n}\}^* \longrightarrow \{a, b\}^*$ given by $h(a_i) = a^i b$ for $1 \le i \le 2n$ and the homomorphical image of the language L_n, the number of letters can be limited to two.

Now, consider $L' = \{a^{2^n} \mid n \ge 1\} \in C(FIN, mc)$ (see Example 1). We assume that $pd_{REG}(L') = k$ for some k. Let $a^{2^n} \in L'$ with $2^n > p$ and $2^{n-1} > kq$, where p and q are the constants associated to L' from Lemma 2. From the condition (ii) of Lemma 2 we obtain that $a^r \in L'$ for some r such that $2^{n-1} < r < 2^n$ which contradicts the structure of L'. In conclusion, $pd_{REG}(L') = pd_{FIN}(L') = \infty$. □

Theorem 8. *The measure pd is not computable for contextual grammars with linear choice.*

Proof. Let $x = (x_1, x_2, \ldots, x_n)$ and $y = (y_1, y_2, \ldots, y_n)$ be two n-tuples of nonempty words over $\{a, b\}$. The language

$$L(y) = \{ba^{i_k} \ldots ba^{i_1}cy_{i_1} \ldots y_{i_k} \mid k \geq 1, 1 \leq i_j \leq n\}$$

is a linear one. If

$$G = (\{a, b, c, d\}, \{c\}, (\{c\}, \{(ba^i, x_i) \mid 1 \leq i \leq n\}), (L(y) \cup \{d\}, \{(\lambda, d)\}))$$

then $pd(G)$ is finite if and only if $pd(G) = 1$ if and only if the Post Correspondence Problem has no solution. Because of the undecidability of the Post Correspondence Problem, $pd(G)$ is not computable for the above G.

Note that G has linear choice. □

Corollary. *The measure pd_{LIN} is not computable for linear languages.*

Finally, we mention some *open problems.*

1. What about the computability of this measure for contextual grammars with finite or regular choice?

2. Is it true that for every contextual grammar G with a finite degree of parallelism, the language $L_{mc}(G)$ is semilinear?

References

Istrail, S. 1978. "Contextual grammars with regulated selection". *Studii si Cercetari Matematic* 30 (3): 287–294.

Marcus, S. 1967. *Algebraic Linguistics. Analitical Models.* New York: Academic Press.

Marcus, S. 1969a. "Contextual grammars". *Revue Roumaine de Mathématiques Pures et Appliquées* 14 (10): 1525–1534.

Marcus, S. 1969b. "Deux types nouveaux de grammaires génératives". *Cahiers de Linguistique Théorique et Appliquée* 6: 69–74.

Marcus, S. (ed). 1978. *La sémiotique formelle du folklore.* Paris: Klincksieck and Bucharest: Publishing House of the Romanian Academy.

Marcus, S., Martín-Vide, C. and Păun, Gh. 1995. "On the power of internal contextual grammars with maximal use of selectors".

Martín-Vide, C., Mateescu, A., Miquel-Vergés, J. and Păun, Gh. 1995. "Internal contextual grammars: minimal, maximal, and scattered use of selectors".

Mitrana, V. 1994. "Contextual grammars: the strategy of minimal competence". In Gh. Păun (ed), *Mathematical Aspects of Natural and Formal Languages.* Singapore: World Scientific Publishing, 319–331.

Păun, Gh. 1982. *Contextual Grammars.* Bucharest: The Publishing House of the Romanian Academy (in Romanian).

Păun, Gh. 1994. "Marcus contextual grammars. After 25 years". *Bulletin of the European Association of Theoretical Computer Science* 52: 263–273.

Păun, Gh. and Nguyen, X.M. 1980. "On the inner contextual grammar". *Revue Roumaine de Mathématiques Pures et Appliquèes* 25 (4): 641–651.

Păun, Gh., Rozenberg, G. and Salomaa, A. 1997. "Contextual grammars: parallelism and blocking of derivations". *Fundamenta Informaticae.* To appear.

Pullum, G.K. 1985. "On two recent attempts to show that English is not a CFL". *Computational Linguistics* 10: 182–186.

Pullum, G.K. and Gazdar, G. 1982. "Natural languages and context-free languages". *Linguistics and Philosophy* 4: 471–504.

Salomaa, A. 1973. *Formal Languages.* New York: Academic Press.

Shieber, S. M. 1985. "Evidence against the context-freeness of natural languages". *Linguistics and Philosophy* 8: 333–343.

The Syntactic Complexity of Internal Contextual Grammars and Languages[1]

Gianina Georgescu

University of Bucharest

Abstract

We investigate the connectedness, the decidability problems and the compatibility of several syntactic measures for internal contextual languages.

Introduction

Contextual grammars were introduced in (Marcus 1969) with motivations from descriptive linguistics. They are based on adjoining contexts (pairs of strings) to strings or parts of strings. In recent years, new types of contextual grammars have been introduced and studied (see (Păun 1994)). An important topic in this area is the study of the syntactic complexity of such grammars and of the class of languages generated.

For a measure of syntactic complexity K, defined for grammars in a class $\mathcal{G}$, the following problems can be formulated:

*P*1. Is there $n_K \in \mathbf{N}$ such that for every $n \geq n_K$ there is a language $L_n \in \mathcal{L}(\mathcal{G})$ such that $K_{\mathcal{G}}(L_n) = n$? (if so we say that K is *connected*).

[1]Research supported by the Academy of Finland, Project 11281.

$P2$. Can $K(G)$ be algorithmically computed for arbitrarily given $G \in \mathcal{G}$?

$P3$. Is there an algorithm for computing $K_{\mathcal{G}}(L(G))$ for an arbitrary grammar $G \in \mathcal{G}$?

$P4_n$. For a given $n \in \mathbf{N}$, can we algorithmically decide whether or not $K_{\mathcal{G}}(L(G)) = n$, for an arbitrary grammar $G \in \mathcal{G}$?

$P5$. Can we algorithmically decide whether $K_{\mathcal{G}}(G) = K_{\mathcal{G}}(L(G))$ or not for an arbitrary grammar $G \in \mathcal{G}$?

$P6$. Is there an algorithm to construct an arbitrary grammar $G \in \mathcal{G}$ a grammar $G' \in \mathcal{G}$ such that $L(G) = L(G')$ and $K(G') = K(L(G))$? (In other words, is there an algorithm to construct the simplest grammar for $L(G)$).

$P7$. Are there languages $L \in \mathcal{L}(\mathcal{G})$ such that $K^{-1}_{1,\mathcal{G}}(L) \cap K^{-1}_{2,\mathcal{G}}(L) = \emptyset$, for two measures K_1 and K_2? (we say that K_1 and K_2 are *incompatible*). ($K^{-1}_{\mathcal{G}}(L) = \{G \in \mathcal{G} \mid K(G) = K_{\mathcal{G}}(L), L = L(G)\}$ is the set of optimal grammars that generates L).

The problems Pi, $i \in \{2, 3, 4_n, 5\}$ are said to be decidable, if and only if there is an algorithm that solves P_i. We shall say that the problem P4 is decidable, if and only if for every integer n the problem $P4_n$ is decidable. We shall say that the problem $P4$ is undecidable, if and only if it is not decidable.

In this paper, we investigate these problems for the class of internal contextual grammars and languages.

Definitions and basic notions

For a vocabulary V we denote by V^* the free monoid generated by V under concatenation; the null element of V^* is denoted by λ. The length of $x \in V^*$ is denoted by $|x|$. The number of occurrences of a symbol a in a string x is denoted by $|x|_a$. For $w \in V^*, w = a_1 \cdots a_n$, where V is an alphabet and $a_1, \cdots, a_n \in V$, we denote by $Mi(w)$ the string $a_n \cdots a_1$.

A *general contextual grammar* is a quadruple $G = (V, B, C, \varphi)$, where V is a finite non-empty alphabet, B is a finite language over V, $C \subseteq V^* \times V^* \times V^* \longrightarrow 2^C$ is the *selection mapping.*

The language generated by G, denoted $L(G)$, is the smallest set $L \subseteq V^*$ which includes B and has the next property: if $x \in L, x = x_1x_2x_3$, with $x_1, x_2, x_3 \in V^*$, and $(u, v) \in \varphi(x_1, x_2, x_3)$, then $x_1ux_2vx_3 \in L$. We also use the notation $x \Longrightarrow y$ for $x, y \in V^*$ if $x = x_1x_2x_3, y = x_1ux_2vx_3$ for some $(u, v) \in C, x_1, x_2, x_3 \in V^*$ such that $(u, v) \in \varphi(x_1, x_2, x_3)$. Then

$$L(G) = \{w \in V^* \mid x \stackrel{*}{\Longrightarrow} w, \text{ for some } x \in B\}.$$

A contextual grammar as above is said to be an *internal contextual grammar* if the mapping φ has the following property:

$$\varphi(x_1, x_2, x_3) = \varphi(x_1', x_2, x_3') \text{ for all } x_1, x_1', x_2, x_3, x_3' \in V^*.$$

For an internal contextual grammar $G = (V, B, C, \varphi)$ we define (see (Păun 1994))

$$\begin{aligned}
Ax(G) &= \text{card } B \\
LAx(G) &= \max \{|x| \mid x \in B\} \\
TAx(G) &= \sum_{x \in B} |x| \\
Con(G) &= \text{card } C \\
LCon(G) &= \max \{|uv| \mid (u, v) \in C\} \\
TCon(G) &= \sum_{(u,v) \in C} |uv| \\
Fi(G) &= \text{card } \{M \subseteq C \mid \textit{there is } x \in V^* \textit{ such that } M = \varphi(x)\} \\
Ass(G) &= sup\{card\ \varphi(x) \mid x \in V^*\}.
\end{aligned}$$

These measures are defined for languages in the natural way:

$$M(L) = inf\{M(G) \mid L = L(G)\},$$

where $M \in \{Ax, LAx, TAx, Con, LCon, TCon, Fi, Ass\}$.

As usual, our proof of undecidability will be based on the undecidability of the Post Correspondence Problem. We denote by $PCP(x, y)$ the Post Correspondence Problem for x and y, where $x = (x_1, \cdots, x_k)$ and $y = (y_1, \cdots, y_k)$ are k–tuples of nonempty words over the alphabet $\{a, b\}$. We say that the problem $PCP(x, y)$ has a solution if there exists a sequence of indices $i_1, i_2, \cdots, i_t$ with $1 \leq i_j \leq k$, such that

$$x_{i_1} x_{i_2} \cdots x_{i_t} = y_{i_1} y_{i_2} \cdots y_{i_t}.$$

Post proved that it is undecidable for arbitrary k–tuples x and y, whether $PCP(x, y)$ has a solution, or not.

The connectedness problem

In (Păun 1982) the connectivity of the measures Ax, Con and Fi on T (the family of languages generated by general contextual grammars) is proved. Thus, we have

Theorem 1. *The measures Ax, Con and Fi are connected on the family of internal contextual languages.*

In [(Georgescu 1994), Theorem 2] it is shown that:

Theorem 2. *Ass is a connected measure on the family of internal contextual languages.*

Theorem 3. *The measures $LAx, TAx, LCon, TCon$ are connected on the family of internal contextual languages.*

Decidability problem

Theorem 4. *It is undecidable whether or not $Ax(G) = Ax(L(G))$ for an arbitrary internal contextual grammar G. (The problem $P5$ is undecidable for Ax.)*

Proof. Let us consider the grammar $G = (V, B, C, \varphi)$, where

$$\begin{aligned}
V &= \{a, b, c, d, e, f\},\\
B &= \{fcf, d, ed\},\\
C &= \{(x_i, Mi(y_i)) \mid 1 \leq i \leq k\} \cup \{(d, \lambda), (e, \lambda)\},\\
\varphi(c) &= \{(x_i, Mi(y_i)) \mid 1 \leq i \leq k\},\\
\varphi(ed) &= \{(e, \lambda)\},\\
\varphi(fzcMi(z)f) &= \{(d, \lambda)\}, \text{ for every } z \in \{a, b\}^+,\\
\varphi(z) &= \emptyset, \text{ otherwise.}
\end{aligned}$$

If $PCP(x, y)$ does not have a solution, then $L(G) = L_1 \cup L_2$, where:

$$L_1 = \{fx_{i_1} \cdots x_{i_t} cMi(y_{i_1} \cdots y_{i_t})f \mid t \geq 0, 1 \leq i_1, \cdots, i_t \leq k\},$$

$$L_2 = \{e^n d \mid n \geq 0\}.$$

But, in this case, $L(G)$ can be generated by the grammar $G_1 = (\{a, b, c, d, e, f\}, B_1, C_1, \varphi_1)$, where $B_1 = \{fcf, d\}$, $C_1 = \{(x_i, Mi(y_i)) \mid 1 \leq i \leq k\} \cup \{(e, \lambda)\}$, and

φ_1 is defined by

$$\begin{aligned}\varphi_1(c) &= \{(x_i, Mi(y_i)) \mid 1 \le i \le k\},\\ \varphi_1(d) &= \{(e, \lambda)\},\\ \varphi_1(z) &= \emptyset, \text{ otherwise.}\end{aligned}$$

Therefore, $Ax(L(G)) \le 2$. More precisely, $Ax(L(G)) = 2$, because the two words from B_1 have distinct letters.

If $PCP(x, y)$ has a solution, then $L = L_1 \cup L_2 \cup L_3$, where

$$\begin{aligned}L_3 = \{&d^n f x_{i_1} \cdots x_{i_t} c Mi(x_{i_1} \cdots x_{i_t}) f \mid t \ge 1, n \ge 1,\ 1 \le i_1, \cdots, i_t \le k,\\ &\textit{and } i_1, \cdots i_t \textit{ is a solution for} PCP(x, y)\}.\end{aligned}$$

Let $G_2 = (V, B_2, C_2, \varphi_2)$ be an internal contextual grammar which generates $L(G) = L_1 \cup L_2 \cup L_3, L_3 \ne \emptyset$. Obviously, if $x \Longrightarrow_{G_2} y$, then $|x| \le |y|$. Because d is the smallest string in $L(G)$, it follows that $d \in B_2$. Suppose that $\varphi_2(d) \ne \emptyset$ and let $(u, v) \in \varphi_2(d)$. So $d \Longrightarrow_{G_2} udv$, and $u = e^p, p \ge 0, v = \lambda$. We also have the following derivation in G_2:

$$d f x_{i_1} \cdots x_{i_t} c Mi(x_{i_1} \cdots x_{i_t}) f \Longrightarrow_{G_2} u d f x_{i_1} \cdots x_{i_t} c Mi(x_{i_1} \cdots x_{i_t}) f = w,$$

where $i_1, \cdots, i_t$ is a solution for $PCP(x, y)$. Thus, $w \in L(G_2)$ has the form $w = udz$, where $z \in L_1$. It follows that $u = \lambda$, so $p = 0$. Hence, to generate a string $e^n d, n > 0$, we need at least one axiom of the form $e^s d, s \ge 1$, in B_2.

On the other hand, to generate L_1 by G_2, we need at least one axiom of the form $f x_{i_1} \cdots x_{i_t} c Mi(y_{i_1} \cdots y_{i_t}) f, t \ge 0$. Because fcf is the smallest string of this form, it follows that $fcf \in B_2$. Thus, $|B_3| \ge 3$, and hence $Ax(L(G)) \ge 3$, because G_2 is an arbitrary internal contextual grammar generating $L(G)$.

In conclusion, $Ax(L(G)) = Ax(G) = 3$ if and only if $PCP(x, y)$ has a solution. Hence, we cannot decide whether or not $Ax(L(G)) = Ax(G)$. □

Theorem 5. *For no integer $n \ge 3$ is it decidable for an arbitrary internal contextual grammar G whether or not $Ax(L(G)) = n$. (The problem P4 is undecidable for Ax.)*

Proof. Let us consider the grammar $G_n = (V_n, B_n, C_n, \varphi_n)$, where

$$\begin{aligned}V_n &= \{a, b, c, d, f\} \cup \{e_i \mid 1 \le i \le n-2\},\\ B_n &= \{fcf\} \cup \{d, e_i d \mid 1 \le i \le n-2\},\\ C_n &= \{(x_i, Mi(y_i)) \mid 1 \le i \le k\} \cup \{e_i, \lambda) \mid 1 \le i \le n-2\} \cup \{(d, \lambda)\\ \varphi_n(c) &= \{(x_i, Mi(y_i)) \mid 1 \le i \le k\},\end{aligned}$$

$$\begin{aligned}
\varphi_n(e_j d) &= \{(e_i,\lambda) \mid 1 \le i \le n-2\}, \text{ for every } 1 \le j \le n-2,\\
\varphi_n(fzcMi(z)f) &= \{(d,\lambda)\}, \text{ for every } z \in \{a,b\}^+,\\
\varphi(z) &= \emptyset, \text{ otherwise.}
\end{aligned}$$

We can prove that $Ax(L(G_n)) = n$ if and only if $PCP(x, y)$ has a solution, which is not decidable. □

The following two theorems have proofs similar to the proof of Theorem 4.

Theorem 6. *Let $n \ge 4$ be an integer. Then:*

a) It is undecidable whether or not $LAx(L(G)) = n$ for an arbitrary grammar G. (P4 is undecidable for LAx.)

b) It is undecidable whether or not $LAx(G) = LAx(L(G))$ for an arbitrary grammar G. (P5 is undecidable for LAx.)

Theorem 7. *Let $n \ge 6$ be an integer. Then:*

a) It is undecidable whether or not $TAx(L(G)) = n$ for an arbitrary grammar G. (P4 is undecidable for TAx.)

b) It is undecidable whether or not $TAx(G) = TAx(L(G))$ for an arbitrary grammar G. (P5 is undecidable for TAx.)

Theorem 8. *The problem P4 is undecidable for Con.*

Proof. Let $n > 4$. Consider the grammar $G = (V, B, C, \varphi)$, where:

$$\begin{aligned}
V &= \{a, b, c, d_1, \cdots, d_{n-k}\},\\
B &= \{c\},\\
C &= \{(x_i, Mi(y_i)) \mid 1 \le i \le k\} \cup \{(d_i,\lambda) \mid 1 \le i \le n-k\},\\
\varphi(c) &= \{(x_i, Mi(y_i)) \mid 1 \le i \le k\},\\
\varphi(zcMi(z)) &= \{(d_i,\lambda) \mid 1 \le i \le n\}, \text{ for every } z \in \{a,b\}^+,\\
\varphi(z) &= \emptyset, \text{ otherwise.}
\end{aligned}$$

Using proof similar to that of Theorem 4, we can prove the theorem.

Theorem 9. *There is an integer k_0 such that for every $n > k_0$ we have:*

a) It is undecidable whether or not $LCon(L(G)) = n$ for an arbitrary grammar G. (P4 is undecidable for $LCon$.)

b) It is undecidable whether or not $LCon(G) = LCon(L(G))$ for an arbitrary grammar G. (P5 is undecidable for $LCon$.)

Proof. a) Let $k_0 = \max\{|x_i y_i| \mid 1 \le i \le k\}$. Take the grammar $G = (V, B, C, \varphi)$, where:

$$\begin{aligned}
V &= \{a, b, c, d\},\\
B &= \{c\},
\end{aligned}$$

$$\begin{aligned} C &= \{(x_i, Mi(y_i)) \mid 1 \le i \le k\} \cup \{(d^n, \lambda)\}, \\ \varphi(c) &= \{(x_i, Mi(y_i)) \mid 1 \le i \le k\}, \\ \varphi(zcMi(z)) &= \{(d^n, \lambda)\}, \text{ for every } z \in \{a,b\}^+, \\ \varphi(z) &= \emptyset, \text{ otherwise.} \end{aligned}$$

We can prove that $LCon(L(G)) = n$ if and only if $PCP(x,y)$ has a solution, which is not decidable.

b) From a), $LCon(G) = n = LCon(L(G))$ if and only if $PCP(x,y)$ has a solution, which is not decidable. □

Theorem 10. *There is an integer k_1 such that for every $n > k_1$:*

a) It is undecidable whether or not $TCon(L(G)) = n$ for an arbitrary grammar G. (P4 is undecidable for $TCon$.)

b) It is undecidable whether or not $TCon(G) = TCon(L(G))$ for an arbitrary grammar G. (P5 is undecidable for $TCon$.)

Proof. Let $k_1 = \sum_{i=1}^{k} |x_i y_i|$. The proof is quite similar to the proof of Theorem 9. We consider the same grammar in which, instead of the context (d^n, λ) we use the context (d^{n-k_1}, λ). □

Theorem 11. *The measure Fi cannot be algorithmically computed for an arbitrary grammar G. (The problem P2 is undecidable for Fi.)*

Proof. Consider the internal contextual grammar $G = (V, B, C, \varphi)$ used to prove Theorem 9, case a). Then, φ has two values, the sets $\emptyset$ and $\{(x_i, Mi(y_i)) \mid 1 \le i \le k\}$ if and only if $PCP(x,y)$ does not have a solution.

But, if $PCP(x,y)$ has a solution, we also have $\varphi(xcMi(x)) = \{(d^n, \lambda)\}$, where $x = x_{i_1} \cdots x_{i_t}$, is a solution for $PCP(x,y)$. Then, $Fi(G) = 3$ if and only if $PCP(x,y)$ has a solution, which is not decidable.

Moreover, we can prove that $Fi(L(G)) = 3$ if and only if $PCP(x,y)$ has a solution and $Fi(L(G)) = 2$ if and only if $PCP(x,y)$ does not have a solution. □

Theorem 12. *The problems $P4, P5$ and $P6$ are undecidable for Fi.*

Proof. Let G be the grammar considered in the proof of Theorem 11.

In [4, Theorem 6.1], the language over $\{e, f, g\}$, $L_n = \{((e^i f)^3 g)^p \mid p \ge 0, i = 1, 2, \cdots, n\}$ is considered and it is proved that $Fi(L_n) = n$.

Now, for $n \ge 3$ we take the language $L(G) \cup L_{n-2}$. This language can be generated by the internal contextual grammar $G_1 = (V_1, B_1, C_1, \varphi_1)$, where

$$\begin{aligned} V_1 &= \{a, b, c, d, e, f, g\}, \\ B_1 &= \{c\} \cup \{(e^i f)^3 g \mid 1 \le i \le n-2\}, \end{aligned}$$

$$\begin{aligned} C_1 &= \{(x_i, Mi(y_i)) \mid 1 \le i \le k\} \cup \{((e^i f)^3 g, \lambda) \mid 1 \le i \le n-2\}, \\ \varphi_1(c) &= \{(x_i, Mi(y_i)) \mid 1 \le i \le k\}, \\ \varphi_1((e^i f)^3 g) &= \{((e^i f)^3 g, \lambda) \mid 1 \le i \le n-2\}, \\ \varphi_1(z) &= \emptyset, \text{ otherwise.} \end{aligned}$$

Obviously, because $L(G)$ and L_{n-2} are languages over two disjoined alphabets, we have $Fi(L(G_1)) = Fi(L(G)) + n - 2$. But, from the proof of theorem 11 we have $Fi(L(G)) = 2$ if and only if $PCP(x, y)$ does not have a solution. Hence, $Fi(L(G_1)) = n$ if and only if $PCP(x, y)$ does not have a solution, which is not decidable. Thus, $P4$ is undecidable for Fi.

Now, from Theorem 11, $Fi(G) = 2 = Fi(L(G))$ if and only if $PCP(x, y)$ has no solution. Hence $P5$ is undecidable for Fi.

Finally, suppose that we can algorithmically find an internal contextual grammar $G' = (V, B', C', \varphi)$ such that $L(G') = L(G)$, $Fi(G') = Fi(L(G))$. But, if $PCP(x, y)$ has no solution, then $L(G) = L_1$, otherwise, $L(G) = L_1 \cup L_2$. (L_1 and L_2 as in Theorem 9, case a). In the first case, $Fi(L(G)) = 2$. In the second case, $Fi(L(G)) = 3$ (see the previous theorem). Thus, for constructing G', we need to know if $L(G) = L_1$ or $L(G) = L_1 \cup L_2$, which is not decidable.

Hence, $P6$ is undecidable for Fi. □

The following lemma is obvious.

Lemma 13. *If P4 is undecidable for a measure K, then P3 is undecidable for K.*

Theorem 14. *The problem P3 is undecidable for Fi.*

Proof. It follows from Theorem 12 and Lemma 13. □

Using a result from (Georgescu 1994) we can prove the following theorem.

Theorem 15. *a) It is undecidable whether or not $Ass(L(G)) = n + 1$ for a given integer $n \ge k$ and for an arbitrary internal contextual grammar G. (P4 is undecidable for Ass.)*

b) It is undecidable whether or not $Ass(G) = Ass(L(G))$ for an arbitrary grammar G. (P5 is undecidable for Con.)

Lemma 16.(Păun 1982) *If P2 is decidable and P4 is undecidable for a measure K, then P3 and P6 are undecidable for K.*

Lemma 17. *The following measures: Ax, LAx, TAx, $Con, LCon$, $TCon, Ass$ are algorithmically computable.*

Theorem 18. *The problems P3 and P6 are undecidable for the measures Ax, LAx, TAx, $Con, LCon, TCon$.*

Proof. It follows from Lemma 16 and Lemma 17.

Compatibility problem

Theorem 19. *All the following pairs* (M_1, M_2) *contain incompatible measures:*

$$\begin{array}{rc} (i) & M_1 \in \{Ax, LAx, TAx\},\ M_2 \in \{Con, LCon, TCon\}, \\ (ii) & M_1 \in \{Ax, LAx, TAx\},\ M_2 = Ass, \\ (iii) & M_1 \in \{Fi, Con\},\ M_2 \in \{LCon, TCon\} \end{array}$$

Proof. i) Consider the language $L = \{d\} \cup \{e^n d \mid n \geq 2\}$.

Clearly, $Ax(L) = LAx(L) = TAx(L) = 1$, because L can be generated by the grammar $G = (\{e, d\}, \{d\}, \{(e, \lambda), (e^2, \lambda)\}, \varphi)$, where φ is defined by:

$$\begin{aligned} \varphi(d) &= \{(e^2, \lambda)\}, \\ \varphi(e^2 d) &= \{(e, \lambda)\}, \\ \varphi(z) &= \emptyset, \text{ otherwise.} \end{aligned}$$

But, if $L = L(G')$, $G' = (\{e, d\}, B', C', \varphi')$ with $Ax(G') = 1$, or $LAx(G') = 1$, or $TAx(G') = 1$, then obviously $B' = \{d\}$ (because d is the shortest string in L). Thus, as $e^2 d$ is the next shortest string, it follows that there is a context $(u, v) \in C'$ such that $(u, v) \in \varphi'(d)$ and $udv = e^2 d$. Therefore, $u = e^2$ and $v = \lambda$. Using this context, we can generate the sublanguage $\{e^{2n} d \mid n \geq 0\}$. But the string e^3 is also in $L(G')$ and it is not an axiom. Thus, there is another context $(u', v') \in C', u'v' \neq \lambda$. Therefore, $Con(G') \geq 2$, $LCon(G') \geq 2$, $TCon(G') > |uv| + |u'v'| = 2 + |u'v'| \geq 3$.

But L can be generated by the grammar $G'' = (V, \{d, e^2 d\}, \{(e, \lambda)\}, \varphi'')$, where

$$\begin{aligned} \varphi''(e^2 d) &= \{(e, \lambda)\} \\ \varphi''(z) &= \emptyset, \ \textit{for } z \neq e^2 d. \end{aligned}$$

Thus, $Con(L) = 1, LCon(L) = 1, TCon(L) = 1$.

(ii) Consider the language:

$$L = \{a^n c b^m \mid n, m \geq 0\},$$

We can prove that $Ax(L) = LAx(L) = TAx(L) = 1$.

If $G' = (V, B', C', \varphi')$ is an internal contextual grammar such that $L(G') = L, Ax(G') = 1$ or $LAx(G') = 1$ or $TAx(G') = 1$, then we can prove that $Ass(G') \geq 2$.

But L can be generated by the grammar $G'' = (\{a,b,c\}, \{a, ac, cb\}, \{(a,\lambda), (\lambda, b)\}, \varphi'')$,

$$\begin{aligned} \varphi''(ac) &= \{(a,\lambda)\}, \\ \varphi''(cb) &= \{\lambda, b)\}, \\ \varphi''(z) &= \emptyset, \textit{ otherwise}, \end{aligned}$$

and, hence, $Ass(L) = 1$.

(iii) We can prove that Fi is incompatible with $LCon$ and $TCon$, considering the language

$$L = \{ba^{2n} \mid n \geq 1\} \cup \{ca^{3n} \mid n \geq 1\}.$$

□

Lemma 20. *Let* $G_i = (V, B_i, C_i, \varphi_i), i = 1,2$ *be two internal contextual grammars such that* $L(G_1) = L(G_2)$ *and let* $C = C_1 \cup C_2$, $\varphi : V^* \longrightarrow V^* \times V^*$, *defined by* $\varphi(z) = \varphi_1(z) \cup \varphi_2(z)$. *Let* $G_i' = (V, B_i, C, \varphi)$, $i = 1,2$. *Then* $L(G_i') = L(G_i)$, $Ax(G_i') = Ax(G_i)$, $LAx(G_i') = LAx(G_i), TAx(G_i') = TAx(G_i)$, $i = 1,2$.

Theorem 21. *The measures* Ax *and* TAx *are compatible.*

Proof. Assume that the two measures are incompatible. Then there is a language L such that $Ax^{-1}(L) \cap TAx^{-1}(L) = \emptyset$. Moreover, there are the internal contextual grammars $G_i = (V, B_i, C_i, \varphi_i)$, $i = 1,2$ such that

$$\begin{aligned} L(G_1) &= L, \ Ax(G_1) = Ax(L), && (1) \\ L(G_2) &= L, \ TAx(G_2) = TAx(L), && (2) \\ Ax(G_1) &< Ax(G_2), && (3) \\ TAx(G_1) &> TAx(G_2). && (4) \end{aligned}$$

We can suppose that $Ax(G_2)$ and $TAx(G_1)$ are minimal with these properties. Also, from Lemma 20, we can suppose that $C_1 = C_2, \varphi_1 = \varphi_2$. Then

$$z \overset{*}{\Longrightarrow}_{G_1} w \text{ if and only if } z \overset{*}{\Longrightarrow}_{G_2} w. \quad (*)$$

Let $B_1 = \{u_1, \cdots, u_s\}$, $B_2 = \{v_1, \cdots, v_t\}$, such that $|u_1| \leq \cdots \leq |u_s|$, $|v_1| \leq \cdots \leq |v_t|$. From 3 and 4 we deduce that

$$s < t \qquad (5)$$

$$\sum_{i=1}^{s} |u_i| > \sum_{i=1}^{t} |v_i|. \qquad (6)$$

Assume that $u_s \notin B_2$. Then, there is $v_j \in B_2$, $1 \leq j \leq t$, such that $v_j \overset{+}{\Longrightarrow}_{G_2} u_s$. Thus $|v_j| < |u_s|$. Also, from $v_j \in L(G_1)$, it follows that there is $u_k \in$

$B_1, 1 \leq k \leq s$, such that $u_k \overset{*}{\Longrightarrow}_{G_1} v_j$, $|u_k| < |u_s|$. It follows that (because of (*)) $u_k \overset{+}{\Longrightarrow}_{G_1} u_s$, so u_s can be eliminated from B_1, a contradiction (B_1 is minimal). Thus, $u_s \in B_2$. Suppose that $u_s = v_i, 1 \leq i < t$ and $|v_i| < |v_t|$. Then, because $v_t \in L(G_1)$, we find that there is $u_{i_0}, 1 \leq i_0 \leq s$, such that $u_{i_0} \overset{*}{\Longrightarrow}_{G_1} v_t$. Because $\max_{1 \leq j \leq s} |u_j| = |u_s| = |v_i| < |v_t|$, it follows that $u_{i_0} \overset{+}{\Longrightarrow}_{G_1} v_t$. Hence $|u_{i_0}| < |v_t|$. From (*) we find that $u_{i_0} \overset{*}{\Longrightarrow}_{G_2} v_t$. But then the grammar $G'_2 = (V, B'_2, C_2, \varphi_2)$, where $B'_2 = (B_2 - \{v_t\}) \cup \{u_{i_0}\}$, generates L and $TAx(G'_2) < TAx(G_2)$, a contradiction.

Thus, it is not possible that $|v_i| < |v_t|$, where $v_i = u_s$. We can suppose that $u_s = v_t$. Let us consider the following sets:

$$\begin{aligned} M_1 &= \{u_1, \cdots, u_{s-1}\}, \\ N_1 &= \{v_1, \cdots, v_{t-1}\}. \end{aligned}$$

Using the same reasoning as above, after eventually renumbering the strings $v_p, \cdots, v_{t-1}$, where $|v_{p-1}| < |v_p| = \cdots = |v_t|$, we obtain $|u_{s-1}| = |v_{t-1}|$.

Repeating this procedure for $u_{s-2}, \cdots, u_2, u_1$, we obtain $u_1 = v_{t-s+1}$. So, $u_1 = v_{t-s+1}, \cdots, u_s = v_t$, which means that $B_1 \subset B_2$ (because we supposed that $t > s$). But this means that $TAx(G_1) = \sum_{u \in B_1} |u| < \sum_{v \in B_2} |v| = TAx(G_2)$, which contradicts the relation 4.

Now, the proof is over. □

Using proof similar to that of the previous theorem, we can prove the following theorem.

Theorem 22. *The measures Ax and TAx are compatible with LAx.*

References

Gruska, J. 1973. "Descriptional complexity of context-free languages". *Proc. Math. Found. Comp. Sci. Symp.* High Tatras, 71–83.

Georgescu, G. 1994. "Infinite hierarchies of some types of contextual languages". In Gh. Păun (ed), *Mathematical Aspects of Natural and Formal Languages.* Singapore: World Scientific Pub. 137–150.

Marcus, S. 1969. "Contextual grammars". *Rev. Roum. Math. Pures Appl.*, 14, 10 (1969). 1525–1534.

Păun, G. 1982. *Contextual Grammars*, Bucureşti: The Publishing House of the Romanian Academy (in Romanian).

Păun, G. 1991. "Further remarks on the syntactic complexity of Marcus contextual languages". *Ann. Univ. Bucharest, Ser. Matem.- Inform.* 3 (1990-1991): 72–82.

Păun, G., Rozenberg, G. and Salomaa, A. 1994. "Contextual grammars: Erasing, determinism, one-sided contexts". In G. Rozenberg and A. Salomaa (eds), *Developments in Language Theory.* Singapore: World Sci. Publ. 370–388.

On Ambiguity in Internal Contextual Languages

Lucian Ilie[1]

Turku Centre for Computer Science

Abstract

Several types of ambiguity in internal contextual languages have already been introduced. We define a new natural type and investigate all types here, mainly in connection with determinism, contextual grammars without choice, and grammars over one-letter alphabets. Several open problems are also formulated.

Introduction

Contextual grammars were introduced in (Marcus 1969), starting from the basic phenomenon in descriptive linguistics of acceptance of a string by a context or vice versa (see (Marcus 1967)). Many variants have already been investigated; the reader is referred to the monograph (Păun 1982) for details (at the level of the year 1981).

---

[1]Research supported by the Academy of Finland, project 137358.

On leave of absence from Faculty of Mathematics, University of Bucharest, Str. Academiei 14, R-70109, Bucharest, Romania.

In the recent paper (Martín-Vide, Miquel-Vergés, Păun, Salomaa 1995), the notion of ambiguity was considered for the first time in this field. Several levels of ambiguity in internal contextual languages were discussed depending on how much information has to be considered in order to describe two distinct derivations: (1) – the axiom and the contexts used; (2) – the axiom and the contexts and selectors used; (3) – (1) together with the order; (4) – (2) together with the order; (5) – the axiom, the contexts used, and the places where they are introduced (that is to say, as much information as possible). For further comments on these types see (Martín-Vide, Miquel-Vergés, Păun, Salomaa 1995).

We introduce here a new type of ambiguity ((0) – only the axiom is taken into account which, as will be seen, is not in the least trivial) and we investigate all the six types mainly from the point of view of determinism, contextual grammars without choice, and grammars over one-letter alphabets.

Basic definitions

For an alphabet V, we denote by V^* the free monoid generated by the alphabet V, λ is the empty string, $V^+ = V^* - \{\lambda\}$, $|x|$ is the length of $x \in V^*$, $|x|_a$ is the number of $a \in V$ occurrences in $x \in V^*$, x_i is the i-th letter of x, and *FIN, REG, CF, CS* are the families of finite, regular, context-free, context-sensitive languages, respectively. For further language theory elements, the reader is referred to (Salomaa 1973).

An *(internal) contextual grammar* is a construct

$$G = (V, B, (D_1, C_1), \ldots, (D_n, C_n)),$$

where V is an alphabet, $B \subseteq V^*$ is a finite language, $D_i \subseteq V^*, C_i \subseteq (V^* \times V^+) \cup (V^+ \times V^*)$, $1 \leq i \leq n$, such that each C_i is a finite set.

The elements of B are called *axioms*, those of C_i are called *contexts*, and D_i is the *selector* associated with the set $C_i, 1 \leq i \leq n$. Note that we do not allow contexts of the form (λ, λ).

If the selectors $D_1, \ldots, D_n$ are languages in a given family F, then we say that G *has F choice.* If $n = 1$ and $D_1 = V^*$, then we say that G is a grammar *without choice*; the set D can then be omitted.

For $w, z \in V^*$ we define

$$w \Longrightarrow z \text{ iff } w = x_1x_2x_3, z = x_1ux_2vx_3, \text{ where } (u,v) \in C_i, x_2 \in D_i, \text{ for some } i, 1 \le i \le n, x_1, x_2, x_3 \in V^*.$$

Then the language generated by G (in the internal mode) is

$$L(G) = \{z \in V^* \mid w \overset{*}{\Longrightarrow} z, \text{ for some } w \in B\},$$

where $\overset{*}{\Longrightarrow}$ is the reflexive and transitive closure of the relation $\Longrightarrow$.

We denote by $IC(F)$ the family of languages generated as above by contextual grammars with F choice and by IC the family of languages generated by contextual grammars with arbitrary choice.

From (Ehrenfeucht, Păun, Rozenberg 1997), (Păun 1982), and (Păun, Nguyen 1980) we know that $REG \subset IC(FIN) \subset IC(REG) \subset CS$, strict inclusions, and $IC(FIN)$ and CF are incomparable.

The above way of giving a contextual grammar is called *the modular presentation*; an equivalent one is the *functional presentation*, based on the *choice mapping* $\varphi : V^* \longrightarrow 2^C$, defined by

$$\varphi(x) = \{(u,v) \mid (u,v) \in C_i, x \in D_i, 1 \le i \le n\}, x \in V^*.$$

(For grammars without choice we get $\varphi(x) = C$ for all $x \in V^*$.) Then we can write the grammar in the form $G = (V, B, C, \varphi)$, where V, B are as above, C is the set of all contexts, and φ is the selection mapping$\varphi : V^* \longrightarrow 2^C$. The derivation relation is defined by

$$w \Longrightarrow z \text{ iff } w = x_1x_2x_3 \text{ for } x_1, x_2, x_3 \in V^*, z = x_1ux_2vx_3 \text{ for } (u,v) \in \varphi(x_2).$$

Conversely, given a grammar in the functional presentation, $G = (V, B, C, \varphi)$, we can write it equivalently as

$$G = (V, B, (D_1, C_1), \ldots, (D_n, C_n)),$$

where $C_i \subseteq C$ and $D_i = \{x \in V^* \mid \varphi(x) = C_i\} \neq \emptyset$, $1 \le i \le n$. (Clearly, $n \le 2^{card(C)}$.)

In what follows we shall use both presentations of contextual grammars and it will be understood from the context which one is being used.

Let us now formally define the six types of ambiguity mentioned in the introduction.

Given a contextual grammar $G = (V, B, C, \varphi)$ and a derivation

$$\delta : w_1 \Longrightarrow w_2 \Longrightarrow \ldots \Longrightarrow w_m, m \geq 1,$$

such that

$$\begin{aligned} & w_1 \in B, \\ & w_i = x_{1,i}x_{2,i}x_{3,i}, \ x_{1,i}, x_{2,i}, x_{3,i} \in V^*, \\ & w_{i+1} = x_{1,i}u_ix_{2,i}v_ix_{3,i}, \text{ for} \\ & (u_i, v_i) \in \varphi(x_{2,i}), 1 \leq i \leq m-1, \end{aligned}$$

the sequence

$$w_1, (u_1, v_1), \ldots, (u_{m-1}, v_{m-1})$$

is called *the control sequence* associated to δ. *The axiom* associated to δ is w_1.

We call *the description* of δ the sequence

$$w_1, x_{1,1}(u_1)x_{2,1}(v_1)x_{3,1}, \ldots, x_{1,m-1}(u_{m-1})x_{2,m-1}(v_{m-1})x_{3,m-1}$$

(the parentheses precisely identify the contexts used and the place of adjoining them).

An intermediate case is to specify only the contexts and their selectors, not the position in which they appear. Thus, we call *complete control sequence* the sequence

$$w_1, ((u_1, v_1), x_{2,1}), ((u_2, v_2), x_{2,2}), \ldots, ((u_{m-1}, v_{m-1}), x_{2,m-1}).$$

If we take into account only the contexts (and selectors) used and not the order of using them, then we obtain the *unordered control sequence* and the *unordered complete control sequence*, respectively.

Briefly, the six types of ambiguity are defined as follows (for more details see (Martín-Vide, Miquel-Vergés, Păun, Salomaa 1995))

$0 - ambiguity$ = two axioms,

$1 - ambiguity$ = two unordered control sequences,

$2 - ambiguity$ = two unordered complete control sequences,

$3 - ambiguity =$ two control sequences,

$4 - ambiguity =$ two complete control sequences,

$5 - ambiguity =$ two descriptions.

A grammar which is not t-ambiguous, for some $t = 0,1,2,3,4,5$, is said to be t-unambiguous. A language $L \in IC(F)$ is *inherently t-ambiguous* if every grammar G (with F choice) generating L is t-ambiguous. A language for which a t-unambiguous grammar exists is called *t-unambigu ous.*

Contextual grammars without choice

First, we are going to show that in the case of grammars without choice, not all types of ambiguity defined in the previous section are non-trivial. We begin with two remarks:

Remark 1. Any internal contextual grammar without choice is 2-ambiguous as long as its set of contexts is non-empty.

Indeed, if there is at least one context, because it can be applied to any selector, it follows that the grammar is 2-ambiguous. (Remember that we cannot have contexts of the form (λ, λ).)

Remark 2. Any internal contextual grammar without choice is 3-ambiguous as long as it has at least two (different) contexts; if it has only one context, then it is 3-ambiguous if and only if it is 0-ambiguous.

Again, because any context can be applied to any selector, it is obvious that if the grammar has at least two contexts, then it is possible to find a derivation in which the order of contexts applied can be changed. Thus the grammar is 3-ambiguous. On the other hand, if the grammar has only one context, then the 3-ambiguity can appear only at the level of axiom, so it is in fact 0-ambiguity.

It is clear now that in the case of internal contextual grammars without choice, we have to consider only two types of ambiguity, namely 0-ambiguity and 1-ambiguity.

In what follows, we give some results which compare the ambiguity between grammars with finite choice and grammars without choice.

Theorem 1. *There are inherently 0-ambiguous languages with respect to* *internal contextual grammars without choice which are 0-unambiguous with respect to internal contextual grammars with finite choice.*

Proof. Consider the language

$$L = \{a, b\}^+$$

and an arbitrary internal contextual grammar without choice $G=(\{a,b\},B,C)$ generating L.

Because all strings in a^+ are in L, it follows that there must be a context of the form $(a^p, a^q), p, q \geq 0, p+q \geq 1$, in C. Applying the same reasoning for b, we find that there must be a context of the form $(b^r, b^s), r, s \geq 0, r+s \geq 1$, in C.

Because the strings $a^p a^q$ and $b^r b^s$ are in L, it follows that there are the axioms $w_1, w_2 \in B$ such that

$$w_1 \overset{*}{\Longrightarrow} a^p a^q,$$
$$w_2 \overset{*}{\Longrightarrow} b^r b^s.$$

(It is possible to have $w_1 = a^p a^q$ and/or $w_2 = b^r b^s$.) Moreover, because L does not contain the empty string, we must have $w_1 \neq w_2$. As G is without choice, we also have the derivations

$$a^p a^q \Longrightarrow b^r a^p b^s a^q,$$
$$b^r b^s \Longrightarrow b^r a^p b^s a^q.$$

Consequently, the string $b^r a^p b^s a^q$ can be obtained starting from two different axioms, w_1 and w_2, so the grammar is 0-ambiguous.

In order to prove that the given language is 0-unambiguous with respect to internal contextual grammars with finite choice, we can take the grammar

$$G' = (\{a,b\}, \{a,b\}, (\{a\}, \{(a,\lambda), (b,\lambda), (\lambda,a), (\lambda,b)\}), (\{b\}, \{(\lambda,b)\})).$$

Obviously, $L(G') = L$. As can be seen, any string in L containing an a can be obtained only from the axiom a and all strings in b^+ can be obtained only from the axiom b, so G' is 0-unambiguous. □

Open problem 1. Are there inherently 0-ambiguous languages with respect to internal contextual grammars without choice which are 1-unambiguous (or t-unambiguous, $t = 2,3,4,5$) with respect to internal contextual grammars with finite choice? (The grammar G' above is 1-ambiguous.) We believe that such languages exist, at least for the 1-ambiguity case.

Theorem 2. *There are inherently 1-ambiguous languages with respect to internal contextual grammars without choice which are 0-unambiguous with respect to internal contextual grammars with finite choice as well as without choice.*

Proof. Consider the language

$$L = \{x \in \{a,b\}^* \mid |x|_a = |x|_b\}.$$

It was proved in (Martín-Vide, Miquel-Vergés, Păun, Salomaa 1995) that L is inherently 1-ambigu ous with respect to internal contextual grammars without choice. For the second part of the theorem, let us consider the grammars

$$G = (\{a,b\}, \{\lambda\}, (\{\lambda\}, \{(a,b),(b,a)\}))$$

(G is with finite choice) and

$$G' = (\{a,b\}, \{\lambda\}, \{(a,b),(b,a)\})$$

(G' is without choice). Obviously, $L(G) = L(G') = L$ and both grammars are 0-unambiguous because each of them has only one axiom. □

Open problem 2. Are there inherently 1-ambiguous languages with respect to internal contextual grammars without choice which are t-unambiguous ($t = 1,2,3,4,5$) with respect to internal contextual grammars with finite choice?

Determinism

An internal contextual grammar $G = (V, B, C, \varphi)$ is called *deterministic* if and only if $card(\varphi(w)) \leq 1$, for any $w \in V^*$. We denote by $DIC(F)$ the family of languages generated by deterministic contextual grammars with F choice and by DIC the family of languages generated by deterministic contextual grammars with arbitrary choice.

From (Ehrenfeucht, Păun, Rozenberg 1997) and (Ehrenfeucht, Ilie, Păun, Rozenberg, Salomaa 1995) we have $DIC(REG) - CF \neq \emptyset$ and $DIC \subset IC$.

First of all, notice that all the six types of ambiguity introduced so far do make sense in the deterministic case, and they are not affected by the fact that here the selector determines the context. On the other hand, we cannot consider here the case of grammars without choice because this would impose the condition that there is at most one context, and the case would be trivial.

Note also that because all the grammars in the proofs of (Martín-Vide, Miquel-Vergés, Păun, Salomaa 1995) are deterministic, the Theorems 1, 2, & 3 give the following result.

Theorem 3. *There are inherently 5-(4-,3-)ambiguous languages with respect to deterministic internal contextual grammars with arbitrary choice which are 4-(2- and 3-, 1- and 2-, respectively) unambiguous with respect to deterministic internal contextual grammars with finite choice.*

We give the following result to compare the ambiguity in the non-deterministic and the deterministic case.

Theorem 4. *There are inherently 4-ambiguous languages with respect to deterministic contextual grammars with finite choice which are 5-unambiguous with respect to non-deterministic internal contextual grammars with finite choice.*

Proof. Consider the language

$$L = c\{a, b\}^*.$$

L is generated by the (non deterministic) internal contextual grammar with finite choice

$$G = (\{a, b, c\}, \{c\}, (\{c\}, \{(\lambda, a), (\lambda, b)\})).$$

Obviously G is 5-unambiguous, for any string $cw \in c\{a, b\}^*, w = w_1 w_2 \ldots w_{|w|}$, $w_i \in \{a, b\}$, $1 \leq i \leq |w|$, the only possible description being

$$c, (\lambda)c(w_{|w|}), (\lambda)c(w_{|w|-1})w_{|w|}, \ldots, (\lambda)c(w_1)w_2 \ldots w_{|w|}.$$

Before showing that L is inherently 4-ambiguous with respect to deterministic internal contextual grammars with finite choice, let us prove that L can indeed be generated by a deterministic internal contextual grammar. Take the grammar

$$G' = (\{a,b,c\}, \{cw \mid w \in \{a,b\}^*, |w| \leq 2\},$$
$$(\{a,b\}, \{(\lambda, a)\}), (\{aa, ab, ba, bb\}, \{(\lambda, b)\})).$$

(The construction is similar to one in (Păun, Rozenberg, Salomaa 1994a).) We prove by induction on $n \geq 1$ that any $w \in c\{a,b\}^*, |w| = n$, can be generated by G'. For $n \in \{1,2,3\}$, this is obvious. Suppose that for some $n \geq 3$, all w with $|w| = n$ belong to $L(G')$ and take $z \in c\{a,b\}^*, |z| = n+1$.

Depending on the last letter of z, we have two cases:

(a) $z = wa, |w| = n$. As $w \in L(G')$ and z can be obtained from w by adding the context (λ, a) around $w_{|w|}$, it follows that $z \in L(G')$.

(b) $z = wb, |w| = n$. Again $w \in L(G')$ and z can be obtained from w by adding the context (λ, b) around $w_{|w|-1}w_{|w|}$, so $z \in L(G')$.

Consequently, $L(G') = L$, and L is a deterministic internal contextual language.

Take now an arbitrary deterministic grammar $G'' = (\{c,a,b\}, B, C, \varphi)$ generating L.

Claim 1. There are (in G'') contexts which can be applied to selectors which do not contain the symbol c.

Proof of Claim 1. Suppose that all contexts in G'' can be applied only to selectors in $c\{a,b\}^*$. It follows that all contexts are of the form $(\lambda, x), x \in \{a,b\}^+$. Suppose also that

$$\max_{cw \in B} |w| = k \geq 1.$$

Without loss of generality we may suppose that

$$B = \{cw \mid w \in \{a,b\}^*, |w| \leq k\}$$

and, for any $cw \in B$, $\varphi(cw) \neq \emptyset$. As $|\varphi(w)| = 1$ for any $w \in B$, for the rest of this proof, we shall denote by $\varphi(w)$ just the non-empty string it contains (i.e. $\varphi(w) = (\lambda, \varphi(w))$). Denote also $\overline{a} = b$ and $\overline{b} = a$ ($\overline{x}$ is the complement of $x \in \{a,b\}$).

Consider the string

$$z = cz_2z_3 \ldots z_{k+2}$$

where $z_i \in \{a,b\}, 2 \leq i \leq k+2$, and, for any $i, 2 \leq i \leq k+2$,

$$z_i = \overline{(\varphi(cz_2z_3 \ldots z_{i-1}))_1}$$

(that is the complement of the first letter of the string $\varphi(cz_2z_3 \ldots z_{i-1})$; note that z_i is well defined for any $2 \leq i \leq k+2$). As can be easily seen, $z \notin L(G'')$, a contradiction.

Claim 2. There are at least two different selectors to which some contexts can be added.

Proof of Claim 2. Suppose, by contradiction, that there is only one selector, say w, to which a context $(\varphi(w))$ can be added. Because we can find in L arbitrarily long strings which do not contain w as a substring, it follows that $L(G'')$ is strictly included in L, a contradiction.

From Claims 1 and 2 we find that there are at least two different selectors, say s_1 and s_2, to which some contexts can be added and, moreover, at least one of them, say s_2, does not begin with c.

Take

$$s_1' = \begin{cases} s_1, & \text{if } s_1 \in \{a,b\}^*, \\ s_1'', & \text{if } s_1 = cs_1'', s_1'' \in \{a,b\}^*. \end{cases}$$

The string $w = cs_1's_2$ is obviously in L and, supposing that $\varphi(s_1) = \{(u_1,v_1)\}$, $\varphi(s_2) = \{(u_2,v_2)\}$ ($u_1 = \lambda$ if $s_1 \in c\{a,b\}^*$), we have the derivations

$$w = cs_1's_2 \Longrightarrow cu_1s_1'v_1s_2 \Longrightarrow cu_1s_1'v_1u_2s_2v_2,$$
$$w = cs_1's_2 \Longrightarrow cs_1'u_2s_2v_2 \Longrightarrow cu_1s_1'v_1u_2s_2v_2.$$

Consequently, we have found two different complete control sequences for the string $cu_1s_1'v_1u_2s_2v_2$, hence G'' is 4-ambiguous. □

Corollary 5. *There are inherently 5-ambiguous languages with respect to deterministic contextual grammars with finite choice which are 5-unambiguous with respect to non-deterministic internal contextual grammars with finite choice.*

Corollary 6. *There are inherently 4-ambiguous languages with respect to deterministic contextual grammars with finite choice which are 4-unambiguous with respect to non-deterministic internal contextual grammars with finite choice.*

Open problem 3. Are there inherently t-ambiguous languages ($t = 0, 1, 2, 3$) with respect to deterministic internal contextual grammars with finite choice which are 5-unambiguous with respect to non-deterministic internal contextual grammars with finite choice? We believe that the example in Theorem 4 is even 0-ambiguous with respect to deterministic internal contextual grammars with finite choice.

What about inherently t-ambiguous languages ($t = 0,1,2,3,4,5$) with respect to deterministic internal contextual grammars with arbitrary choice which are s-unambiguous ($s = 0,1,2,3,4,5$) with respect to non-deterministic contextual grammars with finite choice?

The one-letter case

In this section we consider ambiguity in internal contextual languages and grammars over one-letter alphabets. As expected, all problems are simpler in this case and we are able to give a complete characterization of ambiguous languages and show that all types of ambiguity are decidable for grammars over one-letter alphabets. (This is not true for grammars with arbitrary alphabets (Martín-Vide, Miquel-Vergés, Păun, Salomaa 1995).)

Things are simpler in this case because here the choice is not important, in the sense that the generative power of grammars with arbitrary choice is the same as for finite choice. In what follows, all results are proved for arbitrary choice. The results can be easily modified for grammars without choice.

Theorem 7. *For any internal contextual language $L \subseteq a^*$ we have*

1. L is 4-unambiguous,

2. L is 5-ambiguous if and only if it is infinite.

Proof. Let $L \subseteq a^*$ be an arbitrary internal contextual language. It is rather obvious that, with the possible exception of an initial "mess", L is a finite union of languages over $\{a\}$ such that the length set of each of them is an infinite arithmetical progression. More formally, L can be written as follows

$$L = F \cup \bigcup_{i=1}^{k} L_i,$$

where $F \subset a^*$ is a finite set and, for any $1 \leq i \leq k$, there are some positive integers $m_i \geq 0, n_i \geq 1$, such that

$$L_i = \{a^{m_i + nn_i} \mid n \geq 0\}.$$

Let us take

$$m_0 = \max\{\max\{m_1, m_2, \ldots, m_k\}, \max_{w \in F} |w|\},$$
$$n_0 = \operatorname{lcm}(n_1, n_2, \ldots, n_k).$$

L can be generated by the grammar

$$G = (\{a\}, B, (D, C))$$

where

$$B = F \cup \bigcup_{i=1}^{k} \{w \in L_i \mid |w| \leq m_0 + n_0\},$$
$$D = \{a^r\}, \text{ where } r = \min_{1 \leq i \leq k} (\min\{|w| \mid w \in L_i, |w| > m_0\}),$$
$$C = \{(\lambda, a^{n_0})\}.$$

It can be seen that $L(G) = L$ (the initial "mess" is contained in the axiom set and all languages $L_i, 1 \leq i \leq k$, are generated using only contexts of the form (λ, a^{n_0})). Moreover, for any string in L, there is exactly one possible complete control sequence (because the context in C cannot be applied to a string in F, all strings in F having lengths under m_0). It follows that L is 4-unambiguous.

For the second part of our result, it is obvious that if L is finite, then it is not 5-ambiguous. Let us suppose that L is infinite. In this case, there is at least one context which can be applied to a selector. Because we are working over one letter, it follows that, for long enough strings, we can choose the position of the selectors in several different ways. Hence 5-ambiguity follows. □

Even if all languages over one-letter alphabets are not 4-ambiguous, we can also find 4-ambiguous grammars. Below, we show that any type of ambiguity introduced so far is decidable for grammars in the one-letter case and also that certain types of ambiguity have the same meaning in this case.

Theorem 8. *It is decidable whether or not an arbitrary internal contextual grammar over a one-letter alphabet is 0-ambiguous.*

Proof. Take an arbitrary internal contextual grammar $G = (\{a\}, B, C, \varphi)$. Let us take $B = \{w_1, w_2, \ldots, w_k\}, k \geq 1$. If $k = 1$, then, obviously, G is not

0-ambiguous (having only one axiom). Suppose now that $k \geq 2$ and take, for any $1 \leq i \leq k$,

$$G_i = (\{a\}, \{w_i\}, C, \varphi).$$

For any $i, 1 \leq i \leq k$, the language $L_i = L(G_i)$ is effectively regular so we can decide whether or not there are some $i, j, 1 \leq i, j \leq k, i \neq j$, such that $L_i \cap L_j = \emptyset$. Because G is 0-ambiguous if and only if there are such i and j, the conclusion follows. □

Theorem 9. *It is decidable whether or not an arbitrary internal contextual grammar over a one-letter alphabet is 1-ambiguous.*

Proof. Take an arbitrary internal contextual grammar $G = (\{a\}, B, C, \varphi)$. First, we can decide (by Theorem 8) whether or not G is 0-ambiguous. If it is, then it is also 1-ambiguous. Suppose that G is not 0-ambiguous. Depending on the number of contexts in C, we distinguish two cases

(a) There is at most one context in C. In this case G is not 1-ambiguous.

(b) There are at least two contexts in C. (Of course, we may suppose that there are at least two useful contexts, that is contexts which can be effectively applied to some selectors.) Denote the two contexts by $(a^m, a^n), m \geq 0, n \geq 0, m+n \geq 1$, and $(a^p, a^q), p \geq 0, q \geq 0, p+q \geq 1, (m,n) \neq (p,q)$, and suppose that $(a^m, a^n) \in \varphi(a^r)$, $(a^p, a^q) \in \varphi(a^s)$ for some $r \geq 0, s \geq 0$. We may suppose also that $r \geq s$. It follows that the string $a^{r+(m+n)(p+q)}$ has two different unordered control sequences, namely

$$\{a^r, \underbrace{(a^m, a^n), (a^m, a^n), \ldots, (a^m, a^n)}_{p+q \text{ times}}\}$$

and

$$\{a^r, \underbrace{(a^p, a^q), (a^p, a^q), \ldots, (a^p, a^q)}_{m+n \text{ times}}\}.$$

Consequently, G is 1-ambiguous in this case. □

From the proof of the above theorem we obtain the following result.

Corollary 10. *An internal contextual grammar which is not 0-ambiguous is 1-ambiguous if and only if its set of contexts contains at least two different (useful) contexts.*

Theorem 11. *It is decidable whether or not an arbitrary internal contextual grammar over a one-letter alphabet is 2-ambiguous.*

Proof. Take $G = (\{a\}, B, (D_1, C_1), \ldots, (D_n, C_n)), n \geq 1$, an arbitrary internal contextual grammar. We decide first (by Theorem 9) whether or not G is 1-ambiguous. If it is, then it is also 2-ambiguous. Suppose that G is not 1-ambiguous. By Corollary 10, we find that the set of contexts contains at most one context so $n = 1$ and $G = (\{a\}, B, (D, C))$. If C is empty, then G is not 2-ambiguous, Suppose that $card(C) = 1$. Depending on the number of selectors in D (again we suppose that all selectors in D are useful in the sense that for each of them there is at least one context in C which can be applied) we have two cases

(a) $card(D) = 1$. In this case G is not 2-ambiguous.

(b) $card(D) \geq 2$. Because, for long enough strings, we may suppose that the context in C is applied to different selectors, it follows that G is 2-ambiguous in this case. □

From the proof of the above theorem we obtain the following result.

Corollary 12. *An internal contextual grammar which is not 1-ambiguous is 2-ambiguous if and only if its set of selectors contains at least two different (useful) selectors.*

Theorem 13. *(i) An internal contextual grammar over a one-letter alphabet is 2-ambiguous if and only if it is 4-ambiguous.*

(ii) An internal contextual grammar over a one-letter alphabet is 1-ambiguous if and only if it is 3-ambiguous.

Proof. (i) The "only if" case is obvious. Suppose that an internal contextual grammar G is 4-ambiguous. It follows that there exists a string w which has two different complete control sequences. This is possible only in one of the following three cases

(a) w can be obtained from two different axioms. It follows that G is 0-ambiguous, hence 2-ambiguous.

(b) There are at least two contexts in the context set. By Corollary 10, G is 1-ambiguous and thus 2-ambiguous.

(c) There are at least two selectors in the selector set. In this case G is 2-ambiguous by Corollary 12.

(*ii*) The proof is similar to case (i). □

From Theorems 9, 11, and 13 we get

Corollary 14. *It is decidable whether or not an arbitrary internal contextual grammar over a one-letter alphabet is t-ambiguous, for any* $t \in \{3, 4\}$.

Theorem 15. *An internal contextual grammar over a one-letter alphabet generating an infinite language is 5-ambiguous.*

Proof. See the proof of 2 in Theorem 7. □

Corollary 16. *It is decidable whether or not an arbitrary internal contextual grammar over a one-letter alphabet is 5-ambiguous.*

Final remarks

Finally, we point out two more open problems of the decidability of ambiguity.

It has been proved in (Martín-Vide, Miquel-Vergés, Păun, Salomaa 1995) that ambiguity of any type is undecidable for (non-deterministic) internal contextual grammars. The first open problem concerns the deterministic case.

Open problem 4. Is t-ambiguity ($t = 0, 1, 2, 3, 4, 5$) decidable for deterministic internal contextual grammars?

We believe that ambiguity of any type is also undecidable in the deterministic case but we were not able to reduce the problem to the Post Correspondence Problem, as for the non-deterministic case (Martín-Vide, Miquel-Vergés, Păun, Salomaa 1995).

Another open problem concerns the status of decidability of t-ambiguity for internal contextual grammars without choice. As mentioned in section 3, here we have only two non-trivial types of ambiguity, namely 0-ambiguity and 1-ambiguity.

Open problem 5. Is t-ambiguity ($t = 0, 1$) decidable for internal contextual grammars without choice?

We have no conjecture about 1-ambiguity but we believe that 0-ambiguity is decidable here. (However, such a result would be rather unexpected.) An idea for an algorithm which verifies the 0-ambiguity for internal contextual grammars without choice could be as follows: suppose that $G = (V, B, C)$ is an internal contextual grammar without choice. If $card(B) = 1$, then G is not 0-ambiguous. Suppose that $B = \{w_1, w_2, \ldots, w_k\}, k \geq 2$. Denoting, for any $1 \leq i \leq k$,

$$G_i = (V, \{w_i\}, C)$$

it follows that G is 0-ambiguous if and only if there are $i, j, 1 \leq i, j \leq k, i \neq j$, such that $L(G_i) \cap L(G_j) \neq \emptyset$. But, in order to check this, it would suffice to prove that there exists an a priori computable constant $k_{ij} = k_{ij}(w_i, w_j, C)$ (that is, k_{ij} depends on w_i, w_j, and C) such that $L(G_i) \cap L(G_j) = \emptyset$ if and only if

$$\{w \in L(G_i) \mid |w| \leq k_{ij}\} \cap \{w \in L(G_j) \mid |w| \leq k_{ij}\} = \emptyset.$$

We believe that such a constant exists and the problem is decidable.

References

Ehrenfeucht, A., Păun, Gh. and Rozenberg, G. 1997. "On representing recursively enumerable languages by internal contextual languages". *Theoretical Computer Science*, to appear.

Ehrenfeucht, A., Ilie, L., Păun, Gh., Rozenberg, G. and Salomaa, A. 1995. "On the generative capacity of certain classes of contextual grammars". In Gh. Păun (ed) *Mathematical Linguistics and Related Topics.* Bucharest: The Publishing House of the Romanian Academy, 105–118.

Marcus, S. 1967. *Algebraic Linguistics. Analytical Models*, Academic Press, New York.

Marcus, S. 1969. "Contextual grammars" *Revue Roumaine de Mathématiques Pures et Appliquées* 14: 1525–1534.

Marcus, S., Martín-Vide, C. and Păun, Gh. 1995. "On the power of internal contextual grammars with maximal use of selectors". *Fourth Meeting on Mathematics of Language*, Philadelphia.

Martín-Vide, C., Mateescu, A., Miquel-Vergés, J. and Păun, Gh. 1995. "Internal contextual grammars: minimal, maximal, and scattered use of selectors". In M. Koppel and E. Shamir (eds), *Proc. of The Fourth Bar-Ilan*

Symp. on Found. of Artificial Intelligence (BISFAI'95), Jerusalem, 132–142.

Martín-Vide, C., Miquel-Vergés, J. and Păun, Gh. 1995. "Contextual grammars with depth-first derivation". In A. Nijholt, G. Scollo and R. Steetskamp (eds), *Algebraic Methods in Language Processing (AMiLP'95)*. Proceedings of the Tenth Twente Workshop on Language Technology jointly with First AMAST Workshop on Language Processing (TWLT10), Enschede, University of Twente, The Netherlands, 225–233.

Martín-Vide, C., Miquel-Vergés, J., Păun, Gh. and Salomaa, A. 1995. "Attempting to define the ambiguity of internal contextual languages". In this volume.

Păun, Gh. 1982. *Contextual Grammars.* Bucharest: The Publishing House of the Romanian Academy (in Romanian).

Păun, Gh. 1994. "Marcus contextual grammars. After 25 years". *The Bulletin of the European Association for Theoretical Computer Science* 52: 263–273.

Păun, Gh. and Nguyen, X. M. 1980. "On the inner contextual grammars". *Revue Roumaine de Mathématiques Pures et Appliquées* 25: 641–651.

Păun, Gh., Rozenberg, G. and Salomaa, A. 1994a. "Contextual grammars: erasing, determinism, one-sided contexts". In Rozenberg, G. and Salomaa, A. (eds) *Developments in Language Theory* , Singapore: World Scientific Publishing, 370–388.

Păun, Gh., Rozenberg, G. and Salomaa, A. 1994b. "Marcus contextual grammars: modularity and leftmost derivation". In Păun, Gh. (ed) *Mathematical Aspects of Natural and Formal Languages.* Singapore: World Scientific Publishing, 375–392.

Păun, Gh., Rozenberg, G. and Salomaa, A. 1997. "Contextual grammars: deterministic derivations and growth functions". *Revue Roumaine de Mathématiques Pures et Appliquées*, to appear.

Salomaa, A. 1973. *Formal Languages.* New York and London: Academic Press

Linguistic and semiotic preliminaries to contextual grammars

Solomon Marcus

University of Bucharest

The present article is a preliminary to the book by (Păun, 1997) devoted to the contextual grammars introduced by (Marcus, 1969).

A deep and broad understanding of the linguistic potential of contextual grammars requires a preliminary discussion of the basic bricks of these grammars: strings and contexts. Contexts, in their turn, are related to texts, so we have to consider the texts-contexts interaction.

The context of a situation or event is its spatial and temporal neighbourhood: what does not belong to it, but is spatially or temporally near to it. The contextual analysis of a situation is an investigation of the interaction between it and its context. Contextual analysis is a part of structural analysis, stressing relations and interactions among entities rather than entities in themselves. Structural analysis is a common denominator of both natural and social sciences in the XXth century.

When approaching a system, we distinguish between its internal and its external aspects; the former are concerned with interactions among different parts of the system, while the latter are those interactions betwen the system and what is outside of it. It is this second type of interaction that belongs to contextual analysis.

Contexts may have various levels of analysis and may be of various sizes. In the definition of a context we have used the word "near", which is very fuzzy. So, we have to distinguish between micro-contexts and macro-contexts and consider even more different possible sizes of contexts.

"Contextual" is not a property in itself, it is only a property that can be acquired or abandoned, because it is a relational one. Given two adjacent situations, each of them belongs to the context of the other, so each of them is both text and context. Their interplay is symmetric and, as we shall see, this symmetry is mathematically reflected in the whole theory of descriptive linguistics, under the form of strings-contexts Galois connections.

Dealing with linguistic systems, some authors distinguish between the linguistic context – called "co-text" – and the extralinguistic context, – called "con-text" (in a writing pointing out the *text* entity); it is important to stress, from the beginning, that the co-text, i.e., the linguistic context, is a particular kind of text, while a text can always acquire the hypostasis of a co-text. We can go further and assert that the extralinguistic context is also a text, if we accept a generalized (metaphorical?) concept of a text (acording to which the whole world is a text).

A few words about the etymology of "text". It means 'something woven' and relates to a characteristic of textuality that might be circumscribed as a 'coherent whole'. In the pragmatic view, text is defined by criteria of communication: it is the (verbal) message of an addresser to an addressee. The text is a message within a context.

This brings us to the theoretical status of a "text", and here we discuss some ideas formulated by various authors in the collective book (Petöfi, 1979, 1981). A common denominator of these ideas is the belief that the text cannot be understood by reference only to syntactic and semantic factors; pragmatic aspects cannot be avoided (in contrast with what happens to the status of a sentence, i.e., a grammatical proposition, involving only syntactic and semantic factors). In (Marcus, 1980) we developed a mathematical model of a text, using a mathematical model of cohesion (seen rather as a syntactic property) and a mathematical model of coherence (seen rather as a semantic property), both represented as particular forms of the topological property of connectedness in a graph. All sentences, mathematically represented as rooted trees, are texts and all texts are strings of sentences (but not all strings are texts; as a matter of fact, there are various degrees of textness and it seems to be a fuzzy property). A "formal language status" of the concept of a text was proposed in (Ehrenfeucht et al., 1994), but its linguistic and/or computational motivation has yet to be discussed.

Linguists understand text level as being higher than sentence level. This means that sentences could be conceived as the bricks of a text, the basic problem being what kind of links should exist among sentences in order to obtain, by their concatenation, a text.

Is the text a macrosentence? Does it repeat, at a higher level, the structure of a sentence (= grammatical proposition)? This dilemma remains an important challenge, but most authors respond negatively. Since a context is an ordered couple of strings and since any text is a string (always over a given finite alphabet), we have to expect an interplay of texts and contexts (see (van Dijk, 1977)). A mathematical approach to texts using lattice theory was suggested in (Marciszewski, 1979, 1981), where various types of relations in a text, are discussed.

A textual structure involves some kind of mutual dependence among sentences. This dependence is called sometimes "cohesion" (Halliday, Hasan, 1976). There are various types of cohesive factors ((Crystal, 1987), p. 119): Conjunctive relations (What is about to be said is explicitly related to what has been said before: I left early. However, Mark stayed till the end); Coreference (Features that cannot be semantically interpreted without referring to some other feature in the text. When these relationships look backwards for their interpretations, they are called anaphoric; when they look forwards, they are said to be cataphoric); we should point out that algebraic contextual analysis has already shown its relevance in modeling anaphoric relationships, as can be seen from the work done in (Polkowska, Polkowski, 1995); Substitution (One feature replaces a previous expression: I have got a pencil. Do you have one?); Ellipses (A piece of structure is omitted, and can be recovered only from the preceding discourse: Where did you see the car? In the street); Repeated forms (an expression is repeated in whole or in part); Lexical relationships (one lexical item enters into a structural relationship with another: The flowers were lovely. He liked the tulips best); Comparison (A compared expression is presupposed in the previous discourse: That house was bad. This one's far worse).

Cohesion is rather a matter of degree than a sharp property. Usually, coherent utterances are cohesive, but the converse is not true, as is shown by the famous Chomskian example "Colorless green ideas sleep furiously". Another example, consisting of several sentences, was given in (Enkvist, 1978), mainly p.110: "A week has seven days. Every day I feed my cat. Cats have four legs. The cat is on the mat. Mat has three letters." Like cohesion, coherence too is a matter of degree.

It is clear from the above discussion that a text should have some autonomy, some cohesion and some coherence. Contextual analysis proved to be of some relevance in this respect, but a lot of research remains to be done. This research should include some artificial languages too, mainly programming and other computer languages.

The pragmatic dimension of texts and their extralinguistic context are considered by various disciplines such as pragmatics, speech acts theory, discourse analysis and sociolinguistics. Each of these disciplines is particularly relevant not only to natural languages but also to artificial, and in particular to programming languages.

Pragmatics studies the (implicit or explicit) social rules that govern the way we speak. These rules are related to age, social status, sex, circumstances (formality, politeness, intimacy etc), and social conventions.

Pragmatics, seen in this way, is closely related to pragmatics seen as a semiotic dimension, as the third corner of a triangle the first two corners of which are syntactics and semantics. Like semantics, pragmatics takes into account the intentions of the speaker, the effects of an utterance on the listeners, the various possible ways of expressing something, the presuppositions and the representations about the world upon which people interact. Pragmatics also interferes with stylistics and sociolinguistics in their common concern for the social relationships which exist between participants. Pragmatics and psycholinguistics both investigate the psychological states (attention, memory etc) influencing their performance. Pragmatics and discourse analysis share their interest for the analysis of conversation, of deictic forms, the distribution of information in a sentence, etc.

It is enough to take into account the tremendous importance of problems related to algorithmic complexity and to parallelism, in order to realize the significance of pragmatic aspects for various fields of computer science and specially for algorithmic analysis and for programming languages.

The departure point of speech acts theory is the remark that some utterances are equivalent to actions: I recommend..., I ask..., I warn..., I insist..., I promise..., I renounce..., I require... In each of these cases, we perform an action just by saying something (Austin, 1962). Such utterances are called performatives, and contrast with utterances that convey information (constatives). It should be pointed out that algorithms and programs are rich in performatives and a large part of teaching has the same particularity.

A communicative act considered only in its linguistic aspect is a locutionary act. As soon as we consider "saying" as equivalent to "doing", by directing attention to the act that is performed as a result of the speaker making an utterance (see the above examples), we are dealing with illocutionary acts. If, moreover, we look for the effect of these acts on the listener, we are concerned with perlocutionary acts. Obviously, illocutionary acts and perlocutionary acts occur permanently in man-computer communication.

A classification of illocutionary acts was proposed in (Searle, 1976): a) representatives (the speaker is committed to the truth of a proposition: affirm, believe, conclude, deny, report...); b) directives (the speaker tries to get the hearer to do something: ask, challenge, command, insist, request...); c) commissives (the speaker is committed to a certain course of action: guarantee, pledge, promise, swear, vow...); d) expressives (the speaker expresses an attitude about a state of affairs: apologize, deplore, congratulate, thank, welcome...); e) declarations (the speaker alters the external states or condition of an object or situation solely by making the utterance: I resign, I baptize, You are fired, War is hereby declared...).

If text analysis is mainly directed towards the structure of written language, discourse analysis focuses on the structure of naturally occurring spoken language, as found in such 'discourses' as conversations, interviews, commentaries and speeches. This distinction, introduced mainly by American authors, does not correspond to the usual European interpretation, where the term "text linguistics" is used for the study of the linguistic principles governing the structure of all forms of text, be they spoken or written.

One of the most important topics in discourse analysis is the study of conversation. Let us quote in this respect the "cooperative principle" (proposed in (Grice, 1975)), that should be adopted by people when they communicate (at least, this is Grice's claim). This principle consists of some conversational 'maxims' that underlie the efficient use of language: the maxim of quality (speakers' contributions to a conversation ought to be true; they should not say what they believe to be false, nor should they say anything for which they lack adequate evidence); maxim of quantity (contribution should be as informative as is required for the purposes of the conversation; one should say neither too little, nor too much); maxim of relevance (contributions should clearly relate to the purpose of the exchange); maxim of manner (contributions should be perspicuous – in particular, they should be orderly and brief, avoiding obscurity and ambiguity). Some other maxims are also proposed.

As can be seen, Grice has in view a kind of optimisation of the conversation process. However, the requirements he formulates are to some extent in conflict, because the communication process involves both elements of information and elements of control, in order to make the code we are using able to detect and to correct possible errors. For instance, Grice requires the participants in conversation to be brief and, at the same time, to avoid ambiguity. But these two requirements are usually in conflict, each of them being satisfied at the expense of the other. So, no simultaneous optimisation is possible.

As a culminating point in the approach to texts, we will consider "text semiotics", which is primarily restricted to the study of verbal texts, as an extension of the text metaphor to a universal paradigm, bringing into a common textual framework basic phenomena from both art and science. Text semiotics is a positive answer to the challenge proposed some decades ago under the label "linguistics as a pilot science" (see, for instance, (Marcus, 1974)). But let us remember that the kernel of linguistics as a pilot science is mainly the formal language approach to sciences and to humanities, as can be seen from tens (if not hundreds) of works devoted to this topic. Language, as a universal paradigm, becomes operational to the extent to which the language aspect becomes a form that can be separated from the corresponding specific substance aspect; the whole evolution of linguistic structuralism and of structuralism in general shows that in most considered situations some isomorphism phenomena between language (and linguistics) and other types of systems (and disciplines) prepared the way for successful applications of formal grammars and formal languages to very heterogeneous fields in science and the humanities (programming languages, molecular genetics, anthropology and narrative studies being among the best examples in this respect).

An excellent presentation to text semiotics is by W. Nöth ((Nöth, 1990-1994), pages 329 — 333); we follow him in this respect. Ancient precursors of text semiotics are hermeneutics, rhetoric and poetics. A related topic is the semiotics of metaphor. Text semiotics is today made up of broad areas such as narratives, poeticalness, theater, myths, ideology, theology, law, history, advertising, film, comics, and, perhaps the most important, mass media. Conceived in its first stage as text linguistics, text semiotics was a continuation (mainly in the French tradition) of linguistics; structures beyond the sentence were no longer subject to linguistic research, they were the concern of semiotics, where "the units of analysis are no longer monemes or phonemes, but larger fragments of discourse [...]. Semiology is therefore perhaps destined to be absorbed into a *translinguistics* [...]" (Barthes, 1964-1967). Considering text linguistics as a discipline concerned mainly with text syntax and text semantics, text semiotics is the extension of analysis into the pragmatic dimension of texts (mainly their communicative processes and functions, text reception and the role of the reader).

The concept of text in its broader sense refers to messages of any code: films, ballet performances, happenings, pieces of music, ceremonies or circus acts. For Bakhtin, the text is "the primary datum" of the human sciences; where there is no text, there is neither object of inquiry, nor thought. For B. A. Uspenskii, texts are the primary element (basic unit) of culture, like a message generated by the systems of cultural codes.

"Text" is a central concept in Kristeva's semanalysis (Kristeva, 1969), where semiotics is conceived as a science of the text, seen as a "translinguistic apparatus that redistributes the order of language, relating a communicative 'parole' aiming at direct information to different types of previous or synchronic utterances". Kristeva sees text as productivity. This means, on the one hand, that its relation to the language in which it is situated is redistributive (i.e., destructivo-constructive) and, on the other hand, it is a permutation of texts, an intertextuality; in the space of one text several utterances, taken from other texts, cross and neutralize one another.

There are in Kristeva's approach some points directly related to the preliminary motivations of contextual grammars and to their further perspectives. Productivity leads to generativity, while the destructivo-constructive relation between productivity and language directly suggests the double itinerary: from a given language to its associated contextual grammars and from a given contextual grammar to the language it generates. In contrast to Chomskian generative grammars, where the context is relevant to the structure of the generative rules, contextual grammars use contexts in their intrinsic form, with no auxiliary symbols.

Following Freud, Kristeva considers production to be a process of playful permutation (in contrast with its interpretation as a process of exchange (or use) or meaning (value)). This playful permutation is captured, in contextual analysis, by the texts-contexts interplay, seen as a particular form of the strings-contexts interplay and mathematically modelled by means of the so-called Galois connections (Marcus, 1997). In this respect, Kristeva has in view the extralinguistic context, but considering the universality of the text paradigm, the extralinguistic context becomes a linguistic (in a broader sense) one. That's to say, it becomes a text in the problematics of work as a particular semiotic system (as distinct from that of exchange).

Another key concept, with its source in (Bakhtin, 1929), is that of "intertextuality", where the literary text is seen as a multilayered mosaic of quotations, forming a dialogical and polyphonous structure. Kristeva sees the text as an intersection of texts and codes, the absorbtion and transformation of another text. Considered as a basic concept in current literary criticism, intertextuality is relevant in scientific texts too, due to their step-by-step architecture, where each new contribution is based on previous contributions. Bibliographical references are symptomatic in this respect. We could call this phenomenon macro-intertextuality (or external intertextuality), but we should also pay attention to the micro-intertextuality (or internal intertextuality), related to the internal logical (inferential) construction of a scientific text, where considerations are rigorously ordered, each step being essentially based on the previous steps. Mathematical texts show this aspect by their step-by-step logical structure. Computer programs take advantage of various subprograms. Intertextuality is more visible and by no means less important in scientific than in literary texts.

We can imagine formal models of intertextuality by occurrences of some previous texts in a new one and by various kinds of short distance and/or long distance dependences.

The concept of a text on the alphabet A is defined in (Ehrenfeucht et al., 1994) as a triple $t = (d, m, r)$, where m and r are linear orders on the same domain D, while d is a labelling mapping from D into A. The text appears in this way as a generalization of the idea of a word on A. A text is more structured than a word (string). The idea of introducing a supplementary order in a string was considered in linguistics in (Tesnière, 1959), which distinguished between linear order and structural order in a sentence, by associating to each sentence the graph of its dependency and subordination relations. Tesniere did not truly apply graph theory, but his trees became the main stimulus for introducing dependency grammars (by D. G. Hays), which are very important in the study of natural languages today. Rooted trees, in the sense of graph theory, are constantly used text grammars, as they are conceived in (Ehrenfeucht et al., 1994). However, cohesion and coherency, as basic problems in the linguistic theory of texts, do not yet seem to be explicitly considered in mathematical text theory, as a part of formal language theory. It would be instructive to check the concepts and results of text theory in relation to the mathematical model of a sentence, as it was conceived using graph theory (see, for instance, (Marcus, 1967)). The corresponding problem for contextual grammars is the case when we replace strings by texts; we should obtain in this way some "text contextual grammars".

Since any contextual grammar applied to a natural language will generate a certain level of grammaticality of the considered language L, we have to consider an infinite sequence G_n of contextual grammars generating an infinite corresponding sequence of languages L_n, where L_n is generated by G_n, in such a way that L_n is contained in L_{n+1} for any positive integer n and for any x in L there exists the smallest $n(x)$ such that x is in $L_{n(x)}$. The number $1/n(x)$ shows to what extent x belongs to L. It should be clear that the approximation of L by L_n is not related to the degree of attestability of L_n with respect to L, but by the degree of wellformedness of L_n with respect to L. Fuzzines does not seem to be appropriate to model the status of L.

The text paradigm seems to be a new linguistic universal, to be considered together with all its associated concepts: context, intertextuality, cotext etc. Contextual grammars can in this way be placed within the tradition of linguistic universals.

A more comprehensive framework, recently developed as a general approach to the transgression of the sequentiality of a text, is the hypertext (see, for instance, (Landow, 1992)). As a result of a combination of conceptual devices and computational tools, the hypertext could include all the above aspects – contexts, intertexts and other neighbor notions. Likewise, there may be new ways of developing contextual grammars.

References

Austin, J.L. *How to Do Things with Words*, Oxford Univ. Press, 1962.

Bakhtin, M. *Problems of Dostoevsky's Poetics*, Univ. of Minessota Press, Mineapolis, 1929, republished in 1984.

Barthes, R. *Elements of Semiology*, Cape, London, 1964-1967.

Crystal, D. *The Cambridge Encyclopedia of Language*, Cambridge Univ. Press, 1987, p. 119.

Dijk, T.A. van *Text and Context*, Academic Press, London, New York, 1977.

Ehrenfeucht A., Hoogeboom, H.J., ten Pas, P. and Rozenberg, G. An introduction to context-free text grammars, in *Developments in Language Theory* (G. Rozenberg, A. Salomaa, eds.), World Sci. Publ., Singapore, 1994, 357 - 369.

Enkvist, N. Coherence, pseudo-coherence and non-coherence, in *Cohesion and Semantics* (J. O. Ostman, ed.), Abo Academy Foundation, 1978, 109 - 128.

Grice, H.P. Logic and conversation, in *Speech Acts* (P. Cole, J. L. Morgan, eds.), Academic Press, New York, 1975, 41 - 58.

Halliday, M.A.K. and Hasan, R. *Cohesion in English* London, 1976.

Kristeva, J. *Recherches pour une semanalyse*, Seuil, Paris, 1969.

Landow, G.P. *Hypertext*, The John Hopkins Univ. Press, Baltimore and London, 1992.

Marciszewski, W. A lattice-theoretical approach to the text structure study, in Petöfi, J.S. (ed.), *Text vs. Sentence. Basic Questions of Text Linguistics*, Hamburg, 1979, 1981, 391 - 404.

Marcus, S. *Algebraic Linguistics. Analytical Models*, Academic Press, New York, 1967.

Marcus, S. Contextual grammars, *Revue Roumaine de Mathématiques Théoriques et Appliquées*, 14 (1969), 1525 - 1534.

Marcus, S. Linguistics as a pilot science, in *Current Trends in Linguistics* (Th. Sebeok, ed.), vol. 12, Mouton, The Hague, 1974, 2871 - 2887.

Marcus, S. Textual cohesion and textual coherence, *Rev. Roum. Ling.*, 25, 2 (1980), 101 - 112.

Marcus, S. Contextual grammars and natural languages, chapter 5 in vol. 2 of Grzegorz Rozenberg, Arto Salomaa (eds.), *The Handbook of Formal Languages*, Springer-Verlag, Berlin, Heidelberg, 1997, 215 - 235.

Nöth, W. *Handbook of Semiotics*, Indiana Univ. Press, Bloomington, 1990-1994.

Păun, Gh. *Marcus Contextual Grammars*, Kluwer Academic Publ., Dordrecht, Boston, London, 1997.

Petöfi, J.S. (ed.), *Text vs. Sentence. Basic Questions of Text Linguistics*, Hamburg, 1979, 1981.

Searle, J.R. A classification of illocutionary acts, *Language in Society*, 5 (1976), 1 - 23.

Semeniuk-Polkowska, M. and Polkowski, L.T. *On Some Models of Anaphora Resolution in Mathematical Linguistics*, Warsaw Univ. Press, 1995.

Rozenberg, G. and Salomaa, A. (eds.), *Handbook of Formal Languages*, Springer-Verlag, Berlin, Heidelberg, 1997.

Tesnière, L. *Eléments de syntaxe structurale*, Klincksieck, Paris, 1959.

Attempting to Define the Ambiguity of Internal Contextual Languages

Carlos Martín-Vide[a]
Joan Miquel-Vergés[a]
Gheorghe Păun[b,1]
Arto Salomaa[c,1]

[a] *Rovira i Virgili University*
[b] *Institute of Mathematics of the Roumanian Academy*
[c] *Turku University*

Abstract

A contextual grammar generates strings by starting from certain given *axioms* and iteratively adding *contexts* (pairs of strings), according to given selection restrictions. Several levels of ambiguity can be considered in this framework, depending on the information used for identifying a derivation. We prove that there are inherently ambiguous languages with respect to three of these notions of ambiguity and that the ambiguity is undecidable for internal contextual grammars (even when the selection is defined with respect to finite selectors). A new type of ambiguity is also considered: when a language can be generated by several *optimal* grammars (from the point of view of given complexity parameters), we say that the language is intrinsically ambiguous. Some topics for further research are also mentioned.

---

[1]Research supported by the Academy of Finland, project 11281.

Introduction

Contextual grammars were introduced by S. Marcus (Marcus 1969) as "intrinsic grammars", using no auxiliary symbols. They are based on the phenomenon of acception of certain strings by certain contexts (or conversely) with respect to a given language. This phenomenon is a fundamental one in descriptive linguistics (Marcus 1967), for instance, when defining grammatical categories and, hence, morphological ambiguity.

Roughly speaking, a contextual grammar consists of a given finite set of initial strings (*axioms*) and a given finite set of *contexts* (pairs of strings); sets of contexts are associated with sets of strings (called *selectors*): a context can be adjoined to each string in the associated selector. Starting from an axiom and adjoining contexts according to the selection imposed by the selectors, we obtain a language. When adjoining is allowed only at the ends of the current string, we speak about *external* contextual grammars (this is the kind of grammars considere in (Marcus 1967)). When adjoining is allowed at any place inside the current string, we have an *internal* contextual grammar (as introduced in (Păun and Nguyen 1980)).

For every class of grammars, a natural (and important) problem is that of syntactic ambiguity: given a grammars, are there strings in the generated language that have two syntactic descriptions? "Syntactic description" means intuitively "distinct derivation". For context-free Chomsky grammars the notion is clear: a (distinct) derivation is described by a derivation tree, and so a grammar is ambiguous when there is a string which can be produced by derivations having different derivation trees.

What information we have to consider in order to describe a distinct *derivation* in an internal contextual grammar is not so obvious. A derivation is precisely identified by the axiom, the used contexts, and the *place* where the contexts are used (thus the selectors are also identified). Not all these data are essential from a syntactic point of view; for instance, the order in which contexts are used seems not to be relevant. Thus, we can define several levels of ambiguity, depending on the information used for describing a derivation. We discuss here five variants: (1) the axiom and the contexts used are taken into account but no the order in which the contexts are used; (2) the axiom, the contexts and the selectors used are taken into account but nor the order; (3) as in (1) but considering order, (4) as in (2) but considering the order, (5) the axiom, the contexts and also the palces in which they are used are taken into account (the selectors are also implicitly considered, too). For $t = 1, 2, 3, 4, 5$, this information about a derivation is called *a type-t description* of the derivation.

A grammar is said to be *t-ambiguous*, for $t = 1, 2, 3, 4, 5$, if it can generate a string using two derivations which have different descriptions of type t, in the previously mentioned sense. Otherwise, the grammar is *t-unambiguous.*

From the above discussion, it is clear that 1-ambiguity implies both 2- and 3-ambiguity, that both 2- and 3-ambiguity imply 4-ambiguity, which, in turn, implies 5-ambiguity.

A language is called t-unambiguous if it can be generated by a *t-unambiguous* grammar and *inherently t-ambiguous* if each grammar generating it is t-ambiguous.

Because t-ambiguous grammars are s-ambiguous for $(t, s) \in \{(1, 2), (1, 3), (2, 4), (3, 4), (4, 5)\}$, each inherently t-ambiguous language is inherently s-ambiguous, for t, s as above. We shall find inherently t-ambiguous languages for $t = 3, 4, 5$ which are not inherently $(t - 1)$-ambiguous; the same holds for the pair (4, 2), but the problem remains *open* for inherently 1-ambiguous languages. More precisely, we were able to find inherently 1-ambiguous languages only with respect to internal contextual grammars without choice. Moreover, we prove that ambiguity of any type is not decidable (even for contextual grammars with finite selectors).

Many of the above mentioned inherently ambiguous languages are regular languages in the sense of Chomsky hierarchy. It is known (Salomaa 1973) that the regular Chomsky languages are unambiguous with respect to regular (and context-free) Chomsky grammars. Hence, we lose this property when describing regular languages by means of internal contextual grammars. This result shows that nonterminals are useful from a nonambiguity point of view (the ambiguity can be removed if they are used) and that the notion of ambiguity of types 3, 4 and 5 is too strong (too much information is kept to describe a derivation).

Finally, a new type of ambiguity is introduced, the *intrinsic* one. Consider one or more descriptional complexity parameters and define the notion of an *optimal* grammar for a language (what this means is not always a simple question, because the considered parameters can be incompatible); if a language can be generated by at least two different optimal grammars, then we say that it is intrinsically ambiguous. For the parameters $Ax =$ the number of axioms, Con = the number of contexts, this notion of ambiguity is again shown to be too weak: each infinite internal contextual language with selection is ambiguous.

Internal contextual grammars. Ambiguity

As usual, we denote: V^* = the free monoid generated by the alphabet V, λ = the empty string, $|x|$ = the length of $x \in V^*$, $|x|_a$ = the number of $a \in V$ occurrences in $x \in V^*$, *FIN, REG, CF, CS* = the families of finite, regular, context-free, context-sensitive languages, respectively.

An (internal) *contextual grammar* is a construct

$$G = (V, B, (D_1, C_1), \ldots, (D_n, C_n)),$$

where V is an alphabet, $B \subseteq V^*$ is a finite language, $D_i \subseteq V^*, C_i \subseteq V^* \times V^*$, $1 \leq i \leq n$, such that each C_i is a finite set.

The elements of B are called *axioms*, those of C_i are called *contexts*, D_i is the *selector* associated with the set $C_i, 1 \leq i \leq n$.

If the selectors $D_1, \ldots, D_n$ are languages in a given family F, then we say that G *has F selection*. Thus, we can speak about grammars with finite selection, regular selection, etc. If $n = 1$ and $D_1 = V^*$, then we say that G is a grammar *without selection*; the set D can then be omitted.

For $w, z \in V^*$ we define

$$\begin{aligned} w \Longrightarrow z \quad \text{iff} \quad & w = x_1x_2x_3, z = x_1ux_2vx_3, \text{ where} \\ & (u, v) \in C_i, x_2 \in D_i, \text{ for some } i, 1 \leq i \leq n, \\ & x_1, x_2, x_3 \in V^*. \end{aligned}$$

Then, the language generated by G (in the internal mode) is

$$L(G) = \{z \in V^* \mid w \Longrightarrow^* z, \text{ for some } w \in B\},$$

where $\Longrightarrow^*$ is the reflexive and transitive closure of the relation $\Longrightarrow$.

Equivalently, we can define $L(G)$ as the smallest language L (in the sense of the inclusion relation) such that

$$\begin{aligned} &i) \quad B \subseteq L, \\ &ii) \quad \text{if } w \in L, w = x_1x_2x_3, \text{ for } x_1, x_2, x_2 \in V^*, \\ &\qquad x_2 \in D_i \text{ for some } i, 1 \leq i \leq n, \text{ then} \\ &\qquad x_1ux_2vx_3 \in L \text{ for all } (u, v) \in C_i. \end{aligned}$$

We denote by $IC(F)$ the family of languages generated as above by contextual grammars with F selection.

According to the results in (Ehrenfeuch, Păun and Rozenberg 1997), (Păun 1982), (Păun and Nguyen 1980), we have

$$REG \subset IC(FIN) \subset IC(REG) \subset CS, \text{ strict inclusions,}$$
$$IC(FIN) \text{ and } CF \text{ are incomparable.}$$

The above way of giving a contextual grammar is called *the modular presentation*; an equivalent one is the *functional presentation*, based on *selection mapping*

$$\varphi V^* \longrightarrow 2^C,$$

where

$$C = \bigcup_{i=1}^{n} C_i,$$

defined by

$$\varphi(x) = \{(u, v) \mid (u, v) \in C_i, x \in D_i, 1 \leq i \leq n\}, x \in V^*.$$

(For grammars without selection we get $\varphi(x) = C$ for all $x \in V^*$.) Then we can write the grammar in the form:

$$G = (V, B, C, \varphi),$$

where V, B are as above, C is the set of all contexts, and φ is the selection mapping $\varphi V^* \longrightarrow 2^C$. The derivation relation is defined by

$$w \Longrightarrow z \text{ iff } w = x_1x_2x_3 \text{ for } x_1, x_2, x_3 \in V^*,$$
$$z = x_1ux_2vx_3 \text{ for } (u, v) \in \varphi(x_2).$$

Conversely, given a grammar in the functional presentation, $G = (V, B, C, \varphi)$, we can write it equivalently as

$$G = (V, B, (D_1, C_1), \ldots, (D_n, C_n)),$$

where $C_i \subseteq C$ and $D_i = \{x \in V^* \mid \varphi(x) = C_i\} \neq \emptyset$, $1 \leq i \leq n$. (Clearly, $n \leq 2^{card(C)}$.)

In our considerations below, we shall use the presentation of contextual grammars which seems most appropriate (more economical), but even for grammars given in the modular presentation we use the mapping φ with the implicit definition specified above.

Let us now formally define the five types of ambiguity mentioned in the introduction.

Given a contextual grammar $G = (V, B, C, \varphi)$ and a derivation

$$\delta : w_1 \Longrightarrow w_2 \Longrightarrow \ldots \Longrightarrow w_m, m \geq 1,$$

such that

$$\begin{aligned}
&w_1 \in B,\\
&w_i = x_{1,i}x_{2,i}x_{3,i}, \;\; x_{1,i}, x_{2,i}, x_{3,i} \in V^*,\\
&w_{i+1} = x_{1,i}u_ix_{2,i}v_ix_{3,i}, \text{ for}\\
&(u_i, v_i) \in \varphi(x_{2,i}), 1 \leq i \leq m-1,
\end{aligned}$$

the sequence

$$w_1, (u_1, v_1), \ldots, (u_{m-1}, v_{m-1})$$

is called *the control sequence* associated to δ.

Of course, the control sequence does not identify the derivation, because the contexts might be adjoined to different positions. Thus, we call *description* of δ the sequence

$$w_1, x_{1,1}(u_1)x_{2,1}(v_1)x_{3,1}, x_{1,2}(u_2)x_{2,2}(v_2)x_{3,2}, \ldots,$$

$$x_{1,m-1}(u_{m-1})x_{2,m-1}(v_{m-1})x_{3,m-1}$$

(the parentheses precisely identify the contexts used and the places at which they are adjoined).

An intermediate case is to specify only the contexts and their selectors, not the position where they appear. Thus, we call *complete control sequence* the sequence

$$w_1, ((u_1, v_1), x_{2,1}), ((u_2, v_2), x_{2,2}), \ldots, ((u_{m-1}, v_{m-1}), x_{2,m-1}).$$

If we only take into consideration the contexts (and selectors) used and not the order in which they are used, then we obtain the *unordered control sequence* and the *unordered complete control sequence*, respectively. (They can be formally given as sequences of integers, specifying the number of times each context –and selector– is used; here, we do not enter into such details).

A contextual grammar G is said to be 1-ambiguous if there are two derivations in G which have different unordered control sequences and which generate the same string.

Replacing in this definition the words "unordered control sequences" by "unordered complete control sequences", "control sequences", "complete control sequences", and "descriptions", respectively, we say that the grammar G is 2-, 3-, 4- and 5-ambiguous, respectively.

For clarity, we write, in a concise manner

1-ambiguity = two unordered control sequences,

2-ambiguity = two unordered complete control sequences,

3-ambiguity = two control sequences,

4-ambiguity = two complete control sequences,

5-ambiguity = two descriptions.

A grammar which is not t-ambiguous, for some $t = 1, 2, 3, 4, 5$, is said to be t-unambiguous. A language $L \in IC(F)$ is *inherently t-ambiguous* if every grammar G (with F selection) generating L is t-ambiguous. A language for which a t-unambiguous grammar exists is called *t-unambiguous.*

Of course, in most cases, given a t-unambiguous language, we can also find t-ambiguous grammars generating it. For instance, $L = \{a^n ba^n \mid n \geq 1\}$ is 5-unambiguous, as it can be generated by the grammar

$$G = (\{a, b\}, \{aba\}, (\{b\}, \{(a, a)\}))$$

(there is only one axiom and only one context, which can be adjoined in only one place). However, $L = L(G')$, too, for

$$G' = (\{a, b\}, \{aba\}, (\{b, ab\}, \{(a, a)\})).$$

The grammar G' is not 3-ambiguous (in general, the grammars with only one axiom and only one context are not 3-ambiguous), but it is 5-ambiguous: the string a^2ba^2 can be obtained from aba in two modes

$$aba \Longrightarrow a(a)b(a)a, \quad aba \Longrightarrow (a)ab(a)a.$$

Ambiguity is also discussed in (Păun 1982), but only for external contextual grammars. The notion of ambiguity used is the 3-ambiguity considered here (taking into account the axiom and the ordered sequence of contexts). It is proved (Theorem 5.8 in (Păun 1982)) that the ambiguity of external contextual grammars (even without selection) is undecidable and that there are inherently ambiguous languages with respect to external contextual grammars without selection. It is also proved that the ambiguity and the complexity of external contextual grammars are in general contradictory features: there are unambiguous languages for which grammars of low complexity are ambiguous (complexity here means descriptional complexity: the number of axioms, contexts, etc.). Nothing is done in (Păun 1982) about the ambiguity of internal contextual grammars.

The existence of inherently ambiguous languages

Each inherently t-ambiguous language is inherently s-ambiguous, for $(t, s) \in \{(1, 2), (1, 3), (2, 4), (3, 4), (4, 5)\}$. The converse is not (always) true:

Theorem 1. *There are inherently 5-ambiguous languages (with respect to contextual grammars with arbitrary selection) which are 4-unambiguous (with respect to contextual grammars with finite selection).*

Proof. Consider the language

$$L = \{a^n ba^m \mid n, m \geq 1\}.$$

It can be generated by the grammar

$$G = (\{a, b\}, \{aba\}, (\{a\}, \{(\lambda, a)\})).$$

Clearly, this grammar is not 4-ambiguous, and so L is not inherently 4-ambiguous (even with respect to the most restricted class of contextual grammars, those with finite selection).

However, this language is inherently 5-ambiguous. Indeed, consider a grammar $G = (V, B, C, \varphi)$ generating L. Every axiom in B must be of the form $a^i ba^j, i, j \geq 1$. Hence the contexts in C actually used in derivations of strings of L must be of the form (u, v) with $u, v \in a^*$.

Assume that there is a context (u, v) and a string $a^r, r \geq 0$, such that $(u, v) \in \varphi(a^r)$. So the grammar is ambiguous: the string $a^{r+1}ba$ is in L, and hence there is a derivation $w \Longrightarrow^* a^{r+1}ba$ in G, for some $w \in B$. This derivation can be continued by using the context (u, v) in two positions

$$w \Longrightarrow^* a^r aba \Longrightarrow ua^r vaba$$
$$w \Longrightarrow^* aa^r ba \Longrightarrow aua^r vba.$$

Because $u, v \in a^*$, we have obtained the same string. Hence G is 5-ambiguous.

Therefore, every context (u, v) used in a derivation must be associated with strings of the form $a^r ba^s, r, s \geq 0$ (that is, $(u, v) \in \varphi(a^r ba^s)$). Because all strings of the form $a^k ba$ are in L, there is a context of the form $(a^i, \lambda), i \geq 1$. Because all strings of the form aba^k are in L, there is a context of the form $(\lambda, a^j), j \geq 1$. Consider two strings $a^r ba^s, a^p ba^q$ such that $(a^i, \lambda) \in \varphi(a^r ba^s)$ and $(\lambda, a^j) \in \varphi(a^p ba^q)$. Take the string $a^{r+p}ba^{s+q}$. Because this string is in L, there is a derivation $w \Longrightarrow^* a^{r+p}ba^{s+q}$ in G, for some $w \in B$. This derivation can be continued by using first (a^i, λ) and then (λ, a^j) or conversely

$$\begin{aligned} w \Longrightarrow^* \; & a^p a^r ba^s a^q \Longrightarrow a^p a^i a^r ba^s a^q = a^{i+r} a^p ba^q a^s \Longrightarrow \\ & \Longrightarrow a^{i+r} a^p ba^q a^j a^s = a^{i+r+p} ba^{q+j+s}, \\ w \Longrightarrow^* \; & a^r a^p ba^q a^s \Longrightarrow a^r a^p ba^q a^j a^s = a^p a^r ba^s a^{q+j} \Longrightarrow \\ & \Longrightarrow a^p a^i a^r ba^s a^{q+j} \Longrightarrow a^{p+i+r} ba^{s+q+j}. \end{aligned}$$

We have obtained the same string, so again the grammar is 5-ambiguous.

Observe that in the argument above the type of selector plays no role. Hence G can be of any type. □

Moreover, we have

Theorem 2. *There are inherently 4-ambiguous languages (with respect to contextual grammars with arbitrary choice) which are 2- and 3- unambiguous (even with respect to grammars with finite choice).*

Proof. Take the language

$$L = \{a^n ba^n a^m ca^m \mid n, m \geq 0\}.$$

It can be generated by the grammar

$$G = (\{a, b, c\}, \{bc\}, (\{b, c\}, \{(a, a)\})).$$

This grammar is not 2- or 3-ambiguous (it contains only one context), so L is 2- and 3-unambiguous.

On the other hand, consider an arbitrary grammar $G' = (\{a, b, c\}, B, C, \varphi)$ generating L. From the form of the strings in L, it is easy to see that there are contexts of the form $(a^i, a^i), (a^j, a^j), i, j \geq 1$, such that $(a^i, a^i) \in \varphi(a^k b a^l), k, l \geq 0$, and $(a^j, a^j) \in \varphi(a^p c a^q), p, q \geq 0$. When generating a string $a^n b a^n a^m c a^m$ with large enough n, m, we have to use both the above mentioned contexts. Because their selectors can be disjoint (do not overlap), the order of using these contexts can be changed. We obtain in this way two derivations whose ordered complete sequences differ (it is possible to have $i = j$, and hence the same context, but $b \neq c$, so the selectors differ). This means that G' is 4-ambiguous, which implies that the language L is inherently 4-ambiguous. □

Theorem 3. *There are inherently 3-ambiguous languages (with respect to contextual grammars with arbitrary selection) which are 1- and 2- unambiguous.*

Proof. Consider the language

$$L = \{a^n b^m \mid n, m \geq 1\}$$

and an arbitrary grammar $G = (\{a, b\}, B, C, \varphi)$ generating L. Each string $a^k b$ is in L; such a string can be generated only starting from a string $a^p b, p \geq 1$, and using contexts (u, v) with $u, v \in a^*$. If $(u, v) \in \varphi(a^t)$, then v can be different from λ; if $(u, v) \in \varphi(a^t b)$, then $v = \lambda$. Similarly, because each string ab^k is in L, we have axioms of the form $ab^p, p \geq 1$, and contexts (u', v') with $u', v' \in b^*$. If $(u', v') \in \varphi(b^t)$, then u' can be non-empty, but if $(u', v') \in \varphi(ab^t)$, then $u' = \lambda$.

There are several cases which combine the possibilities discussed above for the contexts $(u, v), (u', v')$ and their selectors. Taking a long enough string z in L (that is a string to which both (u, v) and (u', v') can be adjoined), after adding (u, v) to z we can also add (u', v') and, conversely, after adding (u', v') we can also add (u, v). The strings obtained are equal ((u, v) contributes to the number of occurrences of the symbol a and (u', v') contributes to the number of occurrences of the symbol b), but the two derivations have different descriptions (the order of $(u, v), (u', v')$ is different from one derivation to the other one). Consequently, G is 3-ambiguous.

We leave to the reader the task of examining all the cases suggested and we exemplify the argument with only one case: Take $(a^i, \lambda) \in \varphi(a^t b)$ and $(\lambda, b^j) \in \varphi(ab^s)$. Then, for $z = a^t b^s$ we have

$$w \Longrightarrow^* a^t b^s \Longrightarrow a^i a^t a^s \Longrightarrow a^i a^t b^s b^j,$$
$$w \Longrightarrow^* a^t b^s \Longrightarrow a^t b^s b^j \Longrightarrow a^i a^t b^s b^j, w \in B.$$

The strings obtained are equal, but the derivations are different.

The type of selection plays no role in the previous argument.

The above language L can be generated by the grammar

$$G = (\{a, b\}, \{ab\}, (\{a\}, \{(a, \lambda)\}), (\{b\}, \{(b, \lambda)\})).$$

In order to generate a string $a^n b^m$ we have to use the context (a, λ) and the selector a exactly $n - 1$ times, and the context (b, λ) and the selector b exactly $m - 1$ times. Consequently, G is 2-unambiguous (hence also 1-unambiguous). □

We were not able to find languages which are inherently 2-ambiguous and 1- or 3-unambiguous, or languages inherently 1-ambiguous. This last *open problem* is particularly interesting. We *conjecture* that such languages exist. A partial answer (supporting this conjecture) is the following.

Theorem 4. *There are inherently 1-ambiguous languages with respect to internal contextual grammars without selection.*

Proof. Consider the language

$$L = \{x \in \{a, b\}^* \mid |x|_a = |x|_b\}.$$

Take a grammar (without selection) $G = (V, B, C)$ generating L. Every string of the form $a^n b^n, n \geq 1$, is in L. In order to generate such strings we have to use a context of one of the following forms

$$1) \quad (a^i, b^i), (a^i b^{i_1}, b^{i_2}), i = i_1 + i_2, i_1, i_2 \geq 0, \text{ or}$$
$$(a^{i_1}, a^{i_2} b^i), i = i_1 + i_2, i_1, i_2 \geq 0, \ i \geq 1.$$

Similarly, in order to generate the strings $b^n a^n$ with arbitrarily large $n \geq 1$, the set C must contain a context of one of the following forms

$$2) \quad (b^j, a^j), (b^j a^{j_1}, a^{j_2}), j = j_1 + j_2, j_1, j_2 \geq 0, \text{ or}$$
$$(b^{j_1}, b^{j_2} a^j), j = j_1 + j_2, j_1, j_2 \geq 0, \ j \geq 1.$$

For any one of the possible $3 \times 3 = 9$ cases, consider the string

$$w = a^{ij}b^{ij}a^{ij}b^{ij}.$$

It can be written as

$$w = (\underbrace{a^i \dots a^i}_{j \text{ times}}\underbrace{b^i \dots b^i}_{j \text{ times}})^2.$$

Hence w can be obtained starting from λ (it is in L) and adjoining only contexts of type 1 above. We can also write

$$w = (a^i)^j(b^{ij}a^{ij})(b^i)^j.$$

The string $w' = a^{ij}b^{ij}$ is in L, so w can be obtained from w' by using only contexts of type 2 above, because

$$b^{ij}a^{ij} = \underbrace{b^j \dots b^j}_{i \text{ times}}\underbrace{a^j \dots a^j}_{i \text{ times}}.$$

(A string $a^i \dots a^i b^i \dots b^i$ can be obtained by first producing the external blocks a^i, b^i – this is a context of type 1– and then inserting a^ib^i in the middle and so on. The same for strings $b^j \dots b^j a^j \dots a^j$.)

Consequently, G is 1-ambiguous.

It remains to be proved that L can be generated by an internal contextual grammar without selection. This is obvious: $L = L(G)$, for $G = (\{a, b\}, \{\lambda\}, \{(a, b), (b, a)\})$. □

Observe that the languages used in the proofs of Theorems 1 and 3 are regular in Chomsky's sense, but the languages in Theorems 2 and 4 are context-free non-linear.

The fact that there are regular languages which are inherently t-ambiguous, for various t, contrasts with the fact that regular languages are unambiguous when they are generated with regular grammars. This can be interpreted in the sense that the notion of t-ambiguity, for $t = 3, 4, 5$, is too restrictive. The same conclusion can also be drawn from the result below, and is again in contrast with the result known for context-free languages: every context-free language $L \subseteq V^*$, even an inherently ambiguous one, is a subset of an unambiguous language, namely a regular one, V^*.

Theorem 5. *There are (regular) languages L which are inherently 3-ambiguous and such that each superlanguage $L', L \subseteq L'$, is also inherently 3-ambiguous.*

Proof. Take the language

$$L = \{a^n \mid n \geq 1\} \cup \{b^n \mid n \geq 1\} \cup \{a^n b^m \mid n, m \geq 1\}.$$

Consider a language $L' \subseteq \{a,b\}^*$ such that $L \subseteq L'$ and take a grammar $G = (\{a,b\}, B, C, \varphi)$ generating L'. Because $a^n \in L'$ for all $n \geq 1$, there is a context $(a^{i_1}, a^{i_2}) \in \varphi(a^{k_1}), i_1 + i_2 \geq 1, k_1 \geq 0$; because $b^n \in L'$ for all $n \geq 1$, there is a context $(b^{j_1}, b^{j_2}) \in \varphi(a^{k_2}), j_1 + j_2 \geq 1, k_2 \geq 0$. The string $a^{k_1} b^{k_2}$ is in L', and hence there is a derivation $w \Longrightarrow^* a^{k_1} b^{k_2}$ in G, for some $w \in B$. This derivation can be continued with (a^{i_1}, a^{i_2}), then with (b^{j_1}, b^{j_2}), or conversely. In both cases we obtain the string $a^{k_1+i_1+i_2} b^{k_2+j_1+j_2}$, which means that G is 3-ambiguous. This means that L' (and L, too) is inherently 3-ambiguous.

Of course, the above result is not true for 1- and 2-ambiguity: V^* is unambiguous, because it can be generated by $G = (V, \{\lambda\}, (\{\lambda\}, \{(a,\lambda) \mid a \in V\}))$.

The undecidability of ambiguity

As expected (this is also the case for context-free grammars), the important problem of finding an algorithm able to tell us whether or not an arbitrary contextual grammar is ambiguous has no solution.

Theorem 6. *The ambiguity (of any type t, t = 1,2,3,4,5) of internal contextual grammars (even with finite selection) is undecidable.*

Proof. Take two arbitrary n-tuples of non-empty strings over the alphabet $\{a,b\}$, namely $(x_1, \ldots, x_n), (y_1, \ldots, y_n)$, and construct the contextual grammar

$$\begin{aligned} G &= (\{a,b,c,d,e\}, \{cccdc, ceccc\}, (D_1,C_1), (D_2,C_2), (D_3,C_3), (D_4,C_4)), \\ &\quad (D_1, C_1) = (\{cccdc\}, \{(x_i, a^i b) \mid 1 \leq i \leq n\}), \\ &\quad (D_2, C_2) = (\{ceccc\}, \{(y_i, a^i b) \mid 1 \leq i \leq n\}), \\ &\quad (D_3, C_3) = (\{ccdca\}, \{(e, \lambda)\}), \\ &\quad (D_4, C_4) = (\{acecc, bcecc\}, \{(\lambda, d)\}). \end{aligned}$$

To the axiom *cccdc* we can add only one context from C_1. After using at least one such context, we can use the context in C_3 (the string *ccdca* is present). Thus, we have

$$cccdc \Longrightarrow^* x_{i_1} \dots x_{i_k} cccdca^{i_k}b \dots a^{i_1}b \quad (1)$$
$$\Longrightarrow x_{i_1} \dots x_{i_k} ceccdca^{i_k}b \dots a^{i_1}b, \quad (2)$$

for $k \geq 1, 1 \leq i_j \leq n, 1 \leq j \leq k$. The use of the pair (D_3, C_3) can be iterated

$$(2) \Longrightarrow^* x_{i_1} \dots x_{i_k} ce^r ccdca^{i_k}b \dots a^{i_1}b, \quad (3)$$

for $r \geq 2$. After using the pair (D_3, C_3) twice, no other pair $(D_i, C_i), i \neq 3$, can be used. To a string of form (2) (after one use of (D_3, C_3)) we can also use (D_4, C_4)

$$(2) \Longrightarrow^* x_{i_1} \dots x_{i_k} ceccd^s ca^{i_k}b \dots a^{i_1}b, \quad (4)$$

for $s \geq 2$. To such a string no pair $(D_i, C_i), i \neq 4$, can be used. Finally, to a string of form (2), neither (D_1, C_1), nor (D_2, C_2) can be used.

Similarly, starting from *ceccc* we can obtain (using (D_2, C_2) at least once and then (D_4, C_4))

$$ceccc \Longrightarrow^* y_{j_1} \dots y_{j_l} ceccca^{j_l}b \dots a^{j_1}b \quad (5)$$
$$\Longrightarrow y_{j_1} \dots y_{j_l} ceccdca^{j_l}b \dots a^{j_1}b, \quad (6)$$

for $l \geq 1, 1 \leq j_p \leq n, 1 \leq p \leq l$. The use of (D_4, C_4) can be iterated

$$(6) \Longrightarrow^* y_{j_1} \dots y_{j_l} ceccd^{s'} ca^{j_l}b \dots a^{j_1}b, \quad (7)$$

for $s' \geq 2$. To such a string no pair $(D_i, C_i), i \neq 4$, can be used. To a string of type (6) we can apply (D_3, C_3), too

$$(6) \Longrightarrow^* y_{j_1} \dots y_{j_l} ce^{r'} ccdca^{j_l}b \dots a^{j_1}b, \quad (8)$$

for $r' \geq 2$. Neither (D_1, C_1) nor (D_2, C_2) can be applied to a string of form (6).

Now, comparing the form of the eight types of strings, (1) – (8), we see that the only possible equalities appear in the following cases

(A) $w_1 = w_2$ for w_1 of type (2) and w_2 of type (5). This means

$$w_1 = x_{i_1} \dots x_{i_k} ceccdca^{i_k}b \dots a^{i_1}b,$$
$$w_2 = y_{j_1} \dots y_{j_l} ceccdca^{j_l}b \dots a^{j_1}b,$$

and $w_1 = w_2$ implies $k = l, i_1 = j_1, \ldots, i_k = j_k$ (otherwise we cannot have $a^{i_k}b \ldots a^{i_1}b = a^{j_l}b \ldots a^{j_1}b$) and $x_{i_1} \ldots x_{i_k} = y_{i_1} \ldots y_{i_k}$. Hence there is a solution for the Post Correspondence Problem with respect to the n-tuples $(x_1, \ldots, x_n), (y_1, \ldots, y_n)$.

(B) $w_1 = w_2$ for w_1 of type (3) and w_2 of type (8). This means

$$w_1 = x_{i_1} \ldots x_{i_k} ce^r ccdca^{i_k}b \ldots a^{i_1}b,$$
$$w_2 = y_{j_1} \ldots y_{j_l} ce^{r'} ccdca^{j_l}b \ldots a^{j_1}b,$$

and $w_1 = w_2$ implies $k = l, r = r', i_1 = j_1, \ldots, i_k = j_k$ (otherwise we cannot have $a^{i_k}b \ldots a^{i_1}b = a^{j_l}b \ldots a^{j_1}b$) and $x_{i_1} \ldots x_{i_k} = y_{i_1} \ldots y_{i_k}$. Again the Post Correspondence Problem with respect to the n-tuples $(x_1, \ldots, x_n), (y_1, \ldots, y_n)$ has a solution.

(C) $w_1 = w_2$ for w_1 of type (4) and w_2 of type (7). This means

$$w_1 = x_{i_1} \ldots x_{i_k} ceccd^s ca^{i_k}b \ldots a^{i_1}b,$$
$$w_2 = y_{j_1} \ldots y_{j_l} ceccd^{s'} ca^{j_l}b \ldots a^{j_1}b,$$

and $w_1 = w_2$ implies $k = l, s = s', i_1 = j_1, \ldots, i_k = j_k$ (otherwise we cannot have $a^{i_k}b \ldots a^{i_1}b = a^{j_l}b \ldots a^{j_1}b$) and $x_{i_1} \ldots x_{i_k} = y_{i_1} \ldots y_{i_k}$. The Post Correspondence Problem with respect to the n-tuples $(x_1, \ldots, x_n), (y_1, \ldots, y_n)$ has a solution.

In all cases, the ambiguity of G means 1-ambiguity (because we start from different axioms to generate the considered strings w_1, w_2) and this implies the existence of a solution for the Post Correspondence Problem for the considered n-tuples of words.

Conversely, if the Post Correspondence Problem for $(x_1, \ldots, x_n), (y_1, \ldots, y_n)$ has a solution, then there are $i_1, \ldots, i_k$ such that $x_{i_1} \ldots x_{i_k} = y_{i_1} \ldots y_{i_k}$. Hence, G is clearly 1-ambiguous. For instance, we can find a string

$$w_1 = a_{i_1} \ldots x_{i_k} ceccdea^{i_k}b \ldots a^{i_1}b$$

of type (2) and a string

$$w_2 = y_{i_1} \ldots y_{i_k} ceccdca^{i_k}b \ldots a^{i_1}b$$

of type (6) such that $w_1 = w_2$.

The ambiguity (of any type) of G is equivalent to the existence of a solution for the Post Correspondence Problem, which is known to be undecidable.

A new type of ambiguity: intrinsic ambiguity

Let us start from an example: consider the sentence

Joan sees Carlos singing. (1)

Who sings, Joan or Carlos? The sentence is syntactically ambiguous. Suppose now that this sentence is generated by a contextual grammar. This means that each step of the derivation corresponds to a correct sentence, too. The possible correct sub-sentences of the one above are

Joan sees. (2)

Joan sees Carlos. (3)

Joan sees Carlos singing. (4)

The sentence

**Joan sees singing.* (5)

is not acceptable. This means that in our grammar we can produce the string (maybe it is an axiom) *Joan sees* and we have the contexts (λ, *Carlos*), (λ, *singing*). With these we can produce only the following derivation

Joan sees $\Longrightarrow$ *Joan sees Carlos* $\Longrightarrow$ *Joan sees Carlos singing.*

The derivation

Joan sees $\Longrightarrow$ *Joan sees singing* $\Longrightarrow$ *Joan sees Carlos singing.*

is not possible, (λ, *singing*) is not accepted by *Joan sees.* The ambiguity of (1) does not appear!

However, if we consider the contexts (λ, *Carlos*), (λ, *Carlos singing*), starting from *Joan sees* we get the same three correct sentences (2), (3), (4) as above.

In both cases, we use one starting string and two contexts, and this is the optimal number of axioms and of contexts for this example. Two optimal descriptions of the same language suggests an intrinsic ambiguity which is different from the ambiguity considered in the sections above and usually considered in formal language theory.

The idea, suggested above, is the following: take a natural way to define the take a natural way to define the *optimal* grammars for a language (minimal from given points of view); if a language can be generated by two *different* optimal grammars, then it is considered intrinsically ambiguous.

Two problems emerge here, the easiest of which concerns the definition of *different* grammars. For contextual grammars this is clear, for Chomsky grammars this can mean "different modulo renaming the nonterminals". The important question is what an *optimal* grammar means. Thus, we enter the slippery area of descriptional complexity. For context-free grammars several parameters are considered, which describe their size, eg. the number of nonterminals (Var), the number of productions ($Prod$), the total number of symbols appearing in productions ($Symb$), etc. (see (Gruska 1973) for a survey of notions and results in this area). However, they contradict each other: if we improve one of them, we can lose the quality of the other (there are languages for which there is no optimal grammar from two given points of view).

Two strategies can be followed in such a case: either only one complexity parameter is considered (and therefore the intrinsic ambiguity is defined with respect to this parameter), or several parameters are taken and ordered by a priority relation. For instance, if we take *Var* and *Prod* and we consider that *Var* is more important for us, then a *VarProd*-optimal grammar for a language L means a grammar with the smallest number of productions, selected from the set of grammars with the smallest number of variables generating the language L.

We shall briefly consider here the second strategy for the case of internal contextual grammars. That is to say, we consider the parameters $Ax =$ the number of axioms, $Con =$ the number of contexts. Formally, for a grammar $G = (V, B, C, \varphi)$, we denote

$$Ax(G) = card(B),$$
$$Con(G) = card(C).$$

Then, for a language L, we define

$$M(L) = \min\{M(G) \mid L = L(G)\},\ M \in \{Ax, Con\}.$$

The combined $AxCon$ complexity of L will be

$$AxCon(L) = (Ax(L), \min\{Con(G) \mid L = L(G), Ax(G) = Ax(L)\}).$$

Clearly, $AxCon(L) = (Ax(L), m)$ for some $m \geq Con(L)$.

Each grammar G such that $AxCon(L) = (Ax(G), Con(G)), L = L(G)$, is said to be *AxCon-optimal* for L.

Example. The language $L = a^+ \cup b^+$ can be generated by

$$G = (\{a,b\}, \{a,b\}, (\{a\}, \{(\lambda, a)\}), (\{b\}, \{(\lambda, b)\})),$$

which is $AxCon$-optimal, because it is easy to see that $Ax(L) = 2, Con(L) = 2$. Hence $AxCon(L) = (2,2)$.

The above strategy (and definition of optimal grammars with reference to two measures) is necessary because the two parameters, Ax and Con, are contradictory. Specifically, for a measure M of descriptional complexity and a language L we denote

$$M^{-1}(L) = \{G \mid M(G) = M(L)\}$$

(the set of optimal grammars for L, from the point of view of M). Then, two measures M_1, M_2 are called *incompatible* if there is a language L such that

$$M_1^{-1}(L) \cap M_2^{-1}(L) = \emptyset$$

(the two measures cannot be simultaneously minimized for the grammars generating L).

As expected, we have

Theorem 7. *Ax and Con are incompatible (for internal contextual languages generated by grammars with selection of any type).*

Proof. Consider the language

$$L = \{ba^{2n}, ca^{3n} \mid n \geq 1\}.$$

It can be generated by the grammar

$$G = (\{a,b,c\}, \{ba^2, ca^3\}, (\{b\}, \{(\lambda, a^2)\}), (\{c\}, \{(\lambda, a^3)\})).$$

Hence $Ax(L) \leq 2$. Obviously, both ba^2 and ca^3 must be axioms of any grammar generating L. Hence $Ax(L) = 2$.

Take an arbitrary internal contextual grammar with selection, $G' = (\{a,b,c\}, B, C, \varphi)$, generating L and with $Ax(G') = 2 = Ax(L)$. Clearly,

$B = \{ba^2, ca^3\}$. In order to generate the string ba^4 we need a context (u, v) such that $uv = a^2$. Similarly, in order to generate the string ca^6 we need a context (u', v') with $u'v' = a^3$. Consequently, $Con(G') \geq 2$.

However, $L = L(G'')$, for

$$G'' = (\{a, b, c\}, \{ba^2, ba^4, ba^6, ca^3, ca^6\}, (\{a\}, \{(\lambda, a^6)\})).$$

Hence $Con(L) = 1$. (Therefore, $(Ax(L), Con(L)) = (2, 1)$, but $AxCon(L) = (2, 2)$.) □

Consider now the intrinsic ambiguity with respect to *AxCon*-optimality. Let us denote

$$AxCon^{-1}(L) = \{G \mid AxCon(L) = (Ax(G), Con(G))\}$$

(the set of grammars of complexity equal to $AxCon(L)$, and thus *AxCon*-optimal).

A language L is *intrinsically AxCon ambiguous* if $card(AxCon^{-1}(L)) \geq 2$. In general, if

$$card(AxCon^{-1}(L)) = k, \ k \geq 1,$$

then we say that L is intrinsically *AxCon* ambiguous *of degree k*. If the set $AxCon^{-1}(L)$ is infinite, then we say that L has an infinite degree of ambiguity.

Somewhat surprisingly (and disappointingly), we have

Theorem 8. *Every finite internal contextual language generated by a grammar with selection of any type is unambiguous; every infinite internal contextual language generated by a grammar with selection of any type has an infinite degree of AxCon ambiguity.*

Proof. Take a language $L \subseteq V^*$. If it is finite, then every grammar $G = (V, B, C, \varphi)$ such that $L = L(G)$ must either have $C = \emptyset$, or $\varphi^{-1}((u, v)) \cap Sub(L) = \emptyset$ for all $(u, v) \in C$ (by $Sub(L)$ we have denoted the set of subwords of strings in L), otherwise it generates an infinite language: when $x \Longrightarrow y, x \in L, x = x_1x_2x_3, y = x_1ux_2vx_3$ for $(u, v) \in \varphi(x_2)$ then $y \Longrightarrow z$, too, for $z = x_1uux_2vvx_3$, hence $x_1u^nx_2v^nx_3 \in L$ for all $n \geq 1$ (the context (λ, λ), if it appears, can be removed without changing the generated language). Therefore, $Ax(L) = card(L), Con(L) = 0$. There is exactly one grammar G' with $(Ax(G'), Con(G')) = (card(L), 0)$. Hence L is not ambiguous.

If L is infinite, then $L = L(G)$ for some grammar $G = (V, B, C, \varphi)$ such that there is $(u, v) \in C, uv \neq \lambda$, and $w \in Sub(L), (u, v) \in \varphi(w)$. Take $z \in L, z = x_1x_2x_3$, with $x_2 = w$. Then $x_1u^nx_2v^nx_3 \in L$ for all $n \geq 1$.

Let us consider the grammar $G' = (V, B, C, \varphi')$ with

$$\varphi'(x) = \varphi(x), \text{ for } x \neq u^iwv^i, i \geq 1,$$
$$\varphi'(u^iwv^i) = \varphi(u^iwv^i) - \{(u, v)\}, i \geq 1.$$

We have $L(G) = L(G')$: the use of (u, v) in G associated with the selectors $u^iwv^i, i \geq 1$, can be simulated in G' by using (u, v) associated with w.

Now, consider the grammars

$$G_k = (V, B, C, \varphi_k), \ k \geq 1,$$

where

$$\varphi_k(x) = \varphi(x), \text{ for } x \neq u^iwv^i, i \geq 1,$$
$$\varphi_k(u^iwv^i) = \varphi'(u^iwv^i) \cup \{(u, v)\}, \text{ for } 1 \leq i \leq k.$$

We have $L(G_k) = L(G') = L(G), Ax(G_k) = Ax(G), Con(G_k) = Con(G)$. If G is an $AxCon$-optimal grammar for L, then G_k is optimal. Every two grammars $G_r, G_s, s \neq r$, are different. Hence L has an infinite degree of ambiguity. □

The previous result can be interpreted as showing that our notion of intrinsic ambiguity is still too weak and that other complexity measures, for instance the *length of selectors* (for grammars with finite selection), have to be taken into account.

We hope to make a more detailed study of intrinsic ambiguity in another paper.

We close this section with the remark that our notion of intrinsic ambiguity fits in with what happens in the case of regular languages: they are intuitively unambiguous (also syntactically unambiguous in a precise way) and, significantly, they can be described by a single minimal (as number of states) deterministic finite automaton.

Final remarks

The internal contextual grammars we have considered here are the basic ones, with no restrictions on the use of selectors. It seems that it would also be interesting to investigate ambiguity for restricted classes, such as those with *minimal* or with *maximal* use of selectors, in the sense of (Marcus, Martín-Vide and Păun 1995), (Martín-Vide et al. 1995) (when adjoining a context to a selector, no substring –superstring, respectively– of the selector can be used as a selector), or with leftmost derivations, in the sense of (Păun, Rozenberg and Salomaa 1994), (Păun, Rozenberg and Salomaa 1996). In particular, what can be said about the ambiguity of *deterministic* grammars, such as those investigated in (Păun, Rozenberg and Salomaa 1994), (Păun, Rozenberg and Salomaa 1996)?

As far as intrinsic ambiguity is concerned, in the sense of Section 5, the problem of finding a combination of complexity parameters for grammars such that languages of a given degree $k, 0 < k < \infty$, of ambiguity can be found remains *open*.

Another natural research topic concerns the relation between the syntactic ambiguity of contextual grammars and the morphological ambiguity with respect to their generated languages. The morphological ambiguity is defined taking into account the domination relation between strings, which, in turn, takes into account the contexts which accept the strings. In a contextual grammar we already have a mapping which associates strings and contexts. Can this mapping be used to define the domination relation, and hence the morphological ambiguity?

Let us close this paper with an optimistic interpretation of the results: natural languages are highly ambiguous (see arguments in (Miquel-Vergés 1995)), and we have shown above that internal contextual languages are highly ambiguous, too (from the points of view introduced here); maybe this means that internal contextual grammars are an *adequate* model of natural languages.

References

Ehrenfeucht, A., Păun, Gh. and Rozenberg, G. 1997. "On representing recursively enumerable languages by internal contextual languages". *Theoretical Computer Science* 182.

Gruska, J. 1973. "Descriptional complexity of context-free languages".*Proc. Symp. Math. Found. Computer Sci.*, High Tatras, 71–83.

Marcus, S. 1967. *Algebraic Linguistics. Analytical Models.* New York: Academic Press.

Marcus, S. 1969. "Contextual grammars". *Rev. Roum. Math. Pures Appl.* 14, 1525–1534.

Marcus, S., Martín-Vide, C. and Păun, Gh. 1995. "On the power of internal contextual grammars with maximal use of selectors". *Fourth Meeting on Mathematics of Language, MOL4*, Philadelphia.

Martín-Vide, C., Mateescu, A., Miquel-Vergés, J. and Păun, Gh. 1995. "Internal contextual grammars: minimal, maximal, and scattered use of selectors". In M. Koppel and E. Shamir (eds), *Proc. of The Fourth Bar-Ilan Symp. on Found. of Artificial Intelligence (BISFAI'95)*, Jerusalem, 132–142. Also in M. Koppel and E. Shamir (eds), *Proc. of The Fourth Bar-Ilan Symp. on Foundations of Artificial Intelligence. Focusing on Natural Languages and Artificial Intelligence-Philosophical and Computational Aspects.* AAAI Press, Menlo Park, Ca., 1997, 159-168.

Martín-Vide, C., Miquel-Vergés, J. and Păun, Gh. 1995. "Contextual grammars with depth-first derivation". In A. Nijholt, G. Scollo and R. Steetskamp (eds), *Algebraic Methods in Language Processing (AMiLP'95).* Proceedings of the Tenth Twente Workshop on Language Technology jointly with First AMAST Workshop on Language Processing (TWLT10), Enschede, University of Twente, The Netherlands, 225–233.

Miquel-Vergés, J. 1995. "Ambigedades contextuales en los lenguajes naturales y artificiales". In C. Martín-Vide (ed), *Lenguajes Naturales y Lenguajes Formales, XI.* Barcelona: PPU, 71–91.

Păun, Gh. 1982. *Contextual Grammars.* Bucharest: The Publishing House of the Romanian Academy, (in Romanian).

Păun, Gh. 1994. "Marcus contextual grammars. After 25 years". *Bulletin EATCS* 52: 263–273.

Păun, Gh. and Nguyen, X. M. 1980. "On the inner contextual grammars". *Rev. Roum. Math. Pures Appl.* 25: 641–651.

Păun, Gh., Rozenberg, G. and Salomaa, A. 1994. "Contextual grammars: erasing, determinism, one-sided contexts". In G. Rozenberg and A. Salomaa (eds), *Developments in Language Theory*, Singapore: World Sci. Publ. 370–388.

Păun, Gh., Rozenberg, G. and Salomaa, A. 1994. "Marcus contextual grammars: modularity and leftmost derivation". In Gh. Păun (ed), *Mathematical Aspects of Natural and Formal Languages*, Singapore: World Sci. Publ., 375–392.

Păun, Gh., Rozenberg, G. and Salomaa, A. 1996. "Contextual grammars: deterministic derivations and growth functions". *Rev. Roum. Math. Pures Appl.* 41, 1-2 (1996), 83–108.

Salomaa, A. 1973. *Formal Languages*. New York and London: Academic Press.

Variants of Parallel Communicating Grammar Systems[1]

Valeria Mihalache[2]

Turku Centre for Computer Science

Abstract

Some variants of parallel communicating grammar systems are presented. Motivations from Artificial Intelligence or from other fields are provided for each of these systems. Some of the advantages of using parallel communicating grammar systems in natural language processing are also pointed out.

Introduction

Nowadays a given problem tends to be divided into subproblems and is then solved in a cooperative mode by several "processors". In order to provide a formal representation of such situations, grammar systems have been introduced. Roughly speaking, a grammar system consists of several usual (Chomsky) grammars, see (Salomaa 1973), working together according to a predefined protocol towards generating a common language. There are two

[1]Research supported by the Academy of Finland, project 137358.

[2]On leave of absence from the Faculty of Mathematics, University of Bucharest, Romania.

basic classes of such generative mechanisms: *cooperating distributed* (CD, for short) grammar systems, introduced in (Csuhaj-Varjú and Dassow 1990) (a variant of these appears in (Meersman and Rozenberg 1978), while a particular case was considered in (Atanasiu and Mitrana 1989)), and *parallel communicating* (PC, for short) grammar systems, introduced in (Păun 1989).

In a CD grammar system the component grammars work, by turns, on the same sentential form; the working protocol states the conditions under which a component can become active/inactive during a derivation process. They are well motivated from the Artificial Intelligence point of view by the so-called *blackboard model* in problem solving, (Csuhaj-Varjú, Dassow, Kelemen and Păun 1994).

In a PC grammar system, each of the component grammars has its own sentential form which it modifies according to its rewriting rules; a universal clock which divides time into units is assumed to exist, and the grammars use this to work synchronously; the cooperation among components is performed by communication, which is done on request. The consideration of PC grammar systems is motivated by the intention of formally describing the *classroom model* of Artificial Intelligence, (Csuhaj-Varjú, Dassow, Kelemen and Păun 1994).

Most of the results in the area of grammar systems up to the middle of 1992 can be found in (Csuhaj-Varjú, Dassow, Kelemen and Păun 1994) while more recent results on this topic are surveyed in (Dassow, Păun and Rozenberg 1997), (Păun 1996).

Our intention is to present some variants of PC grammar systems, by parallelizing those defined for the cooperating distributed systems. We start by defining usual PC grammar systems. Then for each of the variants addressed here, we point out the modifications that should be made in the basic definition in order to obtain this new variant. We conclude by emphasizing some characteristics of PC grammar systems that could make them useful in natural language processing.

Basic PC grammar systems

Before giving the definition of PC grammar systems, we need to specify some notations. For basic facts in formal language theory we refer to (Salomaa

1973).

For an alphabet V, V^* denotes the free monoid generated by V; the empty string is denoted by λ, $|x|$ is the length of $x \in V^*$ and $|x|_U$ is the number of occurrences in $x \in V^*$ of symbols of $U \subseteq V$. The set of natural numbers is denoted by $\mathbb{N}$.

Definition 1. *Let $n \geq 1$ be a natural number. A* parallel communicating grammar system *of degree n is an $n+3$-tuple*

$$\Gamma = (N, K, T, G_1, \ldots, G_n),$$

where N is a nonterminal alphabet, T is a terminal alphabet, $K = \{Q_1, Q_2, \ldots \ldots, Q_n\}$ (these sets are mutually disjoint), and

$$G_i = (N \cup K, T, P_i, S_i), 1 \leq i \leq n,$$

are usual Chomsky grammars.

We write $V_\Gamma = N \cup K \cup T$.

The grammars $G_i, 1 \leq i \leq n$, are called *components* of the system, and the elements of K are called *query symbols*; their indices, $1, \ldots, n$, point to the components $G_1, \ldots, G_n$, respectively.

The convention we consider is to denote the start symbol and the production set of a component of a system with the same indices which denote the grammar component. This convention holds for query symbols, too, so we do not need to specify in detail the set of query symbols for a given system.

Definition 2. *Given a PC grammar system $\Gamma = (N, K, T, G_1, \ldots, G_n)$ as above, for two n-tuples $(x_1, x_2, \ldots, x_n), (y_1, y_2, \ldots, y_n), x_i, y_i \in V_\Gamma^*, 1 \leq i \leq n$, we write $(x_1, \ldots, x_n) \Longrightarrow (y_1, \ldots, y_n)$ if one of the next two cases holds:*

(i) $|x_i|_K = 0, 1 \leq i \leq n$, and for each i, $1 \leq i \leq n$, we have $x_i \Longrightarrow y_i$ in the grammar G_i, or $x_i \in T^*$ and $x_i = y_i$;

(ii) there is an i, $1 \leq i \leq n$, such that $|x_i|_K > 0$; then for each such i, we write $x_i = z_1 Q_{i_1} z_2 Q_{i_2} \ldots z_t Q_{i_t} z_{t+1}, t \geq 1$, for $z_j \in V_\Gamma^*, |z_j|_K = 0, 1 \leq j \leq t+1$; if $|x_{i_j}|_K = 0, 1 \leq j \leq t$, then $y_i = z_1 x_{i_1} z_2 x_{i_2} \ldots z_t x_{i_t} z_{t+1}$ [and $y_{i_j} = S_{i_j}, 1 \leq j \leq t$]; when, for some j, $1 \leq j \leq t, |x_{i_j}|_K \neq 0$, then $y_i = x_i$; for all i, $1 \leq i \leq n$, for which y_i is not specified above, we have $y_i = x_i$.

Point (i) defines (componentwise) *derivation steps*, whereas point (ii) defines *communication steps.* In a communication operation, when the communicated string x_j replaces the query symbol Q_j, we say that Q_j is satisfied. Communication has priority over effective rewriting. If some query symbols are not satisfied at a given communication step, they will have to be satisfied at a following one. No rewriting is possible when at least one query symbol is present.

The work of a PC grammar system is blocked in two cases: (1) when a derivation step must be performed and a component x_i of the current n-tuple $(x_1, \ldots, x_n)$ (sometimes we shall call it a *configuration*) is not terminal with respect to G_i, but no rule of G_i can be applied to x_i, and (2) when a *circular query* appears, that is, G_{i_1} introduces Q_{i_2}, G_{i_2} introduces Q_{i_3}, and so on, until $G_{i_{k-1}}$ introduces Q_{i_k} and G_{i_k} introduces Q_{i_1} (because only strings without query symbols can be communicated, none of the query symbols can be satisfied).

The *language generated by a PC grammar system* Γ as above is

$$\begin{aligned} L(\Gamma) \quad = \quad & \{x \in T^* \mid (S_1, S_2, \ldots, S_n) \stackrel{*}{\Longrightarrow} (x, \alpha_2, \ldots, \alpha_n), \alpha_i \in V_\Gamma^*, 2 \leq i \leq n, \\ & \text{and in this derivation there is no intermediate configuration} \\ & \text{with a terminal string as the sentential form of } G_1\}. \end{aligned}$$

If in Definition 2 only grammar G_1 is allowed to introduce query symbols, then we say that Γ is a *centralized* PC grammar system; in contrast, the unrestricted case is called *non-centralized.*

A PC grammar system is said to be *returning* (to axiom) if, after communicating, each component returns to axiom. A PC grammar system is *non-returning* if in point (ii) of Definition 2, the brackets,

$$[and\ y_{i_j} = S_{i_j}, 1 \leq j \leq t],$$

are omitted.

As was mentioned in the Introduction, PC grammar systems are a formal representation of the *classroom model* in Artificial Intelligence. Briefly stated, the classroom model defines the situation when pupils in a class have particular problems to solve: they can use their notebooks, communicate with each other at each step of problem solving or only when the leader of the classroom, who operates on the blackboard, requests them to do so, and the global problem is solved through such cooperation on the blackboard.

In the formal model, pupils correspond to the grammars which make up the system and their notebooks to the sentential forms. The production sets of the grammars therefore encode the knowledge of the pupils. Rewriting a nonterminal symbol in a sentential form can be interpreted as a developmental step of the information contained in the notebooks. A partial solution, obtained by a pupil, corresponds to a terminal word generated in the associated grammar, while the solution to the initial problem is associated to a word in the language generated by the grammar system.

Depending on the variations considered in this basic set-up, the basic definition of the PC grammar systems varies. We shall deal with this in the next section.

Variants

The usual PC grammar systems assume (in the synchronized case) the existence of a universal clock, which divides time into units. In each time unit each of the grammars have to perform a derivation step. If grammars are thought to correspond to pupils (or agents, or processors) involved in solving a problem, then all these agents have the same competence. But in most real-life situations this is not so which is why the so-called *hybrid* CD grammar systems wer introduced. Here "hybrid" means that each grammar has its own mode of derivation, and when it has a sentential form to rewrite, it has to follow that derivation mode.

For the PC case, the feature "hybrid" could be considered with respect to the synchronization of the derivation, or to the communication. The first type of hybridization would mean that there is still a universal clock, but in a time unit grammars can perform a different (but fixed) number of derivation steps (for example one to derive 2 steps, another 5 steps, another being subjected to accomplish terminal derivation, another being allowed to derive unsynchronized). That is, such a system is an $(n+3)$-tuple

$$\Gamma = (N, K, T, (G_1, k_1), \ldots, (G_n, k_n)),$$

where $(N, K, T, G_1, \ldots, G_n)$ is a PC grammar system as in Definition 1, while $k_1, \ldots, k_n \in \mathbb{N} \cup \{\mathrm{u}, \mathrm{t}\}$ indicate how many derivation steps the component grammars $G_1, \ldots, G_n$ have to perform in a time unit; u and t stand for *unsynchronized*, and *terminal* derivation in the corresponding component grammar, see (Csuhaj-Varjú, Dassow, Kelemen and Păun 1994). So the definition of the derivations in a PC grammar system (point i) has to be modified to handle such situations.

The second type of hybrid systems means that after communicating their sentential forms to grammars that have queried them, some components have to continue derivation in the non-returning mode, while others have to do so in the returning mode. Formally, a system of this type is an $(n+3)$-tuple

$$\Gamma = (N, K, T, (G_1, s_1), \ldots, (G_n, s_n)),$$

where $(N, K, T, G_1, \ldots, G_n)$ is a PC grammar system as in Definition 1, while $s_1, \ldots, s_n \in \{r, nr\}$ (r stands for *returning*, nr stands for *non-returning* derivation). Definition 2 is modified accordingly.

It may even be the case that when a grammar is queried by certain components, it then works in the non-returning mode, but when it is queried by other components, it works in the returning mode.

For CD grammar systems, a variant in which there is a *graph control* of the derivation has been considered. This means that the grammars get involved in the derivation process only by following the order imposed by the graph.

A corresponding variant can also be considered in the PC case, where a graph controls not the derivation, but the communication between grammars, instead. That is, a grammar can send its sentential form only to grammars to which it is connected in the graph, and chain communications can be made through, and only through, paths in the graph. Note that this is the situation in the case of computer networks, or in case of systems structured in hierachies, where the flow of information has to follow predefined routes.

A type of CD grammar system which attempts to capture some problems arising in the communication between speakers of different languages is a CD grammar system *with a generalized sequential machine* (gsm, for short, see (Salomaa 1973)) which helps in communication. That is, a grammar derives the common sentential form according to the specified mode of derivation, but when another grammar takes the resulting string and derives it, first a gsm is applied to that string, and then the second grammar operates on the string obtained.

Such restrictions can be considered also for the case of PC grammar systems. Namely, when a grammar is asked to communicate its sentential form to another, a gsm is first applied to this sentential form and the resulting string is communicated to the grammar that has performed the query. This model is useful when each of the grammars has been designated to encode an agent, agents speak different languages, and when an agent is asked to report on his work. Then the system has to translate first the report in the language spoken by the agent who required it; the translation process is represented by a gsm.

A similar type of PC grammar system was considered in (López 1996)(*PC grammar systems with renaming*) but the motivation comes from the *left-dislocation* phenomenon in the syntax of natural languages (in the context of the dichotomy *theme*, or subject a sentence deal with / *rheme*, or enunciation about the subject, left-dislocation refers to the situation when theme has a peripheral position within a sentence, usually at the beginning of it; in the sentence, the left-dislocated constituent has a correlative pronominal, which must be a clitic; moreover, there is a close structural link between the left-dislocated constituent and the clitic one with which it is associated; the left-dislocated element must carry out the same grammatical function and must be given the same thematical role as the pronoun, (López 1996)).

Formally, PC grammar systems with renaming are like usual PC grammar systems, equipped, in addition, with several weak codes which can map a terminal symbol into another one, or can erase a terminal symbol, by means of a λ-production. They are of the form

$$\Gamma = (N, K, T, G_1, \ldots, G_n, h_1, \ldots, h_m),$$

where N, K, T are as in Definition 1, whereas $h_1, \ldots, h_m$ are weak codes from $(N \cup T)^*$ into $(N \cup T)^*$; in addition, a set $K' = \{[h_j, Q_i] \mid 1 \leq i \leq n,\ 1 \leq j \leq m\}$ of composed query symbols is considered, and $G_i = (N \cup K \cup K', T, P_i, S_i)$, for any i, $1 \leq i \leq n$. The system works in the same way as usual PC grammar systems, with the only difference that when a composed query symbol $[h_j, Q_i]$ occurs in a sentential form, it has to be replaced not by x_i, as is the case in usual PC grammar systems, but by $h_j(x_i)$, instead. The role of the weak codes is to encode and maintain the relation between a pronoun and the associated left-dislocated constituent.

A variant of CD grammar systems is CD grammar systems with a *hypothesis language*. In this set-up, a regular language is associated to the system, and when a grammar has accomplished a derivation (in a derivation mode), the derivation is accepted as valid only if the resulted string is in that language.

Similar constraints also can be considered for PC grammar systems: a regular language can be associated to the entire system, and this language can work as a filter for communication. More precisely, this means that when a string is to be communicated, the communication should be allowed only if the string is in that additional language. Formally, a PC grammar system with a hypothesis language is a construction

$$\Gamma = (N, K, T, G_1, \ldots, G_n, R),$$

where $(N, K, T, G_1, \ldots, G_n)$ is a usual PC grammar system, while R is a regular (type 3) language. In order to define a derivation in such a system, in Definition 2, point *ii*), the restriction $x_{i_j} \in R$ should be added; if this is not satisfied for an i_j, then the derivation is blocked.

In a more general framework, regular languages can be considered not as filters for communication, but patterns, or pattern languages, instead. This is intended to model the situation when an agent (processor, pupil) not only needs assistance to perform a job, but needs a particular type of assistance, which is assumed to be known (or at least its "shape" is known) a priori.

Another aspect we want to mention here concerns the existence of *teams* in a grammar system. For CD grammar systems, this problem has already been approached, namely systems have been considered which are enriched with sets consisting of components of the system, and a derivation step is no longer performed in a component grammar of the system, but in such a set of components, instead.

Correspondingly, PC grammar systems with teams can be considered: sets consisting of component grammars are added to the basic definition of PC grammar system. The derivation relation in this case would be defined such that at any derivation step, only the components in a set of grammars (that is, in a team) actually work, in a synchronized manner, whereas the others are inactive (they do not change their sentential forms, by rewriting or by communication). The order in which the teams of grammars can become active/inactive can either be arbitrary, or controlled by a predefined protocol (like, for example, the working protocol in CD grammar systems).

In the original model, for parallel communicating grammar systems it is assumed that all the grammars have the same terminal and nonterminal sets. This is very convenient in terms of the classroom model. Thus, it is quite natural to assume that all the pupils in a classroom have similar background and similar abilities (that is, the associated grammars in the system share the same nonterminal set), and also that they are asked to perform similar tasks (in the corresponding formal model, this implies the same terminal set for all the grammars). However, if one considers that agents, not pupils, are working towards solving a problem, and the protocol is the same as in the classroom model, such assumptions are not natural anymore. Agents may have to perform totally different tasks, and they may have different skills.

This is not a problem at all in the grammar systems set-up. The restriction of all the component grammars of a system having the same terminal and nonterminal sets can be eliminated, by considering that none of the component grammars of the system has its own terminal and nonterminal sets, see (Mihalache 1996). More precisely, such a system is of the form

$$\Gamma = (K, G_1, \ldots, G_n),$$

where $K = \{Q_1, \ldots, Q_n\}$ is the set of query symbols, and $G_i = (N_i \cup K, T_i, P_i, S_i)$ are the (Chomsky) component grammars. The derivation is defined as for basic PC grammar systems. The main difference between these systems and the usual ones is that here the same letter can be terminal in one grammar and nonterminal in another one. Otherwise the change of alphabet is not important.

Final remarks

It is well known that Chomsky grammars are the basis of the syntactic approaches to natural language processing. They were in fact first considered for this purpose. In grammar systems theory, the motivations came from Artificial Intelligence, from multi-agent systems. However, grammar systems seem to offer a lot for natural language processing as well, (Csuhaj-Varjú 1994), (Csuhaj-Varjú 1996), (López 1996).

Parallel communicating grammar systems have the advantage that even when working with context-free or regular sets of productions, their generative power is considerably higher than that of context-free grammars. This may be a great advantage when such generative devices are intnded to be used to process natural languages (because of the context-free rules, the meaning of non-terminals is visible; PC grammar systems can generate the languages $\{a^n b^n c^n \mid n \geq 1\}$, $\{xx \mid x \in \{a, b\}^*\}$, and $\{a^n b^m a^n b^m \mid n, m \geq 1\}$, which are known to model multiple agreements, replication, and crossed dependencies in natural languages, respectively; because the way a grammar obtains its sentential form is of no interest when that sentential form is communicated to another grammar, the components can be viewed as "black-boxes", and then at the level of the system to concern mainly of *what* is to be done rather than *how*; yet PC grammar systems present the advantage of being suitable for use in parallel computing, and so the computational complexity is not a problem anymore).

Moreover, when attempting to use PC grammar systems for natural language generation, note that grammar components can be considered not only for generating phrases in a sentence (like noun phrases, verb phrases, prepositional phrases, and so on), but also for preserving their features (like agreement features) or for preserving phrases such as pronouns to substitute other phrases (just like the register HOLD in augmented transition networks, see (Gazdar and Mellish 1989)).

References

Atanasiu, A. and Mitrana, V. 1989. "The modular grammars". *International Journal of Computer Mathematics* 30: 101–122.

Csuhaj-Varjú, E. 1994. "Grammar systems: a multi-agent framework for natural language generation". In Gh. Păun (ed), *Mathematical Aspects of Natural and Formal Languages*. Singapore: World Scientific Publ., 63–78.

Csuhaj-Varjú, E. "Generalized eco-grammar systems: a framework for natural language generation". *Manuscript.*

Csuhaj-Varjú, E. and Dassow, J. 1990. "On cooperating distributed grammar systems". *Journal of Information Processing and Cybernetics (EIK)* 26: 49–63.

Csuhaj-Varjú, E., Dassow, J., Kelemen, J. and Păun, Gh. 1994. *Grammar Systems*. London: Gordon and Breach Science Publishers Ltd.

Dassow, J., Păun, Gh. and Rozenberg, G. 1997. "Grammar Systems". In G. Rozenberg and A. Salomaa (eds), *Handbook of Formal Languages*. Berlin-Heidelberg: Springer-Verlag, 155–214.

Gazdar, G., and Mellish, C. 1989. *Natural Language Processing in Prolog*. Addison-Wesley Publ. Co.

Jiménez López, M. D. "Grammar systems: possible linguistic motivations", *Research Report of the Grup de Recerca en Linguistica Matematica i Enginyeria del Llenguatge, Tarragona*. To appear (in Spanish).

Jiménez López, M. D. 1996. "Grammar systems and natural languages: intuitive ideas". In C. Martín-Vide (ed), *Lenguajes Naturales y Lenguajes Formales, XII*. Barcelona: PPU, 223–236 (in Spanish).

Meersman, R. and Rozenberg, G. 1978. "Cooperating grammar systems". In *Lecture Notes in Computer Science 64: Proceedings MFCS'78 Symposium*. Berlin: Springer-Verlag, 364–374.

Mihalache, V. "Terminal versus non-terminal symbols in parallel communicating grammar systems". *Revue Roumaine de Mathématiques Pures et Appliquées*. To appear.

Păun, Gh. 1996. "Parallel communicating grammar systems. A survey". In C. Martín-Vide (ed), *Actas del XI Congreso de Lenguajes Naturales y Lenguajes Formales*. Barcelona: PPU, 257–283.

Păun, Gh. and Sântean, L. 1989. "Parallel communicating grammar systems: the regular case". *Annals of the University of Bucharest, Mathematics-Informatics Series* 38: 55–63.

Salomaa, A. 1973. *Formal Languages*. New York and London: Academic Press.

On Contextual Automata

Joan Miquel-Vergés

Rovira i Virgili University
University of Vigo

Abstract

Until now, only two characterizations of contextual languages have been obtained using automata: the first one based on *contraction automata*; and the most recent one based on *restarting automata.* However, in both cases, only a few variants of contextual grammars/languages have been characterized. The aim here is to find a more general framework by introducing a family of *contextual automata.* In order to correspond to the contextual style of working, such a mechanism should be able to execute the operation which is inverse to the insertion of a context: that is, to *erase a context.*

Introduction

Generating the strings which are correct with respect to a given grammar is an important activity but at least equally important is to *analyse* given strings with respect to their correctness as defined by a given grammar. This can be done either by constructing *parsing algorithms* associated to a class of grammars, or by using *automata* equivalent to a class of grammars.

We know the automata which are equivalent to the basic classes of grammars/languages in the Chomsky hierarchy. A similar approach can also be used for contextual grammars.

Contextual grammars

Contextual grammars were introduced by S. Marcus (Marcus, 1969) and are based on a basic phenomenon in descriptive linguistics, that of acceptance of a word by a context (or conversely) (see (Marcus, 1967)). Roughly speaking, a contextual grammar consists of a given finite set of initial strings (*axioms*) and a given finite set of *contexts* (pairs of strings). Sets of contexts are associated with sets of strings (called *selectors*) and a context can be adjoined to each string in the associated selector. Starting from an axiom and adjoining contexts according to the selection imposed by the selectors, we get a language. Since they were introduced over 25 years ago, many variants have already been investigated: determinism, parallelism, etc (see the monograph (Păun, 1982) for details (up to 1981) or to (Păun, 1996; Păun and Rozenberg, 1996) for a recent survey).

Contextual automata

A general image of a contextual automaton is that of a *linear bounded automaton*. That is to say, a simple Turing machine which does not have potentially infinite tape on which to compute but only a portion of tape containing the input string plus two tape squares holding the endmarkers. This tape is scanned by a read/write head, according to the current state of a finite memory. In order to correspond to the contextual style of working, such a mechanism should be able to execute the operation which is inverse to the insertion of a context, that is to *erase a context*.

Until now, only two characterizations of contextual languages have been obtained using automata: the first one, given by Gh. Păun in (Păun, 1982) and based on *contraction automata*; and the most recent one, given by P. Jančar et al. in (Jančar et al., 1994) and based on *restarting automata*. However, in both cases, only some variants of contextual grammars/languages have been characterized.

The aim is to find a more general framework, introducing a family of *contextual automata*. There are several possible variants, some of which characterize families of contextual languages, while others produce new families of languages.

Contextual automata based on deleting automata

Motivated by (natural as well as formal) language analysis, P. Jančar et al. introduced in (Jančar et al., 1996) several types of deleting automata with restart operation and also a new class of contextual grammar with regular selection mapping. The main aim was to compare classes of languages recognized by several versions of deleting automata with restart operation with classes of languages generated by Marcus grammars. Languages generated by contextual grammars with regular selection mapping can be characterized by normal deleting automata with restart operation.

Part of the motivation comes from the area of natural language analysis and resembles the motivation for Marcus contextual grammars in (Marcus, 1969). Another part comes from the area of grammar checking of natural as well as programming languages (Jančar et al., 1994).

Deleting automata, abbr. *D-automata*, are linear bounded automata which cannot rewrite the input cells. They can only delete them. The original definition in (Jančar et al., 1993) differs a little from (Jančar et al., 1996) because the automaton did not have a lookahead window which is, on the other hand, commonly used in parsers for formal and natural languages. The general model is, in a sense, too wide. It seems natural to allow the head only to move to the right (with some bounded lookahead) and to introduce an operation *restart*, where restarting means resuming the work from the very beginning (on a shorter input word). To simplify the description these automata are defined as automata using more complex instructions. One instruction of such an automaton performs a sequence of operations (the length of which is limited by the size of lookahead): move right, and delete, possibly finished by a restart operation.

A *deleting automaton with restart operation*, abbr. DR- *automaton*, M with bounded lookahead is a device with a finite state control unit and one head moving on a finite linear doubly linked list of items. The first item is reserved for a special symbol ¢, the last one for another special symbol \$, and every other item contains a symbol from a finite vocabulary V (not containing ¢, \$). The head has a lookahead "window" of fixed length k, for some $k \geq 0$; this means -besides the current item, M also scans the next k items to the right (or simply the end of the word when the distance to \$ is less than k).

It can be roughly described as follows: it has a finite control unit, a head with a lookahead window attached to a tape, and it works in certain cycles. In one cycle, it moves the head from left to right along the input word on the tape, and at several points it "cuts off" some symbols from the lookahead, and the cycle ends by "restart" -i.e. it resets the control unit to the initial state and places the head on the left end of the (shorter) word. The computation consists of a sequence of cycles and ends by halting in an accepting or rejecting state. In fact, to make the mentioned "cutting off" more natural, the deleting automaton with restart operation uses a doubly linked list of items (cells) rather than the common tape.

In (Jančar et al., 1994) *restarting automata*, abbr. *R-automata*, -a special type of deleting automata with restart operation which have the restart operation tightly bound to the deleting- are defined: immediately after deleting some symbols from the lookahead the automaton restarts, i.e. every instruction with some delete operation ends by restart.

In (Jančar et al., 1995a) the so called *normal restarting automata* were defined, abbr. *norm-R-automata.* They generalized this property to *DR*-automata. Normal *DR*-automata (normal *R*-automata resp.) can in one cycle delete from the current word at most two contiguous subwords the length of which is limited by the size of the lookahead (in the case of normal *R*-automata both these subwords are deleted in a last instruction finished by restart).

When considering a deterministic *DR*-automaton M, it is sometimes convenient to assume it has a *strong cyclic form*, (Jančar et al., 1994) for *R*-automata; this means that the words of length less than k (k being the length of the lookahead) are immediately (in the first cycle) accepted or rejected, and that M performs at least two cycles (at least one restarting) for any longer word. For a nondeterministic *DR*-automaton M, we can assume the *weak cyclic form* , (Jančar et al., 1994) for *R*-automata - any word of $L(M)$ of length at least k can only be accepted by performing at least two cycles. Thus, an *R*-automaton in weak cyclic form can immediately reject a "long" word, but *DR*-automaton in strong cyclic form can immediately only reject "short" words. Moreover, any computation of a *DR*-automaton in (strong) cyclic form is finite (finishing in a halting state).

A *DR*-automaton M is called *external DR-automaton*, abbr. *ext-DR-automaton*, if it is in weak cyclic form and each cycle in any computation by M has the following form: the first instruction used in the cycle can cut off a prefix of the current word, so a sequence of instructions with only move-to-the-right operations can follow with one exception –the last instruction in the cycle (ending by the restart operation) can cut off a suffix of the scanned word; i.e. M can immediately accept only short words, longer words are rejected or shortened by deleting a short (limited by the size of lookahead) prefix and/or suffix of the word in one cycle. Obviously *ext-DR*-automaton is normal.

A *configuration of the* DR-*automaton* M is (u, s, v), where u is the contents of the working list from the left-end marker ¢ to the position of the head, s is the current state and v is the contents of the working list from the scanned item to the right-end marker \$. In the *initial configuration* on an input *word* w, the control unit is in a fixed, initial, state s_0 and the head is attached to the item which contains the left-end marker ¢, i.e. $(\lambda, s_0, ¢w\$)$. (scanning also the first k symbols of the input word w).

The head of the automaton can perform operations of the following three types: 1) *move-to-the-right operation*, abbr. MOV_R. It moves to the right neighbour of the scanned item; 2) *delete operation*, abbr. *DEL*. It deletes of the scanned item with one move to the right; and finally, 3) *restart operation*, abbr. *RST*. It places the head on the first item of the list (containing ¢).

The *computation* of M is controlled by a finite set of *instructions* of the following type: $(s, au) \rightarrow (s', \omega)$. The left-hand side of an instruction determines when it is applicable –s means the current state of the finite control, a means the current symbol which is scanned by the head, and u means the contents of the lookahead window (u being a string of length k or less if it ends with \$). The right-hand side describes the activity to be performed. ω is a sequence of operations MOV_R, *DEL* the length of which is less than or equal to the length of au optionally finished by the operation *RST*. In the instructions with ω ending in *RST* the new state s' is the initial state of M. The operations in the sequence ω are performed from left to right.

We suppose that the states of the finite control are divided into two classes –the *nonhalting states* (there is at least one instruction which is applicable when the unit is in such a state) and the *halting states* (all computations finish by entering such a state); the halting states are further divided into *accepting states* and *rejecting states.*

In general, a *DR*-automaton is *nondeterministic*, i.e. there can be two or more instructions with the same left-hand side (s, au). If this is not the case, the automaton is *deterministic.*

An input word w *is accepted* by M if there is a computation which starts in the initial configuration on w (bounded by ¢,$) on the list and finishes in an *accepting configuration* where the control unit is in one of the accepting states. $L(M)$ denotes the language of all the words accepted by M; we say that M *recognizes the language* $L(M)$.

Any computation of a *DR*-automaton consists of certain *cycles*: in one cycle, the automaton uses instructions with move right and delete operations until a halting state is entered or operation *RST* is executed –in this case the computation is resumed in the initial configuration.

According to the definition, it is possible that the working list (current word) is changed during a cycle until the operation *RST* is performed. Then the computation is resumed in the same initial configuration. But this could be avoided using *DR*-automata in some special form: in a *deleting form* –in all cycles, M either deletes, accepts or rejects at least one symbol.

Normal *DR*-automata are closely related to some classes of Marcus contextual grammars. A contextual grammar works in the opposite direction. Starting with a word from a finite basic set it generates words by inserting two "contexts" in some places of the current word. The insertion is controlled by a selection mapping. Then a natural class of contextual grammar is introduced, where the possibility of an insertion can be decided by a finite automaton –these are the so called contextual grammars with regular selection mapping.

Contextual grammars with regular selection mapping are more general than several classes of contextual grammars studied in the theory of contextual grammars, cf. (Păun, 1985; Păun, 1994). The class of Marcus grammars from (Jančar et al., 1995b) which characterizes the class of languages recognized by normal *R*-automata is also a subclass of these grammars. Moreover, for any contextual grammar G with regular selection mapping a normal *DR*-automaton M can be constructed in such a way, that M not only recognizes the same words, but can follow any derivation by G (in reverse order). Thus, normal *DR*-automata can be used to analyse of languages generated by some classes of contextual grammars. Every word generated by a contextual grammar with regular choice is derived from a short word from base set B. We would like to construct automata which recognize the language generated by the contextual grammar G.

In order to recognize the elements of base B (or axioms), for any *DR*-automaton M we denote $L_1(M)$ –the set of all words accepted by M in one cycle– $L_1(M) = \{ u \mid u \in L(M) \wedge \neg \exists v \in L(M) : u \longrightarrow_M v \}$.

Moreover, the simulating automaton M should satisfy the following property: for any word x, y then $x \Rightarrow_G^* y$ if, and only if, $y \longrightarrow_M^* x$. In particular, one step of a derivation by G should correspond to one cycle of the corresponding *DR*-automaton.

Thus the corresponding *DR*-automaton is required to be normal and in a weak cyclic form. Normality follows from the way in which contextual grammars are derived –at most two contiguous subwords are inserted in a current word in one step of derivation of G. Weak cyclic form ensures that only short words are accepted immediately. Longer words must be shortened or rejected.

In (Jančar et al., 1995a) the relationships between *DR*- automata and contextual grammars are studied. We can summarize the results in the following two theorems about some classes of *DR*-automata "exactly" recognizing some classes of contextual languages with regular selection. The proof is not given in either case.

Theorem 1 *A language L is generated by an external contextual grammar with regular selection, abbr.* ECC(REG) *, if and only if L is recognized by an ext-DR-automaton.*

Theorem 2 *A language L is generated by a regular-prefix finite-infix bounded-suffix contextual grammar with regular selection, abbr.* RFBRCG, *if and only if L is recognized by a norm-R-automaton.*

The present definition of contextual grammar with regular selection can be extended to general families of languages. However, P. Jančar et al. did not consider such more general cases because they are mostly interested in automata recognizing similar classes of languages, and in comparing various kinds of contextual grammars with regular selection with various kinds of deleting automata. Some of these automata seem to be good theoretical background for free-word-order natural language parsing (Czech, for example). For these reasons the restriction to contextual grammar with *regular* selection seems to be sufficient.

Contextual automata based on contraction automata

S.H. von Solms defined in (von Solms, 1975) a new automaton called *contraction automaton of complexity* (n, k), $b \geq 0$, $k \geq 1$, and several well-known classes of formal languages, which had until then only been characterized by grammars, can now be characterized by this new automaton.

Gh. Păun presents in the last chapter of (Păun, 1982) some results about contextual automata which are similar to the *contraction automata* mentioned above. However, only two classes of contextual languages are characterized: the class of simple contextual languages, characterized by *simple contextual automaton*; and the class of ν-contextual programmed languages, characterized by $(right, left)$*-constant contextual automaton.* Unfortunately, the definition of new types of automata which characterize other contextual languages has yet to be considered.

A *contraction automaton of complexity (n,k)*, abbr. (n, k)-C-automaton, is a linear bounded automaton with certain restrictions on its read/write capabilities. Consider a linear bounded automaton $M = (K, V, \Gamma, \delta, s_0, F)$ with the following restrictions and changes: i) $F = \{s_f\}$, ii) K contains a distinguished state s_c, and, iii) Γ contains two distinguished symbols, the start symbol $*$ and the final symbol Ω.

We say two tape symbols A and B are *neighbouring symbols* if they are separated by $t \geq 0$ star symbols. Let $n \geq 0$ and $k \geq 1$ be two constants.

Suppose M always starts in its start state s_0 scanning its right-end marker \$. From here M moves to the left in a read-only mode until its left-end marker ¢ is reached. At any stage during a read-only movement to the left, the state of M depends only on \$ and a subset E of $(\Gamma - V)$, whose symbols appear between the read head and the right marker \$, and with $|E| \leq n$. ($|E|$ is the number of elements in E). Thus, when M reaches its left-end marker ¢, it takes into account that \$ and $m \leq n$ different symbols of $(\Gamma - V)$ appear on its tape.

When ¢ is reached, M changes state and starts moving to the right. During a movement to the right, M may perform $p \leq k$ replacement. Basically M can only perform two *types* of replacement –a *write operation* which replaces a single tape symbol by another tape symbol, or a *star operation* which replaces two neighbouring symbols, the left one by the star symbol, and the right one by any other tape symbol. The star symbol may never be replaced by any other symbol. During a movement to the right, M may thus perform i write and j star operations, provided $i + j \leq k$.

After the last replacement, i.e., number p, M goes into a special state, the *copy state* s_c. In this state M may only copy symbols and move to the right. If \$ is reached in the state s_c, M goes into its start state s_0, and starts another read movement to the left. M goes into the final state s_f and accepts, if the final symbol Ω, together with $r \geq 0$ star symbols, are the only symbols on its tape.

An automaton, as described, is called a contraction automaton of complexity (n,k), abbr. (n,k)-C-automaton. Formally, an (n,k)-C-automaton, $n \geq 0, k \geq 1$, is a 9-tuple $M = (K, V, \Gamma, \delta, s_0, s_c, s_f, \Omega, *)$ where: i) $K = K_L \cup K_R \cup K_C \cup \{s_c, s_f\}$, is the finite, nonempty set of states; K_L, K_R, K_C and $\{s_c, s_f\}$ are mutually disjoint (thus L, R, C in K_L, K_R, K_C correspond to "left", "right","copy", resp.); ii) Γ, is the nonempty, finite set of tape symbols; iii) V, is a subset of Γ, the set of input symbols; V contains two special symbols, ¢ and \$, the left and right end markers, respectively; iv) δ is a function, the *next move function*, from $K \times \Gamma$ into finite subsets of $(K \times \Gamma \times \{R, L\})$, R for right and L for left. (We will not formally consider how the mapping δ works. Our intention is only to consider some basic ideas that can be applied to contextual automata); v) $s_0 \in K, s_c \in K$, and $s_f \in K$, are the start, copy, and final states, respectively; vi) $\Omega \in (\Gamma - V)$, is the final symbol; and, finally, v) $* \in (\Gamma - V)$, is the star symbol.

A *configuration* of an (n,k)-C-automaton $M = (K, V, \Gamma, \delta, s_0, s_c, s_f, \Omega, *)$ is a pair $(s, ¢w_1\underline{A}w_2\$)$, $s \in K$, $w_1, w_2 \in \Gamma^*$, $A \in \Gamma$

The configuration means that M is in state s, scanning the tape symbol A, with $¢w_1$ to the left and $w_2\$$ to the right of A.

The *language accepted by an (n,k)-C-automaton* M is the set $L(M) = \{w \in (V - \{¢, \$\})^* \mid (s_0, ¢w\underline{\$})\} \vdash_M^* (s_f, ¢ *^i \Omega *^j \underline{\$})\}$, where $i + j + 1 = |w|$ and $*^t = * * \ldots *$ (t times).

A *cycle* of an (n,k)-C-automaton M is a movement from its right end marker \$ to its left end marker ¢, and back again. Without loss of generality it can be assumed that during a cycle, M changes its tape in at least one position.

It is clear that if an (n,k)-C-automaton M, as defined above, writes a star symbol, the position on its tape where the star symbol was written becomes "inactive" in the sense that no other symbol may ever be written in that position. Instead of writing a star symbol, M may just as well delete that position from its tape, and shorten its tape by one cell. We say M performs a contraction operation. A star operation is thus replaced by a contraction operation, and as M performs contraction operations, its tape is shortened. M accepts the string if its tape has length 3, and consists of the string $¢\Omega\$$, where Ω is the final symbol. Such an equivalent definition justifies the name "contraction automaton".

Because the star symbol $*$ disappears from the definition, every element $(s', *, R)$ of $\delta(s, A)$ becomes (s', R), and $(s, ¢Y_1Y_2 \ldots Y_p\underline{A}BY_{p+1} \ldots Y_r\$) \vdash_M^* (s', ¢Y_1Y_2 \ldots Y_p * \underline{B}Y_{p+1} \ldots Y_r\$)$ becomes $(s, ¢Y_1Y_2 \ldots Y_p\underline{A}BY_{p+1} \ldots Y_r\$) \vdash_M^* (s', ¢Y_1Y_2 \ldots Y_p\underline{B}Y_{p+1} \ldots Y_r\$)$. In this case, the language accepted by the (n, k)-C-automaton M is the set $L(M)$ such that

$$L(M) = \{w \in (V - \{¢, \$\})^* \mid (s_0, ¢w\underline{\$})\} \vdash_M^* (s_f, ¢\Omega\underline{\$})\}.$$

This machinery is related to our general image of a contextual automaton which is associated to an LBA, i.e. a simple Turing machine which, instead of a potentially infinite tape on which to compute, has a restricted portion of tape containing the input string w plus two tape squares holding the end-markers (¢ and \$). This tape is scanned by a read/write head, according to the current state of a finite memory. In order to correspond to the contextual style of working, such a machinery is able to execute the operation which is inverse to the insertion of a context, that is to *erase a context* (pair of words (u, v), where u is the first component of the context and v is the second component of the context).

In the case of contextual automata the contraction operation is associated to the erase operation. In an initial state s_0, starting with a string w bounded by the markers $¢, \$$, this string w is accepted by the contextual automaton M, if and only if the automaton is able to erase all symbols except $¢, \$$ and it then reaches a final state s_f. Roughly speaking, the work of a contextual automaton consists of cycles: it starts with the read/erase head at the left end of the string, it goes to the right, scanning parts of the string and erasing two of its substrings, then it goes to the left, leaving the string unmodified, until it reaches the left-hand end of the string again. (The work of the automaton is exactly of this type when erasing only in the presence of the end markers, but it is much less specified when not all erasing operations involve the markers $¢, \$$.)

The language associated to this contextual automaton M, in the usual way, would be:

$$L(M) = \{w \in (V - \{¢, \$\})^* \mid (s_0, \underline{¢}w\$)\} \vdash_M^* (s_f, \underline{¢}\$),\ s_f \in F\},$$

The work of a contextual automaton is intuitively described in Figure 1, which shows both the sets of moves (expressed as rewriting rules $P = \bigcup\{P_i\}_{i=\{B,U,R,V,E,L\}}$) used on various segments of the current string (*B*eginning-of-the-string, erasing-string-U, moving-to-*R*ight, erasing-string-V, *E*nd-of-the-string, moving-to-*L*eft, respectively) and the sets of states ($K = \bigcup\{K_i\}_{i=\{B,U,R,V,E,L\}}$) reachable in various moments of the parsing.

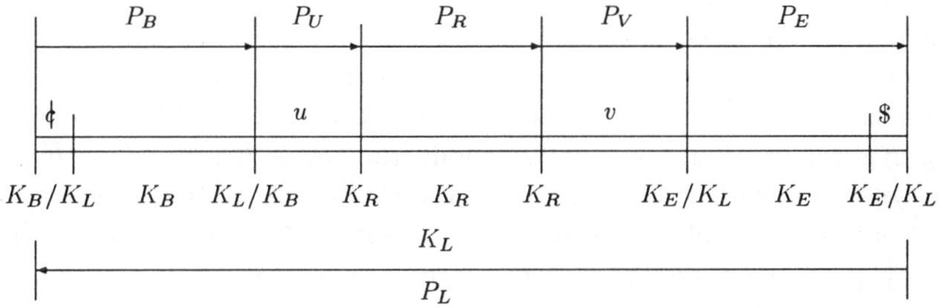

Figure 1

More explicitly, the intuition behind this figure is the following. The states in K_B and the rules in P_B correspond to the scanning of the beginning of a string. The work starts in the state s_0 or in another state from K_B. It is not possible to use any rule in P_B, because the work of P_U can start both in a state from K_B or in a state from K_L. The rules in P_U execute the erasing of a substring of the scanned string (associated with the first term of a context). This string may be empty: rules $s\lambda\lambda \rightarrow \lambda s'$ may appear in P_U. One enters then a state in K_R which determines the move of the automata head to the right, scanning again a substring of the current string. Note that reaching a state in K_R is obligatory, because P_V, and hence the other sets of moves cannot work if P_U does not introduce a state in K_R. However, as we have pointed out above, this can be done, if necessary, by a state-changing rule $s \rightarrow s'$ in P_U. Then, the rules in P_V erase one more substring, possibly the empty one (thus completing the erasing of a context), and there are still rules in P_E, which involve states in K_E, which scan a suffix of the current string. Both the prefix scanned by P_B and the suffix scanned by P_E may consist of only one symbol, the markers ¢, \$, respectively. This possibly single symbol is enough to pass from a state in K_L to one in K_B, by a rule in P_B, or to one in K_R, by a rule in P_R. Similarly, the marker \$ permits the introduction of a symbol in K_L. By rules in P_L one goes from the right to the left, in the presence of states in K_L. Note that during the move operations (rules in $P_B \cup P_R \cup P_E \cup P_L$) the scanned symbols are not changed, only the current state may be modified, and that the markers ¢, \$ are never modified (the erasing rules in $P_U \cup P_V$ also leave them unchanged). This intuitive idea leads to the following definition:

A *contextual automaton* is a construct $M = (K, V, ¢, \$, s_0, F, P)$, where K is a finite set of *states*, V is a vocabulary, ¢, \$ are two special symbols not found in V (*end markers*), $s_0 \in K$ is the *initial state*, $F \subseteq K$ is the set of *final states*, and P is a finite set of *moves*, expressed as rewriting rules; there are four types of states, $K = K_B \cup K_R \cup K_E \cup K_L$, the four sets K_B, K_R, K_E, K_L being mutually disjoint (and $s_0 \in K_B$ and $F \subseteq K_R$), and six types of moves: $P = P_B \cup P_U \cup P_R \cup P_V \cup P_E \cup P_L$, of the following forms: P_B contains rules of the form $sa \to as'$, with $s \in K_L \cup K_B$, $s' \in K_B, a \in V \cup \{¢\}$; P_U contains rules of the form $s\alpha x \to \alpha s'$, with $s \in K_L \cup K_B$, $s' \in K_R, x \in V^*, \alpha \in \{¢, \lambda\}$; P_R contains rules of the form $sa \to as'$, with $s \in K_R$, $s' \in K_R, a \in V$; P_V contains rules of the form $sx\alpha \to s'\alpha$, with $s \in K_R$, $s' \in K_E \cup K_L, x \in V^*, \alpha \in \{\$, \lambda\}$; P_E contains rules of the form $sa \to as'$, with $s \in K_E$, $s' \in K_E \cup K_L, a \in V \cup \{\$\}$ and, finally, P_L contains rules of the form $as \to s'a$, with $s \in K_L$, $s' \in K_L, a \in V \cup \{¢, \$\}$.

According to a contextual automaton we define the rewriting relation $\Longrightarrow$ between strings over $V \cup K \cup \{¢, \$\}$ in the usual way (a contextual automaton can be viewed as a rewriting system, in the general sense). So we can define two languages associated to an automaton M

$$L_0(M) = \{w \in V^* \mid s_0¢w\$ \Longrightarrow^* ¢s_f\$, \text{ for some } s_f \in F\},$$
$$L_t(M) = \{w \in V^* \mid s¢w\$ \Longrightarrow^* ¢s_f\$, \text{ for some } s \in K_B, s_f \in F\}.$$

The language $L_0(M)$ makes use of the initial state of M, and the language $L_t(M)$ is defined by using as a starting state any element of K_B (the subscript t in $L_t(M)$ stands for "total"). In both cases the starting point is a string bounded by the markers ¢, \$; this string is accepted if and only if the automaton is able to erase all symbols except ¢, \$ and then reach a final state.

We can distinguish many types of contextual automata: *marked* automata, with all rules in $P_U \cup P_V$ having $\alpha \neq \lambda$; *unmarked* automata, with all rules in $P_U \cup P_V$ having $\alpha = \lambda$; *b-constant* automata, with all rules having $sa \rightarrow as'$ in P_B with $s = s'$; *r-constant* automata, with all rules having $sa \rightarrow as'$ in P_R with $s = s'$; *r-non-cyclic* automata, each rewriting $sw \Longrightarrow^* ws'$ using rules in P_R has $s \neq s'$; *e-constant* automata, with all rules having $sa \rightarrow as'$ in P_E with $s = s'$; *l-constant* automata, with all rules having $as \rightarrow s'a$ in P_L with $s = s'$ and, finally, *simple* automata, with $card(K_L) = 1$.

Clearly, a simple automaton is also *l*-constant. Moreover, for marked automata the rules in P_B and P_E are of no use, so we can ignore them. This means that marked automata can also be considered *b*- and *e*-constant.

Using this kind of contextual automata based on contraction automata we can characterize "a priori" the whole family of *contextual languages/grammars.* I shall provide only some results with no proof. I refer you to (Martín-Vide et al., 1996) and (Păun, 1996) for proofs, details and more results.

Theorem 3 *(i) A language L is generated by an external contextual grammar without selection, abbr.* EC, *if and only if L is recognized by a marked, r-constant and simple automaton using the "total" mode of derivation. (ii) A language L is generated by an internal contextual grammar without selection, abbr.* IC, *if and only if L is recognized by an unmarked, b-, r- and e-constant and simple automaton using the "total" mode of derivation.*

Theorem 4 *(i) A language L is generated by an external contextual grammar with regular selection, abbr.* ECC(REG) *, if and only if L is recognized by a marked and simple automaton using the "total" mode of derivation. (ii) A language L is generated by an internal contextual grammar with regular selection, abbr.* ICC(REG) *, if and only if L is recognized by an unmarked, b- and e-constant and simple automaton using the "total" mode of derivation.*

Theorem 5 *A language L is generated by a total contextual grammar, abbr.* TC, *if and only if L is recognized by an unmarked and simple automaton using the "total" mode of derivation.*

Theorem 6 *(i) A language L is generated by an external contextual grammar with finite selection, abbr.* ECC(FIN) *, if and only if L is recognized by a marked, r-non-cyclic and simple automaton using the "total" mode of derivation. (ii) A language L is generated by an internal contextual grammar with finite selection, abbr.* ICC(FIN) *, if and only if L is recognized by an unmarked, b- and e-constant, r-non-cyclic and simple automaton using the "total" mode of derivation.*

References

Ehrenfeucht, A., Păun, G. and Rozenberg, G. 1996. *Handbook of Formal Languages*, volume II, chapter Contextual grammars. G. Rozenberg, A. Salomaa, (eds). Berlin and Heidelberg: Springer-Verlag. With a prologue (a linguistic point of view) by S. Marcus.

Jančar, P., Mráz, F. and Plátek, M. 1993. "A taxonomy of forgetting automata". In *MFCS 1993*, volume 711, pages 527–536. Gdańsk, Poland: Springer.

Jančar, P., Mráz, F., Plátek, M., Procházka, M. and Vogel, J. 1995a. "On relations between restarting automata, context-free grammars and Marcus grammars". In *Developments in Language Theory Symposium*, Magdeburg.

Jančar, P., Mráz, F., Plátek, M., Procházka, M. and Vogel, J. 1995b. *Restarting Automata and Marcus Grammars.* Technical Report Math/95/1. Jena: Friedrich Schiller University.

Jančar, P., Mráz, F., Plátek, M., Procházka, M. and Vogel, J. 1996. *Deleting Automata with Restart Operation and Marcus Grammars.* Manuscript.

Jančar, P., Mráz, F., Plátek, M. and Vogel, J. 1994. *Restarting Automata.* Technical Report Math/94/8. Jena: Friedrich Schiller University.

Marcus, S. 1967. *Algebraic Linguistics. Analytical Models.* New York: Academic Press.

Marcus, S. 1969. Contextual grammars. *Revue Roumaine de Mathématiques Pures et Appliquées* 14:1525–1534.

Martín-Vide, C., Miquel-Vergés, J. and Păun, G. 1996. "Contextual Automata". Manuscript.

Păun, G. 1982. *Contextual Grammars.* Bucharest: The Publishing House of the Romanian Academy. In Romanian.

Păun, G. 1985. "On some open problems about Marcus contextual languages". *International Journal of Computer Mathematics* 17:9–23.

Păun, G. 1994. "Marcus contextual grammars. After 25 years". *Bulletin EATCS* 52:263–273.

Păun, G. 1996. *Contextual Grammars. From Natural Languages to Formal Languages and back.* Manuscript.

Solms, S. H. von 1975. "The characterization by automata of certain classes of languages in the context-sensitive area". *Information and Control* 27:262–271.

PART II

SEMANTICS

Nonassociative and Commutative Categorial Grammars and their Languages

Maciej Kandulski

Adam Mickiewicz University

Categorial grammars adhere to the group of formalisms aiming at a description of natural languages in which the syntactic role of expressions is described by means of types. Types are indices of two forms — primitive or compound. Compound types are built inductively by means of three type-forming operators: *left division* $\backslash$, *right division* $/$ and *product* $\cdot$. Thus, formally, for a given set Pr of *primitive types*, the set TP of *types* (with product) is defined as follows: (i) Pr $\subset$ TP, (ii) if x and y are in TP, then x/y, $y\backslash x$ and $x \cdot y$ are in TP. The set of product-free types will be denoted Tp. Primitive types are ascribed to the basic syntactic categories of a language, such as sentences, proper nouns, etc. An expression of a language is assigned a type x/y if it has the role of a functor looking for its argument on the right-hand side, and producing a compound expression of tipe x with an argument of type y. Expressions of the type $x\backslash y$ look for their argument on the left-hand side. The type $x \cdot y$ is ascribed to those expressions which are the concatenation of two expressions of types x and y respectively.

The above ideas can assume the shape of a formal system called the Ajdukiewicz-Bar-Hillel calculus (ABH), cf. (Ajdukiewicz 1935), (Bar-Hillel 1953): ABH formulas are of the shape $X \rightarrow x$, where $X \in \mathrm{TP}^+$ and $x \in$ TP. The only axiom scheme of ABH is

(A0) $\quad x \rightarrow x$, where $x \in$ TP,

and the calculus admits the following three rules of inference:

$$(\mathrm{A}/)\quad \frac{X \to x/y \quad Y \to y}{XY \to x} \qquad\qquad (\mathrm{A}\backslash)\quad \frac{X \to y\backslash x \quad Y \to y}{YX \to x}$$

$$(\mathrm{PR})\quad \frac{X \to x \quad Y \to y}{XY \to x \cdot y}.$$

The product-free version of ABH will be denoted ABH°. The intuitive meaning of a derivable in ABH formula $x_1 x_2 \ldots x_n \to y$ can be stated as follows: if expressions A_i are of types $x_i, 1 \leq i \leq n$, then the expression $A_1 A_2 \ldots A_n$ as a whole is of type y. Assuming $y = s$, where s is a distinguished type of properly built sentence, a criterion is obtained for the sentencehood of sequencess of expressions in the sense of the ABH calculus.

The question of assigning types to elements of vocabulary is crucial for the acceptance or rejection of sequences as coherent sentences. It is definitely not enough to assign only one type to each vocabulary item: it is well known that adverbs can play the role of verb modifiers as well as sentence modifiers, leading to two different readings of sentences like *Someone sings frequently.* On the other hand, assigning types without any restrictions is unacceptable for obvious reasons: *ad hoc* assignment deprives one of the possibility of examining any regularities which may occur between the types assigned to the same element of vocabulary. What we need is a mechanism capable of generating in a regular way new types from finite, generic sets of types ascribed to vocabulary items. Such type changing patterns, linguistically motivated, have been proposed on different occasions, and include, among others, the following schemes:

(M)	$x \to (y/x)\backslash y$	(E)	$x\backslash(y/z) \to (x\backslash y)/z$
	$x \to y/(x\backslash y)$		$(x\backslash y)/z \to x\backslash(y/z)$
(C)	$x/y\ y/z \to x/z$	(G)	$x/y \to (x/z)/(y/z)$
	$x\backslash y\ y\backslash z \to x\backslash z$		$y\backslash x \to (z\backslash y)\backslash(z\backslash x)$

These are known as the Montague, Exchange, Composition and Geach Rules. An instantiation of (G), for example, gives the formula

$$s\backslash s \to (n\backslash s)\backslash(n\backslash s)$$

which means that if an expression plays the role of sentence modifier (sentential adverb) then it can also be a verb phrase modifier (verb phrase adverb), which is precisely the case for the adverb *frequently* in the above example. As can easily be observed, the formulas (M),(E), (C) and (G) cannot be derived in ABH.

J. Lambek in (Lambek 1958) proposed extending ABH to the system L by means of two additional rules of inference:

(R/) $\dfrac{X\,x \rightarrow y}{X \rightarrow y/x}$ (R\) $\dfrac{x\,X \rightarrow y}{X \rightarrow x\backslash y}$

These new rules make it possible to assign new types to vocabulary items by extracting, step by step from the predecessor of a formula, the types of expressions constituting the context in which the item occurrs. One can easily check that the formulas (M),(E), (C) and (G) are derivable in L, so the calculus becomes a common platform for solving a number of syntactic phenomena which are traditionally regarded as an adequate criterion for grammar formalisms. The list of such phenomena includes non-constituent coordination, right- and left-node raising and peripheral extraction in relative clause constructions (see (Morrill 1992), (Steedman 1990)). Nevertheless, there still remain constructions which, from the perspective of the Lambek calculus L, are intractable (for example, topicalization or non-peripheral extraction in relative clauses). The fundamental reason for the incapability of L is the directionality of its type-forming operators or the lack of a mechanism which allows the order of types in the antecedents of formulas of L to be changed. Different measures have been proposed to make Lambek formalism more flexible: enriching the calculus by a new type-forming operator of extraction (see (Moortgat 1988)), adding a modal operator of permutation (see (Morrill et al. 1990)), or taking into account the polymorphic Lambek calculus (see (Emms 1994)). However, a method of changing the order of types can be introduced into the Lambek calculus in a straightforward way, if the system adopts the following rule of permutation:

(P) $\dfrac{XY \rightarrow z}{YX \rightarrow z}$

This, however, results in undesirable consequences. Note that in the Lambek calculus with permutation LP, both formulas are derivable:

$$x/y \rightarrow y\backslash x$$
$$y\backslash x \rightarrow x/y$$

Thus, there is no need to distinguish between the right and left slash, and the system can be formalized in a unidirectional way. Moreover, if the formula $X \rightarrow x$ is derivable in LP, then it is also true for the formula $\pi(X) \rightarrow x$, where $\pi(X)$ is any permutation of the sequence of types in X. But it means that along with any properly built sentence S of a language (i.e. a string of words which has the type s in LP) a phrase in which all words of S are in any order must be accepted as a sentence. No calculus admitting such a general relaxation has any chance of gaining esteem among linguists. However, as J. van Benthem claims (see (van Benthem 1986)): "...the frequent occurrence of permutations of phrases (e.g., in relative clauses or questions) is an undeniable fact of linguistic life". Consequently, in order to build a calculus which better conforms to linguistic reality, permutation has to be introduced in a restricted form. We will describe one such possibility which is based on imposing nonassociativity on the calculus.

The ABH calculus can be extended to L using the rules (R/) and (R\) and, although this increases the flexibility of the calculus, it does have some drawbacks. Lambek in (Lambek 1961) observed that L, along with syntactically coherent sentences, also accepts some ill-formed expressions such as *John likes poor him*, and considers the associativity of L to be the reason for such failures. Consequently, he proposed changing the format of the formulas of the calculus: no longer should their predecessors be treated as strings of types but rather as bracketed strings of types. Formally, we define the set BSTP of *bracketed strings of types* as follows: (i) TP $\subset$ BSTP, (ii) if X and Y are in BSTP, then (XY) is also in BSTP. The nonassociative Lambek calculus NL is a formal system with formulas of the shape $X \to x$, where $X \in$ BSTP and $x \in$ TP, with the axiom scheme (A0) and the rules of inference:

$$(\mathrm{NA}/)\ \frac{X \to x/y \quad Y \to y}{(XY) \to x} \qquad (\mathrm{NA}\backslash)\ \frac{X \to y\backslash x \quad Y \to y}{(YX) \to x}$$

$$(\mathrm{NR}/)\ \frac{(X\,x) \to y}{X \to y/x} \qquad (\mathrm{NR}\backslash)\ \frac{(x\,X) \to y}{X \to x\backslash y}$$

$$(\mathrm{NPR})\ \frac{X \to x \quad Y \to y}{(XY) \to x \cdot y}.$$

The system consisting of (A0), (NA/), (NA\) and (NPR) will be called the nonassociative Ajdukiewicz-Bar-Hillel calculus and denoted NABH. We should point out that the type changing patterns (C), (E) and (G) cease to be derivable in NL, as their derivations essentially employ associativity. On the other hand, in the NLP calculus, which is equal to NL equipped with the nonassociative counterpart of the rule (P):

$$\text{(NP)} \quad \frac{(XY) \to z}{(YX) \to z}$$

permutation can be performed only on a limited scale. It is not admissible between all types but between adjacent bracketed strings.

All the syntactic calculi described so far, as well as their product free versions, can serve as *type reduction systems* in categorial grammars. By *categorial grammar* (CG) based on a *type reduction system* TRS, we mean a quadruple $G = \langle V, I, s, \text{TRS}\rangle$ in which V is a finite *vocabulary*, I is a finite subset of $V \times \text{TP}$ called the *initial type assignment*, $s \in \text{Pr}$, and TRS is a calculus of syntactic types. A categorial grammar G over an associative TRS generates a *string language* L(G) defined as follows: $\text{L}(G) = \{a_1 \dots a_n \in V^+ : \forall 1 \leq i \leq n\ \exists (a_i, x_i) \in\ I\ (\vdash_{\text{TRS}} x_1 \dots x_n \to s)\}$. For a vocabulary V we define the set BS(V) of *phrase structures over* V as the smallest set such that: (i) $V \subset \text{BS}(V)$, (ii) if $A_1, \dots, A_n \in \text{BS}(V)$, then $(A_1 \dots A_n) \in \text{BS}(V)$. In comparison with the definition of BSTP the definition of BS(V) admits structures with more than two direct substructures. As I can be naturally extended to $T \subset \text{BS}(V) \times$ BSTP, a grammar G over a nonassociative TRS generates a *phrase language* $\text{BL}(G) = \{A \in \text{BS}V : \exists X \in \text{BSTP}\ ((A, X) \in T\ \&\ \vdash_{\text{TRS}} X \to s)\}$, and a *string language* L(G) obtained from BL(G) by dropping all brackets in phrase structures from BL(G).

The generative power of a certain grammar formalism is expressed by the class of languages it generates. The Chomsky hierarchy provides a scale for comparing classes of languages, and thus also for comparing different types of grammars. We will describe the position which the languages generated by categorial grammars based on NLP as the type reduction system (NLP-languages) occupy in the Chomsky hierarchy. In addition, we will compare NLP-languages and languages generated by CGs based on other TRSs with those levels of the hierarchy which are considered to be the best approximations to the position of natural languages.

The first result which established the generative power of CGs concerned grammars based on ABH° (ABH°-grammars). The following theorem was proved in (Bar-Hillel, Gaifman and Shamir 1960):

Theorem 1. ABH°*-grammars generate precisely the class of* CF*-languages.*

One of the hypotheses in the above paper was that the class of languages generated by L°-grammars coincided with the class of CF-languages as well.

Despite intense attempts to prove it, this question has had to wait more than thirty years to be solved. In (Pentus 1993) the following result can be found:

Theorem 2. L°*-grammars generate the class of* CF*-languages.*

For LP°-grammars an upper bound in the Chomsky hierarchy is not known. The following theorem gives the lower bound (see (Buszkowski 1984)):

Theorem 3. LP°*-grammars generate at least all permutation closures of* CF*-languages.*

For each result presented above, a separate method of proof had to be found. The situation is different for grammars based on nonassociative calculi: derivations in these calculi share the property of normalizability which provides a certain uniformity to derivation trees. This feature turned out to be essential in establishing the generative power of NL°- and NL-grammars (cf. (Buszkowski 1986b) and (Kandulski 1988a)):

Theorem 4. NL°*-grammars and* NL*-grammars generate the class of* CF*-languages.*

The method of normalization turned out to be applicable to NLP-grammars as well. We are going to show that as far as generative power is concerned, the restrictive ability of nonassociativity is strong enough to suppress the growth in generative power caused by the presence of the rule of permutation. This part of our presentation is based on (Kandulski 1993) and (Kandulski 1995).

As in LP, both formulas $x/y \to y\backslash x$ and $y\backslash x \to x/y$ are derivable in NLP. This suggests that the system can equivalently be axiomatized with unidirectional types. The set TP/ of *unidirectional types with product* is defined inductively as follows: (i) $\mathrm{Pr} \subset \mathrm{TP}/$, (ii) if x and y are in TP/, then x/y and $x \cdot y$ are in TP/. For every type $x \in \mathrm{TP}$ (resp. bracketed string $X \in \mathrm{BSTP}$) we define a type $\|x\|$ (resp. a bracketed string $\|X\|$) called *the unidirectional version of* x (resp. *of* X) inductively as follows: (i) $\|p\| = p$, if $p \in \mathrm{Pr}$, (ii) $\|x \cdot y\| = \|x\| \cdot \|y\|$, $\|x/y\| = \|y\backslash x\| = \|x\|/\|y\|$, (iii) $\|(XY)\| = (\|X\|\,\|Y\|)$. By the *unidirectional version of a formula*

$X \to x$, to be denoted $\|X \to x\|$, we mean the formula $\|X\| \to \|x\|$.
By NCA we denote the syntactic calculus with formulas of the shape $X \to x$, where $X \in$ BSTP/, $x \in$ TP/, admitting the axiom scheme (A0) and the following rules of inference:

$$\text{(NA/)}\ \frac{X \to x/y \quad Y \to y}{(XY) \to x} \qquad \text{(/NA)}\ \frac{X \to x/y \quad Y \to y}{(YX) \to x}$$

$$\text{(NPR)}\ \frac{X \to x \quad Y \to y}{(XY) \to x \cdot y} \qquad \text{(PRN)}\ \frac{X \to x \quad Y \to y}{(YX) \to x \cdot y}$$

NCA can be thought of as the unidirectional version of the calculus NABH with permutation. In order to formalize the unidirectional Lambek calculus equivalent to NLP we need an auxiliary system Ax which can be described as follows: Ax has formulas of the shape $x \to y$, where $x, y \in$ TP/, and admits the rules of inference and the schemata mentioned below for all $x, y, z \in$ TP/:

(A0) $x \to x$

(A1) $(x/y) \cdot y \to x$ (A1′) $y \cdot (x/y) \to x$

(A2) $x \to (x \cdot y)/y$ (A2′) $x \to (y \cdot x)/y$

(A3) $x \to y/(y/x)$ (A4) $x \cdot y \to y \cdot x$

$$\text{(R1)}\ \frac{x \to y}{x/z \to y/z} \qquad \text{(R1′)}\ \frac{x \to y}{z/y \to z/x}$$

$$\text{(R2)}\ \frac{x \to y}{x \cdot z \to y \cdot z} \qquad \text{(R2′)}\ \frac{x \to y}{z \cdot x \to z \cdot y}$$

We write $x \to y \in$ Ax instead of $\vdash_{\mathrm{Ax}} x \to y$. The system NCL arises from NCA by adding the compound rule (C) to this calculus:

$$\text{(C)}\quad \frac{X \to x}{X \to y}, \quad \text{if } x \to y \in \text{Ax and } x \neq y.$$

The equivalence of NLP and NCL is established by the following theorem:

Theorem 5. *If the formula $Y \to y$ is a unidirectional version of a formula $X \to x$, then $\vdash_{\mathrm{NLP}} X \to x$ if and only if $\vdash_{\mathrm{NCL}} Y \to y$.*

For a type $x \in$ TP/ let $c(x)$ denote the *complexity of* x, i.e. the total number of type-forming operators / and $\cdot$ in x. A formula $x \to y \in$ Ax such that $c(x) < c(y)$ (resp. $c(x) > c(y), c(x) = c(y)$) is called an E-formula (resp. R-formula, O-formula). To indicate that $x \to y \in$ Ax is an E- (resp. R-, O-) formula we put the appropriate index above the arrow and write $x \xrightarrow{\mathrm{E}} y \in \mathrm{Ax}$ (resp. $x \xrightarrow{\mathrm{R}} y \in \mathrm{Ax}$, $x \xrightarrow{\mathrm{O}} y \in \mathrm{Ax}$). The fact that formulas $x_i \xrightarrow{I_i} x_{i+1}, i = 1, \ldots, n-1$ are all derivable in Ax will be denoted $x_1 \xrightarrow{I_1} x_2 \xrightarrow{I_2} \cdots \xrightarrow{I_{n-1}} x_n \in \mathrm{Ax}$. The latter sequence will be referred to as a *sequence derivable* in Ax and the string $I_1 I_2 \ldots I_{n-1}$ will be called the *index* of this sequence.

Lemma 1. *If $x \xrightarrow{\mathrm{E}} y \in \mathrm{Ax}$ and $y \xrightarrow{\mathrm{R}} z \in \mathrm{Ax}$, where $x \neq z$, then there exists $\overline{y} \in \mathrm{TP}$ such that $c(\overline{y}) < c(y)$ and $x \rightarrow \overline{y} \in \mathrm{Ax}$ and $\overline{y} \rightarrow z \in \mathrm{Ax}$.*

Lemma 2. *Given a derivable sequence $x_1 \rightarrow \cdots \rightarrow x_{n+3}$ of the index $\mathrm{EO}^n\mathrm{R}$ there exists a derivable sequence $y \rightarrow \cdots \rightarrow z$ whose index is either O^k, where $k \leq n+2$, or $\mathrm{O}^m\mathrm{ERO}^l$, where $m + l \leq n$, such that $x_1 = y$ and $x_{n+3} = z$.*

Proof. First observe that if $x \xrightarrow{\mathrm{E}} y \xrightarrow{\mathrm{O}} z \xrightarrow{\mathrm{R}} v \in \mathrm{Ax}$, and $x \neq v$, then there exists a derivable sequence of one of the indices ER, OER, ERO such that its initial and terminal types are x and v, respectively. The detailed proof of this is long and arduous, and uses nested induction to reflect the inductive definition of the set Ax. Similarly, i.e. inductively, we prove that if $x_1 \rightarrow \cdots \rightarrow x_{n+3}$, $n \geq 1$ and $x_1 \neq x_{n+3}$, is a derivable in the Ax sequence of the index $\mathrm{EO}^n\mathrm{R}$ in which no formula is an instance of (A0), then there exists a sequence $y \rightarrow \cdots \rightarrow z \in \mathrm{Ax}$ whose index is either O^k, where $k \leq n+2$, or $\mathrm{O}^k\mathrm{EO}^l\mathrm{RO}^m$, where $k + l + m \leq n$ and $k + m \neq 0$, such that $x_1 = y$ and $x_{n+3} = z$. This implies that for a given $\mathrm{EO}^n\mathrm{R}$-sequence we can either get rid of the E-formula and the R-formula from this sequence or we can reduce the number of O's between the E- and R-formula without changing the initial and terminal type of the sequence. Now to obtain the conclusion of our lemma we apply induction to n and use both the above mentioned facts. □

An instance of the rule (C) using an E- (resp. R- or O-) formula is called an E- (resp. R- or O-) *instance* of (C). A derivation D of $X \rightarrow x$ in NCL is called *seminormal* if all E-instances of (C) follow R-instances of (C) and all instances of the rules (NA/), (/NA), (NPR) and (PRN). A derivation is *normal* if it is seminormal and all R-instances of (C) precede (NA/), (/NA), (NPR) and (PRN), and also if no O-rule is placed between the latter rules.

Theorem 6. *If* $\vdash_{\mathrm{NCL}} X \to x$, *then any derivation* D *of* $X \to x$ *can effectively be transformed to a seminormal and then to normal form.*

Proof. In order to transform a derivation to a seminormal form we must show how to change the part of the derivation in which a sequence of the index EO^n ($n \geq 0$) precedes one of the rules (NA/), (/NA), (NPR), (PRN) or an R-instance of (C). In all but the last case we can easily change the order of rules. Assume that a sequence S of the index EO^n precedes an R-instance of the rule (C). If $n = 0$ then we employ Lemma 1 to obtain a sequence of any but the ER index. Let $n > 0$. Then, by Lemma 2, S can be transformed to a sequence of the index O^k, where $k \leq n+2$, or of the index $\mathrm{O}^m\mathrm{ERO}^l$, where $m+l \leq n$, with the same initial and terminal types. In the first case nothing can be done, and in the second case we apply Lemma 1 as in the case $n = 0$. The seminormal derivation can be reduced to a normal one by a direct manipulation of the order of applied rules. □

For an NCL-grammar $G_1 = \langle V_{G_1}, I_{G_1}, s_{G_1}, \mathrm{NCL}\rangle$ an NCA-grammar $G_2 = \langle V_{G_2}, I_{G_2}, s_{G_2}, \mathrm{NCA}\rangle$ can be constructed in the following way: $V_{G_2} = V_{G_1}, s_{G_2} = s_{G_1}$, and for $x \in \mathrm{TP}/$ and $v \in V_{G_2}$ let $(v, x) \in I_{G_2}$ if and only if there are types $x_1, \ldots, x_n$ such that $(v, x_1) \in I_{G_1}$, $x_n = x$, $x_1 \to \cdots \to x_n \in \mathrm{Ax}$, and every formula in this sequence is either an R- or O-formula.

Lemma 3. $\mathrm{L}(G_1) = \mathrm{L}(G_2)$.

Proof. As in (Kandulski 1988a), including the essential use of the normalization procedures in NCL established in Theorem 6. □

Let $G = \langle V_G, I_G, s_G, \mathrm{NCA}\rangle$ be an NCA-grammar. We define a CF-grammar $\mathcal{G}$ in the following way: $V_{\mathcal{G}} = V_G, s_{\mathcal{G}} = s_G$ and $U_{\mathcal{G}} = \mathrm{sub}(\{x \in \mathrm{TP}\colon (\exists v \in V_G)((v, x) \in I_G\})$. (For a set T of types $\mathrm{sub}(T)$ stands for the set of all subtypes of types from T). The set $P_{\mathcal{G}}$ of production rules contains all rules of one of the shapes: (i) $x \mapsto v$ where $x \in \mathrm{TP}$, $v \in V_G$, and $(v, x) \in I_G$, or (ii) $x \mapsto x/y\ y$, $x \mapsto y\ x/y$, $x \cdot y \mapsto x\ y$, $x \cdot y \mapsto y\ x$, for all $x, y \in U_{\mathcal{G}}$. As in (Kandulski 1988a), the next lemma can also be proved:

Lemma 4. $\mathrm{BL}(\mathcal{G}) = \mathrm{BL}(G)$.

As a consequence of Lemma 3 and Lemma 4 we have the theorem:

Theorem 7. The class of string languages generated by NCL-grammars is included in the class of CF-languages.

This upper bound for the class of NCA-languages can be made more exact. In order to ascertain this limit we need some additional notions concerning phrase languages.

The set BS(V) of phrase structures over V with the operations

$$f_n(A_1, \ldots, A_n) = (A_1 \ldots A_n), \ n = 2, 3, 4, \ldots$$

forms an absolutely free algebra over V. For any $L \subset$ BS(V) there exists the largest congruence on L (with respect to inclusion), called the *intersubstitutability relation for* L and denoted INT_L (cf. (Buszkowski 1986a) and (Kandulski 1988b)). The index of INT_L will be referred to as the *index of* L and denoted ind(L). A *path* in a phrase structure A is a sequence $A_1, \ldots, A_n$ such that A_1 is a substructure of A and A_{i+1} is a direct substructure of A_i, $i = 1, \ldots n-1$. We define the *degree* deg(A) of a phrase structure $A \in$ BS(V) as the smallest natural number n such that for every substructure B of A there is a path of length $\leq n$ leading from B to an atom from V. For any $L \subset$ BS(V) we call the number

$$\deg(L) = \sup \{\deg(A) \colon S \in \mathrm{L}\}$$

the *degree of the phrase language* L. For $A \in$ BS(V) the *size* s(A) of A is defined as the maximum number of direct substructures in any substructure of A. Given $L \subset$ BS(V) we put

$$\mathrm{s}(L) = \sup\{\mathrm{s}(A) : A \in L\}$$

and call s(L) the *size of* L. The numbers ind(L), deg(L) and s(L) are called the *degrees of complexity of* L.

The two theorems which follow characterize those phrase languages generated by categorial grammars and CF-grammars in terms of degrees of complexity (see (Buszkowski 1986b) and (Thatcher 1967)), respectively:

Theorem 8. *A phrase language* L *such that* s(L) ≤ 2 *is generated by an* NABH°-*grammar if and only if both* ind(L) *and* deg(L) *are finite.*

Theorem 9. *A phrase language* L *is generated by a* CF-*grammar if and only if* s(L) *and* ind(L) *are finite.*

We distinguish a subclass $\overline{\mathrm{CF}}$ of CF-grammars as follows: a CF-grammar $\mathcal{G}$ is a $\overline{\mathrm{CF}}$-grammar if: (i) the set of production rules of $\mathcal{G}$ is closed with respect to permutation of their right-hand sides, (ii) $\deg(\mathrm{BL}(\mathcal{G}))$ is finite. It is easily observed that the context-free grammar $\mathcal{G}$ constructed with the purpose of proving the equality in Lemma 4 fulfils condition (i) of the above definition. Moreover, in (Kandulski 1995), it was proved that for this grammar we also have $\deg(\mathrm{BL}(\mathcal{G})) < \aleph_0$. Consequently, Theorem 7 can be restated in a stronger form:

Theorem 10. *The class of languages generated by* NCL*-grammars is included in the class of languages generated by* $\overline{\mathrm{CF}}$*-grammars.*

Likewise, the reverse implication also holds:

Theorem 11. *For any* $\overline{\mathrm{CF}}$*-grammar* $\mathcal{G}$ *there exists an* NCL*-grammar* G *such that* $\mathrm{L}(G) = \mathrm{L}(\mathcal{G})$.

Proof. Given a $\overline{\mathrm{CF}}$-grammar $\mathcal{G}$, let $\mathcal{G}'$ be a CF-grammar in the Chomsky normal form equivalent to $\mathcal{G}$. We can assume that the right-hand sides of the production rules in $\mathcal{G}'$ are closed with respect to permutation (or, equally, to transpositions, as there are two nonterminals on the right-hand side). We have $\mathrm{L}(\mathcal{G}) = \mathrm{L}(\mathcal{G}')$ but we no longer have $\mathrm{BL}(\mathcal{G}) = \mathrm{BL}(\mathcal{G}')$ since the phrase structure of the elements in $\mathrm{BL}(\mathcal{G}')$ is finer than that in $\mathrm{BL}(\mathcal{G})$. However, for any phrase structures $A \in \mathrm{BL}(\mathcal{G})$ and $A' \in \mathrm{BL}(\mathcal{G}')$ such that $|A| = |A'|$ we have the inequalities:

$$\deg(A') \leq \deg(A)\cdot(\mathrm{s}(\mathrm{BL}(G)) - 1) < \deg(A)\cdot \mathrm{s}(\mathrm{BL}(\mathcal{G})).$$

But $\mathrm{s}(\mathrm{BL}(\mathcal{G}))$ is finite (it is the maximal length of strings on the right-hand sides of production rules from $\mathcal{G}$) and $\deg(\mathrm{BL}(\mathcal{G}))$ is finite as well ($\mathcal{G}$ is a $\overline{\mathrm{CF}}$-grammar). Therefore the following estimation is true:

$$\begin{aligned}\deg(\mathrm{BL}(\mathcal{G})) &= \sup\{\deg(A') : A' \in \mathrm{BL}(\mathcal{G}')\}\\ &\leq \sup\{\deg(A)\cdot \mathrm{s}(\mathrm{BL}(\mathcal{G})) : A \in \mathrm{BL}(\mathcal{G})\ \&|A| = |A'|\}\\ &= \deg(\mathrm{BL}(\mathcal{G}))\cdot \mathrm{s}(\mathrm{BL}(\mathcal{G})) < \aleph_0.\end{aligned}$$

Obviously $\mathrm{s}(\mathrm{BL}(\mathcal{G}')) \leq 2$, and by Theorem 9 $\mathrm{ind}(\mathrm{BL}(\mathcal{G}')) < \aleph_0$. Consequently, by Theorem 8, the language $\mathrm{BL}(\mathcal{G}')$ is generated by a certain NABH°-grammar G_1. Now it suffices to show that $\mathrm{L}(\mathrm{G}_1)$ is generated by a certain NCL-grammar (cf. (Kandulski 1995)). □

Theorems 10 and 11 entirely characterize the class of languages generated by NCL (and NLP) grammars, and can be summarized as

Theorem 12. *The class of* NCL*-languages (*NLP*-languages) consists of* CF*-languages of finite degree generated by grammars whose rules are closed with respect to permutation.*

The above results concerning the generative power of categorial grammars based on different type reduction systems are relevant to the discussion on the place of natural languages in the Chomsky hierarchy. The presence of nested dependencies in natural languages is evidence against their regularity. This was already known to Chomsky in the 50s, and a language $\{a^n b^n : n \geq 1\}$ can serve as a formal counterpart of these phenomena. Only in the mid 80s was a proper argument against the context-freeness of natural languages found —it is connected with the presence of cross-serial dependencies whose structure can be illustrated by a language $\{a^n b^m c^n d^m : n, m \geq 1\}$. According to Gazdar and Pullum (cf. (Gazdar and Pullum 1985)), the upper bound for syntactic phenomena can be found between the class $\mathcal{L}(\mathrm{CF})$ of context-free languages and the class $\mathcal{L}(\mathrm{CS})$ of context-sensitive languages. They say: "No phenomena are known which would lead one to believe that the natural languages fall outside the indexed languages' purview". For the class $\mathcal{L}(\mathrm{IG})$ of languages generated by indexed grammars we have the proper inclusions $\mathcal{L}(\mathrm{CF}) \subset \mathcal{L}(\mathrm{IG}) \subset \mathcal{L}(\mathrm{CS})$ and $\{a^n b^m c^n d^m : n, m \geq 1\} \in \mathcal{L}(\mathrm{IG})$. But at the same time in (Joshi 1985) an opinion was expressed that for an adequate description of natural language the formalism of CF-grammars only need to be strengthened to a small extent, to become the so-called mildly context-sensitive grammars (MCSGs). A formal definition of MCSGs is not given, but the author indicates the minimal conditions which the class $\mathcal{L}(\mathrm{MCSG})$ of languages generated by MCSG should fulfil: (i) $\mathcal{L}(\mathrm{CF}) \subset \mathcal{L}(\mathrm{MCSG})$ and the equality does not hold, (ii) elements of $\mathcal{L}(\mathrm{MCSG})$ must be parsed in polynomial time, (iii) nested dependencies and only a restricted group of cross-serial dependencies can be expressed by means of languages from $\mathcal{L}(\mathrm{MCSG})$, for example a language $\mathrm{L}^* = \{\mathrm{P} \in \{a, b, c\}^* : \#_a\mathrm{P} = \#_b\mathrm{P} = \#_c\mathrm{P}\}$ lacking any regularity in the structure of its words must not belong to $\mathcal{L}(\mathrm{MCSG})$,

(iv) languages in $\mathcal{L}$(MCSG) have to have the so-called constant growth property.

No class of language generated by categorial grammars which are based on the type reduction systems described in this paper fulfil all the above conditions simultaneously— all except LP-grammars generate at most CF-languages, and for LP-languages we have $L^* \in \mathcal{L}(LP)$. On the other hand, other formalisms which have been proposed as descriptions of natural language, such as Tree Adjoining Grammars, Linear Indexed Grammars and Head Grammars, fulfil all these conditions and, significantly, generate the same classes of language, i.e. $\mathcal{L}(TAG) = \mathcal{L}(LIG) = \mathcal{L}(HG)$. One must then ask the question whether there is a syntactic calculus such that languages generated by CGs based on this calculus would satisfy conditions (i)–(iv). The answer is positive, and calculus T, introduced by Steedman serves as an example (see (Steedman 1993)). This calculus arises by affixing two additional rules from ABH°

$$x/y\ (\ldots(y|_1z_1)|_2z_2\ldots|_nz_n) \rightarrow (\ldots(x|_1z_1)|_2z_2\ldots|_nz_n)$$
$$(\ldots(y|_1z_1)|_2z_2\ldots|_nz_n)\ y\backslash x \rightarrow (\ldots(x|_1z_1)|_2z_2\ldots|_nz_n)$$

where $|_i$ is either / or \. Both the above formulas are underivable in L, but the class of language generated by T-grammars coincides with $\mathcal{L}$(TAG), which gives the necessary equality with the aforementioned classes of languages generated by mildly context-sensitive grammars.

References

Ajdukiewicz, K. 1935. "Die syntaktische Konnexität". *Studia Philosophica* 1: 1–27.

Bar-Hillel, Y. 1953. "A quasi-arithmetical notation for syntactic description". *Language* 29: 47–58.

Bar-Hillel, Y., Gaifman C. and Shamir, E. 1960. "On categorial and phrase structure grammars". *Bulletin Res. Council Israel* F9: 1–16.

Benthem, J. van, 1986. *Essays in Logical Semantics.* Dordrecht: Reidel.

Buszkowski, W. 1984. "A note on the Lambek-van Benthem calculus". *Bulletin of the Section of Logic* 131: 31–37.

Buszkowski, W. 1986a. "Typed functorial languages". *Bulletin of the Polish Academy of sciences: Mathematics* 34: 495–505.

Buszkowski, W. 1986b. "Generative capacity of nonassociative Lambek calculus". *Bulletin of the Polish Academy of Sciences: Mathematics* 34: 507–516.

Emms, M. 1994. "Extraction covering extensions of Lambek calculus are not CF". In P. Dekker and M. Stokhof (eds), *Proceedings of the Ninth Amsterdam Colloquium.* ILLC, Department of Philosophy, University of Amsterdam, 269–286.

Gazdar, G. and Pullum, G.K. 1985. "Computationally relevant properties of natural languages and their grammars". *New Generation Computing* 3: 273–306.

Joshi, A.K. 1985. "How much context-sensitivity is necessary for characterizing structural descriptions: Tree adjoining grammars". In D. Dowty, L. Karttunen, and A. Zwicky (eds), *Natural Language Parsing: Psychological, Computational and Theoretical Perspectives.* New York: Cambridge University Press, 206–250.

Kandulski, M. 1988a. "The equivalence of nonassociative Lambek categorial grammars and context-free grammars". *Zeitschrift für mathematische Logik und Grundlagen der Mathematik* 34: 41–52.

Kandulski, M. 1988b. "Phrase structure languages generated by categorial grammars with product". *Zeitschrift für mathematische Logik und Grundlagen der Mathematik* 34: 373–383.

Kandulski, M. 1993. "Normal form of derivations in the nonassociative and commutative Lambek calculus with product". *Mathematical Logic Quarterly* 39: 103–114.

Kandulski, M. 1995, "On commutative and nonassociative syntactic calculi and categorial grammars". *Mathematical Logic Quarterly* 41: 217–235.

Lambek, J. 1958. "The mathematics of sentence structure". *American Mathematical Monthly* 65: 154–170.

Lambek, J. 1961. "On the calculus of syntactic types". In R. Jacobson (ed), *Structure of Language and Its Mathematical Aspects.* Providence, R.I.: American Mathematical Society, 166–178.

Moortgat, M. 1988. *Categorial Investigations: Logical and Linguistic Aspects of the Lambek Calculus.* Dordrecht: Foris.

Morrill, G. 1992. *Type-logical Grammar.* Research Institute for Language and Speech, Rijksuniversiteit Utrecht.

Morrill, G., Leslie, N., Hepple, M. and Barry, G. 1990. "Categorial deductions and structural operations". In G. Barry and G. Morrill (eds), *Studies in Categorial Grammar.* (Edinburgh Working Papers in Cognitive Science, vol. 5). Centre for Cognitive Science, University of Edinburgh.

Pentus, M. 1993. "Lambek grammars are context-free". *IEEE Symposium on Logic in Computer Science.*

Steedman, M. 1990. "Gapping as constituent coordination". *Linguistics and Philosophy* 13: 207–263.

Steedman, M. 1993. "Categorial grammar". *Lingua* 90: 221–258.

Thatcher, J.W. 1967. "Characterizing derivation trees of context-free grammars through a generalization of finite automata theory". *Journal of Computer and Systems Sciences* 1: 317–322.

Words as Modules: a Lexicalised Grammar in the framework of Linear Logic Proof Nets

Alain Lecomte[a]
Christian Retoré[b]

a),b) *INRIA-Lorraine*
a) *Université Pierre Mendès-France*
b) *CRIN-C.N.R.S.*

Abstract

We present a syntactic calculus relying on the notion of proof net, ie. a geometric representation for proofs in linear logic. The lexicon associates a module or partial proof net with each word, and this information completely encodes the syntactic behavior of the word. Parsing a sentence consists of combining the modules associated with its words into a complete proof net. In order to handle word order, this model takes place in a non-commutative extension of linear logic called Pomset logic.

Introduction

In this paper we describe the principles of a syntactic calculus whose building blocks are partial proof-nets or modules. The main idea is to associate with each lexical item one or more modules which encode(s) its syntactic behaviour. The simplest of these modules are obtained by unfolding the components of formulae that would be the type(s) of the lexical items in a type-logical grammar à la (Morrill 1994), while the more sophisticated ones really go beyond the usual type-logical approach. The syntactic analysis within such a paradigm consists of combining these modules into a complete proof-net by a uniform set of plugging rules.

This approach is related to the Partial Proof-Trees as building blocks of a categorial grammar of (Joshi and Kulick 1995,1997), the main difference being the emphasis put on the geometric notion of Proof-Net as in our first attempt (Lecomte and Retoré 1995).

Our main motivation is to obtain a general logical model in which it would be possible to embed calculi such as Lambek grammars on one side and Lexicalised Tree Adjoining Grammars on the other side.

The Lambek calculus is a very elegant syntactic calculus because it is a pure logical calculus enjoying all the properties one can expect: cut-elimination, denotational semantics, truth valued semantics. This is also the reason why it allows a very simple interface with Montagovian semantics. Unfortunately, it suffers from many limitations when applied to linguistic descriptions: for instance it does not handle head-wrapping, cross serial dependencies, right extraction, extraposition from a non-peripheral site etc.

On the other hand, the LTAG model provides us with a very efficient model which succeeds in many cases where the Lambek calculus fails. But, because some problems are also unsolvable in L-TAG (like long-distance scrambling in German, Romance Clitics or Kashmiri wh-extraction), variants of TAG have been developed, like Multi-Component TAG of (Joshi 1987), Multi-Component TAG with Domination Links of (Becker, Joshi and Ranbow 1991) and D-Tree Grammar of (Rambow, Vijay-Shanker and Weir 1995). These models have considerable expressive power, even if their range of complexity is reasonable. But they use an algebraically complex formulation in terms of trees, and as usual with non-logical formalism the relation to semantics is not simple.

In the present paper, we propose a logical system, based on the proof net syntax of Linear Logic which incorporates operations similar to those of TAGs as the plugging rules. The key point in these plugging rules is that they preserve a very simple correctness criterion which states that the objects we construct correspond to *proofs* in the underlying logical system.

We first give an overview of the whole logical system, called POMSET-logic, introduced in (Retoré 1993) — (see (Retoré 1997) for an updated presentation in English). Roughly speaking, this logical calculus is based on Multiplicative Linear Logic enriched with the non-commutative connective *before*, and deals with Partially Ordered Multi-sets instead of ordinary multi-sets of formulae. Then, we present a restricted version of the proof nets of Pomset logic. Indeed this restriction is enough for linguistic descriptions, and its linguistic meaning is easier to understand than the very general first attempt of (Lecomte and Retoré 1995).

Linear logic and word order

Linear Logic (LL) introduced in (Girard 1987) (see (Girard 1995) for an excellent survey) is obtained from classical logic by introducing two modalities ? and ! which control the structural rules of contraction and weakening. Thus the ordinary connectives *or* and *and* split into a *multiplicative* —respectively denoted by $\wp$ and $\otimes$— version and an *additive* one — respectively denoted by $\oplus$ and &. As this system is classical it involves an involutive negation, denoted by $(...)^{\perp}$ which is both an additive and a multiplicative connective. The multiplicative connectives handle the notion of resource management, while the additive ones describe choices.

Our work concerns the multiplicative fragment, which is simpler and more convenient for our purpose — in particular it does not allow any form of contraction or weakening. This logic is classical, in the sense that negation is involutive $(F^{\perp})^{\perp} = F$, and $\wp$ and $\otimes$ are the dual of each other via the following de Morgan rules: $(F \wp F')^{\perp} = F^{\perp} \otimes F'^{\perp}$ and $(F \otimes F')^{\perp} = F^{\perp} \wp F'^{\perp}$. As usual in the classical case, there is an implication defined by means of negation and disjunction: $A \multimap B = A^{\perp} \wp B$.

In order to handle word order, one needs some non-commutativity. If the two connectives are non-commutative, i.e. if the structural rule of exchange is left out like in (Abrusci 1991) one gets the classical extension of the Lambek calculus.

Our approach within the framework of Pomset Logic is completely different: we enrich (commutative) MLL with a non-commutative multiplicative (but still associative) connective called *before*. The de Morgan rules extend to this connective, which is self-dual —$(A < B)^{\perp} = A^{\perp} < B^{\perp}$— and which lies in between $\otimes$ and $\wp$ wrt. linear implication: $A \otimes B \multimap A < B$ and $A < B \multimap A \wp B$. In order to handle this connective, we need to consider that the multiset of conclusions of a proof is partially ordered —in general, a proof has several conclusions in a classical system. This is particularly suitable in natural language processing to handle relatively free word order.

For people familiar with the Lambek calculus we insist that $A^\perp < B$ is very different from $A \multimap B = A^\perp \wp B$. Indeed, the order it introduces has little to do with the order in the Lambek calculus: for instance A and $A^\perp < B$ leads to B only if there is no order between A and $A^\perp < B$.

Proof nets for pomset logic

As a consequence of the aforementioned de Morgan laws we can restrict ourselves to formulae in which negation is only applied to propositional variables. Thus the language that we consider is defined by:

$\mathcal{P}$ a set of propositional variables —positive atoms

$\mathcal{P}^\perp$ the set of negated propositional variables— negative atoms

$\mathcal{F} ::= \mathcal{P} \mid \mathcal{P}^\perp \mid \mathcal{F} \wp \mathcal{F} \mid \mathcal{F} < \mathcal{F} \mid \mathcal{F} \otimes \mathcal{F}$

Note that when we write $G^\perp$, this is just a short hand for the unique formula of this language which is obtained from $G^\perp$ by internalising the negation until it reaches the propositional variables, by means of the de Morgan laws.

Just as the best way of representing proofs in Intuitionistic Logic is to use Natural Deduction (where proofs look like (pseudo-)trees), the natural syntax for Linear Logic (LL) is proof net syntax that was introduced in the original paper (Girard 1987).

As shown in (Retoré 1993) Pomset logic very simply extends the usual proof net syntax and our presentation will follow (Retoré 1997). It is based on the notion of an `R&B`-graph.

Let us call an **`R&B`-graph** an edge bicoloured graph, the two colours of the edges being `B`(bold, blue) and `R`(regular, red). The B-edges are undirected and never adjacent. The R-edges may be undirected or directed, in which case we call them R-arcs. They correspond to connections between formulae (connective-links), or to the partial order between conclusions.

Given a formula F, we define here its **`R&B`-tree** $T(F)$, as an inductively defined R&B-graph. Actually it is not a tree, but looks like the sub-formula tree, hence the name *tree*.

Given an atomic formula c, the discrete graph is the R&B-tree of C, with root c, and leaf c.

If C is a compound formula $A * B$ with $* \in \{\wp, \otimes, <\}$ and if $T(A)$ and $T(B)$ are respectively the R&B-trees of the formulae A and B, Table 1. describes, according to what $*$ stands for, an R&B-tree of C, with root C, and both the leaves of $T(A)$ and $T(B)$ as leaves.

Formula C	$A \wp B$	$A < B$	$A \otimes B$
R&B-tree $T(C)$	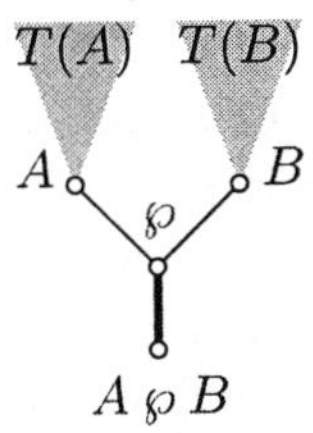	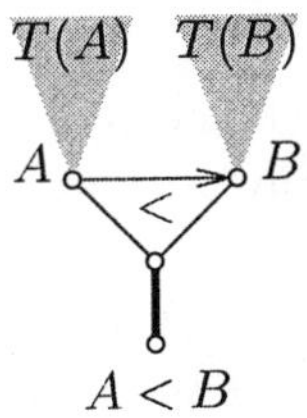	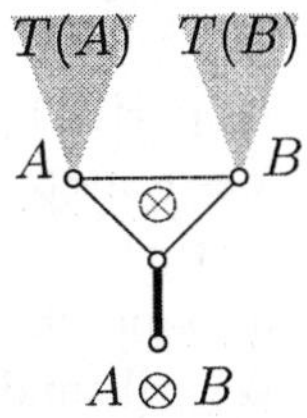

Table 1.

The added edges, arcs and vertices are called a $*$-link: A and B are said to be its premises and $A * B$ its conclusion. Notice that each bottom vertex of a B-edge of the R&B-tree $T(C)$ of a formula C is labelled with a sub-formula of C.

From these R&B-trees we define the R&B-proof-net, whose building blocks are links.

A **partial proof structure** with conclusions and cuts $C_1, \ldots, C_n$ and cuts $G_1^\bullet, \ldots, G_p^\bullet$ —ie. formulae $G_i = X_i \otimes X_i^\perp$ marked as cuts— with order $\Re$ on its conclusions and cuts is an R&B-graph which consists of:

- the family of R&B-trees $T(C_1), \ldots, T(C_n), T(G_1), \ldots, T(G_p)$. This part represents the *syntactic forest*, of the sequent $C_1, \ldots, C_n, G_1, \ldots, G_p$
- a family of B-edges, called *axioms*, every one of which links two leaves which negate each other in such a way that
  (*) for each leaf there exists at most one axiom incident to it.
- a family of R-*arcs*, representing the *order*, i.e. there is one such R-arc from a conclusion or cut X to another Y whenever $X < Y[\Re]$

– a special mark, •, on the roots of the $T(G_i)$ to make a distinction between a cut and a conclusion $X \otimes X^\perp$ which is not considered as a cut.

The leaves which are not incident to any B-edges are called the **hypotheses** of the (partial) proof structure.

A **proof structure** is a partial proof structure with no hypothesis —in this case, there is a B-edge incident to each vertex. Given a proof structure a conclusion is called an **output** whenever it is the positive conclusion a of an axiom $a, a^\perp$ whose negative conclusion $a^\perp$ is the premise of a *times* link. A proof structure is said to be **intuitionistic** whenever it has a single output.

A (partial) proof structure is said to be a **(partial) proof net** whenever it does not contain any alternate elementary (æ) cycle, that is to say a cycle consisting of a sequence of consecutive edges which are alternatively B and R edges in which each vertex appears exactly once.

We will mainly need the following result, which applies to partial proof nets provided a cut does not reach a hypothesis — clearly, if it does, the cut cannot be eliminated. The calculus of ordered proof nets enjoys cut-elimination, which is strongly normalising and confluent: a proof net with conclusions and cuts $F_1, ..., F_n, G_1^\bullet, ..., G_p^\bullet$ ordered by $\Re$ reduces to a cut-free proof net with conclusions $F_1, ..., F_n$ ordered by $\Re|_{F_1,...,F_n}$.

As we do not use proof nets with an order on the conclusions and cuts, the algorithm performing cut-elimination may be described as follows

– a cut link between $A * B$ and $A^\perp \star B^\perp$, where $(*, \star) \in \{(<,<), (\wp, \otimes), (\otimes, \wp)\}$, is erased and replaced with two cut links, one between A and $A^\perp$ and one between B and $B^\perp$

– a cut link between a and $a^\perp$ with $a \in \mathcal{P}$ is suppressed, as well as the two vertices a and $a^\perp$ and their incident B-edges —the two axioms which they are respectively the conclusions of —and a new axiom is added between the $a^\perp$ and a which were previously linked to a and $a^\perp$, respectively.

As we have said above, partial proof nets correspond to words and parsing a sentence or a phrase consists of plugging them in order to obtain a proof net. Here are the two ways we consider of plugging two PPN M_1 and M_2 together:

axiom plugging consists of identifying a hypothesis a of M_1 and a conclusion a of M_2. This corresponds to complementation according to the input or hypotheses sub-categories.

cut plugging consists of linking by a cut-link two dual conclusions and then performing cut-elimination. This corresponds to modification or adjunction.

Actually we shall only make use of the second construction when one of the dual formulae is of the shape $x \otimes x^{\perp}$ with x atomic, ie. when one of the two may be read as a cut on an atomic formula. Such a conclusion/cut will be called a gate.

Labels for expressing and computing word order

Now that we have set the general formalism, we will distinguish, among all possible partial proof nets, the ones which deserve specific linguistic interest. In our system, each word is associated with a partial proof-net. This partial proof-net displays the parts of a formula which express the type of the word: that is to say, *its category and how it must be processed in any context where it occurs.* Vertices at the bottom of a B-edge of a partial proof-net are themselves typed with a sub-formula of the conclusion and labelled with a partial order on strings. These labels will be given for partial proof nets in the lexicon and computed for compound partial proof nets, by rules of unification in the axiom links, and rules of propagation into the links of partial proof nets.

A partial proof net is correctly labelled whenever each (sub)formula is labelled with a pomset of strings which fulfils the following criteria

- **Labelled axiom-link**: it has two conclusions, $(A, \mathfrak{R})$ and $(A^{\perp}, \mathfrak{R})$ where $\mathfrak{R}$ is a partially ordered multi-set of strings —the two labels of the conclusions of an axiom link are equal.

- **Labelled tensor-link**: if the conclusion is labelled by the pomset $\mathfrak{R}$, one of the two premises (we do not know which one) of the tensor-link is labelled with the union of $\mathfrak{R}$ with the pomset $\mathfrak{R}'$ that labels the other premise (thus, if $\mathfrak{R} = \emptyset$, then the two premises are labelled by the same pomset)

- **Labelled before-link**: the conclusion $A{<}B$ is labelled by the pomset $\mathfrak{R} < \mathfrak{R}'$ (where $<$ means that all the elements of $\mathfrak{R}$ are before all the elements of $\mathfrak{R}'$).
- **Labelled par-link**: the conclusion $A \wp B$ is labelled by the pomset $\mathfrak{R} \cup \mathfrak{R}'$ (no order between elements of $\mathfrak{R}$ and elements of $\mathfrak{R}'$).
- **Labelled cut-link**: the cut is labelled by $\emptyset$ and the pomsets of the two premises are equated (particular case of the tensor-link).

This definition is a particular case of the order on axioms we used in (Lecomte and Retoré 1995) and, in the restricted case that we present here, the way the order is computed is clearer. Let us justify this labelling

- Only the *before* connective creates an order on strings.
- The *times* connective preserves the order. Indeed, in a calculus of right handed sequents, a $\otimes$-formula is the dual of an implicative formula, and thus no order is added, since this connective describes a transformation: a sequence of types gives a new type, but the underlying string remains unchanged. Notice that in such a classical system all cases of *par* formulae can be viewed as implicative ones, because of the duality and the De Morgan laws. For instance: $A \wp B = A \multimap B^{\perp}$.
- A $\wp$-formula corresponds to the dual of a $\otimes$-formula. It is therefore natural to retrieve the orderings which occur on the two components, but without creating any new ordering.

From now on we shall call Labelled partial proof nets the ones which are labelled according to the principles we have given above.

It should be noted, in the previous definition, that the labels may be computed from the (Partial) Proof Nets — but this redundant information is useful for underlining word order and for explaining how orders are composed when plugging Partial Proof Nets.

Lexicalised intuitionistic labelled partial proof-nets

Some labelled partial proof nets deserve special attention because they roughly correspond to the elementary trees of TAGs.

An Intuitionistic Labelled PPN is said to be **lexicalised** if and only if

1. it has two conclusions: its output b connected by an axiom link to a $b^\perp$ in some Y_i, and its **main conclusion** which is of the following form $a^\perp \wp (X_1 \otimes Y_1) \wp \ldots \wp (X_m \otimes Y_m)$,

2. $a^\perp$ is labelled by a pomset consisting of one word/string w (which belongs to the lexicon), and the formulae $X_i \otimes Y_i$ by $\emptyset$,

3. $a^\perp$ is linked by an axiom-link to an atom a which occurs in one of the X_i,

4. every X_i is a *par/before* formula, i.e. they do not contain any *times*, connective.

Let us discuss this definition

- If we remember that connectives on the right correspond to their duals on the left, we see that such a conclusion, when moved to the left, leads to a formula: $a \otimes (X_1 \multimap Y_1^\perp) \otimes \cdots \otimes X_m \multimap Y_m^\perp)$.

- Thus, the second condition in the definition makes an occurrence of $a^\perp$ necessary in one of the X_i. This can be interpreted in the following way: the word w is an a-phrase *and* — to be understood as *times*, ie. multiplicative conjunction — when supplied with an X_i-phrase, it yields an $Y_i^\perp$-phrase.

- note that this definition is coherent with our definition of labelled links only the *declarative* part (w *is* an a-phrase) provides an initial pomset. The *procedural* part initially contains no pomset, but in order to fulfill the principles of the labelling in links, at least one of the X_i will receive a pomset (which contains at least w, because of the axiom link between $a^\perp$ and a, (and because X is a *par/before* formula)), and this pomset will be transfered to $Y_i^\perp$, and possibly to the output (if there are axiom links between the Y_j and the X_k).

Following these intuitions the lexical item *loves* has the following type

$$(\{loves\} : v) \otimes ((v < np) \multimap vp) \otimes ((np < vp) \multimap s)$$

which is the type of a transitive verb. It gives a string labelling the verb, and two other pieces of information: if followed by an np, it will give a vp and if this vp is preceded by an np it will give an s. Of course, we need to express the identity of the two occurrences of v and the identity of the two vp. Here, the proof representation is needed, since the only possibility of modelling this identity between two nodes by purely logical means is to link them via an axiom link — (cf. Figure 1.).

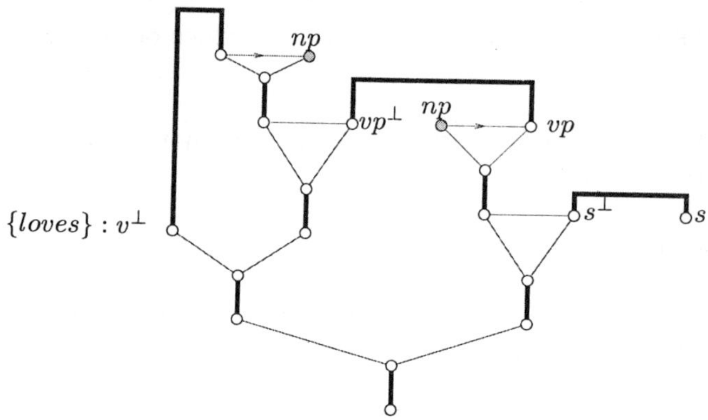

Figure 1.

In Figure 2, we compute, following the rules for labelling, the label of each (sub)formula — labels are denoted by integers. Let us explain how the labelling rules work on this particular example. By the conditions on labelled links, (1) is identified with {loves}. When the np (2) is identified with a real np, thus giving (2) = $\{a < woman\}$ for instance, the conclusion of the before-link will be labelled by: $\{loves < a < woman\}$. This pomset is transmitted to the output $vp^\perp$ (because of the tensor-link). When the second np (3) is instantiated (for instance by $\{a < man\}$), we shall get as a new pomset labelling the conclusion of the second before-link: $\{a < man < loves < a < woman\}$, and this pomset is transmitted to the output $s^\perp$. Notice that the conclusions in the $\otimes$-link remain empty:thus the conclusion of the lexicalised PPN associated with the verbal form *loves* is also labelled by $\{loves\}$.

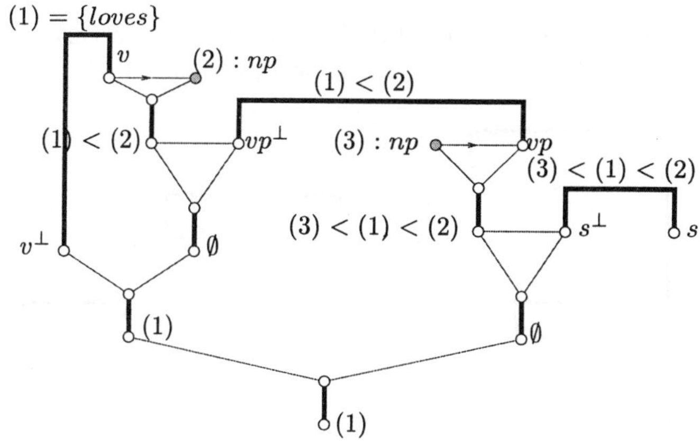

Figure 2.

Thus, plugging by axiom ensures that every hypothesis a with the output a of an a phrase yields the correct word order.

Gates and modifiers

So far, the operation of glugging bu cut-links has a hardly been used and, for the time being, cut formulae are of no obvious interest. However, gates can be considered and used to model modifiers. A gate is a fake conclusion $a \otimes a^{\perp}$ with a being an atomic formula, such that a (resp. $a^{\perp}$) is linked with an axiom link to an $a^{\perp}$ (resp. a) — notice that the absence of an æ-cycle ensures that the two axioms a and $a^{\perp}$ give different conclusions. If we were to reduce this cut, these two axioms and the cut would be replaced with a single axiom linking their dual counterpart. The label of a gate will always be empty, as opposed to the main conclusion which is always labelled, as we have seen above, by the same pomset as the *declarative* B-edge. We shall add such gates along the declarative B-edge of a lexicalised labelled partial proof net.

The only modification consists of replacing an axiom link with a sequence axiom link, cut-link, axiom link, and it is easily observed that such a transformation preserves the property of being an ILPPN.

For instance, if we want to introduce adverbials, like *passionately*, we must open such a *gate* in every LPPN associated with a verb. This will give rise to new LPPNs such as the one shown in Figure 3.

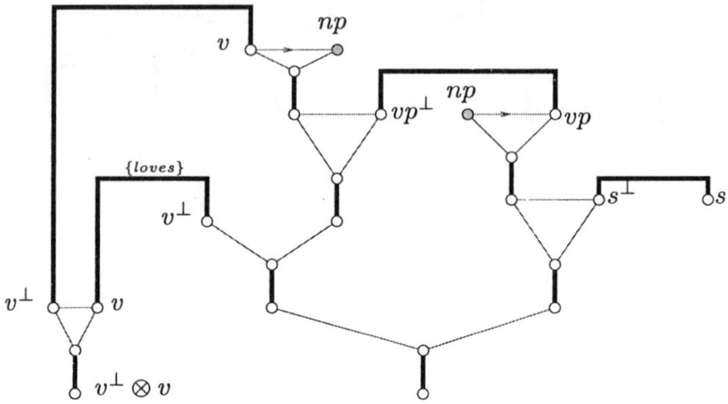

Figure 3.

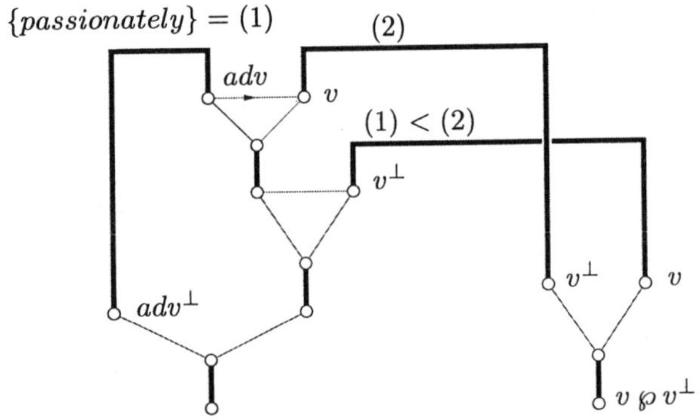

Figure 4.

Such an ILPPN can then be used together with a module which introduces a verb modifier. This modifier LPPN contains a dual conclusion $v^{\perp} \wp v$ (cf. Figure 4). It is then possible to link the two modules by means of a cut. Then, by cut-elimination, two axiom-links are inserted between dual v-nodes, one belonging to the adverbial module and the other to the verbal one. .The label of the v node, and therefore the label of the $vp^{\perp}$ node are transformed and give a correct word order.

This leads us to the following definition. A Modifier-LPP is a Labelled

Partial Proof-Net with two conclusions, one of which is the *par* of two dual atoms x and $x^{\perp}$, where x is the type of object that the module modifies, and the other one is the main conclusion.

Let us explain the behavior of the MLPPN in Figure 4. When linked by a cut link to an LPPN associated to a verbal form (cf. Figure 5), the corresponding *times* formula is labelled by the same pomset (from the definition of labelled cut-links) and so, the highest v-entry in the verbal PPN will be labelled by $\{passionately, loves\}$, but without any ordering on it. It is the operation of cut-elimination which will provide the correct word order.

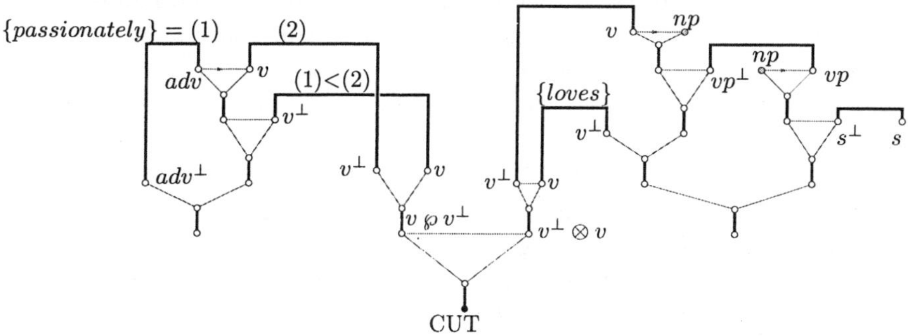

Figure 5.

This operation (which is an intrinsical part of the process of plugging by cut) finally gives us the PPN in Figure 6.

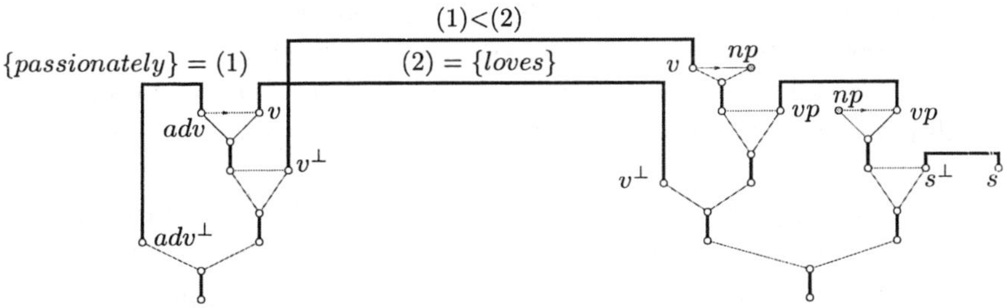

Figure 6.

If there is no modifier, the PPN in Figure 3 is still valid. In this case, cut-elimination amounts to suppressing the *times*-link $v \otimes v^{\perp}$, which is, as has already been said, a mere instance of a cut. It should be pointed out that without cut-elimination, the word order would remain free. It remains to be seen whether we can represent dislocated sentences in this way, that is to say, sentences that result from different orderings of words with particular intonations.

Discontinuous constituents

In order to give an example of the expressive power of our system let us consider an example of a construction which is not handled by the Lambek calculus. Let us consider French negation, which is a discontinuous constituent. We will consider this negation to be *ne ... pas* which wraps the verbal head — the variants *ne ... plus*, *ne ... jamais* etc. being completely similar.

The idea is to associate an MLPPN with this negation, the main conclusion of which is $\{ne\} : neg^{\perp} \wp (\{pas\} : neg \wp ((neg < (v < neg^{\perp})) \otimes v^{\perp})$ and whose secondary conclusion is $v^{\perp} \wp v$.

Let us represent the PPN by a linear expression whose atoms linked by an axiom link are marked by the same label $[i]$, where i is an integer. Then *ne ... pas* is associated with

$$[1] : (\{ne\} : neg^{\perp}) \wp (([2] : \{pas\} : neg) \wp (([1] : neg < ([3] : v < [2] : neg^{\perp})) \otimes [4] : v^{\perp})),$$
$$([3] : v^{\perp}) \wp ([4] : v)$$

The dual formula of the main conclusion (or type of the expression) is

$$([1] : \{ne\} : neg) \otimes (([2] : \{pas\} : neg^{\perp}) \otimes (([1] : neg < ([3] : v < [2] : neg^{\perp})) \multimap [4] : v))$$

The underlying formula expresses that this module provides the context with *ne* and *pas* — whose types are the dual of the other. The axiom links of the module express that a verb v ([3]) wrapped by *ne* and *pas* gives a new verb ([4]).

By cut-link plugging this module with a verbal ILPPN, we obtain the right word order for the negative sentence, for instance *Pierre* **ne** *regarde* **pas** *Marie* (Peter does not look at Mary). Thus, we obtain a simple logical formulation of head-wrapping, as opposed to hitherto considered extensions of the Lambek calculus.

Conclusion

The system we have presented here is specifically a ***resource-conscious system.*** Duality must be interpreted in terms of exchange and communication. Firstly, the plugging of two atomic formulae via an axiom link expresses that some demand of a phrase is satisfied. Secondly, the plugging via a cut-link makes a communication between two processes which can be synchronised by removing the cut — observe that in this case as well, one cut-formula provides what the other formula (the dual one) needs.

This characteristic allows many phenomena to be expressed. For instance, in wh-extraction as well as in cliticization, a word (the wh-word or the clitic word) is supposed to suppress a demand for an np of a given form (for instance an accusative np for *what*, or an np of the same case of the clitic in the clitic-case). But to suppress a demand is to satisfy it, just because of the involutive negation — $(x^{\perp})^{\perp} = x$, i.e. a demand for a demand for a x is equivalent to an x.

This kind of mechanism is typical of a system based on resource consumption as may be observed in categorial grammar, for instance in the type-raising operation. Here, we go beyond this because, as opposed to the Lambek calculus which only has an implicit non-involutive negation, we take advantage of the explicit and involutive negation of linear logic to extend this phenomenon to other situations, and this results in considerable expressive power.

Finally, we should point out that the main advantage of this logic-based system is that *ad hoc* and very particular algebraic operations can be avoided, for instance on trees or strings. Here all the machinery may be summarised as follows: *given the initial LPPNs as they are, build a correct proof-net*, the only requirement being that the correctness criterion, namely *no elementary alternate circuit* is preserved during the construction of the proof net. A future study will investigate the embedding of TAGs and Lambek grammars in this system.

Acknowledgements: Many ideas in this paper have come from discussions in the Calligramme group, especially with Philippe de Groote.

References

Abrusci, V. M. 1991. "Phase semantics and sequent calculus for pure noncommutative classical linear logic". *Journal of Symbolic Logic* 56(4), 1403–1451.

Becker, T., Joshi, A. and Rambow, O. 1991. "Long distance scrambling and tree adjoining grammars". In 5th *EACL*, 21–26.

Girard, J.-Y. 1987. "Linear logic". *Theoretical Computer Science* 50(1):1–102.

Girard, J.-Y. 1995. "Linear logic: its syntax and semantics". In J.-Y. Girard, Y. Lafont and L. Regnier (eds), *Advances in Linear Logic.* (London Mathematical Society Lecture Notes, vol. 222). Cambridge: Cambridge University Press, 1–42.

Joshi, A. 1987. "An introduction to tree adjoining grammars". In A. Manaster-Ramer (ed), *Mathematics of Language* Amsterdam and Philadelphia: Benjamins, 87–114.

Joshi, A. and Kulick, S. 1995. "Partial proof trees as building blocks for a categorial grammar". In G. V. Morrill and R. Oehrle (eds), *Formal Grammar*, FoLLI, 138–149.

Joshi, A. and Kulick, S. 1997. "Partial proof trees, resource sensitive logics and syntactic constraints". In C. Retoré (ed), *Logical Aspects of Computational Linguistics, LACL'96*, (LNCS/LNAI series), Heidelberg and New-York: Springer-Verlag. To appear.

Lecomte, A. and Retoré, C. 1995. "Pomset logic as an alternative categorial grammar". In G. V. Morrill and R. Oehrle (eds), *Formal Grammar*, FoLLI, 181–196.

Morrill, G.V. 1994. *Type Logical Grammar.* Dordrecht and Hingham: Kluwer.

Rambow, O., Vijay-Shanker, K. and Weir, D. 1995. "D-tree grammars". 33rd *Meeting of the Association for Computational Linguistics.*

Retoré, C. 1993. "Réseaux et Séquents Ordonnés". Thèse de Doctorat, spécialité Mathématiques, Université Paris 7.

Retoré, C. 1995. "Pomset logic: a non-commutative extension of classical linear logic". In J. R. Hindley and Ph. de Groote (eds). *Typed Lambda-Calculus and Applications, TLCA'97.* (LNCS, vol. 1210) Heidelberg and New-York: Springer-Verlag, 300–318.

A Metagrammatical Logical Formalism

Vincenzo Manca

Pisa University

Introduction

This paper presents a logical formalism for fundamental concepts of traditional grammar.

In its basic sense a grammar is simply a system of (informal) rules which try to discriminate correct linguistic expressions from ones that are incorrect, according to an ideal speaker of the language considered. The term *traditional grammar* refers to the concepts, methods, and terminology, elaborated over the centuries by grammarians, philosophers and linguists, that constitute (more and less consciously) the average linguistic culture: proposition, predicate, substantive, subject, attribute, complement, modifier, determiner, coordination, subordination, anaphora, ellipsis, deixis, and sentence. These concepts are generally used on the basis of their informal linguistic evidence and often with criteria that depend on the particular language they refer to. Nevertheless, their theoretical relevance is based on very deep roots in Western philosophy from Plato, Aristotle and Dionysius Thrax, to the *Speculative Grammar* of *Scholastic* philosophy (Robins 1951) and the *Grammaire générale et raisonnée* of Port Royal (17th century), where the terminological and conceptual apparatus of traditional Indo-European grammars were elaborated.

We claim that a deep logical analysis of traditional grammar can indicate a linguistic level, or *metagrammatical level*, where the basic meaning of simple conversational language could be formally analyzed and logically represented (cf. Manca 1993 and 1995 for earlier versions of the formalism here considered).

The idea of a logical formulation of classical linguistic analysis was already present in the first investigations of modern mathematical logic. Here we can find, even in the context of mathematical theories, masterpieces of logical analyses of natural language. In this perspective, we can consider: Leibniz's *Characteristica Universalis* (Parkinson 1966); Bertrand Russell's theory of propositions; Frege's *Begriffsschrift* on the symbolization of the predicative structure of mathematical language; and Peano's *Formulario Mathematico* on notations for general mathematical concepts.

The first systematic attempt to use mathematical logic in formal representation of English texts is Reichenbach's *Logic of conversational language* (Reichenbach 1947). Nevertheless, Reichenbah's proposal is simply a collection of interesting examples covering important phenomena of natural language expressiveness, rather than a definition of a rigorous formalism. Several developments emerged from the late 1950s to the early 1970s: Lambek's version of earlier categorial grammar (Lambek 1958), *generative semantics* which extended Chomsky's paradigm (Lakoff 1972, Chomsky 1980) and Montague's approach to natural language in terms of model theory concepts and high order logics (Montague 1974). These approaches (proof theory, generative and model theory) strongly influenced later research on the formal analysis of natural language, and the related fields of knowledge representations and non classical logics (van Benthem 1988, Barwise 1989, Kamp and Reyle 1993).

One feature common to many logical approaches to natural language is their complexity and specificity. One of the main objectives of this paper, on the other hand, is to develop a wide-ranging logical formalism: *Metagramma.* This formalism is comparable with first order logic in the formal description of mathematical theories, or with programming languages in the specification of algorithms. Metagramma consists of symbolic rules with which we can construct formulae built by lexemes of a specific lexicon and symbols expressing logico-grammatical functionalities. The denotative content of simple, but non trivial texts can thus be adequately expressed by sets of *metagrammatical* formulae.

Notations for metagrammatical concepts

In every natural language there are expressions that have the following four fundamental syntactic types: i) *sentence* (assertive, imperative, interrogative), ii) *proposition*, iii) *predicate*, iv) *substantive.*

As a first approximation, we can assume that substantives can represent individuals (of some -maybe high order- universe). Predicates represent properties over individuals. Propositions represent statements, and sentences represent assertions, questions or commands.

Let us call *categorema* any expression that has some fundamental syntactic type. The following are general postulates describing basic aspects common to almost all natural languages.

Postulate 1 *There are elements, usually called* determiners, *that transform predicates into substantives.*

Postulate 2 *Any categorema* φ *of (syntactic) type* τ *includes a categorema* $ker(\varphi)$ *of type* τ *(its* kernel *or its* head*).*

We say that a categorema φ is *nuclear* if $\varphi = ker(\varphi)$. If φ is a nuclear proposition, then its *predicate* is the biggest (w.r.t. the string inclusion) predicate included in φ. For every categorema φ, if it is not nuclear, then the *modifier* of the categorema $ker(\varphi)$ is the string difference $\varphi \setminus ker(\varphi)$.

Postulate 3 *Any nuclear proposition includes a predicate.*

Postulate 4 *Any nuclear proposition that is not a predicate consists of two distinct parts: its predicate and a substantive, called the* subject *of the proposition.*

If φ is a non nuclear predicate including a substantive γ we say that γ is a *complement* of $ker(\varphi)$. If γ is nuclear it is a *direct complement* of φ, otherwise it is an *indirect complement* of φ.

Postulate 5 *When propositions are related to some extra-linguistic elements, called* situations, *they determine assertions.*

Postulate 6 *Some linguistic elements (*anaphoric pronouns *such as in English:* he, she, it*)* refer *to other categoremata.*

Postulate 7 *Some linguistic elements (*deictic pronouns, *i.e. personal and demonstrative pronouns that refer to extralinguistic entities) identify substantives which depend on the situation in which they are used.*

Postulate 8 *Some linguistic elements (*conjunctive particles*) combine categoremata with the same type and produce categoremata of that type.*

Postulate 9 *Some linguistic elements indicate classes and numbers.*

Postulate 10 *Any categorema can be transformed into a substantive.*

The syntactic constructions underlying the above postulates are: *determination, predication, deixis, assertion, complementation, modification, anaphorc coordination, substantivation,* and *pluralization.* We do not claim that this list includes all the constructions of natural languages, only that most texts of any natural language can be represented, in their internal logical structure, by suitable combinations of these syntactical operations.

In Metagramma we adopt three kinds of metagrammatical *determination.* The first one, symbolized by Peano-Russell's *descriptive* iota operator, expresses *definite determination,* i.e., given a predicate *Pred*, it yields the uniquely determined object $\iota Pred$ which satisfies the property represented by *Pred*. The second one, symbolized by Hilbert-Bernays' epsilon operator, expresses the *particular determination,* i.e., given a predicate *Pred*, it yields a particular element $\epsilon Pred$ which satisfies the property represented by *Pred*. The third one is the *indefinite determination* operator η such that, given a predicate *Pred*, $\eta Pred$ represents any element which satisfies the property represented by *Pred*. In Metagramma the predication construct is expressed by equations, therefore, an expression such as "$a \in Pred$" should be seen as an abbreviation for "$a = \epsilon Pred$".

The symbol θ denotes the *speech situation,* that is the *Hic-et-nunc* or *Here-and-now* state of the affairs with respect to which any extralinguistic element (for spatio-temporal-personal deixis) has to be related. A similar symbol has already been used in an analogous way (for "autoreflexive tokens") by Reichenbach (Reichenbach 1947). The symbols $a, b, \ldots$ are individual constants, and $\vdash$ is the *assertion* symbol, already used by Russell, which connects situations and propositions thus producing declarative assertions. Commands or questions are indicated by adding ! or ? to $\vdash$ respectively (possibly adding a pronoun to ?). Anaphoric constants or pronouns

$A, B, \ldots$ play a different role from individual constants. Namely, in natural language, we can speak of things that do not exist, i.e. we have to distinguish between descriptive entities and existential entities. When, w.r.t. a situation s, we assert "$a \in Pred$", we assume that something exists in the situation s which verifies the property *Pred* and we introduce the name a for such an entity. Conversely, given a definite or particular description, if we want to refer to the substantive that it identifies, without any existential commitment, then we put an *anaphora* such as $A := Description$. For this reason we introduce a more precise distinction: we call *term* any descriptive expression obtained by ι, ϵ, η operators, and only when an individual has been equated to a term can it be considered an existential term, i.e. a substantive in a proper sense.

In natural languages, modification and complementation are usually realized by attributive phrases, adverbs, or by complementative particles. A metagrammatical representation of an expression such as "big man" is "$big\langle man \rangle$", where angle parentheses indicate modification. Complementation is expressed by *dot suffixing*; for example, "$eat.b$" indicates that parameter b is added to the predicate *eat* as a direct complement, in order to complete its meaning. Indirect complementation is obtained by combining modification and dot-complementation; for example "eat with the fork" is translated by the metagrammatical formula $eat.(instrument\langle \iota fork \rangle)$, where, in this case, the modification applies to a term and produces a modified term, and the modifier expresses the role of the term in the indirect complementation.

In the following, we assume a set of *atomic predicates* represented by lexemes of a natural language (e.g. English nouns, verbs and adjectives), which will be specified implicitly when they occur.

Let us consider some short examples. A *metagrammatical representation* is a sequence of elementary formulae, each of which is a sentence or an anaphora.

Example 1 *There is a pen on the table.*

This means that, in the situation where the statement is uttered (or written), there is something that is a pen, something that is the table, and the first thing is placed on the second:

$$\theta \vdash \; a \in pen$$

$$\theta \vdash \ b \ = \iota \, table$$
$$\theta \vdash \ a \, \epsilon \, (stay.location\langle b \rangle)$$

Example 2 *Where is the pen?*

$$\theta \vdash a = \ \iota \, pen$$
$$\theta \vdash \ B? \, (a \, \epsilon \, (stay.location\langle B \rangle))$$

Example 3 *Take a pen!*

$$\theta \ \vdash \ a \ = \ \iota \, listen$$
$$B \ := \ \epsilon \, pen$$
$$\theta \ \vdash ! \, (a \, \epsilon \, take.B)$$

The substantivation operator [ ] is very similar to Reichenbach's "event-splitting" operator $[\ ]^*$. Nevertheless, its reformulation in the framework of Metagramma, where a clear distinction between events and situations is adopted, allows us to avoid some aspects of non uniformity and *adhocness* in Reichenbach's formalism. In a statement such as "John believes that Paul is here", if "Paul is here" is represented by a proposition P, then the global sentence has a metagrammatical representation of the following type: $\theta \vdash j\epsilon(believe.[P])$.

In logical languages, anaphora and quantification are realized by means of formal variables and variable-binding constructs, i.e. $\forall$ quantification and Church's lambda abstraction. Reichenbach adopts the same tools in his formalism. In the following examples we show that anaphora and determination can express the universal quantification and relative clauses of natural language in a manner that is very close to the linguistic forms present in almost all languages. Equations $a = \iota Pred$, $a = \epsilon Pred$, and $a = \eta Pred$ represent different kinds of existential denotation, corresponding respectively to "a is the *Pred*", "a is a *Pred*" and "a is some *Pred*" (an existent, but indefinite substantive). Analogously, anaphoric assignments $A := \iota Pred$, $A := \epsilon Pred$ allow us to consider A as its corresponding description, without any existential commitment. However, an anaphoric assignment $A := \eta Pred$ defines an implicit universal quantification that prescribes A to assume all the values which satisfy the predicate $Pred$. The next examples will show how pronouns and descriptive operators can express universal quantification and relative clauses. The first one points out that the order of elementary formulae determines the scopes of quantifications.

Example 4 *Every man loves a woman.*

$$\begin{aligned} S &:= \eta(S \vdash S \,\epsilon\, situation) \\ A &:= \eta\, man \\ B &:= \epsilon\, woman \\ S &\vdash A \,\epsilon\, (love.B) \end{aligned}$$

Example 5 *The child who was crying yesterday is laughing now.*

$$\begin{aligned} \theta &\vdash s \,\epsilon\, yesterday \\ s &\vdash a = \iota(child \wedge cry) \\ \theta &\vdash a \,\epsilon\, laugh. \end{aligned}$$

Formal rules for metagrammatical representations

Consider the following 16 symbols (the commas and the final full stop are not symbols of the alphabet, but punctuation marks). We have already introduced most of them informally. The intuitive meaning of the others is the one that they usually have in informal mathematical language (π is the pluralization modifier indicating *pluralities*, i.e. non empty and non singleton classes of objects satisfying the modified predicate).

$$= \,,\ := \,,\ \vdash \,,\ ! \,,\ ? \,,\ \theta \,,\ \epsilon \,,\ \iota \,,\ \eta \,,\ \pi \,,\ . \,,\ \langle\,\rangle \,,\ [\,] \,,\ \neg \,,\ \wedge \,,\ \vee \,.$$

Consider the following types: Pred, Subst, Prop, Sent, Ind, Sit, Pron, Ref, Num, Cat, Stat, Term (type Cat stands for categoremata, type Term for descriptive terms and Stat for *statements* i.e. propositions or sentences). A *metagrammatical representation* over a lexicon $\mathcal{L}$ is a sequence of formulae such that for each of them, the type Sent or Ref can be assigned according to the rules of the next subsection.

A metagrammatical type system

In the following, **N** is the set of natural numbers. Letters α, β, γ are syntactic variables ranging on the expressions constructed by the 16 logical symbols, a set $\mathcal{I}$ of symbols for individuals, a set $\mathcal{P}$ of symbols for pronouns, a set $\mathcal{S}$ of symbols for situations, and a set $\mathcal{L}$ of lexemes. The symbol $Type$ is a syntactic variable ranging on types. Given an expression α, 'α' stands for its quotation (a name for its linguistic form). The following rules apply to (metagrammatical) type assignment derivations: if the premises occur in a derivation, then the conclusion can be added as its last element. The expression $Free(\alpha)$ is a condition that holds if no anaphoric reference, such as $\alpha := \beta$, occurs in the derivation. The symbol ∇ indicates any determination operator belonging to $\{\iota, \epsilon, \eta\}$, and $\alpha \neq \beta$ means that α and β are two different symbols. Furthermore, "$(\alpha : Type, \ldots)\beta : Stat$" means that the assignment $\beta : Stat$ has been derived by using at some previous step $\alpha : Type, \ldots$ as *assumptions.*

$$\frac{\alpha \in \mathcal{L}}{\alpha : \text{Pred}} \quad \frac{\alpha \in \mathcal{I} \cup \mathcal{S}}{\alpha : \text{Ind}} \quad \frac{\alpha \in \mathcal{P}}{\alpha : \text{Pron}} \quad \frac{\alpha \in \mathcal{S}}{\alpha : \text{Sit}} \quad \frac{\alpha \in \mathbf{N}}{\alpha : \text{Num}} \quad \frac{\alpha \in \mathcal{L}}{\text{`}\alpha\text{'} : \text{Subst}}$$

Axioms

$$\frac{\alpha : \text{Pred}}{\alpha : \text{Cat}} \quad \frac{\alpha : \text{Subst}}{\alpha : \text{Term}} \quad \frac{\alpha : \text{Term}}{\alpha : \text{Cat}} \quad \frac{\alpha : \text{Prop}}{\alpha : \text{Stat}} \quad \frac{\alpha : \text{Sent}}{\alpha : \text{Stat}} \quad \frac{\alpha : \text{Stat}}{\alpha : \text{Cat}}$$

Basic Rules

$$\boxed{\frac{\alpha : \text{Pred}}{(\nabla\, \alpha) : \text{Term}}}$$

Determination

$$\frac{\alpha : \text{Ind},\ \beta : \text{Term}}{\alpha = \beta : \text{Prop}}$$

$$\frac{\alpha : \text{Term},\ \beta : \text{Term}}{\alpha = \beta : \text{Prop}}$$

$$\frac{\alpha : \text{Ind},\ \alpha = \beta : \text{Prop}}{\alpha : \text{Subst}}$$

Predication

$$\frac{\alpha : \text{Pred},\ \beta : \text{Pred}}{(\alpha\langle\beta\rangle) : \text{Pred}}$$

$$\frac{\alpha : \text{Pred},\ \beta : \text{Subst}}{(\alpha\langle\beta\rangle) : \text{Subst}}$$

$$\frac{\alpha : \text{Pred},\ \beta : \text{Term}}{(\alpha\langle\beta\rangle) : \text{Term}}$$

Modification

$$\frac{\alpha : \text{Pred},\ \beta : \text{Term}}{(\alpha.\beta) : \text{Pred}}$$

Complementation

$$\frac{\alpha : \text{Sit},\ \beta : \text{Prop}}{\alpha \vdash \beta : \text{Sent}} \qquad \frac{\alpha : \text{Sit},\ \beta : \text{Prop}}{\alpha \vdash !(\beta) : \text{Sent}}$$

$$\frac{\alpha : \text{Sit},\ \beta : \text{Prop}}{\alpha \vdash ?(\beta) : \text{Sent}} \qquad \frac{\alpha : \text{Sit},\ \gamma : \text{Pron},\ Free(\gamma),\ (\gamma : \text{Term})\beta : \text{Prop}}{\alpha \vdash \gamma ?(\beta) : \text{Sent}}$$

Assertion

$$\frac{\alpha : \text{Pred}}{[\alpha] : \text{Subst}} \qquad \frac{\alpha : \text{Prop}}{[\alpha] : \text{Subst}} \qquad \frac{\alpha : \text{Sent}}{[\alpha] : \text{Subst}}$$

Substantivation

$$\frac{\alpha : Type}{\neg(\alpha) : Type} \qquad \frac{\alpha : Type,\ \beta : Type}{(\alpha \wedge \beta) : Type} \qquad \frac{\alpha : Type,\ \beta : Type}{(\alpha \vee \beta) : Type}$$

Coordination

$$\frac{\alpha : \text{Num},\ \beta : \text{Pred}}{\alpha(\beta) : \text{Pred}} \qquad \frac{\alpha : \text{Pred}}{\pi(\alpha) : \text{Pred}}$$

Pluralization

$$\frac{\alpha : \text{Pron}, Free(\alpha), (\alpha : \text{Sit}, \alpha : \text{Term})\beta : \text{Stat}}{\nabla(\alpha \vdash \beta) : \text{Sit}}$$

Deixis

$$\frac{\alpha : \text{ Pron},\ Free(\alpha),\ \beta : \text{ Cat}}{(\alpha := \beta) : \text{ Ref}}$$

$$\frac{\alpha : \text{ Pron},\ \alpha := \beta : \text{ Ref},\ \beta : Type}{\alpha : Type}$$

$$\frac{\alpha : \text{ Pron},\ Free(\alpha),\ (\alpha : \text{Term})\beta : \text{Stat}}{(\nabla\beta) : \text{Term}}$$

$$\frac{\begin{array}{c}\alpha : \text{ Pron},\ \gamma : \text{ Pron},\ Free(\alpha),\ Free(\gamma),\ \alpha \neq \gamma, \\ (\alpha : \text{Term})\beta : \text{ Stat}, (\alpha : \text{Term})(\gamma := \beta)\ : \text{Ref}\end{array}}{\gamma : \text{ Pred}}$$

Anaphora

The reader can verify that all the examples considered above can be formally derived as metagrammatical representations by using the considered rules.

Example 6 *The child who was crying yesterday is laughing now.*

1) $\theta : Sit$	*Ax*
2) $yesterday : Pred$	*Ax*
3) $s : Sit$	*Ax*
4) $s : Ind$	*Ax*
5) $\epsilon\, yesterday : Term$	*Determination* 2
6) $s\, \epsilon\, yesterday : Prop$	*Predication* 4,5
7) $\boxed{\theta \vdash s\, \epsilon\, yesterday} : Sent$	*Assertion* 1,6
8) $child : Pred$	*Ax*
9) $cry : Pred$	*Ax*
10) $child \wedge cry : Pred$	*Coordination* 8,9
11) $\iota(child \wedge cry) : Term$	*Determination* 10
12) $a : Ind$	*Ax*

13) $a = \iota(child \wedge cry) : Prop$	*Predication* 12, 11
14) $\boxed{s \vdash a = \iota(child \wedge cry)} : Sent$	*Assertion* 3, 13
15) $laugh : Pred$	*Ax*
16) $\epsilon\, laugh : Term$	*Determination* 15
17) $a\, \epsilon\, laugh : Prop$	*Predication* 12, 16
18) $\boxed{\theta \vdash a\, \epsilon\, laugh} : Sent$	*Assertion* 1, 17

The boxed formulae are the metagrammatical representation of Example 5.

Conclusions

An interesting feature of Metagramma is its easy usage in the representation of texts where commonly used logical formalisms are completely inadequate due to the complexity of the generated formulae. We tested Metagramma in several applications: i) instructions for the use of a heater, or for assembling the parts of a personal computer; ii) children's stories such as *Cinderella*; iii) statements and proofs of theorems of elementary geometry; iv) Latin texts of considerable syntactical complexity (a Letter by Cicero). Usually the length of the metagrammatical representation (number of lines) is no more than twice the number of lines in the original texts. However, almost all the formalizations considered retain the global intelligibility of the associated texts. More thorough testing with Metagramma should help to highlight its weaknesses and pave the way for improvements and possible extensions.

Another open issue is the formal aspect of Metagramma; for example, its relationship with logical systems dealing formally with situations and intensions (Montague 1974, van Benthem 1988, Barwise 1989, and Devlin 1991). A more proof theory oriented analysis could individuate inference rules for deriving assertions from other assertions. Such rules would add a new level to the formal description of metagrammatical notions. We only give two fragments of derivations in the formal generation of *metagrammatical paraphrases.* For example, consider the metagrammatical representations of "a is walking fast to b". The following is a simple derivation, obtained by using suitable rules, of a metagrammatical paraphrase that in English corresponds to "if a is walking fast to b then a's walking to b is fast":

$$\frac{\theta \vdash a\, \epsilon\, ((fast\langle walk\rangle).(destination\langle b\rangle))}{\theta \vdash ([walk.(destination\langle b\rangle)].a)\, \epsilon\, fast}$$

Analogously, the next is a (trivial) derivation for: "if a is walking fast to b then a is walking":

$$\frac{\theta \vdash a \,\epsilon\, ((fast\langle walk\rangle).(destination\langle b\rangle))}{\theta \vdash a \,\epsilon\, (fast\langle walk\rangle)}$$

Another important aspect of metagrammatical representations is the lexicon on which these representations are constructed. In order to get a true interlingual character, a metagrammatical formula has to contain lexemes without any semantic ambiguity. This aspect entails a thorough analysis of *archetypal lexicons*, their nature and their structure. A subject for future work would be to find some possible connection between Thom's 16 archetypal *logoi* determined by topological analyses and logical approaches to natural language (Thom 1970, Fenstad 1976, and Manca 1996). If lexicons used in metagrammatical representations are well chosen, then a person who knows Metagramma, and who consults a suitable bilingual dictionary, should be able to produce a corresponding metagrammatical representation based on the lexicon of a language that he/she does not know, in order to communicate with a speaker of that language (who knows Metagramma). In this sense, metagrammatical representations can be seen as a sort of formal counterpart of the linguistic projects on artificial languages (Large 1985), intimately connected to knowledge representation, semi-automatic translation, linguistic typology, and to the old and fascinating theme of *universal* grammar (Greenberg 1963 and Comrie 1981).

References

Barwise, J. 1989. *The Situations in Logic.* CSLI Lecture Note N. 17. Stanford (CA.): Center for the Study of Language and Information.

Benthem, J. van 1988. *A Manual of Intensional Logic.* CSLI Lecture Note N. 1. Stanford (CA.): Center for the Study of Language and Information.

Chomsky, N. 1980. *Rules and Representations.* New York: Columbia University Press.

Comrie, B. 1981. *Language Universals and Linguistic Typology, Syntax and Mophology.* Oxford: Basil Blackwell.

Devlin, K. 1991. *Logic and Information.* Cambridge (Mass.): Cambridge University Press.

Fenstad, J. E. 1976. "Models for natural languages". In J. Hintikka, I. Niniluoto and E. Saarinen (eds), *Essays on Mathematical and Philosophical Logic.* Dordrecht, Boston and London: Dordrecht Reidel Publishing Company, 315–340.

Greenberg, J. H. (ed). 1963. *Universals of Language.* Cambridge (Mass.): The MIT Press.

Kamp, H. and Reyle, U. 1993. *From Discourse to Logic.* Dordrecht, Boston and London: Kluwer Academic Publishers.

Lambek, J. 1958. "The mathematics of sentence structure". *American Mathematical Monthly* 65: 154–170.

Large, A. 1985. *The Artificial Language Movement.* Oxford: Basil Blackwell.

Lakoff, G. 1972. "Linguistics and natural logic". In D. Davison and G. Harman (eds), *Semantics of Natural Languages.* Dordrecht, Boston and London: Dordrecht Reidel Publishing Company.

Manca, V. 1993. "Typology and logical structure of natural language". In K. Sikkel and A. Nijholt (eds), *Parsing Natural Language*, Proc. of 6th TWLT Workshop. Enschede: Universiteit Twente, 23–36.

Manca, V. 1995. "A logical formalism for intergrammatical representations". In A. Nijholt, G. Scollo, and R. Steetskamp (eds), *Algebraic Methods in Language Processing*, Proc. of 10th TWLT & 1st AMiLP Workshop. Enschede: Universiteit Twente, 247–254.

Manca, V. 1996. "Thom's Logoi in Metagrammatical Representations". In C. Martín-Vide (ed), *Lenguajes Naturales y Lenguajes Formales.* Barcelona: P.P.U., 237–250.

Montague, R. 1974. *Formal Philosophy.* Thomason R. H. (ed). London: Yale University Press.

Parkinson, G. H. R. 1966. *Leibniz Logical Papers.* Oxford: Clarendon Press.

Reichenbach, H. 1947. *Elements of Symbolic Logic.* New York: MacMillan Limited.

Robins, R. H. 1951. *Ancient and Medieval Grammatical Theory in Europe.* London: G. Bell & Sons LTD.

Thom, R. 1970. "Topology and linguistics". In A. Haeflinger and R. Narasimhan (eds), *Essays on Topology and Related Topics.* Berlin: Springer-Verlag.

Word Meaning, Logic and the Informative Entailment Relation

Ángel Nepomuceno Fernández
Francisco J. Salguero Lamillar

University of Sevilla

A dynamic perspective of meaning in natural language has to deal with all those phenomena related to information inference from the linguistic expressions uttered in normal discourse. We can designate the set of these phenomena by means of the pragmatic term *semantic enrichment*. There are several modes of semantic enrichment in discourse. Some of the most fundamental of these are:

1. Logical inference, based on the rules of classical predicate logic, that can be applied to complete sentences.

2. Contextual reference assignment to anaphoric terms, such as pronouns, demonstratives, temporal adverbs, etc.

3. Information inference from the lexicon belonging to major categories: nouns, adjectives and verbs.

Our work discusses this third kind of semantic enrichment. We deal with it from a logical point of view within a classical framework rather than a modal one. This means that the previous linguistic analysis of the lexicon sets aside modal operators, well known in the linguistic literature, in order to be based mainly on meaning postulates and on what we call the *informative entailment relation*, an inference relation different from the traditional relation of logical inference.

Dynamic theories of meaning and lexical relations

Discourse interpretation cannot be considered from a compositional perspective only. It depends on several processes of enrichment that can be divided into two main categories: semantic and pragmatic enrichment.

In a wide perspective, semantic enrichment is concerned with the speaker's knowledge about logic and language, while pragmatic enrichment deals with everything related to the speaker's knowledge about the world. Roughly speaking way, the process of discourse interpretation can be seen as an application to linguistic utterances of Grammar Rules, Logical Rules and the underlying information obtained by the speakers/hearers from their previous knowledge of the world.

But it is evident that, defined in such a way, both sorts of enrichment are excessively general, and therefore it is important to distinguish among the different kinds of processes involved within them. It also seems that it is not a reasonable strategy to consider the different components of discourse interpretation as separate modules.

We will consider discourse interpretation on the basis of concrete enunciative sentence utterances as an application of Grammar Rules + Logical Rules + Lexical Information Rules + World Knowledge. We will deal with lexical information rules as part of the logical rules rather than as part of the rules of the grammar. This is because we consider lexicon from a denotational semantic perspective, not from a morphological one. Therefore, our aim is to integrate the lexical information rules into a general logical theory for the interpretation of enunciative utterances in natural discourse. This means we must analyze the lexical meaning belonging to major categories and establish an appropriate entailment relation for discourse inferences depending on lexicon. To do this, we define a formal language L for the interpretation of enunciative sentences.

Lexical information rules are seen as a part of meaning postulates and must be defined previously. These rules describe the lexical relations that occur among the words belonging to the main categories in a language.

These relations are well known in lexical semantics, but their importance for logical inference has not been adequately recognized by logicians.

Essentially, we can distinguish between two kinds of lexical relation: paradigmatic relations, or *sense relationships*, and syntagmatic relations. When some of these relations are between common nouns or adjectives, for example, their logical semantic treatment is not a problem: we have two predicates of the same adicy such that their semantic values are related by means of basic set theory relations. This is the case of words like "dog" and "animal", for example. For these words we can define a paradigmatic relation called *hyponymy*. This means that the denotation of "dog" is a subset of the denotation of "animal", and so we can establish why it is possible to infer the sentence "Pluto is an animal" from the sentence "Pluto is a dog". So, we have first

$$\|dog\| \subset \|animal\|$$

where $\|dog\|$ and $\|animal\|$ are the denotational semantic values of the words "dog" and "animal", and so we have that

$$dog(pluto) \models animal(pluto)$$

What kind of "logical" relation is $\models$, above? Really, it is not the usual one, but the inference is valid and we can express it even in a more general way:

$$\models \forall x(dog(x) \rightarrow animal(x))$$

This is not only the case of hyponymy. We can find the same problem in other paradigmatic relations such as *synonymy*, where the denotations of words are identical sets and we may establish a logical equivalence between sentences including them. This is also the case of certain syntagmatic relations.

A well-known problem arises when we have certain relations between two predicates of different adicy, as in the case of some adjectives and verbs. It is evident that logical inference is made from a sentence like "John opened the door" to the sentence "The door was open". This inference does not depend on propositional or predicate logic, but in lexical relations, again. And it is evident that the denotation of the transitive verb "open" cannot be equivalent to or included in the denotation of the adjective "open", because the transitive verb denotes a set of pairs and the adjective denotes a set of individuals.

This problem has been explained using a decompositional analysis of meaning and formally established using meaning postulates. Nevertheless, this is a more frequent problem in lexical semantics than it seems to be. So, meaning postulates are needed to explain why we can infer one sentence from another when there is no logical relation between them, only lexical relations between terms that even denote different extensional objects. Therefore these meaning postulates must be based on a previous analysis of the logical relations between the words in the sentence and on a new type of "logical" relation that cannot be the classical logical inference.

The language L and its semantics

Our formal language L is a First Order Predicate Language with individual and predicate parameters called terms. Language L is defined as usual and it includes the classical logical connectives as well as the existential and general quantifiers.

The semantics of L is also the usual one. For any term t and any sentence α of the formal language, $\|t\|$ and $\|\alpha\|$ represent their semantic values. In other words, for any term t, any sentence α and an interpretation $\Im$, $\|t\| = \Im(t)$ and $\|\alpha\| = \Im(\alpha)$.

The semantic value of a sentence α of L is one of the two members of the set $\{1, 0\}$, as usual. So $\Im(\alpha) = 1$, otherwise $\Im(\alpha) = 0$. On the other hand, given a non-empty set U, for $u \in U$, I_u is the principal ultrafilter generated by $\{u\}$ in the following sense:

$$I_u = \{S \subseteq U | u \in S\}.$$

The semantics of L is defined by the following clauses, each of which has a different semantic level.

1. If $t \in L$ is an individual term, then $\|t\| = I_u$ for one $u \in U$
2. If $R \in L$ is a k-adic predicate, for $k \geq 1$, then $\|R\| \in \wp(U^k)$
3. If $\alpha \in L$ is a sentence, $\|\alpha\| \in \{1, 0\}$

Clause number 3 is developed in the usual way for all those logical signs which are the main symbol in α. The basic clause is the following one:

> If α is of the form $Rb_1 \ldots b_n$, $\|\alpha\| = 1$ iff $\langle u_1 \ldots u_n \rangle \in \|R\|$ provided that $\|b_i\| = I_{u_i}$ for every $i \leq n$.

Quantification is taken in a substitutional sense. The clause for existential quantification is:

> If α is of the form $\exists x\beta$, $\|\alpha\| = 1$ iff $\|(\beta(b/x)\| = 1$ for at least one term b that does not occur in β.

In the semantic levels 1 and 2 the following relation can be defined. Given $s, t \in L$, $s \preceq t$ iff:

- both are individuals or predicates of the same adicy and $\|s\| \subseteq \|t\|$ or
- both are predicates and if the adicy of s is higher than the adicy of t, then $\|s\| = \|t\| \times \|w\|$, where w is another term of L.

Informative content of sentences and the informative entailment relation

The informative entailment relation is defined in terms of the non-logical content of a sentence (lexicon), which we will call *informative content of a sentence*, and its logical content (the logical semantic value of the sentence). In other words, the information that a sentence α provides may be seen as a semantic value of the terms in α and its logical content, defined as usual in predicate logic.

So, the information provided by any sentence α of L is seen as a function of its informative content and its logical content. The informative content of a sentence α, provided by the semantic value of the terms in α, becomes a central point in the interpretation of sentences.

We can recursively define the notion of informative content as follows: Let C_α represent the informative content of α, $\Sigma(\alpha)$ express the semantic value of the terms in α and $\langle\{0,1\}, -, +, \times, 0, 1\rangle$ be a Boolean algebra, as usual. So:

1. If α is $Rb_1 \ldots b_n$, $\Sigma(\alpha) = \langle \|R\|, \langle \|b_1\| ... \|b_n\| \rangle\rangle$; then $C_\alpha = \langle \Sigma(\alpha), \|\alpha\| \rangle$
2. If α is $\neg\beta$, $C_\alpha = \langle \Sigma(\beta), 1 - \|\beta\| \rangle$
3. If α is $\beta \vee \gamma$, $C_\alpha = \langle \Sigma(\beta), \Sigma(\gamma), \|\beta\| + \|\gamma\| \rangle$
4. If α is $\beta \wedge \gamma$, $C_\alpha = \langle \Sigma(\beta), \Sigma(\gamma), \|\beta\| \times \|\gamma\| \rangle$
5. If α is $\beta \rightarrow \gamma$, $C_\alpha = \langle \Sigma(\beta), \Sigma(\gamma), 1 - \|\beta\| + \|\gamma\| \rangle$
6. If α is $\exists x\beta(x)$ or $\forall x\beta(x)$, $C_\alpha = \langle \Sigma(\beta(b/x)), \|\beta(b/x)\| \rangle$

Given a set of informative contents K, K is semicomplete iff there is a set T of elemental sentences such that:

1. For all $\alpha \in T$, $C_\alpha \in K$
2. If $C_\alpha \in K$, $C_{\neg\neg\alpha} \in K$
3. If C_α, $C_\beta \in K$, $C_{\alpha\wedge\beta} \in K$
4. If $C_{\neg(\alpha\wedge\beta)} \in K, C_{\neg(\alpha\vee\beta)} \in K, C_{\neg(\alpha\rightarrow\beta)} \in K, C_{\neg\exists x\beta} \in K$ and $C_{\neg\forall x\beta} \in K$, then $C_{\neg\alpha\vee\neg\beta} \in K, C_{\neg\alpha\wedge\neg\beta} \in K, C_{\alpha\wedge\neg\beta} \in K$ and $C_{\forall x\neg\beta}, C_{\exists x\neg\beta} \in K$, respectively
5. If $C_{\exists x\beta} \in K$, then there is a parameter b such that $C_{\beta(b/x)} \in K$
6. If $C_{\forall x\beta} \in K$, then $C_{\beta(b/x)} \in K$ for every parameter b belonging to a set associated with K (the set of the inhabitants of K)
7. $C_\alpha \in K$ iff $C_{\neg\alpha} \notin K$

Some logical operations for informative contents can be defined. In order to do this, we will use the usual logical symbols:

$$\neg C_\alpha \equiv C_{\neg\alpha}$$
$$C_\alpha \wedge C_\beta \equiv C_{\alpha\wedge\beta}$$
$$C_\alpha \vee C_\beta \equiv C_{\alpha\vee\beta}$$
$$C_\alpha \rightarrow C_\beta \equiv C_{\alpha\rightarrow\beta}$$

Now we can define the *informative entailment relation* $\preceq$ with regard to the third semantic level, its arguments being informative contents instead of sentences. Given the sentences α and β in a language L, the relation $C_\alpha \preceq C_\beta$ is defined by the following rules:

1. If α and β are atomic sentences, the predicate R occurring in α and the predicate S in β, then $C_\alpha \preceq C_\beta$ iff:

   a) $R \preceq S$ and

   b) whatever $\|\alpha\|$ and $\|\beta\|$ may be, $\|\alpha\| \leq \|\beta\|$

2. If $C_\alpha \preceq C_\beta$ then $\neg C_\beta \preceq \neg C_\alpha$

3. If α is $\eta \wedge \delta$ then either $C_\eta \preceq C_\beta$ or $C_\delta \preceq C_\beta$ or there is a C_φ such that $C_\eta \preceq C_\beta \vee C_\varphi$ or $C_\delta \preceq C_\beta \vee C_\varphi$

4. If β is $\eta \vee \delta$ then either $C_\alpha \preceq C_\eta$ or $C_\alpha \preceq C_\delta$ or there is a C_φ such that $C_\alpha \preceq C_\eta \vee C_\varphi$ or $C_\alpha \preceq C_\delta \vee C_\varphi$

5. If β is $\eta \rightarrow \delta$ then $C_\alpha \preceq \neg C_\eta \vee C_\delta$

6. If α is $\eta \rightarrow \delta$ then $C_\eta \preceq C_\beta$

Semantic entailment is a relation defined over formulas, but it may be explained by means of the relation $\preceq$ defined above. Given a finite set of sentences Γ, $\Gamma_\wedge$ represents the formula obtained by means of the conjunction of the formulas that belong to Γ. Then we can define the concept of *informative consequence* in the following way:

$$\Gamma \models_I \psi \text{ iff } C_{\Gamma_\wedge} \preceq C_\psi$$

In this sense, we can prove the following theorem which can be interpreted as meaning that the informative entailment relation is considered prior to the logical entailment relation.

Theorem. *For any finite set of sentences* $\Gamma = \{\varphi_1 \ldots \varphi_n\}$ *and a sentence* ψ*, whatever its interpretation may be, if* $\Gamma \models \psi$ *then* $\Gamma \models_I \psi$*.*

Proof. The proof is given briefly. We examine several cases on the basis of the length of ψ. First, if $\Gamma_\wedge \models \psi$ then in all cases it is evident that $\|\Gamma_\wedge\| \leq \|\psi\|$. If ψ is atomic, there are two predicates R and S in Γ and ψ respectively, such that $R \preceq S$. Thus, by definition, $C_{\Gamma_\wedge} \preceq C\psi$. Suppose ψ is the formula $\neg\beta$; then $\beta \models \neg\Gamma_\wedge$ and because of the inductive hypothesis $C_\beta \preceq C_{\neg\Gamma_\wedge}$. So by the second clause of the definition of the informative relation $C_{\Gamma_\wedge} \preceq C_{\neg\beta}$ and therefore $C_\Gamma \preceq C_\psi$. Should there be some quantified formula among the premises, then we must study formulas of the form $\forall x\psi$ or $\exists x\psi$ in Γ. The proof for this case and the others is analogous to the proof of the cases studied above. □

Informative structures. A relevant calculus for informative contents

From any consistent set of elemental sentences, we are able to define filters that can be considered as systems of information. In this sense, a *basic system of information* is defined as any set Γ of elemental sentences $\{\varphi_1 \ldots \varphi_n\}$.

An *informative structure* is a set Δ of the informative content of the sentences in Γ such that Δ is a filter on the set of informative contents of Γ in the following way:

1. If $\varphi \in \Gamma$, then $C_\varphi \in \Delta$
2. If $C_\varphi, C_\psi \in \Delta$, then $C_\varphi \wedge C_\psi \in \Delta$
3. If $C_\varphi \in \Delta$ and $C_\varphi \preceq C_\psi$, then $C_\psi \in \Delta$
4. $C_\varphi \in \Delta$ iff $\neg C_\varphi \notin \Delta$
5. If $C_\varphi, C_\psi \in \Delta$ and $C_\varphi \preceq C_\psi$, then $C_\varphi \rightarrow C_\psi \in \Delta$
6. If $C_{\varphi(b/x)} \in \Delta$, then $C_{\exists x\varphi(x)} \in \Delta$
7. If $\{b_1 \ldots b_k\}$, where $k \geq 1$, is the set of all the parameters that occur in the formulas of Δ and $C_{\varphi(b_1/x)}, \ldots, C_{\varphi(b_k/x)} \in \Delta$ then $C_{\forall x\varphi(x)} \in \Delta$

Clauses 2, 3 and 4 make Δ a filter on the set of informative contents, generated by a basic system of information.

Theorem. *Informative structures are semicomplete sets (Hintikka sets) of informative contents.*

Proof. Given an informative structure Δ, we shall prove that Δ is a Hintikka set.

1. By definition, there is a basic system of information that generates Δ. Let this system be T. This fulfills the first condition in the definition of semicomplete sets.

2. Now, let $C_\alpha \in \Delta$. Since $\neg\neg C_\alpha$ and C_α are equivalent, $C_\alpha \preceq C_{\neg\neg\alpha}$ and by clause 3 of the definition of informative structures, $C_{\neg\neg\alpha} \in \Delta$.

3. Let $C_\alpha, C_\beta \in \Delta$. By clause 2 in the definition of Δ, $C_\alpha \wedge C_\beta \in \Delta$ and so $C_{\alpha\wedge\beta} \in \Delta$.

4. Let $C_{\neg(\alpha\wedge\beta)} \in \Delta, C_{\neg(\alpha\vee\beta)} \in \Delta, C_{\neg(\alpha\rightarrow\beta)} \in \Delta, C_{\neg\exists x\beta} \in \Delta$ and $C_{\neg\forall x\beta} \in \Delta$. Then, by the definitions of the logical signs and the concept of informative content, $C_{\neg\alpha\vee\neg\beta} \in \Delta, C_{\neg\alpha\wedge\neg\beta} \in \Delta, C_{\alpha\wedge\neg\beta} \in \Delta, C_{\forall x\neg\beta} \in \Delta$ and $C_{\exists x\neg\beta} \in \Delta$, too.

5. Let $C_{\exists x\beta} \in \Delta$. By clause 6 in the definition of Δ it is a sufficient condition that $C_{\beta(b/x)} \in \Delta$.

6. Let $C_{\forall x\beta} \in \Delta$. Then, by definition of Δ, it is enough that $C_{\beta(b_i/x)} \in \Delta$ for every parameter b_i such that $i = 1, 2, 3, \ldots k$.

7. By clause 4 in the definition of Δ, $C_\alpha \in \Delta$ iff $\neg C_\alpha \notin \Delta$ and then $C_\alpha \in \Delta$ iff $C_{\neg\alpha} \notin \Delta$. □

Now, let L' be the non-implicative fragment of the language L. Given any informative structure Δ, we define the truth function ϕ as follows: if φ and ψ are formulas of L', then

1. $\phi(\varphi, \Delta) = 1$ iff $C_\varphi \in \Delta$

2. $\phi(\neg\varphi, \Delta) = 1$ iff $\phi(\varphi, \Delta) = 0$

3. $\phi(\varphi \wedge \psi, \Delta) = 1$ iff $\phi(\varphi, \Delta) = 1$ and $\phi(\psi, \Delta) = 1$

4. $\phi(\varphi \vee \psi, \Delta) = 1$ iff $\phi(\varphi, \Delta) = 1$ or $\phi(\psi, \Delta) = 1$

5. $\phi(\varphi \rightarrow \psi, \Delta) = 1$ iff $\phi(\varphi, \Delta) = 1$ and $C_\varphi \preceq C_\psi$

6. $\phi(\exists x\varphi, \Delta) = 1$ iff $\phi(\varphi(b/x), \Delta) = 1$ for a parameter b in the formulas of Δ

7. $\phi(\forall x\varphi, \Delta) = 1$ iff $\phi(\varphi(b_k/x), \Delta) = 1$ for every parameter b_k in the formulas of Δ such that $k \geq 1$

On the basis of the concepts defined above, we can construct a calculus for a logic of informative contents. The following is a Relevant axiomatic Calculus for Informative Contents (RCIC) based on Belnap's relevant logic.

Axioms:

A1. $C_\alpha \preceq C_\alpha$

A2. $C_\alpha \preceq C_\alpha \vee C_\beta$

A3. $C_\alpha \wedge C_\beta \preceq C_\alpha$

A4. $C_\alpha \wedge (C_\beta \vee C_\gamma) \preceq (C_\alpha \wedge C_\beta) \vee C_\gamma$

A5. $(C_\alpha \rightarrow C_\beta) \wedge (C_\alpha \rightarrow C_\gamma) \preceq C_\alpha \rightarrow (C_\beta \wedge C_\gamma)$

A6. $(C_\alpha \rightarrow C_\gamma) \wedge (C_\beta \rightarrow C_\gamma) \preceq (C_\alpha \vee C_\beta) \rightarrow C_\gamma$

Rules:

R1. $C_\alpha, C_\alpha \preceq C_\beta \vdash C_\beta$

R2. $C_\alpha, C_\beta \vdash C_\alpha \wedge C_\beta$

R3. $C_\alpha \preceq C_\beta, C_\gamma \preceq C_\delta \vdash (C_\beta \rightarrow C_\gamma) \preceq (C_\alpha \rightarrow C_\delta)$

Theorem. (Soundness of RCIC) *For every informative structure* Δ, *if* $C_\alpha \preceq C_\beta$ *and* $\phi(\alpha, \Delta) = 1$, *then* $\phi(\beta, \Delta) = 1$.

Proof: As usual, proving soundness for all the axioms and rules. □

References

Alonso, E. 1992. "Tratamiento formal de la noción de contenido". In C. Martín Vide (ed): *Lenguajes Naturales y Lenguajes Formales, VII.* Barcelona: PPU, 239-246.

Anderson, A. R. and Belnap, P. 1975. *Entailment: the Logic of Relevance and Necessity*. New York: Princeton University Press.

Anderson, A. R. and Belnap, P. 1992. *Entailment: the Logic of Relevance and Necessity II*. New York: Princeton University Press.

Benthem, J. van. 1991. *Language in Action. Categories, Lambdas and Dynamic Logics*. Amsterdam: North Holland.

Cruse, D. A. 1986. *Lexical Semantics*. Cambridge: Cambridge University Press.

Dowty, D. 1979. *Word Meaning and Montague Grammar*. Dordrecht: Reidel.

Dunn, M. J. 1986. "Relevance logic and entailment". In D. Gabbay (ed): *Handbook of Philosophical Logic*. Dordrecht: Reidel, 117-224.

Keenan, E. L. and Faltz, L. M. 1985. *Boolean Semantics for Natural Language*. Dordrecht: Reidel.

Monk, J. D. and Bonnet, R. (ed). 1989. *Handbook of Boolean Algebra*. Vol 1. Amsterdam: North Holland.

Nepomuceno Fernández, Á. 1995. "Un estudio formal de aspectos relevantes de estructuras informativas". *Ágora* 14/2: 23-30.

Nepomuceno, Á. and Salguero, F. J. 1993. "La relación de consecuencia informativa". In C. Martín Vide (ed): *Lenguajes Naturales y Lenguajes Formales, IX*. Barcelona: PPU, 363-369.

Priest, G. and Sylvan, R. 1992. "Simplified semantics for basic relevant logics". *Journal of Philosophical Logic*. 21/2: 215-232.

Accessible Similar Worlds and French Coherent Infinitival Constructions

Lisa A. Reed

The Pennsylvania State University

Introduction

The goal of this paper is to develop a formal analysis of one type of direct and indirect causation. The terms *direct* and *indirect* causation were coined by Shibatani (Shibatani 1973; Shibatani 1976, 31–32), who used them to describe the difference in meaning associated with lexical and periphrastic causative pairs like (1a,b):

(1) a. Mary stood the child up.
    b. Mary got the child to stand up.

In particular, Shibatani proposed that lexical causatives like (1a) encode direct causation and periphrastic causative sentences like (1b), indirect causation since in the former type of causative sentence, the causee is understood to be less agentive than he or she is in the latter type of causative sentence. Thus, the difference in meaning between (1a,b) can be characterised as in (2a,b):

(2) a. *Direct causation*
    A causative sentence in which the causee is understood to be non-agentive.

b. *Indirect causation*
A causative sentence in which the causee is understood to be Agentive.

Although this was clearly not Shibatani's intent, Hyman & Zimmer (Hyman & Zimmer 1976, 193), Talmy (Talmy 1976, 106– 107), and many other authors have since extended his characterisations to cover similar, although not identical, meaning contrasts involving the various types of periphrastic causative verbs. Consider, as an illustrative example, the following pair of sentences:

(3) a. Mary made her children eat their oatmeal.

b. Mary got her children to eat their oatmeal.

As the preceding examples make clear, a verb like *make* can be said to encode direct causation and a verb like *get*, indirect causation, since in the former case the causee is clearly understood to be less Agentive than he or she is understood to be in the latter one.

It is this type of direct and indirect causation which will be the focus of the present paper. The goal will be to develop a novel, logic-based account of the distinction, one which builds naturally from earlier hypotheses by Dowty (Dowty 1972), Lewis (Lewis 1973a; Lewis 1973b), and McCawley (McCawley 1976) whose work on conditional sentences generally, and on causative sentences particularly, has already led to a relatively clear understanding of neutral causation.

The discussion will proceed as follows. It will first be shown that the direct/indirect contrast is quite systematically encoded in the French language. That is, every causative verb in this language will be shown to explicitly encode the distinction via the use of an "unexpected" Case pronoun, making this language the ideal object of study in this area. However we will see that the present definition of the contrast, which makes use of a primitive notion of Agentivity, leads to an apparent paradox. It will be argued that this paradox can be resolved by reconsidering the definitions of direct and indirect causation and by examining the interaction of these notions with the lexical semantics of the verbs in question.

The data and the apparent paradox

Let us begin with the French data given below in (4)–(6). As alluded to in the preceding paragraph, two interesting generalisations emerge from a close consideration of these sentences.

First, it is clear from these examples that French is indeed a language in which the direct/indirect contrast can be explicitly encoded with every member of the class of causative verbs, a set of verbs which has long been known to include *faire* 'to get/make,' *laisser* 'to let,' and the various perception verbs, such as *voir* 'to see,' *entendre* 'to hear,' etc.

(4) *Faire* 'make/get':

a. *Marie les faisait apprendre l'anglais.*
Marie them-ACC made to-learn the English
'Marie made/?*got them (to) learn English.'

b. *Bill Clinton lui a fait téléphoner à Bob Dole.*
Bill Clinton him-DAT has made to-call up Bob Dole
'Bill Clinton ?*made/got him (to) call up Bob Dole.'

(5) *Laisser* 'to let X do Y when one feels like it/X feels like it':

a. *Je lui laisserai téléphoner à sa mère quand ça me chante./ ??quand ça lui chante.*
I her-DAT will-let to call up her mother when it me sings/ when it her sings
'I'll let her call up her mother whenever I feel like it./ ??whenever she feels like it.'

b. *Marie les laisse conduire sa voiture quand ça leur chante./ ??quand ça lui chante.*
Marie them-ACC lets to-drive her car when it them sings/ when it her sings
'Marie lets them drive her car ??whenever she feels like it./ whenever they feel like it.'

(6) *Voir* 'to see X act of X's accord/of Y's accord':

a. *J'ai vu briller le soleil./?J'ai vu le soleil briller.*
I have seen to-shine the sun/I have seen the sun to-shine
'I saw the sun shine./?I saw the sun (choose to) shine.'

b. *Je les ai vus tuer des cailles chez le voisin ??quand ça lui chantait./quand ça leur chantait.*
I them-ACC have seen to-kill some quail at the neighbor when it him sang/when it them sang
'I would see them killing quail over at the neighbor's place ??whenever he (the neighbor) felt like it/whenever they (the embedded subject) felt like it.'

In particular, an application of the definitions of direct and indirect causation given earlier in (2) reveals that the (a) member of each of the pairs in (4)–(6) involves direct causation, and the (b) member, indirect causation. In the case of the *faire* 'to make/get' sentences such as the ones in (4), for example, the contrast can be most easily rendered into English as in (7a,b). And, similarly, the parallel contrasts involving *laisser* 'let' and the perception verbs can be rendered via the addition of adverbial clauses, as shown in (8) and (9) respectively.

(7) English equivalents of *faire*:

a. Mary *made* her children learn English.

b. Mary *got* her children to learn English.

(8) English equivalents of *laisser*:

a. Whenever Mary feels like it, she lets her children drive the family car.

b. Mary's such a wimp that she lets her children drive the family car whenever they feel like it.

(9) English equivalents of *voir*:

a. Mary saw the roots twisting under the force of the heat of the sun.

b. Mary saw the roots twisting around the throat of their helpless victim.

In sum, we have seen that a consideration of the French data reveals that the degree of Agentivity of the embedded subject can be explicitly encoded with every causative verb in this language. What the data also reveal, and this is much more important for the purposes of this paper, is that the manner in which the direct/indirect contrast is encoded in this language is both productive and systematic, although somewhat paradoxical if one compares the behavior of certain causative verbs with that of other members of the class.

Let us consider then exactly how the direct/indirect contrast is encoded in French. One very productive means by which this is achieved is via the use of an *unexpected* Case pronoun. The sentences in (10a) and (11a) contain two illustrative examples of this phenomenon; the data in (4)–(6), of course, contain others.

(10) Unexpected Accusative Case: *Faire* 'make'

a. *Marie les faisait apprendre l'anglais.*
Marie them-ACC made to-learn the English
'Marie made them learn English.'

b. *Marie faisait apprendre l'anglais à ses enfants.*
Marie made to-learn the English to her children-DAT
'Marie made/got her children (to) learn English.'
Data originally observed by Girault-Duvivier (Girault-Duvivier 1856); interpretive import first observed by Hyman & Zimmer (Hyman & Zimmer 1976)

(11) Unexpected Dative Case: *Faire* 'got'

a. *Bill Clinton lui a fait téléphoner à Bob Dole.*
Bill Clinton him-DAT has made to-call to Bob Dole
'Bill Clinton got him to call up Bob Dole.'

b. *Bill Clinton a fait téléphoner Charles Taylor à Bob Dole.*
Bill Clinton has made call Charles Taylor-ACC to Bob Dole
'Bill Clinton made/got Charles Taylor (to) call up Bob Dole.'
Data originally due to Morin (Morin 1980); interpretive import first observed by Reed (Reed 1990; Reed 1992)

As demonstrated by (10a), the Accusative Case pronoun *les* 'them-ACC' in this sentence is said to be *unexpected* because the lexical DP counterpart given in (10b) is in a Dative Case position. Similarly, the Dative pronoun *lui* 'him-DAT' in (11a) is *unexpected* since the lexical DP counterpart in (11b) is in an Accusative Case position. Thus, *unexpected* Case can be characterised as in (12):

(12) *Unexpected Case Sentences:*
Periphrastic causative sentences in which the embedded subject appears as a clitic pronoun which bears a Case feature distinct from that which the lexical DP counterpart would receive in a cohesive/incorporated structure.

The data in (4)–(6) contain *unexpected* Case examples for the various causative verbs. However, if one compares the verb *faire* 'to make/get' with the other verbs (*laisser* 'to let' and the perception verb *voir* 'to see'), one immediately notices that the class of causative verbs exhibits a split and even paradoxical behavior with respect to the manner in which a particular unexpected Case feature is used to encode either direct or indirect causation. In particular, what the data indicate, and as I have summarized below in (13a,b), is that *faire* 'to get/make' uses unexpected Accusative Case to encode direct causation and unexpected Dative Case to encode indirect causation. But the perception verbs and *laisser* 'to let' do just the opposite: clearly, the unexpected Accusative Case encodes indirect causation with these verbs, while the unexpected Dative Case examples which are attested encode direct causation.

(13) *The Paradox:*

a. Unexpected Accusative Case examples:
faire 'make' encodes direct causation (causee is [-Agentive])
laisser 'to let *X* act of *X*'s own accord' and perception verbs encode indirect causation (the causee is [+Agentive]).

b. Unexpected Dative Case examples:
faire 'get' encodes indirect causation (causee is [+Agentive])
laisser 'to let X do Y when one wishes' encodes direct causation (the causee is [-Agentive]);
perception verb examples are not attested due to the lack of a Dative Case feature in the Case grid of these verbs. (The semantic behavior of perception verbs and *laisser* 'let' in cohesive/non-cohesive structures

indicates that they are to be treated as semantic likes. See Achard (Achard 1993a; Achard 1993b).)

Why should the class of causative verbs exhibit this paradoxical behavior? Shouldn't it be the case that every member of the class of causative verbs encodes a direct or an indirect reading with the same unexpected Case feature? In the analysis to be developed below, it is suggested that, in fact, they do. In particular, I will argue that what appears to be divergent semantic behavior among the causative verbs with respect to direct and indirect causation is, in fact, due to a misunderstanding of the meaning of direct and indirect causation, coupled with a failure to take into consideration certain crucial meaning differences which distinguish the various causative verbs from one other.

Analysing the direct/indirect contrast: Necessary versus probable cause

As our point of departure, let us briefly review how neutral causative sentences have been analysed in the semantic literature. Once this has been made clear, then it will be possible to turn to a modification of this analysis to cover the direct/indirect contrast.

David Dowty (Dowty 1972) and David Lewis (Lewis 1973b) were the first to (independently) develop formal semantic analyses of neutral causation. Their analyses, which differ slightly for the technical reasons discussed at length by McCawley (McCawley 1976), are both based on David Hume's (Hume 1912) insight that causative sentences are really *hidden* modal sentences. That is, Hume has suggested that causative sentences not only express what the world actually is like, but also what it would be like if a very specific set of circumstances were different. To capture this idea formally, Dowty and Lewis have made use of the material implication. In particular, Dowty has associated neutral causative sentences like (14a) with the Logical Forms in (14b,c):

(14) a. John's smoking *caused* him to get cancer.

b. [John smoked. AND John got that cancer.]$_i$ AND [John didn't get that cancer. $N \rightarrow$ John didn't smoke.]$_{S_i}$

c. $[P \text{ AND } Q]_i \text{ AND } [\neg QN \rightarrow \neg P]_{S_i}$

The Logical Forms in (14b,c) state that if a speaker utters *John's smoking caused him to get cancer.* then that speaker is asserting two things. First, he or she is asserting that it is, in reality, true that John both smoked and he got cancer. (This is the meaning of the first conjunct in (14b,c).) Secondly, that speaker is asserting that in some set of worlds that are pretty much like this one, except for the fact that John didn't get that particular cancer, John also did not smoke. (This is the meaning of the second conjunct in (14b,c).) In sum, under this approach, one can truthfully utter *Event X causes Event Y* if X and Y occurred in the real world and if in some set of similar worlds in which Y fails to obtain, so does X. In order for the semantic system to interpret these Logical Forms, the definitions given in (15) through (18) are required. These definitions are due to Lewis (Lewis 1973a, 13– 14), who was himself inspired by earlier work by Stalnaker (Stalnaker 1968) and Stalnaker and Thomason (Stalnaker and Thomason 1970).

(15) Let \$ be an assignment to each possible world i of a set $\$_i$ of sets of possible worlds. Then \$ is called a (centered) system of spheres, and the members of $\$_i$ are called spheres around i (designated S_i), if and only if, for each world i, the following conditions hold:

a. $\$_i$ is centered on i.

b. $\$_i$ is nested.

c. $\$_i$ is closed under unions.

d. $\$_i$ is closed under (nonempty) intersections.

e.

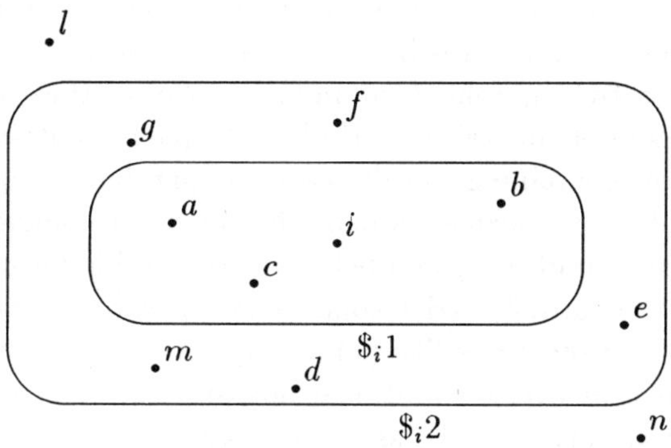

The function of the definitions in (15) is to set up a means by which we may consider what the real world would be like if certain factors were different. These alternative states of affairs are called accessible similar worlds, which are worlds that resemble ours with respect to any number of factors (often left vague), but which differ from ours with respect to other, very specific ones. The assignment function which sets up this means of comparison is symbolised by the $\$_i$ and it organises the accessible worlds in a particular way, described by each of the clauses in (15). The initial clause, (15a) ensures that the real world, symbolised i, will be the world we consider to be most similar to itself. The clause in (15b) ensures that if we have two accessible possible worlds a and e which are different from each other in the exact degree to which they are similar to the real world, then it will be possible to determine once and for all which of the two worlds, a or e, is the one most similar to i; this world will be assigned to a sphere of accessible worlds closer to the sphere containing the real world. The clauses in (c) and (d) ensure that we make a difference between worlds which are comparable to ours and worlds which are not. In particular, the clause in (c) ensures that if we have two possible worlds a and n, only one of which is to any degree comparable to the real world, then only that similar world will be assigned to an accessibility sphere around the real world i. The inaccessible world will not be in any sphere around i. The clause in (d) has a very similar effect. It ensures that if there is a world j that is a member of a number of accessibility spheres around i, and if there is also a different world n that is in no way similar to the real world i, then only j will be assigned to the appropriate spheres of worlds accessible from i. The sum total effect of these definitions will be to organise worlds similar to ours in the fashion illustrated in graphic form in (15e). We see the real world i in the center of a system of spheres of worlds: each sphere contains equally similar worlds; spheres containing worlds most comparable to ours are found closest to i. Worlds to no degree comparable to ours are outside the spheres.

The definitions given below in truth table form are also needed to interpret the variably strict conditional operator found in the Logical Form of causative sentences like (14a). In particular, Lewis (Lewis 1973a) has proposed that every conditional operator, be it of the variably or constantly strict variety, must be associated with the same standard truth table given in (16). In other words, (16), under this approach, will apply to each of the conditional sentences in (17):

(16)

P	Q	P conditional operator Q
t	t	t
t	f	f
f	t	t
f	f	t

(17) a. If she had fewer than 25 students in the course, then she definitely gave essay tests.

b. If she has fewer than 25 students in the course, then she will definitely give essay tests.

c. If she had had fewer than 25 students in the course, then she would certainly have given essay tests.

In order to differentiate between the various types of conditional sentences in (17), Lewis (Lewis 1973a, Chapter 1) has put forth the definitions given in (18), which specify exactly which worlds must be considered in evaluating the truth of a given conditional sentence.

(18) a. Strict indicative conditionals (symbolised $\rightarrow$): Worlds at which we evaluate the truth of $[P \rightarrow Q]$: the real world only.

b. Strict modal conditionals (symbolised $N[P \rightarrow Q]$): Worlds at which we evaluate the truth of $[P \rightarrow Q]$: every accessible world.

c. Variably strict (a.k.a. counterfactual) conditionals (symbolised $[PN \rightarrow Q]$): Worlds at which we evaluate the truth of $[P \rightarrow Q]$: every world in some sphere of accessible worlds.

In particular, to determine the truth of a strict indicative conditional like the one in (17a), one can only consider the real world; in evaluating the truth of a strict modal conditional like (17b), however, every accessible world must be considered. Finally, in the case of variably strict conditional or counterfactual sentences like (17c), only one sphere of accessible worlds needs to be considered.

In sum, the current logical analysis of neutral causation has associated these sentences with the Logical Form in (14c). Given this background, we can now turn to the issue of direct and indirect causation. It is important to first note that the analysis just reviewed was not formulated to account for the English contrasts given below in (19a,c), nor for their French counterparts summarized earlier in (13a,b). In particular, the current analysis of causation was intended only to apply to neutral causal relations, without making distinctions with respect to direct and indirect causes. The current analysis would therefore associate all of the sentences given below with the LF in (19d), thus failing to capture subtle semantic distinctions between them.

(19)
a. Mary *made/got* her children (to) eat their oatmeal.
b. Mary *lets* her kids drive the family car whenever she feels like it./whenever they feel like it.
c. Mary *saw* the roots twisting under the force of the sun's heat./ around the throat of their helpless victim.
d. $[P \text{ AND } Q]_i \text{ AND } [\neg QN \rightarrow \neg P]_{S_i}$

To account for these distinctions, I would like to introduce two refinements to the current theory of causation. The first will involve a complete redefinition of the notions; the second will relate to certain differences in the lexical meaning of the various causative verbs which act in conjunction with the direct and indirect contrast to give rise to the paradoxical Agentivity contrasts discussed at length in relation to the examples in (4)–(6).

Beginning with the first modification, I have mentioned that I am rejecting the idea that the direct/indirect contrast is to be defined in terms of some primitive notion of Agentivity, as has been previously assumed. I am doing so because the French data clearly show that this notion cannot be used to explain why different unexpected Case features are used to encode the same type of causation. With what then do I propose to replace this notion in order to arrive at a unified account of the phenomenon? I would like to suggest that direct causation does not correlate with a feature [-Agentive], but rather relates to a situation in which the events denoted by the matrix and embedded clauses are inevitably causally linked or causally dependent. That is, we have a situation of direct causation any time it is the case that if the embedded event fails to occur, then so too must the event denoted by the matrix clause. In other words, direct causation means that Event X is a necessary cause of Event Y. In contrast, indirect causation will refer to situations in which these two events are not inevitably linked. That is, we have a situation of indirect causation if we allow for the event denoted by the embedded clause to fail to take place, even though the event denoted by the matrix sentence did. Thus, Event X is now only a probable cause of Event Y. To put this in yet another way, direct causation involves universal quantification over a sphere of accessible worlds, whereas indirect causation is simply existential quantification over such a sphere. To formally capture this idea, I would like to suggest that direct causative sentences be associated with the LF in (20a), whereas indirect causative sentences be associated with the LF in (20b). As (20a,b) also make clear, I am assuming a unified semantic definition of the direct/indirect contrast in the French language: unexpected Accusative Case will always encode direct causation, whereas unexpected Dative Case will always encode indirect causation.

(20) a. *Direct causation:*
Universal quantification over accessible worlds
$[P \text{ AND } Q]_i \text{ AND } [\neg QN \rightarrow \neg P]_{S_i}$
(Encoded in French via unexpected Accusative Case or a non-cohesive structure, provided that the causative verb syntactically allows for both cohesive and non-cohesive options.)

b. *Indirect causation:*
Existential quantification over accessible worlds
$[P \text{ AND } Q]_i \text{ AND } [\neg Q \text{ POSS} \rightarrow \neg P]_{S_i}$
(Encoded in French via unexpected Dative Case or a cohesive structure, provided that the causative verb syntactically allows for both cohesive and non-cohesive options.)

My second modification will capture the rather curious fact that direct causation with *faire* 'to make,' correlates with a low degree of Agentivity on the part of the embedded subject, whereas in similar sentences involving *laisser* 'to let X do as X wishes' and *voir* 'to see X do as X wishes,' this individual is understood to be highly Agentive (and vice versa, of course, in the case of indirect causative sentences). This apparent paradox, I will suggest, is to be attributed to the interaction of direct and indirect causation with the contrasting lexical semantics of the various causative verbs. What I would like to suggest is this. A verb which means *make* or *get* differs from a verb meaning *let* or *see* in that when one makes someone or gets someone to do something, one is primarily responsible for that event's occurrence. However, when one lets or sees an event occur, one is not the primary cause of the embedded event's taking place. An example will make this clear. If I weren't around to make or get my kids to eat their oatmeal, well, then quite likely, they wouldn't eat it at all. But if I weren't around to let or see my kids drive the family car, that's a very different matter. Quite likely, they would go ahead and drive it anyway. To formally capture these intuitions, I would like propose that the LF of the verb *faire* 'to make/get' contains the clause in (21a), while the LF's of *laisser* 'to let' and the perception verbs contain the clause in (21b).

(21) a. Lexical semantics of causative *faire* 'to get/make':
$[Q = 0]$ at some S in $\$_i$ where $\$_i$ picks out accessible worlds in which the matrix subject does *not* exist.

b. Lexical semantics of causative *laisser* 'to let' and perception verbs:
$[Q = 1]$ at some S in $\$_i$ where $\$_i$ picks out accessible worlds in which the matrix subject does *not* exist.

As indicated above in (21), I am proposing that these intuitions can be formally captured by considering whether the event denoted by the embedded clause is true or false in some sphere of accessible worlds in which the matrix subject does not even exist. If the event denoted by the embedded sentence in a causative structure would not take place under such conditions, then the matrix subject made or got the embedded subject to act as he or she did in the real world. If, on the other hand, the event denoted by the embedded clause would have taken place anyway, without the matrix subject's influence, then, clearly, the matrix subject simply let or saw the event take place.

These are my proposals. I will conclude by demonstrating how they account for the apparent paradoxes involving Agentivity. In (22a) and (23a) below, two unexpected Accusative Case examples have been given. If the two refinements discussed in the preceding paragraphs are incorporated into the present Logical Forms of these sentences, one arrives at the complete logical translations given in (22b) and (23b) respectively:

(22) *Direct causation:* Unexpected Accusative Case with *faire* 'to make'

a. *Je l'ai fait manger sa soupe.*
I him-ACC have made to-eat his soup
'I *made* him eat his soup.'

b. $[P \text{ AND } Q]_i$ AND $[\neg QN \rightarrow \neg P]_{S_i}$
where $\$_i$ picks out accessible worlds in which the matrix subject *exists* AND $[Q = 0]_{S_i}$ where $\$_i$ picks out accessible worlds in which the matrix subject does *not* exist.

(23) *Direct causation:* Unexpected Accusative Case with *laisser* 'to let X do as X wishes' and *voir* 'to see X do as X wishes' (as well as non-cohesive examples with these verbs)

a. *Marie les a laissé/vus conduire sa voiture.*
Marie them-ACC has let/seen to-drive her car
'Marie finally relented and let them drive her car.'
'Marie *saw* them go driving off in her car.'

b. $[P \text{ AND } Q]_i$ AND $[\neg QN \rightarrow \neg P]_{S_i}$
where $\$_i$ picks out accessible worlds in which the matrix subject *exists* AND $[Q = 1]_{S_i}$ where $\$_i$ picks out accessible worlds in which the matrix subject does *not* exist.

The first conjunct of the LF's of these examples is identical. It simply requires that the events denoted by the matrix and embedded clauses in all causative sentences take place in the real world. The second conjuncts of the LF's of these sentences, which are the ones which express direct causation, are also identical. These conjuncts say that the two events denoted by the matrix and embedded clauses are inevitably linked in every world in some sphere of worlds like this one in which the matrix subject exists. The third conjuncts of these LFs differ from one another and interact with the second conjunct to give rise to the apparent paradox. First, in the case of the verb *faire* 'to get/make,' the third conjunct says that the matrix subject is the primary cause of the embedded event's taking place. Without him or her, this event would probably not have taken place at all. In contrast, the third conjunct of the verbs meaning *let* and *see* do not attribute this primary responsibility to the matrix subject. How does this account for the apparent paradox concerning the degree of Agentivity of the embedded subject? Recall that direct causation entails that the two events are causally linked in every accessible world in a sphere around the real world and that the meaning of *faire* 'to get/make' says that the matrix subject is *the* primary cause of the embedded event's taking place. Given this, we conclude that the two events are so inevitably linked because the matrix subject is extremely powerful. That is, he or she will not allow for any other possible outcome. The embedded subject, therefore, cannot act in any way but in accordance with the influence of the matrix subject; hence, the non-Agentive reading for the embedded subject in direct causative sentences involving *faire* 'to make.' On the other hand, since verbs like *laisser* 'to let' and *voir* 'to see' do not attribute primary responsibility for the embedded event's occurrence to the matrix subject, the inevitably of the two events' being causally linked will, in these sentences, be attributed to the strong influence of the embedded subject. Hence, the highly Agentive reading associated with the embedded subject in direct causative sentences with these verbs. The paradox involving indirect causative sentences will be resolved in a like manner. In particular, the indirect causative example in (24a), as well as the two in (25a) and (25b), will be associated with the LF's in (24b) and (25c) respectively:

(24) *Indirect causation:* Unexpected Dative Case with *faire* 'to get'

a. *Je lui ăi fait téléphoner à ses parents.*
I him-DAT have made to-call up his parents
'I *got* him to call up his parents.'

b. $[P \text{ AND } Q]_i$ AND $[\neg Q \text{ POSS} \rightarrow \neg P]_{S_i}$ where $\$_i$ picks out accessible worlds in which the matrix subject *exists* AND $[Q = 0]_{S_i}$ where $\$_i$ picks out accessible worlds in which the matrix subject does *not* exist.

(25) *Indirect Causation*: Unexpected Dative Case with *laisser* 'X lets Y do Z whenever X chooses to' (as well as cohesive lexical DP examples with both *laisser* and *voir* 'X sees Y acting under the influence of Z')

a. *Je lui laisserai téléphoner à sa mère quand ça me chante.*
I her-DAT will-let to call up her mother whenever it me sings
'I'll let her call up her mother whenever I feel like it.'

b. *J'ai vu briller le soleil.*
I have seen to-shine the sun
'I saw the sun shining.'

c. $[P \text{ AND } Q]_i \text{ AND } [\neg Q \text{ POSS} \rightarrow \neg P]_{S_i}$ where $\$_i$ picks out accessible worlds in which the matrix subject *exists* AND $[Q = 1]_{S_i}$ where $\$_i$ picks out accessible worlds in which the matrix subject does *not* exist.

Once again, the first conjuncts of these LF's (which are identical) must be satisfied in the real world: it must be the case that both the matrix subject did X and that the embedded subject did Y. The second conjuncts (which are also identical) express indirect causation. In contrast to direct causation, indirect causation does *not* entail that the events denoted by the matrix and embedded clauses be inevitably linked in every accessible world in a sphere around this one in which the matrix subject exists. They need only be linked in one other world like this one. In other words, the speaker has now allowed for the possibility that there is some world like this one in which one of the events occurs without the other. This second conjunct will interact with the third one (which distinguishes the verb *faire* 'to get/make' from the other causative verbs) to give rise to the apparent paradox. In the case of a verb like *faire* 'to get/make,' the third conjunct says that the matrix subject is *the* primary cause of the embedded event's taking place. Given that, we assume that the two events may fail to be linked because the matrix subject is not all that powerful. That is, he or she could have failed to get the embedded subject to act in the desired manner. Hence, the Agentive reading for the embedded subject in indirect causative sentences with this causative verb. In contrast, the third conjunct of the verbs *laisser* 'to let' and *voir* 'to see' says that the matrix subject is not *the* primary cause of the embedded event's taking place, from which we infer that the embedded subject is. Now the lack of a strong causal link between the two events will be attributed to the lack of a strong influence on the part of the embedded subject. Hence, the non-Agentive reading associated with the embedded subject in indirect causative sentences with verbs like *laisser* 'to let' and *voir* 'to see.'

To summarise, I have argued in this paper that the phenomenon of direct and indirect causation does not correlate with a primitive notion of Agentivity, as has been assumed up until now. Instead, it has been suggested that direct and indirect causation actually involves universal versus existential quantification over a sphere of accessible worlds. In particular, direct causation entails that the two events be causally linked in every accessible world in a sphere around the real world, whereas indirect causation requires this to be the case in just one of them. Under this approach, the Agentive/Non-Agentive readings previously thought to *be* direct and indirect causation are actually shown to be artifacts of the interaction of this quantification with the lexical semantics of the causative verb in question.

References

Achard, M. 1993a. *Complementation in French: A Cognitive Perspective.* Unpublished Ph.D. dissertation, University of California, San Diego.

Achard, M. 1993b. "Causative structures in French: Word order following *faire*, *laisser*, and *forcer*". In J. Guenter, B. Kaiser, C. Zoll (eds), *Proceedings of the Nineteenth Annual Meeting of the Berkeley Linguistics Society.* Berkeley: University of California, 1–12.

Dowty, D. 1972. "On the syntax and semantics of the atomic predicate CAUSE". In *Papers from the Eighth Regional Meeting, Chicago Linguistic Society.* Chicago: University of Chicago, 62–74.

Girault-Duvivier, Ch.P. 1856. *Grammaire des grammaires, ou analyse raisonnée des meilleurs traités sur la langue française.* Paris: Cotelle.

Hume, D. 1912. *An Enquiry Concerning Human Understanding and Selections from a Treatise of Human Nature* (Section VII). Chicago: Open Court Publishing Company.

Hyman, L. and Zimmer, K. 1976. "Embedded topic in French". In C. N. Li (ed), *Subject and Topic.* New York: Academic Press, 191–211.

Lewis, D. 1973a. *Counterfactuals.* Cambridge: Harvard University Press.

Lewis, D. 1973b. "Causation". *The Journal of Philosophy* LXX: 556–572.

McCawley, J. 1976. "Remarks on what can cause what". In M. Shibatani (ed), *Syntax and Semantics* (vol. 6). New York: Academic Press, 117–129.

Morin, Y.Ch. 1980. "Les bases syntaxiques des règles de projection sémantique: L'interprétation des constructions en faire". *Lingvisticae Investigationes* IV: 203–212.

Reed, L. 1990. "On clitic Case alternations in French causatives". Paper presented at the Twentieth Annual Linguistic Symposium on Romance languages. University of Ottawa, Canada. (Published as Reed 1992.)

Reed, L. 1992. "On clitic Case alternations in French causatives". In P. Hirschbühler and K. Koerner (eds), *Romance Languages and Modern Linguistic Theory*, Amsterdam and Philadelphia: Benjamins, 205–223.

Shibatani, M. 1973. *A Linguistic Study of Causative Constructions*. Unpublished Ph.D. dissertation. Berkeley: University of California. (Distributed by the Indiana University Linguistics Club, Bloomington, Indiana.)

Shibatani, M. 1976. "The grammar of causative constructions: A conspectus". In M. Shibatani (ed), *Syntax and Semantics* (vol. 6). New York: Academic Press, 1–40.

Stalnaker, R. 1968. "A theory of conditionals". In N. Rescher (ed), *Studies in Logical Theory*. (American Philosophical Quarterly Monograph 2). Oxford: Basil Blackwell, 98–112.

Stalnaker, R. and Thomason, R. 1970. "A semantic analysis of conditional logic". *Theoria* XXXVI: 23–42.

Talmy, L. 1976. "Semantic causative types". In M. Shibatani (ed), *Syntax and Semantics* (vol. 6). New York: Academic Press, 43–116.

PART III

NATURAL LANGUAGE PROCESSING

Machine Translation of Motion Verbs from English into Spanish

J. Gabriel Amores[a]
Juan Pablo Mora[b]

a) *University of Sevilla*
b) *University of Huelva*

Abstract

In this paper we propose an account of motion verbs within JULIETTA, an English to Spanish Machine Translation prototype. The system is implemented in Prolog, and follows a transfer approach to Machine Translation (MT). From a linguistic point of view, it is based on Lexical–Functional Grammar (Kaplan & Bresnan 1982), and has as one of its goals the solution of difficult problems in English to Spanish Machine Translation. One of those problems is the translation of motion verbs. In English these verbs encode the manner (or cause) of movement, whereas Spanish encodes the path in the verb. Thus, the appropriate translation of *roll out of the room* from English into Spanish would not be *rodar fuera de la habitación* but *salir de la habitación rodando.* Although verbs of this type have been studied from many perspectives, they have rarely been approached in the context of MT. JULIETTA manages to translate these sentences successfully with transfer rules based on the semantic features of the verb, thus generalizing over all verbs at once, without having to resort to particular rules for each one.

Motion events in English and Spanish

The automated translation of English and Spanish sentences with verbs of motion faces the hurdle posed by the one–to–many and many–to–one correspondences between the verbs that head them. The following sentences with the English verb *roll*, used only in its motion sense, are illustrative of the difference between the two languages:

(1) The ball rolled for two hours.
La pelota rodó durante dos horas.
(2) The ball rolled into the house.
La pelota entró en la casa (rodando).
lit. The ball entered the house (rolling).
(3) The ball rolled out of the house.
La pelota salió de la casa (rodando).
lit. The ball exited the house (rolling).
(4) The ball rolled up the hill.
La pelota subió la colina (rodando).
lit. The ball ascended the hill (rolling).
(5) The ball rolled down the hill.
La pelota bajó la colina (rodando).
lit. The ball descended the hill (rolling).
(6) The ball rolled across the bridge.
La pelota cruzó el puente (rodando).
lit. The ball crossed the bridge (rolling).
(7) The balls rolled together.
Las pelotas se juntaron (rodando).
lit. The balls came together (rolling).
(8) The balls rolled apart.
Las pelotas se separaron (rodando).
lit. The balls separated (rolling).
(9) The ball rolled around the pole.
La pelota dio vueltas alrededor del poste (rodando).
lit. The ball revolved around the pole (rolling).
(10) The ball rolled under the chair.
La pelota se metió debajo de la silla (rodando).
lit. The ball introduced itself under the chair (rolling).

(11) The ball rolled away.
La pelota se alejó (rodando).
lit. The ball went away (rolling).
(12) The ball rolled off the table.
La pelota se salió de la mesa (rodando).
lit. The ball went off the table (rolling).
(13) I rolled the ball for two hours.
Hice rodar la pelota durante dos horas.
lit. I made the ball roll for two hours.
(14) I rolled the ball into the house.
Metí la pelota dentro de la casa (rodando).
lit. I introduced the ball into the house (rolling).
(15) I rolled the ball out of the house.
Saqué la pelota de la casa (rodando).
lit. I took the ball out of the house (rolling).

Since the manner of movement in Spanish *rodando* (rolling) would usually be left out, the English verb *roll* would correspond to at least fifteen Spanish verbs. If the translation is from Spanish into English, the problem is magnified. A single Spanish verb such as *salir* could correspond to hundreds of verbs in English.[1] A few examples will suffice:

(16) *Salió del garaje en coche.*
lit. exited (3rd person) the garage by car.
He drove out of the garage.
(17) *Salió del garaje corriendo.*
lit. exited (3rd person) the garage running.
He ran out of the garage.
(18) *Salió del garaje a gatas.*
lit. exited (3rd person) crawling.
He crawled out of the garage.
(19) *El coche salió del garaje retumbando.*
lit. the car exited the garage rumbling.
The car rumbled out of the garage.

This contrast has been studied by a number of scholars(Talmy 1985; Talmy 1991; Slobin 1996; Aske 1989; Sebastian & Slobin 1994). They have come to the conclusion that the languages of the world can be classified into two groups: those which encode the path or trajectory of the movement inside the verb, and those which encode it as a satellite to the verb.[2] Spanish belongs to the first group and English to the second, as the examples above illustrate.

Spanish will tend to express in the main verb the trajectory the object has followed in the movement. This explains why the translation of *roll* in the sentences above is a path verb, when a trajectory is present in English. Spanish will have an inventory of these verbs which will usually be the head of directed motion sentences. Some of them are: *salir* (exit), *entrar* (enter), *dirigirse* (direct oneself), *cruzar* (cross), *subir* (go up), *bajar* (go down), *caer* (fall), *juntarse* (get together), *separarse* (come apart), *atravesar* (go across), *pasar* (go past/by), *avanzar* (go forward), *retroceder* (go back), *meter* (put in), *sacar* (take out), etc.

English, on the other hand, will encode in the verb the manner or the cause of the movement. The inventory of these verbs in English is quite large: *crawl, tiptoe, bus, drive, shuffle, pad, rustle, leap, jump, pull, push, shove*, are just a few examples (cf. Levin 1993:264–269). Typically, the verbs encoding cause will correspond to the transitive use of the verb, if there is one (see examples 13–15).

All this means that it will be easier to accumulate a number of paths in one clause in English, since these are expressed by non–verbal satellites. This accumulation will not be natural in Spanish. Consider the sentence:

(20) He ran down into the cellar.
(Él) bajó y entró en el sótano.
lit. (He) went down and entered the cellar.

The Spanish translation requires two clauses to keep all the information. On the other hand, the manner of movement will have to be expressed by an adverbial in Spanish, although quite often it is omitted altogether, relying on extralinguistic knowledge for its recovery. In this line, studies like (Slobin 1996) have reported that in literary translation, going from English into Spanish, the manner of movement is lost in 51% of the cases, and information about trajectory in 76%.

It should be borne in mind that these are tendencies. Thus, English has path verbs similar to the Spanish ones (ascend, descend, enter, advance, escape, exit, cross) but most of them are borrowings from Romance languages, and are not used widely, as the unnaturalness of the literal translations in 1 to 15 attest. Spanish, on the other hand, has verbs that encode the manner of movement. But as Slobin (1996) has pointed out, they will tend to appear without trajectories, and will tend to be interpreted as atelic, i.e., as activities rather than accomplishments (Vendler 1957). Thus, a sentence like *He ran downstairs into the cellar* can also have as translation *Corrió escaleras abajo hasta el sótano* (lit. (he) ran downstairs to the cellar), with two ground elements, or path descriptors, in Spanish.

However, sentences with more than one path element are uncommon in Spanish. Besides, the sentence above does not mean exactly the same as its English counterpart. The entering cannot be contradicted in English, but it can in Spanish:

(21) (a) *He ran downstairs into the cellar, but did not go in.
(b) *Corrió escaleras abajo hasta el sótano, pero no entró.*
lit. (He) ran downstairs as far as the cellar, but did not go in.

The only translation into Spanish that would keep all the information would require a coordination of two clauses, with two path verbs:

(c) *Bajó las escaleras y entró en el sótano, (corriendo).*
lit. (He) went down the stairs and entered the cellar, (running).

As usual, the manner of movement is optional, but in this case the pause is needed because otherwise the *running* would be understood as applying only to the second verb.

What seems clear is that on many occasions, especially with the prepositions IN, OUT and ACROSS, the manner of movement cannot be kept in the Spanish translation and a path verb has to be used obligatorily. Some authors, like (Aske 1989), have connected this fact with the telicity or atelicity of the situation described. Manner of movement verbs can be used in Spanish with atelic events, as in *Corrió escaleras abajo.* With telic events, a path verb has to be used: *Entró en el sótano.* Other authors, like(Talmy 1991; Slobin 1996), have introduced the notion of boundary–crossing. Thus, when a boundary is crossed, as is usually the case with INTO, OUT, and ACROSS, Spanish must use a path verb to describe the situation.

Motion constructions in English and Spanish have been related to the resultative construction. For example, Goldberg (1995:81) views resultatives as a metaphorical extension of the caused-motion construction. The following are a few examples of resultatives:

(22) He pushed the door shut.
Cerró la puerta (de un empujón).
lit. (He) closed the door (of a push).

(23) He drank himself to death.
Se mató de tanto beber.
lit. He killed himself by drinking a lot.

Slobin and Talmy consider that, as in the case of boundary crossing, resultatives exhibit a change of state. Since languages like Spanish have a restriction against expressing these changes of state as secondary predicates, they must be encoded in the main verb.

JULIETTA

This section describes JULIETTA, a Lexical-Functional Grammar--based Machine Translation prototype implemented in Prolog, and designed originally for the translation of medical abstracts from English into Spanish (Amores 1992).

JULIETTA follows a transfer approach to Machine Translation. Any transfer-based MT system contains three main modules: analysis, transfer and generation. The input sentence is analyzed by a parser, obtaining a syntactico-semantic representation which is then transferred to an equivalent representation in the target language (Spanish). The target representation is used to generate the final translation. The transfer architecture fits perfectly with the representations assigned by an LFG grammar. In LFG, every sentence is first analyzed in terms of its constituent structure (c-structure). This level contains categorial and word-order information, which is discarded by JULIETTA during analysis. A deeper, syntactic representation containing functional and grammatical information (f–structure) is then obtained after the appropriate functional equations have been solved. The f–structure is represented as a feature–value matrix, common to most unification–based approaches to grammar (Shieber 1986). Transfer takes as input a source f–structure and returns as output a target f–structure. Finally, the generation component takes an f–structure as input and returns the corresponding c–structure.

JULIETTA is currently capable of handling most structures of the English language, including coordination (CLs, VPs, NPs and PPs), relative clauses, complementation and modification (of verbs, nouns and adjectives), hyphenation patterns, resultative constructions, reflexivization, ergativity, question formation, comparative constructions, phrasal verbs, passives, etc.

Translating motion verbs with JULIETTA

As has been pointed out above, the translation of motion verbs from English into Spanish poses many challenges, even for human translators. As regards Machine Translation, the translation of motion verbs seems to contain a generalization which should be formalized in the system. However, the main challenge for an MT system is that the internal structure of sentences with motion verbs in English and Spanish is very different. Usually, MT systems apply translation rules of two types: lexical transfer rules and structural transfer rules. Lexical transfer rules trigger different translations of lexical items based on contextual information. For example, the verb **raise** translates differently into Spanish depending on the type of object:

raise + plant-object = *cultivar*
raise + animate-object = *criar*
raise + 'flag' = *izar*
raise + 'question' = *plantear*

Structural transfer rules modify the internal structure of the sentence, such as translating a passive into an active. Motion verbs pose the problem that it is the semantic features of the verb that trigger both a lexical transfer rule and a structural transfer rule at the same time. In effect, we need a rule that translates a particular construction in English into its corresponding equivalent in Spanish. This, in turn, poses the problem of identifying the limits of the construction.

An additional problem comes from the amount of information which has to be transferred from one language to the other. It has been argued above that human translators usually lose information in their translations of motion verbs, relying on background information to fill the translation gap. However, this strategy is extremely difficult and dangerous in MT since it is almost impossible to decide what information is already known by the reader and therefore could be dispensable in the translation process.

JULIETTA uses a combination of source language and contrastive information to solve the problem. Since the motion construction may appear with different patterns, the sections that follow will describe how JULIETTA handles each one, even though the strategy is similar for all cases.

Motion verbs with one prepositional object

Consider examples 2–6, 9 and 10 above. In all of them the verb of movement is followed by a prepositional object headed by a preposition which indicates the path. In the suggested Spanish translation, the preposition has been translated as a verb which expresses the trajectory described by the preposition. Thus, for every preposition in English there must be a corresponding verb. Finally, the original English verb has been translated as a manner adverbial. Let us see how JULIETTA proceeds step by step. First, the lexical entry for the verb *roll* must be coded as `vtype:motion`, admitting any of the prepositions listed in its `pobj` specification, as follows:

```
dic(v,roll,[pred:roll,ggf:[subj,pobj],vtype:motion,
            pobj:[pcase:[across,to,into,past,up,through,down,
                  along,under,off,out_of,away_from,around]],
            subj:[role:theme]]).
```

With this information, JULIETTA will obtain the following (simplified) result for a sentence like *The ball rolled into the house*:

```
>> the ball rolled into the house.

 pred:roll
 tense:past
```

```
vtype:motion
ggf:[subj,pobj]
pobj:pred:house
     spec:the
     pcase:into
subj:pred:ball
     spec:the
```

The transfer rule which performs the modifications mentioned above is shown below:

```
([P,pobj:pcase == Pcase,
    vtype == motion]) >>
    ([], ([P] => [P1|_]),true,
     (manner(P1,Manner),
       prep_verb_corresp(Pcase,Pred,OtherFeats)))
     => ([pred:Pred,manner:[form:Manner]|OtherFeats]).
```

The rule may be glossed as follows: for any predicate **P**, if it is marked as `vtype:motion`, and contains a prepositional object, then obtain its translation (`[P] => [P1|_]`) and its adverbial manner form (e.g. from *roll* we would first get *rodar* and then *rodando*). Next, the preposition head is changed into its verbal counterpart (`prep_verb_corresp(Pcase, Pred, OtherFeats)`). The resulting f structure will be headed by the new predicate **Pred** followed by the manner adjunct. The result of applying this rule will be:

```
pred:entrar
vtype:motion
tense:past
manner:form:rodando
subj:pred:pelota
     spec:el
pobj:pred:casa
     spec:el
     pcase:en
```

Which, after generation, produces:

```
La pelota entro en la casa rodando.
```

Motion verbs with one path particle only

Alternatively, we may find an adverbial particle expressing the path, with no terminal location to the movement. It is the case of examples 7, 8 and 11: *The balls rolled together.* The translation rule will change minimally, but the general strategy is the same: obtain the verbal counterpart of the particle and change the original verb into a manner adjunct:

```
([P,adj2:form == Form,
    vtype == motion]) >>
       ([adj2:_],
        ([P] => [P1|_]),
         true,
        (manner(P1,Manner),
          prep_verb_corresp(Form,Pred,OtherFeats)))
        => ([pred:Pred,adj2:[form:Manner]|OtherFeats]).
```

More than one path

As mentioned above, English permits the accumulation of paths in the motion construction. Accumulation may be achieved in two ways. First, we could add more path particles (one or two at most, according to data) before the prepositional object, as example (20) above and the following one show:

(24) He ran back down into the cellar.
Volvió, bajó y entró en el sótano, corriendo.
lit. he came back, came down and entered the cellar, running.

In this situation, the translation rule is quite complex, since a single clause must be translated as a coordination of verb phrases in Spanish, with the manner adverbial at the end. The following rule handles this problem:

```
([P,pobj:adj2:form == Form,
```

```
    pobj:pcase == Pcase,
    vtype == motion,
    tense == T,num == N, per == Per])
    >>>>
        ([pobj:POBJ],
         ([P] => [P1|_]),
        (manner(P1,Manner),
          prep_verb_corresp(Form,Pred,OtherFeats),
          lextrf(POBJ,POBJ2,POBJ),
          delfeat(adj2:_,POBJ2,POBJ3),
          prep_verb_corresp(Pcase,Pred2,_)))
        => ([pred:Pred,
             conj:[coor:y,tense:T,num:N,per:Per,
                   pred:Pred2,pobj:POBJ3,
                   adj2:[form:Manner]|OtherFeats]]).
```

Alternatively, the event may be expanded adding more than one prepositional object with the same motion verb, as for example in:

(25) The boy ran up the hill, past the flag, into the house.
El niño subió por la colina, pasó por delante de la bandera y entró en la casa, corriendo.
lit. The boy ascended the hill, passed the flag and entered the house, running.

This example is even more difficult, since in addition to translating a prepositional object as a coordination of verb phrases, the original prepositional objects must also be translated and be made dependent on each of the new predicates. The rule below handles this case.

```
([P,pobj:pcase == Pcase,
    pobj:conj:pcase == Pcase2,
    pobj:conj:conj:pcase == Pcase3,
    vtype == motion,
    tense == T, num == N, per == Per]) >>>>
        ([pobj:POBJ],
          ([P] => [P1|_]),
          (manner(P1,Manner),
```

```
          prep_verb_corresp(Pcase,Pred1,_),
          prep_verb_corresp(Pcase2,Pred2,_),
          prep_verb_corresp(Pcase3,Pred3,_),
          lextrf(POBJ,POBJ2,POBJ),
          member(conj:Conj1,POBJ2),
          member(conj:Conj2,Conj1),
          delfeat(conj:Conj1,POBJ2,POBJ3),
          delfeat(conj:Conj2,Conj1,Conj3),
          delfeat(coor:_,Conj2,Conj22),
          delfeat(coor:_,Conj3,Conj33)))
        => ([pred:Pred1,
             pobj:POBJ3,
             conj:[coor:comma,pred:Pred2,tense:T,num:N,
                   per:Per,pobj:Conj33,
                   conj:[coor:y,pred:Pred3,tense:T,num:N,
                         per:Per,pobj:Conj22,
                         adj2:[form:Manner]]]]).
```

Motion verbs with causative meaning

So far we have provided examples of intransitive uses of the motion verb. These verbs may also be found in transitive patterns, exhibiting the same type of transformation when they are translated into Spanish. The only difference lies in the verb associated with the preposition. If, for example, the predicate associated with the preposition *into* is *entrar*, in the causative meaning, it will be *meter*. Also, in addition to being marked as `vtype:motion`, the verb must be in its transitive use and marked `caus:yes`, for causative.

```
([P,pobj:pcase == Pcase,
    vtype == motion,
    caus == yes]) >>
    ([], ([P] => [P1|_]),true,
         (manner(P1,Manner),
           prep_caus_verb_corresp(Pcase,Pred,OtherFeats)))
     => ([pred:Pred,manner:[form:Manner]|OtherFeats]).
```

Finally, if none of the patterns above has been found, the system makes use of the default translation of the original verb.

Results and conclusions

Bellow there is a battery of examples translated with JULIETTA.

```
Sentence 114  the ball rolled into the house.
La pelota entro en la casa rodando.

Sentence 115  the ball rolled out of the house.
La pelota salio de la casa rodando.

Sentence 116  the ball rolled down the hill.
La pelota bajo por la colina rodando.

Sentence 117  the ball rolled across the bridge.
La pelota cruzo por el puente rodando.

Sentence 118  the balls rolled together.
Las pelotas se juntaron rodando.

Sentence 119  the balls rolled apart.
Las pelotas se separaron rodando.

Sentence 120  the ball rolled around the pole.
La pelota dio la vuelta al poste rodando.

Sentence 121  the ball rolled away.
La pelota se alejo rodando.

Sentence 122  the boy rolled the ball into the house.
El muchacho metio la pelota en la casa rodando.

Sentence 123  the boy rolled the ball out of the house.
El muchacho saco la pelota de la casa rodando.
```

```
Sentence 124  the ball rolled for two hours.
La pelota rodo durante dos horas.

Sentence 125  he ran down into the cellar.
Bajo y entro en el sotano corriendo.

Sentence 126  he ran back down into the cellar.
Volvio, bajo y entro en el sotano corriendo.

Sentence 127  the boy ran up the hill, past the flag,
              into the house
El muchacho subio por la colina, paso junto a la bandera
            y entro en la casa corriendo.
```

The results show that it is possible to formalize the contrastive difference between motion verbs in English and in Spanish. A small group of transfer rules in JULIETTA is capable of translating most patterns in which motion verbs may appear in English. Nevertheless, there are some cases in which this strategy would generate the wrong translation, as for example in *He walked into the street*, which would be translated as *??Entró en la calle (andando)*. Examples like these seem to be subject to pragmatic constraints, since one does not usually 'enter a street', as stated in the Spanish translation.

Notes

1. A casual examination of (Garrudo 1991, 1996) has shown that there are a large number of verbs that can be translated as *salir*. Levin (1993: 234–235) lists 118 verbs of sound emission. These verbs could be translated as *salir* when followed by a prepositional phrase headed by *out*.
2. Talmy (1991: 486) defines satellite as the grammatical category of any constituent other than a nominal complement that is in a sister relation to the verb root.

References

Amores, J.G. 1992. *A Lexical-Functional Grammar-Based Machine Translation System for Medical Abstracts*. Ph.D. Thesis. Universidad de Sevilla.

Aske, J.. 1989. "Path predicates in English and Spanish: a closer look," *Berkeley Linguistics Society* 15, 1–14.

Kaplan, R. and Bresnan, J. 1982. "Lexical–functional grammar: a formal system for grammatical representation". In J. Bresnan (ed), *The Mental Representation of Grammatical Relations.* Cambridge, Mass: MIT Press, 173–281.

Garrudo, F. 1991, 1996. *Diccionario Sintáctico del Verbo Inglés.* Barcelona: Ariel.

Goldberg, A.E. 1995. *Constructions: A Construction Grammar Approach to Argument Structure.* Chicago, IL: The University of Chicago Press.

Levin, B. 1993. *English Verb Classes and Alternations: A Preliminary Investigation.* Chicago, IL: The University of Chicago Press.

Talmy, L. 1985. "Lexicalization patterns: semantic structure in lexical forms". In T. Shopen. *Language Typology and Syntactic Description. Vol III: Grammatical Categories and the Lexicon.* Cambridge: Cambridge University Press.

Sebastian, E. and Slobin, D.I. 1994. "Development of linguistic forms: Spanish". In R. Berman and D. Slobin. *Relating Events in Narrative: A Crosslinguistic Developmental Study.* Hillsdale, NJ: Erlbaum, 239–284.

Shieber, S.M. 1986. *An Introduction to Unification–based Approaches to Grammar.* Stanford, CA: CSLI Lecture Notes.

Slobin, D.I. 1996. "Two ways to travel: verbs of motion in English and Spanish". In M. Shibatani & S. A. Thompson (eds), *Grammatical Constructions: Their Form and Meaning.* Oxford: Oxford University Press, 195–219.

Talmy, L. 1991. "Paths to realization: a typology of event conflation." *Berkeley Linguistic Society 17,* 480–519.

Vendler, Z. 1957. "Verbs and times". *Philosophical Review* 56,143–160.

On the Complexity of Pronominal Anaphora Resolution in Machine Translation

Ruslan Mitkov[a]
Paul Schmidt[b]

[a] *University of Wolverhampton*
[b] *IAI, Saarbrücken*

Introduction: Latest developments in anaphora resolution

After considerable and successful initial research in anaphora resolution (Wilks 1975; Hobbs 1976; Webber 1978; Sidner 1979) and after years of relative silence in the early eighties, the late eighties and early nineties saw a revival of interest with various projects reported. We could classify the most well-known works into "integrated"/"knowledge-based" approaches (integrating various traditional linguistic constraints and preferences and knowledge sources) and "alternative" (making use of non-traditional techniques and resources such as corpora, neural networks, uncertainty reasoning) approaches. Among the integrated approaches worth mentioning are D. Carter's shallow processing approach (Carter 1987), E. Rich and S. LuperFoy's distributed architecture (Rich & LuperFoy 1988), J. Carbonell and R. Brown's multi-strategy approach (Carbonell & Brown 1988), C. Rico Pérez' scalar product coordinating approach (Rico Pérez 1994), and Mitkov's combined approach (Mitkov 1994). Successful alternative approaches reported include Nasukawa's knowledge-independent approach

(Nasukawa 1994), Dagan and Itai's statistical/corpus processing approach (Dagan & Itai 1990), Connolly, Burger and Day's machine learning approach (Connolly, Burger & Day 1994), Mitkov's uncertainty-reasoning approach (Mitkov 1995), Mitkov's practical approach (Mitkov 1996b) and Kennedy and Boguraev's (1996) tagger-based approach. There is a trend towards developing corpus-based, parser-free, knowledge-independent and practical approaches (Dagan & Itai 1990; Nasukawa 1994; Mitkov 1996b; Kennedy & Boguraev 1996) which aim to overcome the notoriously difficult (and inaccurate) task of knowledge representation and processing.

In this paper we would like to address a largely neglected area of pronominal anaphora resolution: Machine Translation (MT). As the following sections of the paper will show, anaphora resolution, which is arguably among the toughest probems in Natural Language Processing, is particularly complex in MT.

The paper consists of two main parts. The first part investigates those problems which occur specifically in MT. The second part indicates "practical" solutions on a more general level, though referring to a concrete implementation in the CAT2 system (Mitkov, Choi & Sharp 1995).

Anaphora in Machine Translation

Brief survey

The establishment of the antecedents of anaphors is of crucial importance for correct translation. When translating into languages which mark the gender of pronouns, for example, it is essential to resolve the anaphoric relation. Equally, anaphora resolution is vital when translating discourse rather than isolated sentences since the anaphoric references to preceding discourse entities have to be identified.

However vigorous the latest research in anaphora resolution may have been and however challenging the applications envisaged may be (e.g., automatic identification of automatic links in corpora, see (Mitkov 1997)), there is one application area which has not benefited greatly from the new developments: Machine Translation (MT). Several works have ventured to take Machine Translation beyond the (simple) sentence by successfully resolving anaphoric links although the number of these MT-related works is just a small percentage of all reported projects on anaphora resolution. It is almost certain that the lack of attention is due to the additional complexities posed by MT. We should mention specifically Wada's implementation of the Discourse Representation Theory in an LFG-based English-to-Japanese MT program (Wada 1990), Chen's algorithms for resolving personal and reflexive pronouns in English-to-Chinese/ Chinese-to-English MT (Chen 1992), Nakaiwa's approaches for zero pronoun resolution in Japanese-to-English MT (Nakaiwa & Ikehara 1995; Nakaiwa et al. 1995; Nakaiwa et al. 1994; Nakaiwa & Ikehara 1995), Preuß, Schmitz, Hauenschild, Umbach et al.'s works on the development of an anaphora resolution module in the English-to-German MT system KIT-FAST (Hauenschild et al. 1993; Preuß et al. 1994), Saggion and Carvalho's implementation of pronoun resolution in a Portuguese-to-English MT system and Mitkov et al.'s extensions of the Korean-to-English MT system MATES and the English-to-German/German-to-English MT CAT2 (Mitkov et al. 1994; Mitkov et al. 1995) by the development of additional anaphora resolution modules.

'Discrepancies' in coreference

Is anaphora resolution optional? — the problem of carrying over ambiguities, the case of Korean

While in most European language pairs anaphora resolution is "compulsory" (otherwise in certain cases we risk rendering quite unacceptable translations), there are certain language pairs where anaphora resolution may seem "optional". As an illustration, consider the sentences (Hutchins & Somers 1992):

(1) The monkey ate the banana because it was hungry.
(2) The monkey ate the banana because it was ripe.
(3) The monkey ate the banana because it was tea-time.

In each case the pronoun "it" refers to something different: in (1) the monkey, in (2) the banana and in (3) — the abstract notion of time. If we have to translate the above sentences into German, then anaphora resolution is unavoidable, since the pronouns take the gender of their antecedents and the German words "Affe" — (masculine, "monkey"), "Banana" (feminine, "banana") and "es" (neutral — "it" for time notion) are of different genders.

Consider now the translation of sentences (1) - (3) from English to Korean and their literal descriptions in English.

(1′) pay.ko.pha.se wuen.swung.i.nun pa.na.na.lul mek.ess.ta
hungry-causal monkey-nom banana-acc eat-past, decl.

(2′) ik.e.se wuen.swung.i.nun pa.na.na.lul mek.ess.ta
ripe-causal monkey-nom banana-acc eat-past, decl.

(3′) hi.tha.im.i.e.se wuen.swung.i.nun pa.na.na.lul mek.ess.ta
tea time-causal monkey-nom banana-acc eat-past, decl.

Note that in the above Korean translations there are no pronouns. These examples might seem to suggest that in translating from English to Korean, we could bypass the tough problem of anaphora resolution. However, such a conclusion would be mistaken.

The assumption that anaphoric expressions in the source language can be easily mapped to the corresponding anaphors in the target language, or that in many cases they can simply be ignored in the transfer phase, is unfounded. It is not hard to find English sentences for which anaphora resolution is necessary in order to obtain their correct translation into Korean. Consider the sentences:

(4a) Although programmers usually write good programs, they may still make a mistake.

(4b) Although programs are usually written by good programmers, they may still contain mistakes.

In Korean, there are two types of pronouns corresponding to "they", one for human beings and the other for non-human beings. In order to assign the proper Korean pronouns to the English pronoun "they", the system should be able to resolve "they" picking out one of the two possible antecedents, "programmers" and "programs".

Anaphora resolution becomes a particularly serious business when we aim at achieving high-quality translation. The translation of (4a) and (4b) into Korean, with the successful assignment of pronouns, may still sound awkward to Koreans, because in Korean it is stylistically more natural not to mention explicitly anaphors in subordinate clauses that are coreferential with nominal expressions in the main clause. It is somewhat similar to English participle constructions whose subject is "understood." The best translation of (4b) in Korean could be described literally in English as:

(5) Being usually written by good programmers, programs may still contain mistakes.

Thus, if we are able to arrive at the translation of (4a) and (4b) without overt pronouns, the translation is better. Thus, anaphora resolution is crucial (also) in English-to-Korean MT because we must resolve the pronominal "they" in order to replace it by proper nominal expressions.

'Optional' anaphora resolution means preserving anaphoric ambiguity in case no anaphora resolution is undertaken. It may seem that carrying ambiguities over translation is even more 'authentic' from the point of view of having a mirror translation of the source text. However, not resolving anaphoric ambiguity means that during the translation process the text is not fully understood. Note that the goal of the analysis is to produce an unambiguous intermediate representation (Isabelle & Bourbeau 85).

Moreover, a system relying heavily on the 'ambiguity preservation' method (i) offers no computational advantage when ambiguity-preserving situations have to be identified dynamically, and (ii) is extremely vulnerable in situations where the lexicon is growing while the system is in use or when additional languages must be introduced (Nirenburg et al. 1992). Every new word sense added to the lexicon can potentially ruin the possibility of retaining ambiguity in translation for all previous entries. This means that extra attention must be paid to the maintenance of the lexicons.

'Discrepancies' in translating anaphors (Romance and some Far East languages)

Assuming that the coreferential links have been established, the translation of anaphors in the target language is not always a straightforward task. In the majority of language pairs (and cases), the pronouns in the source language are translated by target language pronouns which correspond to the antecedent of the anaphor. However, there are exceptions. In some languages, the pronoun is translated directly by its antecedent. In English-to-Malay translation, for instance, there is a tendency to replace 'it' with its antecedent. Replacing a pronominal anaphor with its antecedent means, however, that the translator (program) must first be able to identify the antecedent.

Very often, pronominal anaphors are simply omitted in the target language. For example, though English personal pronouns have their correspondences in Spanish, they are frequently not translated because of the typical Spanish elliptical zero-subject constructions. Other languages with typical elliptical (zero) constructions corresponding to source English pronouns are Italian, Thai, Chinese and Japanese. A recent study on the translation of English pronouns into Japanese (Uehera 1996) shows that 60% the source pronouns are translated as zero-pronouns.

Another interesting example is English-to-Korean translation. English pronouns can be omitted elliptically, translated by a definite noun phrase, by their antecedent, or by one or two possible Korean pronouns, depending on the syntactic information and semantic class of the noun to which the anaphor refers (Mitkov, Kim, Lee & Choi 1994).

Gender and number "discrepancies"

In addition to the "discrepancies" in target language anaphor selection described in section 4, an additional complexity in MT is due to gender "discrepancies" across languages, to number "discrepancies" of words denoting the same concept, to "discrepancies" in gender inheritance of possessive pronouns.

(i) There are gender discrepancies across languages. In French gender is assigned arbitrarily (although not as arbitrarily as in German), so that translation problems occur where the gender of the source does not carry over to the target language.

Je prends le livre. Il est bon.
Ich nehme das Buch. Es ist gut.

Since English has natural gender, this may create problems in translation into languages that assign gender grammatically.

I take the 9 o'clock train. It is usually late.
Ich nehme den 9 Uhr Zug. Er ist gewöhnlich zu spät.

(ii) There are also a number of discrepancies between nouns which are referred to by a singular pronoun in one of the languages and by a plural noun in the other.

Die Informationen sind falsch. Sie verursachten aber eine Panik.
The information is wrong. But it (not they) caused a panic.

The police are coming. They are just in time.
Die Polizei kommt gerade. Sie kommt gerade noch rechtzeitig.

(iii) There are problems with discrepancies of gender inheritance across languages such as those between French and German, e.g.:

Jacques a détruit sa voiture.
Jacques hat sein (not: ihr) Auto zerstört.

General problems

There are three general problems concerning anaphora in MT:

a. There is first and foremost the problem of analysis. The fundamental prerequisite for any treatment of anaphora in MT is the determination of the coreference relation in analysis. To determine coreference relations, one must turn to one of the strategies (or a combination of them) mentioned in the introductory section of this paper. They offer a range of syntactic, semantic, pragmatic, world-knowledge-based, discourse based factors; wherever rule-based approaches cannot be used, heuristic or statistics-based methods are to be applied.
There are three general problems concerning anaphora in MT: Whatever the approach, the result has to be the complete detection of coreference relations: this is the prerequisite to resolving all the translation problems mentioned above, for all of the languages to which we have referred.

b. Secondly, there is a problem of generation. As described above, for Malay and Korean, coreference need not necessarily be expressed by anaphor-antecedent relations, but may be expressed by other language-specific means (e.g., rementioning the antecedent). The input for generation must be the coreference relation; the generation module then has to produce a cohesively linked text in the target language. This may result in an antecedent and an anaphor, but it may also result in completely different expressions as shown by the examples in section *'Discrepancies' in coreference.*

c. Thirdly, there is a problem related to the treatment of referring expressions in transfer. It comes down to what exactly should be transferred. Is it to be a detailedly specified linguistic object? Is it just an index, i.e. a coreference relation between antecedent and anaphor? Is it some other kind of abstract representation?

Given the problems in various languages highlighted above, there is only one real option, namely some abstract representation of the coreference relation.

In effect, this means that anaphors are not translated, but reconstructed on the basis of coreference relations established in the source language and transferred to the target.

A workable example

Constraints and preferences applied

Our approach to anaphora resolution for MT is based on a combination of syntactic and semantic constraints and preferences. Constraints serve as filters to rule out unacceptable candidates, whereas preferences propose the most likely antecedent from a set of acceptable candidates.

A. Syntax constraints

Various syntactic constraints for the elimination of otherwise acceptable antecedents in resolution are used. The most obvious constraint is the almost obligatory agreement of the pronoun and its antecedent in number, person and gender.

(a) A pronoun can refer to an NP only if they agree in number, person and gender.

Example (we have used identical indexes to denote coreference; different indexes mean the NPs cannot be coreferential):

Mary$_i$ told John$_j$ and her friends$_k$ that she$_i$ was in love.

Apart from these constraints, we have used the c-command constraints as formulated in (Ingria & Stallard 1989).

(b) A non-pronominal NP cannot overlap in reference with any NP that c-commands it.

He$_i$ told them about John$_j$.

(c) The antecedent of a bound anaphor must c-command it.

John$_i$ likes pictures of himself$_i$.

(d) A personal pronoun cannot overlap in reference with an NP that c-commands it.

John$_i$ told Bill$_j$ about him$_k$.

B. Syntactic preferences

(a) Syntactic parallelism preference

Preference is given to antecedents with the same syntactic role as the pronoun.

The programmer$_i$ successfully combined Prolog$_j$ with C, but he$_i$ had combined it$_j$ with Pascal last time.

The programmer$_i$ successfully combined Prolog with C$_j$, but he$_i$ had combined Pascal with it$_j$ last time.

(b) Topicalisation preference

Topicalised structures are first searched for possible anaphoric referents.

It was Asia$_i$ who told Zahara to go to Kuala Lumpur. Why did she$_i$ do it?

Topicalisation is a preference, rather than a constraint. Consider the sentence "It was Zahara who told Mano to go to Kuala Lumpur. Why did he do it?" [he=Mano]. The same syntactic and semantic structures yield "Mano" as the referent for "he", because the local constraints so dictate, regardless of who is topicalised.

C. Semantic constraints and preferences

(a) Verb case role constraints

Case-role semantics impose constraints on what can fill them.

If filled by the anaphor, the verb case role constraints must be satisfied also by the referent of the anaphor.

> Vincent removed the diskette from the computer$_i$ and then disconnected it$_i$.
>
> Vincent removed the diskette$_i$ from the computer and then copied it$_i$.

(b) Semantic networks constraints (semantic consistency)

Semantic networks indicate the possible links between concepts as well as concepts and their attributes.

> Do not run the program$_i$ on this computer because it$_i$ is encoded.
>
> Do not run the program on this computer$_i$ because it$_i$ is broken.

(c) Semantic parallelism preference

Those antecedents are favoured which have the same semantic role as the pronoun.

> Vincent gave the diskette to Sody$_i$. Kim also gave him$_i$ a letter.
> Vincent$_i$ gave the diskette to Sody. He$_i$ also gave Kim a letter.

Implementation in CAT2

A strategy similar to the one described above can be seen in the anaphora resolution demo module of the unification-based MT system CAT2 (Mitkov, Choi & Sharp 1995). CAT2 was developed at IAI, Saarbrücken, as a sideline implementation to the Eurotra Project. The translation strategy is based on tree-to-tree transduction, where an initial syntactico-semantic tree is parsed, then transduced to an abstract representation ("interface structure"), designed for simple transfer to a target language interface structure. This is then transduced to a syntactico-semantic tree in the target language, whose yield provides the actual translated text.

The current version of the anaphora resolution model implemented in CAT2 is based exclusively on syntactic and semantic constraints and preferences. Syntax constraints include the almost universal agreement of the pronoun and its antecedent in number, person and gender as well as c-command constraints as formulated in (Ingria & Stallard 1989). Syntactic preferences used are syntactic parallelism and topicalisation. Syntactic parallelism gives preference to antecedents with the same syntactic role as the pronoun, whereas topicalised structures are searched first for possible anaphoric referents.

Semantic constraints and preferences include verb case role constraints, semantic network constraints (semantic consistency) and semantic parallelism preference. Verb case role constraints stipulate that if they are filled by the anaphor, they must also be satisfied by the antecedent of the anaphor. Semantic networks indicate the possible links between concepts as well as concepts and their attributes; semantic parallelism preference favours antecedents which have the same semantic role as the pronoun.

The project concentrates primarily on intersentential anaphora resolution, but since CAT2, like most other MT systems, operates only on single sentences, we simulate the intersententiality by conjoining sentences, as in:

The decision was adopted by the council; it published it.

The task is to resolve the pronominal references in the second 'sentence' with the antecedents in the first. The implementation, which successfully handles pronominal resolution in the context of English-to-German translation, can be carried over to multiple-sentence input.

The noun phrase features relevant for anaphora resolution are collected in the complex feature "anaph", consisting of two additional features, "ref" (referential features) and "type". The referential features include the noun's agreement features (person, number, gender), lexical semantic features (e.g., animacy), and its referential index; the type feature indicates whether the noun is a pronoun or not:

anaph={ref={agr=A,sem=S, index=I},type=T}

All non-pronominal nouns receive a unique index by a special index generator within CAT2; each pronoun takes its index value by way of unification with its antecedent, as outlined below.

Anaphora resolution in CAT2 has two main steps. First, all "anaph" features within a sentence are collected in a "cand" (candidates) feature and percolated to the S node, so that anaphora resolution between sentences can take place locally under the topmost node (intrasentential anaphora resolution will already have occurred). Then, for each pronoun in the second sentence, its "ref" feature is resolved with those of the antecedents in the first sentence. Backtracking provides for all combinations, under the condition that the "ref" features agree, i.e. unify.

Correct pronoun resolution is shown in the translations by CAT2 of the sentences "The council adopted the decisions; the commission published them" (Der Rat verabschiedete die Beschlüsse; die Kommission veröffen--tlichte sie.), "The council adopted the law; it published it." (Der Rat verabschiedete das Gesetz; er veröffentlichte es.), "The commission published the law; it was adopted by the council." (Die Kommission veröffentlichte das Gesetz; es wurde von dem Rat verabschiedet.) and the sentence "The decision was adopted by the council; it published it." (Der Beschluss wurde von dem Rat verabschiedet; er veröffentlichte ihn.)

Improvement of the model

Although the syntactic and semantic criteria for the selection of an antecedent are very strong, they are not always sufficient to distinguish among a set of possible candidates. In case of antecedent ambiguity it is the most salient element among the candidates for antecedent which is usually the top runner. This most salient element is referred to in computational linguistics as focus, e.g., (Sidner 1979) or center e.g., (Grosz, Joshi & Weinstein 1983) though terminology is much more diverse (Hirst 1981; Mitkov 1995a).

It is now clear that very often when two or more candidates "compete" for the antecedent, the task of resolving the anaphor is shifted to the task of tracking down the center/focus of the sentence (clause).

To further improve our model for anaphora resolution, we envisage the integration of a center tracking engine. Based on empirical studies from the sublanguage of computer science, we have developed a statistical approach to determine the probability of a noun phrase being the center of a sentence. Unlike the approaches reported so far, our method is able to propose the center with high probability in every discourse sentence, including the first one. The approach uses an inference engine based on Bayes' formula which draws an inference in the light of some new piece of evidence. This formula calculates the new probability, given the old probability plus some new piece of evidence (Mitkov 1994b).

In addition, we envisage the implementation of heuristic and domain modules, which, together with a referential expression filter, are expected to improve the performance of anaphora resolution in the CAT2 Machine Translation system.

References

Carbonell, J. and R. Brown. 1988. "Anaphora Resolution: A Multi-Strategy Approach". *Proceedings of the 12th International Conference on Computational Linguistics (COLING-88)*, Budapest, Hungary.

Carter, D.M. 1987. *Interpreting Anaphora in Natural Language Texts.* Chichester: Ellis Horwood.

Chen, H.H. 1992. "The Transfer of Anaphors in Translation". *Literary and Linguistic Computing* 7:4.

Connoly, D., Burger, J. and Day, D. 1994. "A Machine Learning Approach to Anaphoric Reference". *Proceedings of the International Conference on "New Methods in Language Processing"*, UMIST, Manchester, 14-16 September 1994.

Dagan, I. and Itai, A. 1990. "Automatic Processing of Large Corpora for the Resolution of Anaphora References". *Proceedings of the 13th Interna-*

tional Conference on Computational Linguistics (COLING-90), Helsinki, Finland.

Halliday, M. and Hasan, R. 1976. *Cohesion in English (Longman English Language Series 9)*. London: Longman.

Hirst, G. 1981. *Anaphora in Natural Language Understanding*. Berlin: Springer Verlag.

Hobbs, J. 1978. "Resolving Pronoun References". *Lingua* 44.

Hutchins, J. and Somers, H. 1992. *An Introduction to Machine Translation*. London: Academic Press.

Ingria, R. and Stallard, D. 1989. "A Computational Mechanism for Pronominal Reference". *Proceedings of the 27th Annual Meeting of the Association for Computational Linguistics (ACL'89)*. Vancouver, British Columbia.

Isabelle, P. and Bourbeau, L. 1985. "TAUM-AVIATION: Its Technical Features and Some Experimental Results", *Computational Linguistics* 11.

Kennedy, C. and Boguraev, B. 1996. "Anaphora for Everyone: Pronominal Anaphora Resolution without a Parser". *Proceedings of the 16th International Conference on Computational Linguistics (COLING-96)*. Copenhagen, Denmark.

Mitkov, R. 1994. "An Integrated Model for Anaphora Resolution". *Proceedings of the 15th International Conference on Computational Linguistics (COLING-94)*, Kyoto, Japan.

Mitkov, R. 1995. "An Uncertainty Reasoning Approach to Anaphora Resolution". *Proceedings of the Natural Language Pacific Rim Symposium*. Seoul, Korea.

Mitkov, R. 1996a. "Anaphora Resolution in Natural Language Processing and Machine Translation". *Proceedings of the International Colloquium on Discourse Anaphora and Anaphora Resolution*. Lancaster, (keynote speech).

Mitkov, R. 1996b. "Pronoun Resolution: The Practical Alternative". *Proceedings of the International Colloquium on Discourse Anaphora and Anaphora Resolution*, 17-19 July 1996. Lancaster, UK.

Mitkov, R. 1997. "Towards Automatic Identification of Anaphoric Links in Corpora". (forthcoming)

Mitkov, R., Choi, S.K. and Sharp, R. 1995. "Anaphora Resolution in Machine Translation". *Proceedings of the Sixth International Conference on Theoretical and Methodological Issues in Machine Translation*, 5-7 July 1995. Leuven, Belgium.

Mitkov, R., Kim, H.K., Lee, H.K. and Choi, K.S. 1994. "The Lexical Transfer of Pronominal Anaphors in Machine Translation: The English-to-Korean Case". *Proceedings of the SEPLN'94 conference*, 20-22 July 1994. Cordoba, Spain.

Nakaiwa, H. and Ikehara, S. 1992. "Zero Pronoun Resolution in a Japanese-to-English Machine Translation System by Using Verbal Semantic Attributes". *Proceedings of the 3rd Conference on Applied Natural Language Processing (ANLP'92)*, Trento, Italy.

Nakaiwa, H., Yokoo, A. and Ikehara, S. 1994. "A System of Verbal Semantic Attributes Focused on the Syntactic Correspondence between Japanese and English". *Proceedings of the 15th International Conference on Computational Linguistics (COLING-94)*. Kyoto, Japan.

Nakaiwa, H. and Ikehara, S. 1995. "Intrasentential Resolution of Japanese Zero Pronouns in a Machine Translation System Using Semantic and Pragmatic Constraints". *Proceeedings of the International Conference on Theoretical and Methodological Issues in Machine Translation (TMI'95)*. Leuven, Belgium.

Nakaiwa, H., Shirai, S., Ikehara, S. and Kawaoka, T. 1995. "Extrasentential Resolution of Japanese Zero Pronouns Using Semantic and Pragmatic Constraints". *Proceedings of the AAAI 1995 Spring Symposium Series: Empirical methods in discourse interpretation and generation.*

Nasukawa, T. 1994. "Robust Method of Pronoun Resolution Using Full-Text Information". *Proceedings of the 15th International Conference on Computational Linguistics (COLING-94)*, 5-9 August 1994. Kyoto, Japan.

Nirenburg S., Carbonell, J., Tomita, M. and Goodman, K. 1992. *Machine Translation: A Knowledge-Based Approach*, Morgan Kaufmann Publishers.

Preuß S., Schmitz, B., Hauenschild, C. and Umbach, C. 1994. "Anaphora Resolution in Machine Translation". *Studies in Machine Translation and Natural Language Processing*, Volume 6 "Text and Content in Machine Translation: Aspects of Discourse Representation and Discourse Processing" ed.

by W. Ramm, Office for Official Publications of the European Community, Luxembourg.

Rich, E. and LuperFoy, S. 1988. "An Architecture for Anaphora Resolution". *Proceedings of the Second Conference on Applied Natural Language Processing*, 9-12 February 1988, Austin, Texas.

Rico Pérez, C. 1994. "Resolución de la Anáfora Discursiva Mediante una Estrategia de Inspiración Vectorial". *Proceedings of the SEPLN'94 conference*, 20-22 July 1994. Cordoba, Spain.

Saggion, H. and Carvalho, Ar. 1994. "Anaphora Resolution in a Machine Translation System". *Proceedings of the International Conference "Machine translation, 10 years on"*, 12-14 November, 1994. Cranfield, UK.

Schmidt, P. 1993. "Pronominal Anaphora in Multilingual MT". Unpublished draft, IAI, Saarbrücken.

Sidner, C. L. 1979. "Towards a Computational Theory of Definite Anaphora Comprehension in English Discourse", Technical Report No. 537. M.I.T. Artificial Intelligence Laboratory.

Uehara, S. 1996. "Anaphoric Pronouns in English and Their Conterparts in Japanese". *Proceedings of the International Colloquium on Discourse Anaphora and Anaphora Resolution*, 17-19 July 1996. Lancaster, UK.

Wada, H. 1990. "Discourse Processing in MT: Problems in Pronominal Translation". *Proceedings of the 13th International Conference on Computational Linguistics (COLING-90)*, Helsinki.

Webber, B.L. 1978. *A Formal Approach to Discourse Anaphora*, Garland.

Weisweber, W. 1994. "The Experimental MT System of the Project KIT-FAST—Complementary Research for Eurotra-D". *Proceedings of the International Conference "Machine translation, 10 years on"*, 12-14 November, 1994. Cranfield, UK.

Wilks, Y.A. 1975. "Preference Semantics". *The Formal Semantics of Natural Language* ed. by E. Keenan. Cambridge: Cambridge University Press.

An Interval Algebra for Temporal Relations Conveyed by a Text

Irene Pimenta Rodrigues[a]
Gabriel Pereira Lopes[b1]

[a)] *Universidade de Évora*
[b)] *Universidade Nova de Lisboa*

Abstract

In this paper we present and justify the use of an Interval Algebra (AI5) that reveals the temporal relations (between eventualities) conveyed by a text. Making these relations explicit is the task of the pragmatic interpretation of the text's temporal entities. The set of qualitative temporal relations, abducted during the pragmatic interpretation process, allows us to represent and propagate the temporal constraints between the text's eventualities. It enables us to model state persistence in the knowledge base with the text facts. The algebra presented is also suitable for implementing two modes (*ask* and *tell*) of satisfying the temporal constraints.

[1]Research supported by JNICT.

Introduction

It is our goal to process texts in order to extract the information conveyed by the sentences of these texts. In order to obtain the meaning of a text sentence, we must relate the entities of each sentence to those introduced by the previous sentences, and by so doing solve discourse phenomena such as: definite nominal anaphora, pronominal anaphora, verbal and nominal ellipsis, sentence tense and aspect interpretation, etc. The process that enables a computer to relate the entities of each text sentence to those introduced by previous text sentences is referred to in the literature as *pragmatic interpretation of discourse entities* (Pereira and Pollack 1991; Grosz and Sidner 1986; Hobbs, Stickel, Appelt, and Martin 1990). This process takes into account world knowledge, the situation described by the text already processed and the salience of the entities introduced by the sentences in the discourse (Webber 1988; Grosz and Sidner 1986). The pragmatic interpretation of sentence tense and aspect requires a discourse structure (Webber 1988; Hobbs, Stickel, Appelt, and Martin 1990; Rodrigues and Lopes 1992a), a knowledge base with general knowledge about events, states and time intervals, and the representation of the events and states already described by the text (Lascarides, Asher, and Oberlander 1992; Rodrigues and Lopes 1993a; Kamp and Reyle 1993). One of the results of the pragmatic interpretation of tense and aspect of a sentence is the temporal anchoring of that sentence's main eventuality. A temporal anchoring of an eventuality is a temporal relation between the eventuality's time interval and the time interval(s) of eventuality(ies) of previous text sentences (Webber 1988; Moens and Steedman 1988; Kameyama, Passonneau, and Poesio 1993).

In this paper we present and justify an Interval Algebra (AI5) that can represent the temporal relations (between text eventualities) conveyed by a text as a consequence of the pragmatic interpretation of that text's temporal entities. This Algebra is a subset of Allen's Algebra (Allen 1984). It has 37 relations that are closed under the intersection, composition and inversion operations. In the next section we present the set of five qualitative temporal relations that we need in order to represent the interpretation of sentence tense and aspect. We then present the other (31) qualitative relations that we need to consider in order to be able to propagate the constraints built with the initial set of five relations. Finally, we discuss some of the advantages of having this small set of relations, for instance the possibility of obtaining a model for the knowledge base containing the text facts that model state persistence.

The pragmatic interpretation of sentence tense and aspect

The pragmatic interpretation of a text sentence in the context provided by the interpretation of the previous sentences, namely temporal anaphora resolution, requires a set of previously introduced referents which can be used as anaphoric referents (Kamp and Reyle 1993; Lascarides, Asher, and Oberlander 1992; Rodrigues and Lopes 1993a). In order to obtain the set of possible referents for the pragmatic interpretation of each text sentence's tense and aspect, we must build a discourse structure: the text temporal structure that we have presented in our earlier work (Rodrigues and Lopes 1993b). This structure provides the visible entities (the most salient ones) for the pragmatic interpretation process.

Relation	Inv.	Meaning	Point relation (extremes)	equivalent in Allen Algebra
a < b	>	$a\rceil \quad \lceil b$	$t_{a_f} < t_{b_i}$	a **b** b
a ⊂ b	⊃	$\lceil b \quad \lceil a \quad a\rceil \quad b\rceil$	$t_{b_i} \leq t_{a_i}$, $t_{a_f} \leq t_{b_f}$	a **d s f eq** b
a ∝ b	$\dot{\propto}$	$\lceil x \quad \lceil y \quad \rceil x \quad y\rceil$ $(x = a \wedge y = b) \vee (x = b \wedge y = a)$	$t_{a_i} \leq t_{b_f}$, $t_{b_i} \leq t_{a_f}$	a **o oi eq m mi d di s si f fi** b

Table 1: The initial set of five qualitative relations

This structure is made up of discourse segments that reflect how the eventualities introduced by new sentences relate temporally to salient (visible) eventualities of the temporal discourse structure. Each text segment has features for *kind*, *time*, *eventuality* and *subsegments*. According to the kind of segment, its subsegments must obey some temporal constraints, and the features *time* and *eventuality* are computed bottom-up from the features of its subsegments. Every sentence is represented by a segment, and to be pragmatically interpreted it has to be inserted into the text's temporal structure. Since the segmentation is based on the temporal properties of the segments, there are some temporal relations that must be inferred in order to be able to insert a new segment into the text's temporal structure.

These five relations are $\{<, >\supset, \subset, \propto\}$ (see table 1), and give rise to five different discourse segment types that impose different temporal relations between their subsegments.

As far as the pragmatic interpretation process is concerned, we use the proposal of (Hobbs, Stickel, Appelt, and Martin 1990) and view pragmatic interpretation as abduction. This means that the interpretation of a text is the minimal explanation of why the text would be true. So, the interpretation of sentence tense and aspect is the explanation of why the main sentence eventuality would be true in the context of the previously acquired temporal facts. As a sentence eventuality is always a *state* or an *event*, the explanation of the eventuality is always a set of assumptions that will allow the eventuality to be *predictedn* or *explained* from its interpretation context. In (Rodrigues and Lopes 1993b) a sentence interpretation process is driven by the attempt to justify the sentence's main eventuality. So the tense interpretation theory, given an intermediate sentence semantic representation, gives rise to a set of abducted predicates that explain the sentence from knowledge acquired with the previously interpreted text sentences. However, the sentence tense is interpreted in the sentence context, i.e. only the information contained in visible segments of the text's temporal structure is taken into account. Some of the solutions to tense interpretation may contradict with the information conveyed by previous text sentences that are no longer in visible segments. To eliminate these solutions we have to check the consistency of the knowledge base with the information conveyed by the previous sentences updated with the new sentence representation. To perform this consistency checking operation on the knowledge base we shall implement the knowledge base in a logic programming framework, a contradiction removal system (Pereira, Damásio, and Alferes 1993). This implementation also allows us to check whether an expression is a logical consequence of the knowledge base. This operation is important during the pragmatic interpretation of sentence tense, namely for testing the preconditions for the abduction of a contingency relation (cause, consequence, etc) between two eventualities.

The basic temporal entities of the language we use are *events*, *states* and *time intervals*; predicates are used to explicitly represent contingency relations (Moens and Steedman 1988) between eventualities (events or states). With this language we are able to handle state persistence, and the prediction of events and states during the process of temporal anaphora resolution.

These two forms of temporal reasoning (persistence and prediction) are well documented in the literature related to temporal reasoning. However they are not sufficiently dealt with in important works on tense interpretation and temporal anaphora resolution (Webber 1988; Lascarides, Asher, and Oberlander 1992).

The temporal structure

Our approach takes into account linguistic knowledge and world knowledge to determine the temporal relation between the new sentence eventuality and a temporal focus. In order to obtain the *temporal focus* we build up a discourse structure (tree structure) from constructors called *segments.* This structure supplies the possible temporal focus for the tense interpretation of each new sentence. A segment has the following features: segment referent: s_i; sort: $sort_i \in \{\mathbf{none}, \mathbf{bef}, \mathbf{aft}, \mathbf{cont}, \mathbf{icont}, \mathbf{over}, \mathbf{basic}\}$; tense: a verb tense; time: t_i; eventuality: e_i; temporal predicate: occurs(e_i, t_i) or holds(e_i, t_i); logic form: the sentence logic form; and subsegments: an ordered list of segment referents (possibly empty).

A segment in a subsegment list must verify the restrictions imposed by its parent sort (Rodrigues and Lopes 1992a): given segment s, consider subsegments$(s) = \{s_1, s_2, \ldots, s_n\}$, let $t_{s_k} \equiv$ time(s_k), the meaning of sort(s)[2] is: **bef**– $\forall i < k, t_{s_i} < t_{s_k}$; **aft**– $t_{s_1} > t_{s_2}$; **cont**– $t_{s_1} \subset t_{s_2}$; **icont**– $t_{s_1} \supset t_{s_2}$; **over**– $\forall i, k\ t_{s_i} \propto t_{s_k}$ (the intersection of t_{s_i} and t_{s_k} is non empty); **none**– $\forall t_{s_j}, t_{s_k}$ there is no temporal relation that they must obey; **basic**– $n = 0$ i.e. subsegments$(s)=\emptyset$.

The features of a nonbasic segment are inherited from its subsegment features. A segment of sort **none, bef** or **over** inherits: tense (last subsegment tense), time referent (the composition of all its subsegment times), eventuality referent(the composition of all its subsegment eventualities). A segment of sort **aft**, **cont** or **icont** (having only 2 subsegments) inherits *the tense, the time referent, the eventuality referent, the temporal predicate* from its first subsegment.

The discourse structure that we obtain is used to provide a *temporal focus* for the interpretation of a sentence. In this structure the possible temporal foci are the eventualities in visible segments. Whenever a new

[2]Segments of sort *aft, cont* and *icont* have only 2 subsegments.

segment is attached to the text temporal structure, there is a set of temporal constraints that the new segment eventuality must obey because of the segments' sort definition. These temporal constraints are satisfied if they are backed by world knowledge or if the current set of temporal constraints implies them.

Visibility (of a segment): the text segment (ie. the root of the structure) is *visible*. The last subsegment of a visible segment is *visible*. *Properties of visible segments*: a new sentence's segment may only be attached to a visible segment. The eventualities and time referents of visible segments are the possible *temporal foci* or *temporal referents* for a new sentence tense and aspect interpretation.

Consider the text: *Mary pushed John (1). John fell (2).*

The first sentence will be represented by the segment of sort *basic* s_1. The second sentence will be represented by the segment of sort *basic* s_2. In order to interpret the second text sentence, its segment must be inserted in the text temporal structure. The text structure for the interpretation of this sentence is the segment s_1. The result of the interpretation of this sentence tense should be that $t_1 < t_2$ because of the use of the simple past in both sentences and because there is no contingency relation between the two eventualities that predict other temporal relation. So, the segment that groups the two sentences should be of sort *bef* s_{1_1}:

s_{1_1}	bef	simple past
$t_1 \cup t_2$	$e_1 \cup e_2$	occurs($e_1 \cup e_2, t_1 \cup t_2$)

s_1	basic	simple past
t_1	e_1	occurs(e_1, t_1)
evt(e_1, push(Mary,John)).		

s_2	basic	simple past
t_2	e_2	occurs(e_2, t_2)
evt(e_2, fall(John)), $t_1 < t_2$		

Representing text temporal facts

The temporal ontology of the knowledge base containing text facts should be as close to natural language temporal concepts as possible, in order to facilitate the temporal reasoning necessary for the pragmatic interpretation of the temporal entities. States and events introduced by natural language expressions are represented by discourse entities to simplify the process of anaphora resolution. States and events are always associated with a temporal preposition (the event or state type) and with a time interval. In order to eliminate the proliferation of lemmas about states and events, the time interval associated with these entities is always a maximal interval, i.e. the maximal interval where the event occurs or the maximal interval where the state holds. In the knowledge base language, we consider the following temporal entities: *events*, *states* and *time intervals*. *Time intervals.* The temporal relations considered between time intervals are $\{<, >, \subset, \supset, \propto\}$[3]. *Events.* An event E_1 is associated with its occurrence time T_1 by the predicate *occurs*(E_1,T_1). An event E_1 is associated with a temporal proposition R (the event type) by the predicate *evt*(E_1,R). *States.* A state S_1 is related to the time T_1 where it is holding by the predicate *holds*(S_1,T_1). A state S_1 is associated with a temporal proposition (the *state* type) by the predicate *evt*(S_1,R). In natural language, an eventuality should be represented as an event or a state depending on the verbal aspect and the temporal modifiers. For instance, sentence 1 gives rise to an eventuality that should be represented as a state.

(1) The plane was landing at Faro airport.

While sentence 2 should be represented as an event.

(2) The plane landed at Faro airport.

Pragmatic interpretation of sentence tense and aspect requires the consideration of possible relations between eventualities conveyed by that sentence and those previously introduced by the text (e.g. cause, sub-action and consequence). Texts 3 to 5 have the same syntactic form (sentence tenses are simple past) but they may have different interpretations:

(3) Mary fell. John pushed her.

(4) Mary fell. John helped her.

(5) John cooked a salmon. He cut it in small pieces.

Text 3 can have the following two interpretations: "John pushing" happens before "Mary's fall" only if we assume that "pushing" caused the "fall" (Webber 1988; Lascarides, Asher, and Oberlander 1992); and "John pushing" happens after "Mary's fall" (Kamp and Reyle 1993; Webber 1988; Lascarides, Asher, and Oberlander 1992). Text 4 is interpreted as: "John helping" happens after "Mary's fall". Text 5 can be interpreted as: "John cutting" happens during "John cooking" only if we assume that "John cooked the salmon by cutting it in small pieces", i.e "John cutting" is a sub-action or is in the preparatory phase of "John cooking" (Moens and Steedman 1988; Webber 1988); and "John cutting" happens after "John

[3] $t_i \propto t_j$ means that the intersection of the two time intervals is nonempty.

cooking". So, to take into account the possible relations between the eventualities, we assume that generally an event, e, has the following structure:

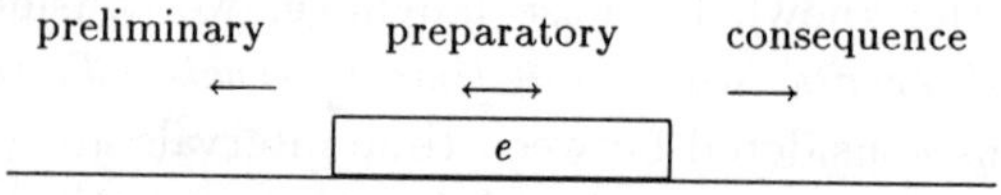

Due to the qualification problem (Shoham 1988), in general, knowledge about events and state types is defeasible. We represent the event/state structure by explicit predicates such as: cause(e_j,e_i) to represent that event e_i has event e_j in its preliminary phase; prep(e_j,e_i) to represent that event e_i has event e_j in its preparatory phase; and consq(e_j,e_i) to represent that event e_j has state e_i as a consequence.

The AI5 algebra

Temporal constraints (Vilain and Kautz 1986) (obtained by the pragmatic interpretation of temporal entities) need to be propagated through all the time intervals associated with temporal entities in order to check whether they are temporally consistent. In order to be able to propagate the constraints we need to have the set of temporal relations closed under composition, intersection and inversion of relations. The initial set of five relations is not closed under composition and intersection of relations. In order to propagate the constraints imposed by the initial set of five relations we have to consider 31 relations in addition to the 5 basic temporal relations. In this paper we show how to obtain these 31 relations in order to have an algebra. Almeida (1987), van Eynde (1990) and Song (1991) claim that there are other sets of temporal relations that are subsets of Allen's Algebra. Allen's Interval Algebra (Allen 1984) is built with the disjunction of the 13 possible relations between two time intervals, so Allen's Algebra considers 2^{13} qualitative relations. The main disadvantage of this algebra is that there are no polynomial-time algorithms to check whether a given set of constraints is consistent. Another problem is that in order to understand natural language we don't need to consider all the possible relations between two time intervals (van Eynde 1990; Song 1991) because most of the temporal relations cannot be expressed by natural language expressions. So the algebra AI5 is built by starting with the initial set of five relations and then adding the relations needed to ensure that the new set of relations becomes closed under composition, intersection and inversion of relations.

o	$<$	$>$	$\subset$	$\supset$	$\propto$	$\propto_<$	$\propto^1_<$	$\propto_>$	$\propto^1_>$	$\propto_1$	$<_\propto$	$<^1_\propto$
$<$	$<$	?	$\propto_<$	$<$	$\propto_<$	$\propto_<$	?	?	$<$	$\propto_<$	$\propto_<$	?
$>$	?	$>$	$\propto_>$	$>$	$\propto_>$	?	$>$	$\propto_>$	?	$\propto_>$	?	$\propto_>$
$\subset$	$<$	$>$	$\subset$	?	?	$\propto_<$	?	$\propto_>$	?	?	?	?
$\supset$	$\propto^1_>$	$\propto^1_<$	$\propto_1$	$\supset$	$\propto$	$<_\propto$	$\propto^1_<$	$<^1_\propto$	$\propto^1_>$	$\propto_1$	$<_\propto$	$<^1_\propto$
$\propto$	$\propto^1_>$	$\propto^1_<$	$\propto$	?	?	$<_\propto$	?	$<^1_\propto$	?	?	?	?
$\propto_<$	$<$	?	$\propto_<$	?	?	$\propto_<$	?	?	?	?	?	?
$\propto^1_<$	?	$\propto^1_<$	$<^1_\propto$	$\propto^1_<$	$<^1_\propto$	?	$\propto^1_<$	$<^1_\propto$	?	$<^1_\propto$	?	$<^1_\propto$
$\propto_>$	?	$>$	$\propto_>$	?	?	?	?	$\propto_>$	?	?	?	?
$\propto^1_>$	$\propto^1_>$	?	$<_\propto$	$\propto^1_>$	$<_\propto$	$<_\propto$	?	?	$\propto^1_>$	$<_\propto$	$<_\propto$	?
$\propto_1$	$\propto^1_>$	$\propto^1_<$	$\propto_1$	?	?	$<_\propto$	?	$<^1_\propto$	?	?	?	?
$<_\propto$	$\propto^1_>$	?	$<_\propto$	?	?	$<_\propto$	?	?	?	?	?	?
$<^1_\propto$	?	$\propto^1_<$	$<^1_\propto$	?	?	?	?	$<^1_\propto$	?	?	?	?

Table 2: Table with the composition of two relations

The composition of two relations r_1 and r_2 is the relation r_3 such that $r_3 = r_1 o\ r_2 = \{(x,y) \in \mathcal{I} \times \mathcal{I} | (x,z) \in r_1 \wedge (z,y) \in r_2\}$. *The intersection of two relations* r_1 and r_2 is the relation r_3 such that r_1, r_2 i $r_3 = r_1.r_2 = \{(x,y) | (x,y) \in r_1 \wedge (x,y) \in r_2\}$. *The inverse of a relation* r is the relation r^{-1} such that $r^{-1} = \{(x,y) \in \mathcal{I} \times \mathcal{I} | (y,x) \in r\}$.

In order to close the set of relations under these 3 operations we translated the initial set of five relations into Point Algebra (Vilain and Kautz 1986) (see table 1). Then we built a graph where nodes represent time intervals and edges represent temporal relations. We were then able to run the path consistency algorithm (Vilain and Kautz 1986). This algorithm checks whether the edges are correctly labeled by considering groups of 3 nodes. Note that this algorithm gives the correct result because our initial set of five relations has a translation into the point algebra that does not need disjunction (this is not the case with Allen's Algebra). Table 2 displays the the set of relations that we must consider in order for them to be closed under composition[4], (see table 4 for the meaning of the new relations).

[4]This table can also be obtained by translating the initial set of five relations into Allen's Interval Algebra (see table 1) and consulting Allen's relations composition table.

.	$<$	$>$	$\subset$	$\supset$	$\propto$	$\propto_<$	$\propto_<^1$	$\propto_>$	$\propto_>^1$	$\propto_1$	$<_\propto$	$<_\propto^1$
$<$	$<$	$\emptyset$	$\emptyset$	$\emptyset$	$\emptyset$	$<$	$\emptyset$	$\emptyset$	$<$	$\emptyset$	$<$	$\emptyset$
$>$		$>$	$\emptyset$	$\emptyset$	$\emptyset$	$\emptyset$	$>$	$>$	*set*	$\emptyset$	$\emptyset$	$>$
$\subset$			$\subset$	$\frac{\subset}{\supset}$	$\subset$	$\frac{\subset}{\propto_<}$	$\emptyset$	$\frac{\subset}{\propto_>}$	$\emptyset$	$\subset$	$\subset$	$\subset$
$\supset$				$\supset$	$\supset$	$\emptyset$	$\frac{\supset}{\propto_<^1}$	$\emptyset$	$\frac{\supset}{\propto_>^1}$	$\supset$	$\supset$	$\supset$
$\propto$					$\propto$	$\frac{\propto}{\propto_<}$	$\frac{\propto}{\propto_<^1}$	$\frac{\propto}{\propto_>}$	$\frac{\propto}{\propto_>^1}$	$\propto_1$	$\frac{\propto}{<_\propto}$	$\frac{\propto}{<_\propto^1}$
$\propto_<$						$\propto_<$	$\emptyset$	$\frac{\propto_<}{\propto_>}$	$\frac{\propto_<}{\propto_>^1}$	$\frac{\propto_<}{\propto_1}$	$\propto_<$	$\frac{\propto_<}{\propto_1}$
$\propto_<^1$							$\propto_<^1$	$\frac{\propto_<^1}{\propto_>}$	$\frac{\propto_<^1}{\propto_>^1}$	$\frac{\propto_<^1}{\propto_1}$	$\frac{\propto_<^1}{\propto_1}$	$\propto_<^1$
$\propto_>$								$\propto_>$	$\emptyset$	$\frac{\propto_>}{\propto_1}$	$\frac{\propto_>}{\propto_1}$	$\propto_>$
$\propto_>^1$									$\propto_>^1$	$\frac{\propto_>^1}{\propto_1}$	$\propto_>^1$	$\frac{\propto_>^1}{\propto_1}$
$\propto_1$										$\propto_1$	$\propto_1$	$\propto_1$
$<_\propto$											$<_\propto$	$\propto_1$
$<_\propto^1$												$<_\propto^1$

Table 3: Table with the intersection of two relations.

In order to get a closed set of relations under intersection, we obtain the set of relations that is presented in table 3 and the following four relations: $\propto.\propto_<.\propto_>^1$ and its inverse; and $\propto_<.\propto_>^1.\propto_1$ and its inverse.

In order to propagate the constraints we must be able to deal with edges (relations) that are not completely reduced under intersection because: $(r_1.r_2) \circ r_3 = (r_1 \circ r_3).(r_2 \circ r_3)$; $r_1 \circ (r_2.r_3) = (r_1 \circ r_2).(r_1 \circ r_3)$; and $(r_1.r_2)^1 = {r_1}^1.{r_1}^1$.

Our constraint system only has to consider the set of relations in table 4, instead of the 36 relations needed by the algebra AI5.

With this set of relations, we are able to perform constraint propagation in polynomial time (N^3 where N is the number of time intervals). And, as we will explain in the next section, we are able to handle two modes of constraint satisfaction (*tell* and *ask*), and also to obtain state persistence information.

Conclusions

In order to pragmatically interpret the tense of a sentence there are some forms of temporal reasoning that our knowledge base must be able to handle. Namely, it must be able to:

• Predict another eventuality based on the current knowledge. This form of reasoning is used when we want to identify the current sentence eventuality with a phase (preparatory, preliminary or consequence) of a previously introduced eventuality. In related literature in Artificial Intelligence (Pinto and Reiter 1993; Baker 1989; Kakas, Kowalski, and Toni 1992; Shoham 1988; Hanks and McDermott 1987) this form of reasoning is normally referred to as "prediction". In a previous section we have shown how this form of reasoning is supplied by our system.

• Prefer the models of the knowledge base where states temporally overlap events. In related work documented in the literature (Pinto and Reiter 1993; Baker 1989; Kakas, Kowalski, and Toni 1992; Shoham 1988; Hanks and McDermott 1987) this form of reasoning is referred to as "state persistence". We will show why this form of temporal reasoning is important in order to pragmatically interpret a sentence's tense and how our system can provide it.

Relation	R^{-1}	Meaning	Point relation (extremes)	equivalent in Allen's Algebra
a < b	>	$a\rceil \quad \lceil b$	$t_{a_f} < t_{b_i}$	a **b** b
a ⊂ b	⊃	$\lceil b \quad \lceil a \quad a\rceil \quad b\rceil$	$t_{b_i} \leq t_{a_i}$, $t_{a_f} \leq t_{b_f}$	a **d s f eq** b
a ∝ b	∝	$\lceil x \quad \lceil y \quad \rceil x \quad y\rceil$ $(x = a \wedge y = b) \vee (x = b \wedge y = a)$	$t_{a_i} \leq t_{b_f}$, $t_{b_i} \leq t_{a_f}$	a **o oi eq m mi d di s si f fi** b
a $\propto_<$ b	$\propto^1_<$	$a\rceil \quad b\rceil$	$t_{a_f} < t_{b_f}$	a **b m s o d** b
a $\propto_>$ b	$\propto^1_>$	$\lceil b \quad \lceil a$	$t_{a_i} > t_{b_i}$	a **bi mi f oi d** b
a $\propto_1$ b	$\propto_1$	$\lceil x \quad \lceil y \quad \rceil x \quad y\rceil$ $(x = a \wedge y = b) \vee (x = b \wedge y = a)$	$t_{a_i} < t_{b_f}$, $t_{b_i} < t_{a_f}$	a **o oi eq d di s si f fi** b
a $<_\propto$ b	$<^1_\propto$	$\lceil a \quad b\rceil$	$t_{a_i} < t_{b_f}$	a **b m s si f fi d di o oi eq** b

Table 4: The set of relations between two intervals, a e b

• Be able to check:

— if a particular temporal relation is consistent with the set of all temporal relations. In the literature on Constraint Systems this is referred to as a "Tell" operation. This operation is performed whenever we update the knowledge base with the result of a pragmatic interpretation of a text sentence. Given two time intervals t_1 and t_2, a temporal relation r_1, and a set of constraints G, in order to check if $t_1 r_1 t_2$ is consistent with G (tell), we must build the constraint graph, and reduce it with the path consistency algorithm (propagate the constraints). If the label between the nodes that represents t_1 and t_2 is r_2 then $t_1 r_1 t_2$ is consistent with G if and only if $r_2.r_1 \neq \emptyset$.

— if a particular temporal relation is implied by the set of all temporal relations. In the literature on Constraint Systems this is referred as an "Ask" operation. This operation is performed during the pragmatic interpretation when we have to check whether a temporal relation is implied by the previously interpreted text. Given two time intervals t_1 and t_2, a temporal relation r_1, and a set of constraints G, in order to check if $t_1 r_1 t_2$ is implied by G (ask), we must build the constraint graph, and reduce it with the path consistency algorithm (propagate the constraints). If the label between the nodes that represents t_1 and t_2 is r_2 then $t_1 r_1 t_2$ is implied by G if and only if $r_2.r_1 = r_2$.

State persistence

Consider text 6. The second sentence gives rise to a state where "John was writing a letter".

(6) Mary arrived home at 12 o'clock (1). John was writing a letter (2). She cooked a meal (3) and they ate it (4). She went out at 3 pm (5) and mailed John's letter (6).

The interpretation of the tense of this sentence leads us to a situation where the time interval of the first sentence's eventuality is contained in the time interval of the second. For the interpretation of sentence 3 one possibility is to consider that "Mary cooked after she arrived home". With this interpretation we will get the constraints:

$t_{arrive} \subset t_{writing} \wedge t_{arrive} < t_{cook}$

Note that, with this interpretation, the constraint $t_{writing} < t_{cook}$ is consistent with the above set of constraints. However, an interpretation where $t_{writing} \supset t_{cook}$ would be preferred. This interpretation will be the one where we have state persistence, i.e. we assume that a state ends just when there are reasons to believe that it has ended.

In order to get state persistence using our system, we just have to transform the constraints graph into another graph that models persistence. This transformation requires the following steps:

1. Build a sorted (ascending in time) structure with the time intervals that are associated with states.

2. Build a sorted (ascending in time) structure with the time intervals that are associated with events.

3. Pick up the first state in the structure and the first event in the structure:

3.a. If the relation "the time interval of the state" $\supset$ "the time interval of the event" is consistent with the set of constraints, add the relation to the set of constraints.

3.b. Pick the next event and perform the previous step, if there are no more events pick the next state and start with the first event.

After this transformation we obtain a new graph that models state persistence. We have to sort the states (and the events) because persistence must go from the past into the future. In this way we ensure that a state will overlap as many events as it can.

References

Allen, J. 1984. Towards a general theory of action and time. *Artificial Intelligence 23*, 123–154.

Almeida, J.M. 1987. *Reasoning About the Temporal Structure of Narrative.* Ph. D. thesis, State University of New York, Buffalo, NY.

Baker, A.B. 1989. A simple solution to the yale shooting problem. In *Proceedings of KR.* Morgan and Kaufmann Pub, Inc.

Eynde, F. van 1990, October. The semantics of tense and aspect. In M. Filgueiras et al. (eds), *EAIA'90 2nd Advanced School in AI.* Springer Verlag.

Grosz, B. and Sidner, C. 1986. Attention, intention, and the structure of discourse. *Computational Linguistics 12*(3), 175–204.

Hanks, S. and McDermott, D. 1987. Nonmonotonic logic and temporal projection. *Artificial Intelligence 33.*

Hinrichs, E. 1988, June. Tense, quantifiers, and contexts. *Computational Linguistics 14*(2), 3–14.

Hobbs, J., Stickel, M., Appelt, D. and Martin, P. 1990, December. Interpretation as abduction. Technical Report 499, SRI International.

Kakas, A.C., Kowalski, R.A and Toni, F. 1992. Abductive Logic Programming. *Journal of logic and computation 2*(6), 719–770.

Kameyama, M., Passonneau, R., and Poesio, M. 1993. Temporal centering. In *Proceedings of the* 31st *Annual Meeting of the ACL.*

Kamp, H. and Reyle U. 1993. *From Discourse to Logic.* Dordrecht: D. Reidel.

Kowalski, R. and Sergot, M. 1986. A logic-based calculus of events. *New Generation Computing 4*, 67–95.

Lascarides, A., Asher, N. and Oberlander, J. 1992. Inferring discourse relations in context. In *Proceedings of the 30th Annual Meeting of ACL.*

Moens, M. and Steedman, M. 1988, June. Temporal ontology and temporal reference. *Computational Linguistics 14*(2), 15–28.

Pereira, F. and Pollack, M. 1991. Incremental interpretation. *Artificial Intelligence 50*, 40–82.

Pereira, L., Damásio, C. and Alferes, J. 1993. Diagnosis and debugging as contradiction removal. In L. M. Pereira and A. Nerode (eds), *Proceedings of the 2th International Workshop on Logic Programming and Non-monotonic Reasoning*, pp. 316–330. The MIT Press.

Pinto, J. and Reiter, R. 1993. Temporal reasoning in logic programming. In D. S. Warren (ed), *Proceedings of the 10th ICLP.* MIT Press.

Rodrigues, I.P. and Lopes, J.G. 1993a. Building the text temporal structure. In *Progress in Artificial Intelligence: 6th EPIA.* Springer-Verlag.

Rodrigues, I.P. and Lopes, J.G. 1993b. Text processing in a logic programming framework. In *Proceedings of NLULP'4.*

Rodrigues, I.P. and Lopes, J.G.P. 1992a. Discourse temporal structure. In *Proceedings of the COLING'92.*

Shanahan, M. 1989. Prediction is deduction but explanation is abduction. In *Proceedings of IJCAI 89.* Morgan Kaufmann Pub, Inc.

Shoham, Y. 1988. Chonological ignorance. *Artificial Intelligence 36*, 279–331.

Song, F. 1991. *A Processing Model for Temporal Analysis and its Aplication to Plan Recognition.* Ph. D. thesis, University of Waterloo, Canada.

Vilain, M. and Kautz, H. 1986. Constraint propagation algorithms for temporal reasoning. In *Proceedings of AAAI.* Morgan Kaufmann Pub. Inc.

Webber, B.L. 1988, June. Tense as discourse anaphor. *Computational Linguistics 14*(2), 61–73.

Approximate Reasoning about Natural Language: A Certain Distributional–Mereological Model

Lech T. Polkowski[a]
Maria Semeniuk–Polkowska[b]

[a] *Warsaw University of Technology*
[b] *Warsaw University*

Abstract

We propose an approach to approximate reasoning about natural language based on combining the ideas of two paradigms: algebraic-distributional models of language and rough mereology. We outline possible applications of this model of approximate reasoning to the important areas of Artificial Intelligence: knowledge extraction from texts, text classification and data mining in texts.

Introduction

Techniques of Artificial Intelligence and Computer Science are applied currently to many problems concerning natural language. Among such problems we may mention information retrieval from texts (see Cowie & Lehner 1996, Kraft & Boyce 1995), text clasification (see Lewis & Sparck Jones 1996) and data minig in texts (see Feldman et al. 1997, Mannila et al.

1994). Among some of the techniques proposed in this area, a role of rough-set theoretic approximations has been stressed in Srinivasan (1991). We propose here some techniques which can prove useful in this respect by applying a deeper concept of rough mereology presented fully in Polkowski & Skowron (1997). We also discuss models of anaphoric reference (see Polkowski & Semeniuk-Polkowska 1994) and algorithms for anaphoric resolution of a text along with rough mereological notions of a rough inclusion and a mereological distance. We suggest how these techniques can be combined with other techniques (e.g. Bayesian hierarchical clustering (see e.g. Iwayama & Tokunaga 1994)) to form a conceptual scheme for text classification as well as for pattern recognition in texts. In particular, the approach presented here may be applied as a new technique for finding interesting patterns in texts: instead of finding prioritized dependencies among concepts from a given hierarchy, we could apply the algorithms for anaphora resolution in order to produce new texts in which patterns consist of the most specific concepts. These patterns would then form the domain in which one could search for interesting relations. The search parameters can be optimized using natural computation techniques e.g. neural networks or genetic algorithms, using training sets of examples.

Distributional models

The syntactic description of language adopted here is based on the algebraic-distributional approach; we recall here the basic notions of this approach. A language is regarded here as a set of strings (phrases) over a fixed vocabulary V; the set of all finite strings i.e. strings of the form $v_1v_2...v_k$ where $v_1, v_2, ..., v_k \in V$ is denoted by $\Sigma(V)$. Endowed with the operation of juxtaposition which for any two given strings $v_1v_2...v_k$ and $w_1w_2..w_m$ produces the string $v_1v_2...v_kw_1w_2...w_m$, $\Sigma(V)$ is the free semigroup over the generator set V. Thus a language L is a subset $L \subseteq \Sigma(V)$.

The primitive word predicate $D_L(x, y)$ on $\Sigma(V)$, called the *domination* (in the sense of Dobrushin) *relative to the language* L is defined as follows: for any pair x, y of strings over V, we let $D_L(x, y)$ be true if and only if the following condition is satisfied for any pair u, v of strings in $\Sigma(V)$: if $uxv \in L$ then $uyv \in L$. In particular, the restriction $D_L|L$ is the domination on the language L.

The equivalent extension R_L of the domination predicate D_L is defined (obviously) as: $R_L(x,y)$ if and only if $D_L(x,y) \wedge D_L(y,x)$; the word predicate R_L is the *contextual equivalence relative to the language L*. The restriction $R_L|L$ is the contextual equivalence on the language L. We can also consider word predicates $D_L|V$ and $R_L|V$.

The predicates of domination (also in the ramified versions by Franclova, Nebesky, Novotny, Kunze, Trybulec, Semeniuk-Polkowska) found many important applications in the study of language (cf. Marcus 1966). We mention here the configurational models of language based on the notion of a configuration by Kulagina; the recurrent definition of configuration is based on predicates D_L and R_L (cf. Semeniuk-Polkowska 1983). For the sake of illustration, we recall here the definition of $G-$configurations (configurations in the sense of Gladkii).

A phrase $x \in L$ is a *$G-$ configuration of degree 1* in the language L whenever the following conditions are satisfied:

(i) the length of x is at least 2;

(ii) there exists a word $a \in V$ with the property that $R_L(x,a)$;

A word a is said to be a *resultant* of x.

Assuming that $G-$configurations of degrees $1, 2, ..., n-1$ have been defined, we say that a phrase $x \in L$ is a *$G-$ configuration of degree n* if and only if the following conditions are satisfied:

(i) the length of x is at least 2;

(ii) there exists a word $a \in L$ such that

 (a) $D_L(a,x)$;

 (b) if $uxz \in L$ and for no $G-$configuration y of degree less than n we have that y is a substring of uxz and y meets x in uxz but y is no substring of x, then $uaz \in L$.

A word a is said to be a *resultant* of x.

To illustrate some applications of this notion, we say that a phrase $x \in L$ is *$G-$ atomic* (respectively: *$G-$ simple*) if and only if x contains no $G-$configuration (respectively: x is a $G-$ configuration and no $G-$ configuration other than x is a substring of x). The *Gladkii theorem* states that a language L is of type 2 in the Chomsky hierarchy if and only if the sets of atomic phrases in L and $G-$ simple phrases in L are finite.

Apart from classificational results the configuration theory proved useful in the analysis of deep syntactic relationships in a language (cf. Semeniuk-Polkowska 1983).

Another area of research associated with domination predicates is the study of anaphoric predicates (cf. Polkowski & Semeniuk- Polkowska 1994). Bellow we outline some of the basic notions of this research area

Domination predicates

In this section, we modify the notion of a language by considering paradigmatic partitions on the vocabulary V of a language L. In this approach (cf. Marcus 1966) a language is a triple (V, L, P) where V is a vocabulary, $L \subseteq \Sigma(V)$ is a language over V and P is a partition (i.e. an equivalence relation) on the set V (in a natural language interpretation, P is usually the approximate partition of words into classes of flexional forms). The predicates D_L and R_L are introduced as above. The equivalence classes of R_L are called *distributional classes*; we denote by the symbol $dc(x)$ the distributional class of x. Obviously, we may extend the predicate D_L to the domination predicate $\hat{D}_L$ over distributional classes: $\hat{D}_L(dc(x), dc(y))$ is true if and only if $D_L(x, y)$ is true. This relation does not depend on the choice of representatives x, y.

A class $dc(x)$ is said to be *initial* if and only if the following condition is fulfilled: if $\hat{D}_L(dc(y), dc(x))$ is true then $dc(x) = dc(y)$. For an initial distributional class $dc(x)$, the set $\bigcup\{dc(y) : \hat{D}_L(dc(x), dc(y))$ is called the *grammatical category generated by* x, denoted symbolically by $gc(x)$. For a grammatical category $gc(x)$, we denote by $\hat{D}_{L,x}$ the restriction $\hat{D}_L|gc(x)$ of the word predicate $\hat{D}_L$ to the grammatical category $gc(x)$ and we introduce the strong domination predicate $s\hat{D}_{L,x}$ restricted to the grammatical category $gc(x)$ by letting $s\hat{D}_{L,x}(dc(y), dc(z))$ be true if and only if the condition

$$\hat{D}_{L,x}(dc(y), dc(z)) \wedge non\hat{D}_{L,x}(dc(z), dc(y))$$

is true.

The strong domination predicate allows us to introduce the numerical function $rank_x$ on the grammatical category $gc(x)$; this idea was proposed by S. Marcus (see Polkowski & Semeniuk-Polkowska 1994). We will call a sequence $(dc(x_0), dc(x_1), ..., dc(x_k))$ of elements of $gc(x)$ a *path* (of *length* k) with the end-class $dc(x_k)$ in the case when $s\hat{D}_{L,x}(dc(x_i), dc(x_{i+1}))$ is true for each $i < k$. A path $(dc(x_0), dc(x_1), ..., dc(x_k))$ is *maximal* when there is no class $dc(y)$ in $gc(x)$ with the property that either $s\hat{D}_{L,x}(dc(y), dc(x_0))$ or $s\hat{D}_{L,x}(dc(x_k), dc(y))$ or $s\hat{D}_{L,x}(dc(x_i), dc(y))$ and $s\hat{D}_{L,x}(dc(y), dc(x_{i+1}))$ for some $i = 1, 2, ..., k-1$.

A path $(dc(x_0), dc(x_1), ..., dc(x_k))$ is called *initial* when $x_0 \in dc(x)$. For any $y \in gc(x)$, we define the rank of y by letting $rank_x(y) = \max\{k : \textit{there exists}$ an initial maximal path of length k with the end-class $dc(y)\}$. By default, $rank_x(x) = 0$. We collect in the set $Trans(y)$ all initial maximal paths to the class $dc(y)$ of length equal to $rank_x(y)$. The paths in $Trans(y)$ will be interpreted as lists of phrases ordered according to decreasing contextual replaceability and replaceable by y in all contexts; maximality of paths means taking into account phrases with maximal acceptability (in the given language) which dominate y (i.e. can be replaced with y in any context).

Anaphoric predicates

We will introduce here some new word predicates related to the problem of *anaphoric reference.* Anaphoric reference is one of techniques used for linking sentences hence it is naturally associated with finite sequences of sentences i.e. with *texts.*

We recall (cf. Polkowski & Semeniuk- Polkowska 1994) that anaphoric reference in a certain sequence of phrases (a text) T is the set of pairs (x, y) of phrases such that x precedes y in the natural linear order of precedence of occurrences in T and x, y co-refer to the same object with respect to the semantic interpretation of the language. By necessity, the anaphor y has greater replaceability in contexts of the language than the antecedent x.

For strings u, v, we say that u has an *occurrence* in v if and only if there exist strings w, t such that $v = wut$. For a sequence $T = (t_1, t_2, ..., t_n)$ of strings in L and a string x,we will call an *occurrence* of x in T any triple (i, w, t) such that $t_i = wxt$.

We recall that we work with the language $\mathcal{L} = (L, V, P)$ where P is a (paradigmatic) partition on the vocabulary V. The partition P extends to a product partition on $\Sigma(V)$ and we will denote by the same symbol P the restriction of this extension to L i.e. for a string $v_1v_2...v_k$, we take as the class $P(v_1v_2...v_k)$ the Cartesian product $P(v_1)\times P(v_2)\times ... \times P(v_k)$ of classes of $v_1, v_2, .., v_k$.

We say that an occurrence (i, w, t) of a string x in T *accepts paradigmatically* a string y if and only if there exists $y' \in P(y)$ with the property that $wy't \in L$. The word predicate $Pacc(i, w, t, y)$ is true when the occurrence (i, w, t) accepts paradigmatically the string y.

The predicate $\lhd(x, y)$ denotes the natural precedence order in T i.e. $\lhd(x, y)$ is true if and only if x precedes y in T.

We now recall the notion of an anaphoric pair (cf.Polkowski & Semeniuk-Polkowska 1994).

For occurrences $(i, u, w), (j, v, t)$ in T where $t_i = uxw, t_j = vyt$, we say that (x, y) is an *anaphoric pair over the grammatical category* $gc(z)$ *relative to* T when the following conditions are fulfilled:

(i) $\lhd(x, y)$;

(i) there exist $x', y' \in gc(z)$ such that $x \in P(x'), y \in P(y')$;

(iii) there exists an initial path $(dc(x_0), dc(x_1), .., dc(x_p))$ in $Trans(x')$ (i.e. $x_p = x'$) with $x_0 = z$ and $y' = x_i$ for some $i < p$;

(iv) $vx't \in L$ a fortiori $Pacc(j, v, t, x')$.

The notion of an anaphoric pair captures the essential features of the phenomenon of anaphoric reference: (a) the co-referring (on the syntactic level) to the same object (by (iii), (iv)); (b) precedence of the antecedent over the anaphor (by (i)); (c) a greater acceptability of the antecedent than that of the anaphor (by (iii)). Based on this notion is the notion of anaphoric resolvent (anaphora resolution) (see Polkowski & Semeniuk-Polkowska 1994). In the discussion which follows, we still work with the grammatical category $gc(z)$ and a fixed sequence T of elements of L.

The word predicate $Occ(i, z)$ is true when there exists a string x in $gc(z)$ of $rank_z(x) = i$ which has an occurrence in T; in the case when $Occ(i, z)$ is true, we denote by $Occ\_set(i, z)$ the set of all such occurrences denoted by their respective strings in the order of precedence i.e. $x_1 \lhd x_2 \lhd \ldots \lhd x_{m(i)}$. We denote by the symbol $segm(i, j)$ the initial segment of length j of $Occ\_set(i, z)$ i.e. the segment $x_1 \lhd x_2 \lhd \ldots \lhd x_j$ where $j = 1, 2, \ldots, m(i)$.

Anaphoric resolutions

A*partial anaphoric resolution of degree* (k, l) is a word function f whose domain $dom(f)$ satisfies the equation $dom(f) = segm(k, j)$ for some $j \leq m(k)$

and which takes the values in the set $Occ\_set(l,z)$ where $l > k$. Informally, f assigns to each anaphor $x_i \in segm(k,j)$ the antecedent $f(x_i) \in Occ\_set(l,z)$. These partial functions are ordered linearly by means of the Brouwer-Kleene ordering $\sqsubseteq$: for partial anaphoric resolutions $f \neq g$ of degree (k,l), we let $f \sqsubseteq g$ if and only if $f(\alpha(f,g)) \triangleleft g(\alpha(f,g))$ where $\alpha(f,g)$ is the first x with respect to the ordering $\triangleleft$ such that $f(x) \neq g(x)$.

We restate here the algorithm (cf. Polkowski & Semeniuk- Polkowska 1994) generating partial anaphoric resolutions of primary character (meaning, informally, that anaphors are "close" to antecedents in the sense given by the notion of a marked interval, below).

For a given pair (k,l) where $k < l$, a partition $\{c_1, c_2, .., c_m\}$ on the set $Occ\_set(k,z)$ is the *partition into marked intervals* if it is the case that

(i) each c_i is an interval $[x_{k(i)}, ..., x_{k(i)+u(i)}]$ with respect to $\triangleleft$;

(ii) for each i there exists $y \in Occ\_set(l,z)$ such that (a) $x_{k(i-1)+u(i-1)} \triangleleft y \triangleleft x_{k(i)}$; (b) $(y, x_{k(i)+j})$ is an anaphoric pair for each $j \leq u(i)$;

(iii) there is no $y \in Occ\_set(l,z)$ such that $x_{k(i)+r} \triangleleft y \triangleleft x_{k(i)+r+1}$ and $(y, x_{k(i)+r+t})$ is an anaphoric pair for some $0 \leq r \leq u(i) - 1$ and some $t \geq 1$.

For any marked interval c_i, we set $X(c_i, l) = \{y : y$ satisfies (a),(b) in (ii)$\}$; for a given x, we denote by $c(x)$ the marked interval which contains x.

We add a semantic ingredient by introducing a set $Forb \subseteq L$ of *forbidden sentences*; this follows an idea by Revzin 1966. For strings x and y such that $Pacc(i,w,t,y)$ is true where (i,w,t) is the occurrence of x and $wy't \in L$ for an appropriate $y' \in P(y)$, we denote by $T[x/y']$ the sequence T in which t_i is replaced by $wy't$. We denote by T_g the sequence obtained by replacing in T each $x \in dom(g) \cap Occ\_set(k,z)$ with an adequate $g(x)' \in P(g(x))$. We say that $T[x/y']$ is *acceptable,* which we denote by the symbol $\models T[x/y']$, when it is not the case that $T[x/y'] \in Forb$. Similarly, $\models T_g$ is defined.

We restate the algorithm which outputs all partial anaphora resolutions of the degree $(i, i+1)$.

ALGORITHM

INPUT: $T, gc(z), i$; {*a sequence (text) over* L, *a grammatical category the rank of anaphors*; $i+1$ *is the rank of antecedents*}

INITIALIZE:

$c_1, c_2, .., c_k$: *marked intervals in* $Occ\_set(i,z)$;

Calculate $X(c_1, i+1) : \{y_1 \lhd y_2 \lhd .... \lhd y_m\}$
Calculate $g_{1,p}(x_1) : if \models T[x_1/y'_p]$ then y'_p else undefined;
$\{x_1$ *is the first element in* $c_1\}$

For $k = 1$ **to** $cardinality(Occ\_set(i, z))$ **do**
$\{x_k$ *is the* $k-th$ *element in* $Occ\_set(i, z)$; $c(x_k) = c_{j(k)}\}$
$\{g_1 \sqsubseteq g_2 \sqsubseteq ... \sqsubseteq g_n$ *are functions defined already on* $\{x_1, x_2, .., x_{k-1}\}\}$
$\{X(c_j, i+1) = \{y_{1,j} \lhd y_{2,j} \lhd .... \lhd y_{m(j),j}\}\}$
For $j = 1, 2, ..., n$ and $u = 1, 2, ..., m$ **do**
$g_{k,j,u} =$ **if** $\models T[x_k/y_u]$ **then** $g_j \cup \{(x_k, y_u)\}$ **else** g_j
#
#

The algorithm generates a set $M\_A(i, i+1)$ of anaphoric (partial) resolvents for T.
It should be pointed out that by composing the above algorithms for $i = 0, 1, 2, \ldots, \max\_rank$, we generate sets $M\_A(0, i)$ for $i = 1, 2, \ldots, \max\_rank$ where $\max\_rank$ denotes the maximal possible rank for a given antecedent (i.e. the antecedent which is the most specialized in the given context is chosen).

Knowledge abstraction from a text

We outline here a scheme for abstracting knowledge from texts by classifying a given text in a specified domain. To this end, we apply the technique composed of the three basic ingredients: mereological measure of closeness between objects, anaphoric resolution technique of sect. 2. 3 and hierarchical (Bayesian) clustering.

Mereology of Lesniewski

Mereological set theories were initiated in 1916 by Stanislaw Lesniewski (cf. Lesniewski 1992). The primitive notion of Lesniewski's mereological theory is the relation part *of being a part.* This relation needs to be irreflexive (meaning that it is not true for any x that $prt(x, x)$) and transitive i.e. for any x, y, z, from $prt(x, y) \wedge prt(y, z)$ it follows that $prt(x, z)$. The relation *prt* introduces into the universe U a hierarchy based on the decomposition of complex objects into simpler (proper) parts.

The notion of a (possibly) improper part is rendered by the relation *ingr* of being an *ingredient*, defined as follows: for any objects $x, y \in U$, the relation $ingr(x, y)$ is true if and only if either $prt(x, y)$ or $x = y$. Then *ingr* is a partial order on the universe U i.e. *ingr* is reflexive (meaning $ingr(x, x)$ for any x), weakly anti-symmetric (meaning that the condition $ingr(x, y) \wedge ingr(y, x)$ implies $x = y$, for any pair x, y of objects), and transitive.

The relation *ingr*, in turn, is the starting point towards the Lesniewski set theory. Consider a property (unary predicate) F which is defined for objects in the universe U and such that the sentence $F(x)$ is true for at least one object in U. Then the notion of a *set of objects* with the property F (*set* F, for short) is introduced in the following way; an object x is said to be a *set of objects having the property* F (x *set* F, for short) if and only if the following condition holds: given any y with $ingr(y, x)$, there exists an object z such that $ingr(z, y)$ and for some w the condition $ingr(z, w) \wedge ingr(w, x) \wedge F(w)$ is true.

If, in addition to the condition x *set* F, the object x satisfies the condition that $ingr(t, x)$ for every t such that $F(t)$ is true, then we say that x is a *class of objects having the property* F (x *class* F, for short).
The mereology of Lesniewski collapses the Cantorian hierarchy: $class(class\ F) = class\ F$ (see Lesniewski 1992).

We introduce into mereology the notion of an *element* by means of a predicate *elm* defined as follows: $elm(x, y)$ if and only if we have $F(x) \wedge (y\ class\ F)$ for some non-void predicate F.

Similarly, the notion of a *subset* is introduced via the following predicate *sub*: $sub(x, y)$ iff for every object z we have: $ingr(z, x)$ implies $ingr(z, y)$.

Then, the following are equivalent for any pair a, b of objects: (i) $ingr(a, b)$; (ii) $elm(a, b)$; (iii) $sub(a, b)$.

The hierarchy of exact parts established in the universe U by the relation *prt* can be regarded as the counterpart of e.g. the exact derivation of a formula in a syntactic logical calculus and a fortiori as the proof of existence of a complex object. In most applications of Artificial Intelligence, however, our knowledge about the objects in U is not complete or it is uncertain; consequently, we cannot establish the exact relation of decomposition into parts and we can only consider the relation of being a part in a degree (cf.

Polkowski & Skowron 1997).

Rough mereology

Formally, we introduce on the universe U a binary function μ (cf. Polkowski & Skowron 1997) also called a *rough inclusion.* Any rough inclusion μ, written as a ternary predicate on the product $U \times U \times [0,1]$, satisfies, among others, the following basic requirements stemming from our intuitive understanding of the nature of partial containment (in what follows, $r, s \in [0,1]$):

(i) $\mu(x,x,1)$ for any $x \in U$;

(ii) $\mu(x,y,1) \Rightarrow [\mu(z,y,r) \wedge \mu(z,x,s) \Rightarrow (r \geq s)]$;

(iii) $\mu(x,y,1) \wedge \mu(y,x,1) \Rightarrow [\mu(x,z,s) \wedge \mu(y,z,r) \Rightarrow (s = r)]$.

The formula $\mu(x,y,r)$ is read "the object x is a part of the object y in degree at least r". If the predicate $I(\mu)$ is defined as follows: $I(\mu)(x,y)$ is true if and only if $\mu(x,y,1)$ is true, we define a partial ordering of the universe U. The relation $prt(\mu)$ is defined as follows: $prt(\mu)(x,y)$ if and only if $I(\mu)(x,y) \wedge (\neg I(\mu)(y,x))$ satisfies the requirements for the relation of being an (exact) part in Lesniewski's mereology (cf. Polkowski & Skowron 1997).

A useful set of rough inclusions can be produced in the case when objects in the universe U are described in terms of *attributes* (*features*) and their values: given objects x, y, we consider the subset $DIS(x,y)$ of the attribute set A defined as follows: $DIS(x,y) = \{a \in A : a(x) \neq a(y)\}$; then we let $\mu(x,y) = cardinality DIS(x,y)/cardinality A$. Subtler versions of μ can be obtained by partitioning the set A of attributes into subsets $C_1, C_2, ..., C_m$, assigning positive weights $w_1, w_2, ..., w_m$ such that $\Sigma_i w_i = 1$ to $C_1, C_2, ..., C_m$, respectively, and letting $\mu(x,y) = (cardinality A)^{-1} \Sigma_i w_i cardinality(C_i \cap DIS(x,y))$. In particular, this approach may be applied when our objects are coded as subsets of the universe: given sets A, B, we consider a partition $\mathcal{P}$ on the set A along with a set of weights $\{w(C) : C \in \mathcal{P}\}$ where each $w(C) \geq 0$ and $\sum_{C \in \mathcal{P}} w(C) = 1$. Then we let $\mu_{w,\mathcal{P}}(A,B) = \sum_{C \in \mathcal{P}} w(C)(\frac{card(C \cap B)}{card(B)})$. The convenience of this approach lies primarily in the fact that the weights $w(C)$ can be learned from training examples by means of natural computation techniques e.g. neural networks.

The mereological distance function $dist(\mu)(x,y)$ will be defined in terms of the mereological similarity predicate $\tau(\mu)(x,y,r)$. We state: $\tau(\mu)(x,y,r)$

is true if and only if $\mu(x,y,r) \wedge \mu(y,x,r)$ is true. Then we let $dist(\mu)(x,y) = \sup\{r : \tau(\mu)(x,y,r)\}$; although $dist(\mu)$ is a generalized metric, it satisfies a triangle inequality of the form $dist(\mu)(x,z) \leq f(\ dist(\mu)(x,y), dist(\mu)(y,z))$ for a certain class of functions f in adequately constructed models (cf. Polkowski & Skowron 1994).

Observe that our notion of mereological distance differs from the standard notion of topological distance: here, objects x, y which are μ-identical (i.e. they satisfy the condition $(x,y) \in ingr(\mu) \wedge (y,x) \in ingr(\mu)$) satisfy the condition $dist(\mu)(x,y) = 1$ (and not, as in the standard metric theory, $dist(\mu)(x,y) = 0$).

To sum up, we may introduce into the universe U the measure μ of partial containment; we may then reconstruct Lesniewski's mereology (sect. 3.1) on the universe U via the ingredient relation $I(\mu)$ and this sets the hierarchy of exact parts in U. Observe that, as in Lesniewski's mereology the notions of a subset, an element and an ingredient are equivalent (sect. 3.1). Our relation μ can be also regarded as a fuzzy membership function (cf. Polkowski & Skowron 1997). The function $dist(\mu)$ can be regarded as a similarity measure among objects, and in particular, can be applied to tell us how close a given object x is to being an exact part of an object y. These ideas form a basis for a scheme of approximate reasoning presented in Polkowski & Skowron (1997). We apply the above similarity measure to the problem of a text classification.

Text classification

We consider a class of texts concerning a domain whose key phrases form a gramatical category C ordered by the relation of domination D_C. We assume that a set St of standard texts is given. The algorithm for text classification given below is based on the algorithm for anaphora resolution (sect. 2.3). This algorithm acts on a given text T as well as on standard texts from the set St and its effect is to replace concepts of higher ranks in these texts with the most specific concepts of maximal ranks. The resulting texts can be regarded as containing the most specific patterns. These patterns then undergo a clustering. The outcome is a family of clusters. Clusters regarded as sets are then estimated with respect to a similarity measure $dist(\mu)$ for an appropriate rough inclusion μ. The outcome is the set $\{dist(\mu)(T,T') : T' \in St\}$; on the basis of this set of distance values, a decision procedure classifies the text T in the subdomain represented by a standard text T'.

ALGORITHM

INPUT: T, *St*; {*a given text, a set of standard texts*}

Step 1. For a given text T, and texts in St, apply algorithm for anaphora resolutions.

Outcome: sets $M\_A(i, i+1)(T)$, $M\_A(i, i+1)(T')$ for $T' \in St$, $i = 0, 1, 2, \ldots, \max\_rank$

Step 2. To the texts of the form T_g, respectively T'_g, where

$g \in \bigcup_i [M\_A(i, i+1)(T) \cup M\_A(i, i+1)(T')]$ apply hierarchical aggregation algorithm (see Appendix, below).

Outcome: hierarchical aggregates structure for each of the texts in Step 1.

Step 3. Calculate a mereological distance

$dist(i, \mu_{w,\mathcal{P}})(M\_A(i, i+1)(T), M\_A(i, i+1)(T'))$ for each $T' \in St$ as follows:

$dist(i, \mu_{w,\mathcal{P}})(M\_A(i, i+1)(T), M\_A(i, i+1)(T')) = \min_{g,h}\{dist(i, \mu_{w,\mathcal{P}}) \cdot (T_g, T'_h)\}$ where $g \in M\_A(i, i+1)(T), h \in M\_A(i, i+1)(T')$ and

$dist(i, \mu_{w,\mathcal{P}})(T_g, T'_h) = \min_j\{dist(i, \mu_{w,\mathcal{P}})(Cl_j T_g, Cl_j T'_h)\}$ where $Cl_j T$ is the $j-th$ aggregate (cluster) set of the text T.

Calculate $\min_i\{dist(i, \mu_{w,\mathcal{P}})(M\_A(i, i+1)(T), M\_A(i, i+1)(T'))\}$

$= dist(\mu_{w,\mathcal{P}})(T, T')$ for $T' \in St$.

Step 4. Apply a decision procedure based on calculated distances

$\{dist(\mu_{w,\mathcal{P}})(T, T') : T' \in St\}$ e.g. for a given threshold tr, if $dist(\mu_{w,\mathcal{P}})(T, T') > tr$ then we classify T as belonging to the subdomain represented by the standard T'.

In this approach, each pair (i, g) can be perceived as an autonomous intelligent agent: the final outcome is the result of interactions among these agents.

Appendix

We quote an exemplary algorithm for hierarchical aggregation (a textual version of the Iwayama-Tokunaga (1994) algorithm based on Bayesian ideas).

ALGORITHM

INPUT: For given i: the set D of contexts in which antecedents of rank $i+1$ (their number m) substituted anaphors of rank i in the given text T by a function g in $M\_A(i, i+1)$.
Let $D = C_1$.

Calculate: for the current aggregate C_k find
$\mathbf{P}(C_k|D) = \prod_{c \in C_k, d \in D} P(c|d)$ where $\mathbf{P}(c|d) = \mathbf{P}(d|c)\mathbf{P}(c)\mathbf{P}(d)^{-1}$ and
$\mathbf{P}(d|c) = \mathbf{P}(d) \sum_v \mathbf{P}(V = v|d)\mathbf{P}(V = v|c)\mathbf{P}(V = v)^{-1}$;
$\mathbf{P}(V = v|d)$ is the frequency of the antecedent v among all antecedents accepted by the context d;
$\mathbf{P}(V = v|c)$ is the frequency of the antecedent v among all antecedents accepted by contexts in c;
$\mathbf{P}(V = v)$ is the frequency of the antecedent v among all antecedents.
Find: c_i, c_j such that $C_{k+1} = C_k - \{c_i, c_j\} \cup \{c_i \cup c_j\}$ satisfies
max $\mathbf{P}(C_{k+1}|D)$.
Repeat until one aggregate

OUTPUT: aggregates $C_1, C_2, .., C_m$

References

Cowie, J. and Lehner, W. 1996. "Information extraction", *Communications ACM* 39(1), 80–91.

Feldman, R., Kloesgen, W. and Zilberstein, A. 1997. "Document Explorer: discovering knowledge in document collections", In *Proceedings Intern. Symposium on Methodologies for Intelligent Systems ISMIS 97, Lecture Notes in Artificial Intelligence*, to appear.

Iwayama, M. and Tokunaga, T. 1994. "A probabilistic model for text categorization based on a single random variable with multiple values". *Proceedings of the 4th Conference on, Applied Natural Language Processing.*

Kraft, D.H. and Boyce, B.R. 1995. "Approaches to intelligent information retrieval", *Advances in Databases and Artificial Intelligence*, (vol.1). JAI Press. 243–261.

Lesniewski, S. 1992. "Foundations of the general theory of sets", In S.J. Surma, J.T. Srzednicki, D.I. Barnett & V.F. Rickey (eds), *Stanislaw Lesniewski. Collected Works.* Dordrecht and Warsaw: Kluwer and Polish Scientific Publishers, 128–173.

Lewis, D.D. and Sparck, K. Jones. 1996. "Natural language processing for information retrieval", *Communications ACM* 39(1), 92–101.

Mannila, H., Toivonen, H. and Verkamo, A. 1994. "Efficient algorithms for discovering association rules" *KDD-94: AAAI Workshop on Knowledge Discovery in Databases*, 181–192.

Marcus, S. 1966. *Algebraic Linguistics: Analytical Models.* Academic Press, New York and London.

Polkowski, L. and Semeniuk-Polkowska, M. 1994. "A model of anaphora resolution based on distributional-algebraic approach in Analytical Models theory of Algebraic Linguistics" In C. Martín-Vide (ed), *Current Issues in Mathematical Linguistics.* Amsterdam: North Holland, 29–38.

Polkowski, L. and Skowron, A. 1997. "Rough mereology-a new paradigm for approximate reasoning" *Intern. J. Approximate Reasoning*, in print.

Revzin, I.I. 1966. *Models of Language*, London: Methuen.

Semeniuk-Polkowska, M. 1983. "The theory of configurations in Algebraic Linguistics", *Intern. J. Computer Mathematics* 14: 239–257.

Srinivasan, P. 1991. "The importance of rough approximations for information retrieval", *Intern. J. Man-Machine Studies* 34: 657–671.

Bidirectional and Event–Driven Parsing with Multi Virtual Trees

José F. Quesada

Centre for Scientific Informatics, Andalucía

Abstract

This paper deals with the problem of efficiency in Natural Language Processing. Basically, our main goal in this work is the design of a parsing kernel for real time applications. We propose a complete framework which includes: first, a new parsing technique based on a bottom–up, bidirectional and event–driven parsing strategy; second, a well founded formal definition of a set of predicates and relations that serve as the mathematical background of the parser; and third, a specific computational model that affects the memory organization for efficient storage of compiled Context–Free Grammars (CFG), as well as the data model used during parsing, which we have called multi virtual trees. All these components have been defined in a completely unified model.

More specifically, this paper concentrates on the mathematical foundations of the model, carefully describing the notions of partial derivability and adjacency, which permit the incorporation of strong top–down predictions over bottom–up strategies.

Bidirectional, event–driven and bottom–up parsing, with top–down predictions, based on multi virtual trees

The efficiency and robustness of a parser may be said to depend, among others, on three factors: the parsing algorithm itself, the mathematical model which serves as a base for the representation of grammatical relations, and the computational model or data structures which represent the objects to be manipulated by the parser.

A new parsing framework: linguistic, mathematical and computational issues

We have developed a complete framework which includes original ideas with respect to the three criteria mentioned above.

As regards the mathematical model, we use the specification of a CFG to define relations of coverage, partial derivability and adjacency, based on bottom–up derivations. These relations, defined mathematically as sets of objects associated with each symbol in the grammar, constitute the formal model generated after compiling the grammar and will be used directly by the parser.

The choice of the mathematical model above is dependent on the parsing algorithm. Basically, it consists of a bottom–up, bidirectional and event–driven parser. The events behave as analysis objects which are triggered by coverage tables. Moreover, there is also a hierarchy of filters which use the information available from the *plane of bidirectional analysis* and the tables of derivations and adjacencies in order to reject multiple events in the first stages of analysis.

For deterministic analyses, the parser actually manipulates a *surface of analysis* which evolves in time, until it reaches the root node in the grammar. For ambiguous grammars it is necessary to refer to a *plane of analysis* and this heads to the problem of defining computationally efficient structures to store so much information. We propose the creation of multi virtual trees, a novel approach to the notion of analysis forests, which is based on virtual relations among the components of the forest and on the separation of tree skeletons from the contents of each node. As a result, the contents of the node become independent of the node itself and are therefore reusable.

Finally, the model includes a series of computational strategies for the representation of symbolic information.

These ideas have been implemented in C on a medium–size workstation. The results obtained by the parser in the analysis of complex linguistic phenomena such as recursivity and local and non–local dependencies show that the parser can achieve a computational complexity in the order of $O(n\ log(n))$, where n is the length of the input string.

Also, the implementation has yielded results of between 2000 and 12000 words analyzed per second for the previous linguistic phenomena.

The combination of bottom–up and top–down strategies

Bottom–up parsing enriched with top–down predictions is one of the most common strategies in the design of parsers for context–free grammars.

Bottom–up models have been defended because of their efficiency (Pereira 1985), (Tomita 1987), (Carter 1990), (Shan 1991). The additional incorporation of top–down predictions improves the overall efficiency of the parser (Andrews and Brown 1993), (Dowding et al 1994), (Carroll 1994). As a result, we could say that these parsers are controlled simultaneously by the data (the input string) and the goal (the grammar).

This bivalent strategy is already present in the Earley algorithm. There, the predictor operator takes on the role of top–down prediction while the scanner operator in conjunction with the look–ahead component incorporates the bottom–up strategy (Earley 1970).

In the case of LR parsers, the action and goto tables are responsible for the bottom–up strategy being the basic strategy in the model (Aho and Ullman 1972), (Chapman 1987), (Tomita 1991). However, LR parsers are not exclusively bottom–up since the stack (or the graph) usually stores the left context of the symbol being analyzed. This information actually behaves as a predictive component which may be used to solve shift–reduce and reduce–reduce conflicts, as suggested by (Pereira 1985) and (Shieber 1983).

The bottom–up and top–down combination is also found in chart–based parsers (Kay 1980).

In the following sections we will present a parser which incorporates both strategies in a novel way. The core of the bottom–up component is a bidirectional generator of analysis events whose strategy is theoretically founded in a chart model. In our case the events will take on the roles of both active and inactive edges in a chart. Nevertheless, a pure chart generates an overhead of edges during analysis which reduces the overall efficiency of the system. To avoid this, a top–down component will act upon the bottom–up generator and impose strong restrictions. This will result in the elimination of edges (events) with no possibility of success.

Mathematical foundations

The top–down predictor component must be mathematically sound for the elimination of an event to be an irrefutable decision. With this goal, we define a set of relations in the domain of context–free grammars which will serve as the basis for the definition of top–down predictions.

Bottom–up derivations

In this section we provide a formal definition of the bottom–up derivation relation for a context–free grammar.

Context–free productions. Given a non empty set, X, we will call p a context–free production over X, where $p =< \delta, \Delta >$, written as $\delta \longrightarrow \Delta$, iff $\delta \in X$ and $\Delta \in X^*$. Given a non empty set, X, we will call P a set of context–free productions over X, iff $P \subseteq X \times X^*$

A set of productions, P, over a set X, defines three subsets of X:

- Set of non-terminals $P_N = \{\delta \in X : \exists \Delta \in X^*(\delta \longrightarrow \Delta \in P)\}$
- Set of terminals
  $P_T = \{\delta \in X : \delta \notin P_N \wedge \exists \lambda \in X, \exists \Gamma, \Omega \in X^*(\lambda \longrightarrow \Gamma\delta\Omega \in P)\}$
- Vocabulary $P_V = P_N \cup P_T$

Context–free grammars. Given a set of productions, P, and a set R, such that $R \subseteq P_N$, we define a context–free grammar, G, as $G =< P, R >$. Given a context–free grammar, $G =< P, R >$, the following sets can be obtained: productions of G: $G_P(= P)$; roots of G: $G_R(= R)$; terminal symbols of

G: $T(=P_T)$; non–terminal symbols of G: $N(=P_N)$; and vocabulary of G: $V(=P_V)$.

Direct bottom–up derivation in G. Let $\delta \in V$, and $\Delta, \Gamma, \Omega \in V^*$. We define the direct bottom–up derivation in G, $\longrightarrow_G$, as follows

$$\Gamma\Delta\Omega \longrightarrow_G \Gamma\delta\Omega \text{ iff } \delta \longrightarrow \Delta \in G_P$$

Bottom–up derivation in G. Let $\Gamma, \Omega \in V^*$. We define the bottom–up derivation in $G \Longrightarrow_G$, as follows

$$\Gamma \Longrightarrow_G \Omega \text{ iff } \exists\Delta_1, \ldots, \Delta_n \in V^* \text{ such that } \forall i_{(1 \leq i < n)} \Delta_i \Longrightarrow_G \Delta_{i+1}$$
$$\text{where } \Delta_1 \equiv \Gamma, \Delta_n \equiv \Omega$$

Mathematically, the bottom–up derivation is the reflexive and transitive closure of the direct bottom–up derivation.

Sentences in G. Let $\Delta \in T^*$. We will say that Δ is a sentence in G

$$S_G(\Delta), \text{ iff } \exists\delta \in G_R(\Delta \Longrightarrow_G \delta)$$

Language generated by a grammar G. Finally, we define the concept of context–free language as usual

$$L_G = \{\Delta \in T^* : S_G(\Delta)\}$$

Partial derivability and adjacency relations

Next we define the predicates and relations used by the top–down predictor. Let $\alpha, \beta \in V$:

Root symbols. α is a root symbol, $R(\alpha)$, iff $(\alpha \in G_R)$.

Epsilon symbols. α is an epsilon symbol, $E(\alpha)$, iff $(\varepsilon \Longrightarrow_G \alpha)$ [1].

[1] ε is the empty string; we will assume $E(\varepsilon)$.

String of epsilon symbols. Δ is a string of epsilon symbols, $E(\Delta)$, iff $\forall\delta \in \Delta(E(\delta))$.

Left partial derivability. β is a left partial derivation of α, $\alpha \longmapsto_l^* \beta$, iff $\exists\Gamma, \Delta, \Omega \in V^*(\Gamma\alpha\Delta \Longrightarrow_G \Gamma\beta\Omega)$.

We define $LPD(\alpha) = \{\beta \in V\alpha \longmapsto_l^* \beta\} \cup \{\alpha\}$ [2].

Right partial derivability. β is a right partial derivation of α, $\alpha \longmapsto_r^* \beta$, iff $\exists\Gamma, \Delta, \Omega \in V^*(\Gamma\alpha\Delta \Longrightarrow_G \Omega\beta\Delta)$.

We define $RPD(\alpha) = \{\beta \in V\alpha \longmapsto_r^* \beta\} \cup \{\alpha\}$ [3].

Primary adjacency. β is a primary adjacent of α, $\alpha \Uparrow \beta$, iff $\exists\delta \in V$ and $\exists\Gamma, \Omega, \Delta \in V^*(\delta \longrightarrow \Gamma\alpha\Delta\beta\Omega \in G_P \wedge E(\Delta))$.

Left adjacency. β is a left adjacent of α, $\alpha \Uparrow_l^* \beta$, iff $\exists\gamma \in LPD(\alpha) \wedge \exists\delta \in RPD(\beta)$ such that $(\delta \Uparrow \gamma)$

We define $LA(\alpha) = \{\beta \in V : \alpha \Uparrow_l^* \beta\}$.

Right adjacency. β is a right adjacent of α, $\alpha \Uparrow_r^* \beta$, iff $\exists\gamma \in RPD(\alpha) \wedge \exists\delta \in LPD(\beta)$ such that $(\gamma \Uparrow \delta)$.

We define $RA(\alpha) = \{\beta \in V : \alpha \Uparrow_r^* \beta\}$.

Left partial self–derivability. α is left partial self–derivable, $LPSD(\alpha)$, iff $\alpha \longmapsto_l^* \alpha$.

Right partial self–derivability. α is right partial self–derivable, $RPSD(\alpha)$, iff $\alpha \longmapsto_r^* \alpha$.

Left–most symbol. α is a left–most symbol, $LM(\alpha)$, iff $\exists\delta \in V(\alpha \longmapsto_l^* \delta \wedge R(\delta))$.

Right–most symbol. α is a right–most symbol, $RM(\alpha)$, iff $\exists\delta \in V(\alpha \longmapsto_r^* \delta \wedge R(\delta))$.

---

[2] We will consider that every symbol is a left partial derivation of itself.

[3] We will consider that every symbol is a right partial derivation of itself.

Coverage of the symbols in a grammar G

Next we will define three types of coverage. This information is used by the bottom–up component of the parser to generate the analysis events.

For each symbol, α, of a grammar ($\alpha \in G_V$), their left, $LC(\alpha)$, medium, $MC(\alpha)$, and right, $RC(\alpha)$, coverages are defined as sets of productions in the following way

$$\begin{aligned} LC(\alpha) &= \{\delta \longrightarrow \alpha\Delta : \Delta \in V^*\} \\ MC(\alpha) &= \{\delta \longrightarrow \Omega\alpha\Delta : \Omega, \Delta \in V^+\} \\ RC(\alpha) &= \{\delta \longrightarrow \Omega\alpha : \Omega \in V^+\} \end{aligned}$$

Bidirectional parsing and the plane of analysis

The choice of the mathematical model above is mutually dependent on the parsing algorithm. Basically, it consists of a bottom–up, bidirectional and event–driven parser. The events behave as analysis objects which are triggered by coverage tables. Moreover, there is also a hierarchy of filters which use the information available from the *plane of bidirectional analysis* and the tables of derivations and adjacencies in order to reject multiple events in the first stages of analysis.

Next, we will study how we can incorporate some strong top–down predictions based on the mathematical model presented over a classical bottom–up chart parser.

Chart parsing: analysis rules

A chart may be described roughly as a set of trees. Each tree is actually a directed acyclic graph (DAG), in which the leaves correspond to the words in the input sentence and each of the internal nodes corresponds to a syntactic structure of the grammar. This would be a *static* definition, mainly describing the result of parsing with a chart.

On the other hand, a *dynamic* definition of the parsing process distinguishes basically between nodes and arcs. Nodes have the role described above and arcs apply a rule of the grammar over a set of nodes. An arc is *inactive* when it has obtained all the nodes required on the right-hand side of the production which generated it. Otherwise, the arc will be *active*.

Let's illustrate these notions with the following grammar

```
(1:S ->NP VP)
(2:NP->np)
(3:NP->det n)
(4:VP->v)
(5:VP->v NP)
```

First, upon receiving a string of words to be parsed, each of the spaces between words is numbered sequentially

```
1 Peter 2 eats 3 the 4 cakes 5.
```

A node is represented by indicating the initial and final positions defining its interval and the symbol associated. In turn, an arc must contain information about the limits of its application interval, the rule which generated it and the number of symbols on the right-hand side of the rule already consumed. Thus, any arc will be represented as a four-tuple: <i,j,rule,pos>.

The pair (rule,pos) is usually represented in the literature by means of dotted rules. For example, the arc <1,2,2,2> = <1,2,NP->np.> represents the application of rule number 2 (NP -> np) in the interval 1-2. The arc has obtained all the symbols on the right-hand side and, therefore, is inactive. Now, the following arc <1,2,1,2> = <1,2,S->NP.VP> is an active arc which has applied rule number 1 (S -> NP VP) in the interval 1-2 and has only consumed an NP symbol so that it expects a VP symbol in the interval 2-N.

Obviously, every inactive arc automatically generates a node. In order to facilitate their representation, henceforward we will show inactive arcs between square brackets, indicating the application interval and the node generated, as follows [1,2,NP]

The combination rule. The basic rule of chart parsing is called the *combination rule* (CR), defined as follows: if a chart contains two adjacent nodes of the form $< i, j, \alpha \longrightarrow \Delta.\beta\Omega >$ and $< j, k, \beta \longrightarrow \Psi. >= [j, k, \beta]$ then we must generate a new arc with the form $< i, k, \alpha \longrightarrow \Delta\beta.\Omega >$. The new arc generated will be active or inactive depending on whether Ω is null or not.

Bottom–up rule. A bottom-up chart algorithm is obtained by applying the CR rule in combination with the *bottom–up rule* (BR): each time a new inactive arc is added to the chart, for example $< i, j, \alpha \longrightarrow \Psi. >= [i, j, \alpha]$, for each rule in the grammar of the form $(\lambda \longrightarrow \alpha\Omega)$, we must add a new active arc of the form $< i, i, \lambda \longrightarrow .\alpha\Omega >$.

Top–down rule. Finally, a top-down chart algorithm is obtained by applying the CR rule in combination with the *top–down rule* (TR): each time a new active arc is added to the chart, for example $< i, j, \alpha \longrightarrow \Delta.\beta\Omega >$, for each rule in the grammar of the form $(\beta \longrightarrow \Psi)$ we must include a new active node with the following form $< j, j, \beta \longrightarrow \Psi >$.

Bidirectional bottom–up rule, event–driven parsing and the use of the coverage tables

Next, we will concentrate on the use of a bottom–up strategy, such as the one obtained with the above combination and bottom–up rules. And we will analyze how to impose strong top–down predictions on this model by means of the mathematical model presented above.

In our proposal, we use the notion of event as a generalization of the notion of arc. We also justify a bidirectional strategy for parsing.

The most important consequence of this model is the modification of the classical bottom–up rule. Instead, we propose the following one:

Bidirectional bottom–up rule. Each time a new node (inactive arc) is added to the stack of the parser, for example $< i, j, \alpha \longrightarrow \Psi. >= [i, j, \alpha]$

- For each production $p \in LC(\alpha)$, that is, $p \equiv \lambda \longrightarrow \alpha\Omega$, we must add a new event of the form $< i, j, \lambda \longrightarrow .\alpha.\Omega >$ [4]
- For each production $p \in MC(\alpha)$, that is, $p \equiv \lambda \longrightarrow \Delta\alpha\Omega$, we must add a new event of the form $< i, j, \lambda \longrightarrow \Delta.\alpha.\Omega >$
- For each production $p \in RC(\alpha)$, that is, $p \equiv \lambda \longrightarrow \Delta\alpha$, we must add a new event of the form $< i, j, \lambda \longrightarrow \Delta.\alpha. >$

[4]The bidirectional strategy permits the use of double-dotted events. If Ω is empty, then, the event generated is closed on both sides: $[i, j, \lambda]$.

Imposing top–down predictions: partial derivability and adjacency

With this linguistic and computational model, we can obtain a formal definition of the processes of analysis of derivations and adjacencies as follow:

Analyses of partial derivations are applied over the open extremes of an event. Basically, we have to check whether the symbol needed is partially derivable from the real symbol. We will distinguish two types of analyses of derivations depending on the direction of the open extreme of the event.

Left–derivation analysis. Let us suppose that an event is applying the production $\delta \longrightarrow \delta_1 \ldots \delta_n$ over the surface $\Gamma\delta_1 \ldots \delta_i\omega\Omega$ where $1 \leq i < n$. In fact, this event is making a prediction of the (required) symbol δ_{i+1} over the (real) symbol ω. In this case, we have to check if $\delta_{i+1} \in LPD(\omega)$.

Right–derivation analysis. Let us suppose that an event is applying the production $\delta \longrightarrow \delta_1 \ldots \delta_n$ over the surface $\Gamma\varphi\delta_i \ldots \delta_n\Omega$ where $1 < i \leq n$. In fact, this event is making a prediction of the (required) symbol δ_{i-1} over the (real) symbol φ. In this case, we have to check if $\delta_{i-1} \in RPD(\varphi)$.

Analyses of adjacencies are applied over the closed extremes of an event. Basically, we have to check the adjacency relation between the symbol that the event will generate (the left–hand side of the production) and the symbol that appears next to the closed extreme of the event. We will distinguish two types of analyses of adjacencies depending on the direction of the closed extreme of the event.

Let us suppose that an event is applying the production $\gamma \longrightarrow \gamma_1 \ldots \gamma_n$ over the surface $\Delta\Gamma\Omega$ where $\Gamma \equiv \gamma_1 \ldots \gamma_n$.

Left–adjacency analysis. If Δ is non–empty ($\Delta \equiv \ldots\delta$), then we have to check if $\delta \in LA(\gamma)$. If Δ is empty ($\Delta \equiv \varepsilon$), then we have to check if $LM(\gamma)$

Right–adjacency analysis. If Ω is non–empty ($\Omega \equiv \omega\ldots$), then we have to check if $\omega \in RA(\gamma)$. If Ω is empty ($\Omega \equiv \varepsilon$), then we have to check if $RM(\gamma)$

Event driven parsing and multi virtual trees

In this section we introduce multi virtual trees, a novel approach to the notion of analysis forests, which are based on virtual relations among the components of the forest and on the separation of tree skeletons from the contents of each node.

The basic goal of our proposal has been to make the nodes of a tree or a forest of analyses and the structures and algorithms manipulated by the parser completely independent. This independence has been achieved by using *MvtNod* (node of a multi virtual tree) and *MvtCaD* (collection and diffusion of events in a multi virtual tree) structures in such a way that when the parser finishes we do not obtain a compact tree but a set of *MvtNod's*, each of which contains pointers to one or more possibilities of analysis. This is why the adjective *virtual* is used to describe the model. What are actually virtual are the relationships between the *MvtNod's*. In turn, these relations are transparent for the parsing algorithm, which only takes into account the events which depart from, or arrive at, each *MvtCaD*.

The basic idea underlying the parser is that analysis is an operation internal to a *MvtCaD*. As a consequence, we will be able to delete, merge[5], transfer or run an event. Whenever an event is modified, the affected *MvtCaD's* will be marked using some of the flags in the *MvtCaD* structure.

Experimental results

These ideas have been implemented in C on a medium–size workstation and have yielded results of between 2,000 and 12,000 words analyzed per second. The experimental results also show a real complexity of the order *O(n log(n))* which depends on the length of the input string for grammars including recursive constructions and local and non–local dependencies.

Next, we show the predicted model obtained for each type of grammar. The dependent variable T is the time used for the complete analysis (in seconds) and the factor used, W, is the length of the input string (number of words).

[5]The process of merging two events, due to the bidirectional strategy, must control some possible conflicts between events. These conflicts are detected by means of the self–partial derivability relation: $LPSD(\alpha)$ and $RPSD(\alpha)$

We show the results obtained with a Simple Lineal Regression Test for two cases. The first one uses T as the response and $W\ log(W)$ as the factor. The second one uses T/W as the response and the same factor $W\ log(W)$. In addition, we have included Pearson Correlation Coefficients (PCC) for both cases.

- Recursive Constructions

$$T = -5.183 + 219E - 7 * (Wlg(W)); PCC(T, Wlg(W)) = 0.999$$
$$T/W = 0.0001 + 46E - 13 * (Wlg(W)); PCC(T/W, Wlg(W)) = 0.974$$

- Local Dependencies

$$T = -17.82 + 352E - 7 * (Wlg(W)); PCC(T, Wlg(W)) = 0.993$$
$$T/W = 0.0002 + 38E - 12 * (Wlg(W)); PCC(T/W, Wlg(W)) = 0.998$$

- Non-local Dependencies

$$T = -1.031 + 851 - 8 * (Wlg(W)); PCC(T, Wlg(W)) = 0.998$$
$$T/W = 0.0002 + 14E - 12 * (Wlg(W)); PCC(T/W, Wlg(W)) = 0.998$$

Conclusion

Efficiency in Natural Language Processing involves three main factors concerning the linguistic, mathematical and computational bases. This paper proposes a parsing strategy that includes research in these three aspects.

From the linguistic perspective, the parser may be described as a bidirectional bottom–up event–driven system. The mathematical component defines a set of relationships which permit the incorporation of strong top–down predictions over the general bottom–up strategy. The computational level incorporates specifically designed data structures aimed at an efficient representation of all the information involved in the process. This paper concentrates on the mathematical foundations of this parsing model.

References

Aho, A.V. and Ullman, J.D. 1972. *The Theory of Parsing, Translation and Compiling. Vol. I: Parsing.* Englewood Cliffs, N.J.: Prentice Hall.

Andrews, N.A. and Brown, J.C. 1993. "A high–speed natural language parser". *AISB Quarterly* 86, 12-19.

Carroll, J. 1994. "Relating complexity to practical performance to natural–language processing". *CMP-LG e–print archive cmp-lg/9405033.*

Carter, D. 1990. "Efficient disjunctive unification for bottom–up parsing". *COLING'90*, 70-75.

Chapman, N. P. 1987. *LR Parsing. Theory and Practice.* Cambridge: Cambridge University Press.

Dowding, J., Moore, R., Andry, F. and Moran, D. 1994. "Interleaving syntax and semantics in an efficient bottom–up parser". *Proceedings of the 32nd Annual Meeting of the ACL*, 110-16.

Earley, J. 1970. "An efficient context–free parsing algorithm". *Communications of the ACM* 13(2), 94-102.

Kay, M. 1980. "Algorithm schemata and data structures in syntactic processing". *CSL-80-12 Xerox Palo Alto Research Center.*

Pereira, F.C.N. 1985. "A structure–sharing representation for unification–based grammar formalisms". *Proceedings of the 23rd Meeting of the ACL*, 137–144.

Shan, P. 1991. "Experiments with GLR and chart parsing". In (Tomita 1991), 17-34.

Shieber, S.M. 1983. "Sentence disambiguation by a shift–reduce parsing technique". *IJCAI'83*, 699-703.

Tomita, M. 1987. "An efficient augmented context–free parsing algorithm". *Computational Linguistics* 13(1-2), 31-46.

Tomita, M. (ed) 1991. *Generalized LR Parsing.* London: Kluwer Academic Publishers.

References

[illegible]

An LALR Extension for DCGs in Dynamic Programming

Manuel Vilares Ferro
Miguel Á. Alonso Pardo

University of A Coruña

Abstract

We propose a parsing model for natural languages based on the concept of definite clause grammar. Our work embodies in a common frame a dynamic programming construction developed for logical push-down automata, and techniques that restrict the computation to a useful part of the search space inspired by LALR parsing. Unlike preceding approaches, our proposal avoids backtracking in all cases, providing computational sharing and operational completeness for definite clause grammars without functional symbols.

Introduction

The popularity of definite clause grammars (DCGs) is often related to natural language processing. In comparison with other formalisms, they seem to be particularly well-suited to control the perspicuity with which linguistic phenomena may be understood and expressed in actual language descriptions. However, descriptive appropriateness does not guarantee operational efficiency, and computational tractability is required if we intend to use descriptions for the mechanical processing. Though much research has been devoted to this subject, most of the practically usable work deals with the reduction of backtracking phenomena when parsing. To attain this goal, authors often follow two different approaches:

- Reduce the search space, using control techniques. Here, we distinguish between dynamic techniques when control is made by rewriting programs (Bancilhon et al. 1986; Nilsson 1991) and static ones when control is made by an external driver, which determines the action to be performed (Nilsson 1986). Some authors (Rosenblueth and Peralta 1994) try to integrate both strategies.

- Incorporate dynamic programming techniques (Lang 1991; Pereira and Warren 1983) , which ensure that all parses are made in parallel, eliminating backtracking processes.

Our goal is to combine the advantages of the preceding approaches, while eliminating their drawbacks. We attempt to do three tings: improve the quality of sharing, while reducing dependence on the syntactic context, avoid extra evaluation work and reduce the search space by indexing the parse, and implementing a garbage collector facility. As the operational model we chose the logical push-down automaton (LPDA), a formal engine introduced by B. Lang (Lang 1991) that generalizes the dynamic programming aspects of earlier evaluation strategies.

In the following sections of this article, we introduce dynamic programming in LPDA's and we describe our evaluation scheme, as well as our dynamic programming framework and its complexity bounds for both time and space. A general consideration on the quality of the system is presented, as well comparisons with preceding proposals. The article ends with a discussion of the work.

The general framework

In essence, an LPDA is a push-down automaton that stores logical atoms and substitutions on its stack and uses unification to apply transitions. We consider a simple variation from the original notion of B. Lang (Lang 1991).

Formally, an LPDA is a 7-tuple $\mathcal{A} = (\mathcal{X}, \mathcal{F}, \Sigma, \Delta, \$, \$_f, \Theta)$, where: $\mathcal{X}$ is a denumerable and ordered set of variables, $\mathcal{F}$ is a finite set of functional symbols, Σ is a finite set of extensional predicate symbols, Δ is a finite set of predicate symbols used to represent the literals stored in the stack, $\$$ is the *initial predicate*, $\$_f$ is the *final predicate*; and Θ is a finite set of *transitions* of three kinds:

- *Horizontal:* $B \longmapsto C\{A\}$. Applicable to the stack $E.\rho\ \xi$, iff there exists the *most general unifier* (mgu), $\sigma = \text{mgu}(E, B)$ such that $F\sigma = A\sigma$, for a fact F in the extensional database. We obtain the new stack $C\sigma.\rho\sigma\ \xi$.

- *Pop:* $BD \longmapsto C\{A\}$. Applicable to stacks of the form $E.\rho E'.\rho'\ \xi$, iff there is $\sigma = \text{mgu}(< E, E'\rho >, < B, D >)$, such that $F\sigma = A\sigma$, for a fact F in the extensional database. The result will be the new configuration $C\sigma.\rho'\rho\sigma\ \xi$.

- *Push:* $B \longmapsto CB\{A\}$. We can apply it to configurations $E.\rho\ \xi$, iff there is $\sigma = \text{mgu}(E, B)$, such that $F\sigma = A\sigma$, for a fact F in the extensional database. We obtain the stack $C\sigma.\sigma\ B.\rho\ \xi$.

where B,C and D are literals in the algebra of terms $T_\Delta[\mathcal{F} \cup \mathcal{X}]$ and A is in $T_\Sigma[\mathcal{F} \cup \mathcal{X}]$, representing a control condition. Henceforth, we shall talk about *stacks* or *configurations* to refer to finite sequences of pairs *literal/substitution* denoted by $A.\sigma$, with the top on the left.

A *dynamic programming interpretation* of an LPDA $\mathcal{A}$ is the systematic exploration of a search space, whose elements $[\xi]$ are the classes of an equivalence relation $\mathcal{R}$ on the stacks ξ, that we call *items*. To manipulate this space, we define an operator *Op* adapting the transitions in $\mathcal{A}$ to their use with items. We use the term *dynamic frame* (Vilares Ferro 1992; Villemonte de la Clergerie 1993) to refer pairs $(\mathcal{R}, Op)$, and we denote by S^T the standard dynamic frame where *Op* is the identity and each stack is an item. Whichever the dynamic frame is, it must verify three properties in relation to S^T. Firstly, each computation in S^T has its corresponding counterpart in the dynamic frame (cf. compatibility). Secondly, all final configuration in S^T has its corresponding counterpart in the dynamic frame (cf. completeness). Finally, all final configurations found in our dynamic frame must correspond to final ones in S^T (cf. correctness).

The parsing algorithm builds items from the initial configuration, by applying transitions to existing ones until no new application is possible. To ensure fairness and completeness, an equitable selection order must be established in the search space. To ignore redundant items a subsumption-based relation must be put into place.

Improving sharing and efficiency

Due to the non-determinism of DCGs, it is advisable to merge the search space as much as possible. This saves on the space needed to represent items, and also on their processing.

The dynamic frame S^1

We exploit the possibilities of dynamic programming by taking S^1 as the dynamic frame (Vilares Ferro 1992; Villemonte de la Clergerie 1993). We take items of the form $[A.u] := \{A.u\xi\}$, which means that stacks are represented by their top. So, we reduce as much as possible the dependence on the syntactic context. To replace this lack of information during pops, we define the operator *Op* as follows:

- *Horizontal case:* $Op(B \longmapsto C)([A]) = [C\sigma]$, where $\sigma = \mathrm{mgu}(A, B)$.
- *Pop case:* $Op(BD \longmapsto C)([A]) = \{D\sigma \longmapsto C\sigma\}$, where $\sigma = \mathrm{mgu}(A, B)$, and $D\sigma \longmapsto C\sigma$ is the *dynamic transition* generated by the pop transition. This transition is applicable not only to the configuration resulting from the first transition, but also to those transitions to be generated and which share the same syntactic structure.
- *Push case:* $Op(B \longmapsto CB)([A]) = [C\sigma]$, where $\sigma = \mathrm{mgu}(A, B)$.

Reducing the search space

We index the parse by string position. So, we limit the search space at the time of recovery, as parsing progresses, by deleting information relating to earlier string positions. This relies on the concept of *itemset* (Earley 1970), for which we associate a set of items to each token in the input string, that represents the state of the parsing process at that point of the scan.

We extend itemsets to include dynamic transitions and decrease the number of such structures generated. To do this, it is sufficient to consider itemsets as synchronization points, and they are generated one by one. So, dynamic transitions in an itemset are only necessary once an empty reduction has been performed and ambiguity arises in the scope of the itemset (Vilares Ferro 1992).

We attach a *back pointer* to the itemset associated to the input symbol at which we began to look for that configuration of the LPDA, as well as a pointer to the current itemset. Items are now triples $[A, \text{itemset}, \text{back-pointer}]$, where $A \in T_\Delta[\mathcal{F} \cup \mathcal{X}]$.

The control strategy

S^1 guarantees the best sharing quality for a given evaluation scheme, but the choice of this scheme can noticeably alter the results (Vilares Ferro 1992). A balance between computational and sharing efficiency, and parser size is the best basis to decide. We focus on LALR(1)-like methods, which have a moderate splitting state phenomenon, and which improve both sharing and efficiency.

To build the driver, we recover the context-free backbone $\mathcal{G}^f$ of the DCG $\mathcal{G}$. We obtain terminals from the extensional database and non-terminals from heads in the intensional one. Terms with the same functor, but different number of arguments correspond to different symbols in $\mathcal{G}^f$. We then build the LALR(1) automaton, probably non-deterministic, for $\mathcal{G}^f$, that is adapted to context-free parsing in S^1 (Vilares Ferro 1992). To communicate the driver and the logical engine, we augment items with the state in which the driver is, to obtain quadruples $[A, \text{itemset}, \text{back-pointer}, \text{state}]$. We illustrate the work with the Dyck-language with one type of brackets. Throughout the rest of this paper, the following DCG is our running example

$$
\begin{array}{lllll}
\gamma_1 : & s(\text{nil}) & \rightarrow & \varepsilon \\
\gamma_2 : & s(s(\text{T}_1, \text{T}_2)) & \rightarrow & s(\text{T}_1)\ s(\text{T}_2) \\
\gamma_3 : & s(s([, \text{T},])) & \rightarrow & [\ s(\text{T})\ ]
\end{array}
$$

In this case, $\mathcal{G}^f$ is given by the context-free rules

$$\gamma_0^f : \Phi \rightarrow S \dashv \quad \gamma_1^f : S \rightarrow \varepsilon \quad \gamma_2^f : S \rightarrow S\,S \quad \gamma_3^f : S \rightarrow [\,S\,]$$

To control pops in a reduction, given a clause γ_k defined by $A_{k,0} \rightarrow A_{k,1}, \ldots, A_{k,n_k}$ in a DCG $\gamma_{1..m}$, we consider: The vector $\vec{T}_k$ of the variables occurring in γ_k, and the predicate symbol $\nabla_{k,i}$. An instance of $\nabla_{k,i}(\vec{T}_k)$ indicates that all literals from the ith literal in the body of γ_k have been proved. So, our evaluation scheme is given by the transitions

$$\begin{array}{lll}
1. & [A_{k,n_k}, it, bp, st] & \longmapsto \; [\nabla_{k,n_k}(\vec{T}_k), it, it, st]\,[A_{k,n_k}, it, bp, st] \\
 & & \qquad \{\text{action}(st, \text{token}_{it}) = \text{reduce}(\gamma_k^f)\} \\
2. & [\nabla_{k,i}(\vec{T}_k), it, r, st_1] & \\
 & [A_{k,i}, r, bp, st_2] & \longmapsto \; [\nabla_{k,i-1}(\vec{T}_k), it, bp, st_2] \\
 & & \qquad \{\text{action}(st_2, \text{token}_{it}) = \text{shift}(st_1)\},\ i \in [1, n_k] \\
3. & [\nabla_{k,0}(\vec{T}_k), it, bp, st] & \longmapsto \; [A_{k,0}, it, bp, st]
\end{array}$$

for the reduction mode, and

$$\begin{array}{lll}
4. & [A_{k,i}, it, bp, st_1] & \longmapsto \; [A_{k,i+1}, it+1, it, st_2]\,[A_{k,i}, it, bp, st_1] \\
 & & \qquad \{\text{action}(st_1, \text{token}_{it}) = \text{shift}(st_2)\},\ i \in [0, n_k) \\
5. & [\$, 0, 0, 0] & \longmapsto \; [A_{k,0}, 0, 0, st]\,[\$, 0, 0, 0] \\
 & & \qquad \{\text{action}(0, \text{token}_0) = \text{shift}(st)\}
\end{array}$$

for the scanning one. Briefly, we can interpret these transitions as follows:

1. *Selection of a clause* Select the clause γ_k whose head is to be proved; then push $\nabla_{k,n_k}(\vec{T}_k)$ on the stack to indicate that none of the body literals have yet been proved.

2. *Reduction of one body literal:* The position literal $\nabla_{k,i}(\vec{T}_k)$ indicates that all body literals of γ_k following the ith literal have been proved. Now, for all stacks having $A_{k,i}$ just below the top, we can reduce them and in consequence increment the position literal.

3. *Termination of the proof of the head of clause γ_k:* The position literal $\nabla_{k,0}(\vec{T}_k)$ indicates that all literals in the body of γ_k have been proved. Hence, we can replace it on the stack by the head $A_{k,0}$ of the rule, since it has now been proved.

4. *Pushing literals:* The literal $A_{k,i+1}$ is pushed onto the stack, assuming that they will be needed in reverse order for the proof.

5. *Initial push transition:* The initial predicate will only be used in push transitions, and exclusively as the first step of the LPDA computation.

Correctness and completeness are easily obtained from (Vilares Ferro 1992) and (Villemonte de la Clergerie 1993), based on these results for LALR(1) context-free parsing and bottom-up evaluation without functional symbols[1], both using S^1 as dynamic frame.

Complexity bounds

Unrestricted DCGs have Turing machine power. So, it makes no sense to give a useful notion of computational complexity. Following F. C. N. Pereira and D. H. D. Warren (Pereira and Warren 1983) we differentiate between *online* and *offline* parsing algorithms using unification constraints that are considered as soon as rules are applied, or as a supplementary filtering phase after a classic context-free parsing. Given that the *offline* case seems to be the only one that is linguistically relevant at the same time as the parsing problem is decidable, we estimate the complexity of doing online unification for offline parsable grammars. Assuming an input string of length n, our algorithm takes a time $\mathcal{O}(n^3)$ and a space $\mathcal{O}(n^2)$, in the worst case. The reasons are:

- The number of variables to access in an item and their ranges are both bounded. Only the value for the back pointer depends on i, and it is bounded by n. As a consequence, the number of items associated to the string position i is $\mathcal{O}(i)$, and the algorithm needs a space $\mathcal{O}(\Sigma_{i=0}^{n} i) = \mathcal{O}(n^2)$.

- Both push and horizontal transitions execute a bounded number of steps per item in any itemset, while pop ones can execute $\mathcal{O}(i)$ steps because they may have to add $\mathcal{O}(l)$ items for the itemset in the position l pointed back to. So, it takes a time $\mathcal{O}(i^2)$ in the itemset in

[1]The general case is not always decidable (Pereira and Warren 1983) .

the position i, in the worst case, and time complexity for a successful parsing, including online unification and subsumption checking is $\mathcal{O}(\Sigma_{i=0}^{n} i^2) = \mathcal{O}(n^3)$.

For the class of *bounded item grammars*, the number of items is bounded whichever the itemset is, and the time and space on the length of the input string are linear. This has a practical aplication because this class of grammar includes the LALR(1) family and, in consequence, linear parsing can be performed while local determinism is present.

A comparison with previous works

We shall compare our work with some of the most representative approaches based on inference systems for logic programs. As a reference we have taken the work of U. Nilsson (Nilsson 1986; Nilsson 1991), F. Bancilhon et al. (Bancilhon et al. 1986) , B. Lang (Lang 1991), E. Villemonte de la Clergerie (Villemonte de la Clergerie 1993), and D. Rosenblueth and J. Peralta (Rosenblueth and Peralta 1994) .

U. Nilsson (Nilsson 1986) and D. Rosenblueth and J. Peralta (Rosenblueth and Peralta 1994) propose SLR(1)-like evaluators, which are more efficient than grammar-oriented algorithms because they drastically limit backtracking. The difference between these approaches is the way in which they incorporate the contextual information present in DCGs. U. Nilsson ignores this information when generating the driver, and does not take it into account until reduction occurs. To prevent this from happening, D. Rosenblueth and J. Peralta concentrate the contextual information in the clauses of the extensional database, and this forces the original DCG to be rewritten in a non trivial manner the original DCG, while the application domain is restricted to fixed-mode DCGs. Both (Nilsson 1986; Rosenblueth and Peralta 1994) work in S^T but do not consider an indexing technique. Consequently, the sharing quality is low.

Control can also be introduced by a goal-oriented strategy, whose efficiency depends on the amount of significant work required to evaluate the control predicates introduced. This is the case of the Magic Set methods(Bancilhon et al. 1986; Nilsson 1991) , which disregard the sharing problem.

B. Lang and E. Villemonte de la Clergerie exploit the dynamic program-

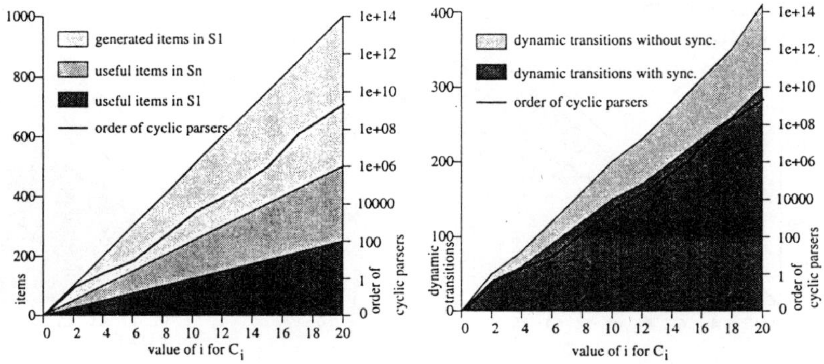

Figure 1: *Number of items and dynamic transitions*

ming construction of LPDAs, but they always consider state-less automata, which reduces the efficiency of evaluation. The size of the search space depends only on the evaluation scheme and efficiency depends closely on the DCG and the corpus of sentences to be analyzed, as is proved by M. Vilares (Vilares Ferro 1992).

Our proposal guarantees completeness and correctness, when ther are no functional symbols, for unrestricted DCGs. Control is given by an LALR(1) driver, with a moderate state splitting phenomenon and large deterministic domain. The dynamic programming construction avoids backtracking, and the dynamic frame S^1 ensures optimal sharing for the evaluation scheme. The use of itemsets such as synchronization structures facilitates the reduction of the search space and the detection of cycles, a point that none of the preceding authors touch on.

Experimental results

We have selected a scenario that cannot be qualified as advantageous. We search for DCGs with the following characteristics: the language should include sentences with a high density of ambiguities, to prove the suitability of the algorithm for sharing computations, the grammar should tackle the problem of recursive evaluation, and the data should contain cycles to prove that they adapt to this feature and, finally, garbage collection should not

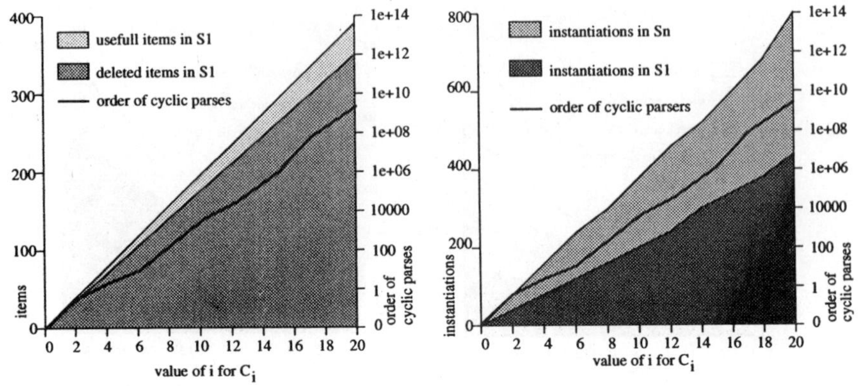

Figure 2: *Unified pairs and garbage collector*

be trivial.

As far as these requeriments are concerned, our running example seems to be a good candidate. Reductions involve, in the worst case, two terminals separated by another reduction. So, the the use of indexes does not allow large memory recovery. Sentences of the form $[.\overset{i}{.}.\,[\,]\,.\overset{i}{.}.]$, are taken as input strings. Because the grammar contains a rule $S \rightarrow S\ S$, the number of cyclic parses grows exponentially with i. This number is

$$C_0 = C_1 = 1 \quad \text{and} \quad C_i = \binom{2i}{i}\frac{1}{i+1}, \text{ if } i > 1$$

On this basis, the left-hand scheme in Figure 1 gives the number of useful and useless items generated in S^1 and also compares the number of generated useful items generated in S^1 and S^T, while the right-hand scheme shows the number of dynamic transitions generated in S^1 considering and not considering synchronization on itemsets. Finally, the left-hand scheme in Figure 2 shows the behavior of the garbage collector facility, while the right-hand one represents the number of pairs unified during the parse process. Additional costs due to the computation of the driver are irrelevant.

We cannot really provide a comparison with other DCG parsers because of their problems dealing with cyclic structures. However we can take results on S^T as a reference for non-dynamic SLR(1)-like methods (Nilsson 1986; Rosenblueth and Peralta 1994) , since in this case the SLR(1) driver is closed to ours due to the little impact of the lookahead facility. Naïve dynamic bottom-up methods (Lang 1991; Villemonte de la Clergerie 1993) can be assimilated to S^1 results without synchronizing either garbage collector, also because the little impact of state splitting in the example.

Conclusion

We have described a strategy for implementing DCG parsers. Our operational frame is an LPDA in dynamic programming. The architecture is a bottom-up evaluation scheme optimized with a predictive control given by an LALR(1) driver. The system ensures an optimal treatment of sharing of computations, and completeness and correctness for DCGs without functional symbols.

Although preliminary results seem robust, there is still some work to be done to exploit the potential of our proposal to the fullest. In particular, future improvements will include an incremental facility in order to provide interactive parsing.

Acknowledgments

This work was partially supported by Xunta de Galicia (Projects XUGA 20403B95 and XUGA 10505B96) and Government of Spain (*Acción integrada* HF96-36).

References

Bancilhon, F., Maier, D., Sagiv, Y. and Ullman, J. 1986. "Magic-set and other strange ways to implement logic programs". *Proc. of the 5th ACM SIGMOD-SIGACT Symp. on Principles of Database Systems.*

Earley, J. 1970. "An efficient context-free parsing algorithm". *Communications of the ACM* 13(2):94–102.

Lang, B. 1991. "Towards a uniform formal framework for parsing". In M. Tomita (ed), *Current Issues in Parsing Technology.* Norwell: Kluwer Academic Publishers, 153–171.

Nilsson, U. 1986. "AID: An alternative implementation of DCGs". *New Generation Computing* 4:383–399.

Nilsson, U. 1991. "Abstract interpretation: A kind of magic". *Proc. of PLILP'91.*

Pereira, F.C.N. and Warren, D.H.D. 1983. "Parsing as deduction". *Proc. of the 21st Annual Meeting of the Association for Computational Linguistics*, 137-144.

Rosenblueth, D.A. and Peralta, J.C. 1994. "LR inference: Inference systems for fixed-mode logic programs, based on LR parsing". In M. Bruynooghe (ed), *Logic Programming. Proceedings of the 1994 International Symposium (ILPS'94).* Cambridge: The MIT Press, 439–453.

Vilares Ferro, M. 1992. *Efficient Incremental Parsing for Context-Free Languages*, PhD thesis, University of Nice, France.

Villemonte de la Clergerie, E. 1993. *Automates à Piles et Programmation Dynamique*, PhD thesis, University of Paris VII, France.

PART IV

VARIA

Parsing Unrestricted Text into Prosodic Units. A Formal Description

David Casacuberta
Rafael Marín
Lourdes Aguilar

Autonomous University of Barcelona

1 Introduction

Applications in natural language processing and speech technologies such as text-to-speech or recognition systems require text analysis procedures that are able to run in real time with a low computational cost, and that are robust enough to deal with unrestricted input text. Attempts to automatize the processes of obtaining and analyzing data are being made (Hirschberg 1991, Ostendorf and Veilleux 1994); however, to achieve this goal, a model is needeed in which units and levels of analysis are defined. This paper[1] presents the axiomatization of a procedure for segmenting texts into prosodic units, which can be implemented in a text-to-speech (TTS) system.

In the domain of TTS systems, interest in applying automatic procedures is steadily expanding, mainly due to the development of multilingual systems in laboratories and to the growth of vocal services using speech synthesis. Moreover, there is an attempt to overcome one of the main problems in TTS systems: the lack of naturalness due to deficiencies in prosodic and linguistic information. Although it is generally agreed that an appropriate allocation of pauses improves the overall quality of a TTS system, it is not clear why this should be so. It could be said that it is chiefly due to the contribution of prosody to speech perception (Nooteboom *et al.* 1978). Pauses help to segment words because pauses coincide with word boundaries and word groups, and tend to signal semantically and syntactically coherent groups; moreover, pauses provide the human processor with additional time to cope with linguistic information. Obviously, these perceptual functions become more important in synthetic speech where the signal does not include any acoustic-phonetic redundancy.

However, although we agree on the need for an adequate strategy for assigning pauses, it is not an easy task. On the one hand, a multiplicity of factors is involved in the prosodic segmentation performed by a speaker (Dechert and Raupach 1980); on the other hand, some pauses are optional and are therefore difficult to systematize.

The problem of how to deal with these matters and their application to TTS systems is the main concern in a growing family of prosodic segmentation algorithms. Assumptions concerning the relation among the linguistic modules of the system influence the form of the algorithm, varying from systems performing a complete syntactic analysis which is then reinterpreted in prosodic terms (Frenkenberger *et al.* 1994) to systems that merely perform a morphological analysis without considering syntactic information (Emerard *et al.* 1992). The most successful approach is nevertheless the one that at the same time considers the importance of both syntactic and non-syntactic factors in the prediction of prosodic boundaries (Bachenko and Fitzpatrick 1990, Hirschberg and Prieto 1996). Following this approach, it is assumed that suprasegmental phenomena cannot be derived exclusively from one source of information.

On the other hand, the theoretical model establishes the units and the levels of analysis that will be used in the algorithm. For instance, Hirschberg and Prieto 1996 adopt Pierrehumbert's theory of intonational description for English (Pierrehumbert 1980) to develop a phrasing module for a TTS system for Mexican Spanish, whereas Bachenko and Fitzpatrick 1990 formalize the psychological model described in Gee and Grosjean 1983.

Within this framework of studying the relation between disciplines such as syntax and prosody, and the limitations dictated by the application in a TTS system, our study has a three-fold aim. First, we describe a methodology for automatically assigning pauses in texts; second, we propose a formal description of this methodology; and finally, we test the reliability of the procedure by implementing it in a system.

2 The empirical facts

Before presenting the empirical facts to be explained by the formal model, we will devote some space to the units used in this model.

2.1 Units

The stress group (SG) is conceived as a string, formed by zero or more unstressed words preceding a lexically stressed word. For example, the string *el pelo* ("the hair") is an SG consisting of an unstressed word preceding the stressed one, whereas *ventana* ("window") is an SG with only one element, the noun *ventana*. Following traditional Spanish linguistic descriptions, the appearance of stress can be related to the lexical category of the word. Open categories (that is, nouns, verbs, adjectives and adverbs) are considered to be lexically stressed words, while closed categories –prepositions, determiners or conjunctions– are unstressed[2].

A categorial stress group (CSG) can be seen as an SG which includes syntactic properties, that is, a prosodic unit carrying syntactic information.

When labeling an SG to obtain a CSG, it is necessary to differentiate between SGs formed by only a stressed word and SGs with one or more unstressed words preceding the stressed one. As for the first, we simply indicate the syntactic category to which the stressed word belongs. We refer to this category as the head of the CSG. Thus, an SG such as *ventana* is labeled as noun group (ng).

To deal with SGs formed by more than one word, the category of the first unstressed word of the CSG, as well as the category of the stressed word, has to be indicated. In this case, the category of the first word will be considered the head of the CSG, and the category of the last word the modifier of the CSG. Going back to the example given above, *el pelo* is a CSG in which the first category is a quantifier[3] and the last one a noun. We will abbreviate this as qg(n), where 'q' stands for 'quantifier', 'g' for 'group', and 'n' for 'noun'. The letter before 'g' refers to the head and the one in brackets to the modifier.

The list of stressed categories and the corresponding CSGs is as follows: adjective (ag), adverb (adg), gerund (g), infinitive (i), noun (ng), participle (pt) and verb (vg).

The list of CSGs formed by more than one word is the following:

–cg: head: conjunction; possible modifiers: a, ad, g, i, n, pt, v.

–ccg: head: coord. conjunction; possible modifiers: a, ad, g, i, n, pt, v.

–clg: head: clitic; possible modifier: v.

–pg: head: preposition; possible modifiers: a, ad, g, i, n, pt, v.

–qg: head: quantifier; possible modifiers: a, ad, pt, v.

We thus have two levels of specification: one which takes into account only the head and one which also specifies the modifier. Consequently, in a sentence such as *Darwin tuvo que reconocer el fracaso de su teoría,* two labelings are possible

(1) *[Darwin]ng [tuvo]vg [que reconocer]cg [el fracaso]qg [de su teoría]pg*
Darwin was forced to accept the failure of his theory.

(2) *[Darwin]ng [tuvo]vg [que reconocer]cg(i) [el fracaso]qg(n) [de su teoría]pg(n)*

In (2), the letter appearing after the name of the CSG indicates its modifier. Thus, for example, the CSG [*de su teoría*]pg(n) is a prepositional group which has a noun as modifier.

2.2 A definition of pause

A pause can be defined as an interruption of the sound stream, which is acoustically marked by a silence and is perceptible to the listener. Since we are dealing with read speech, it is worth distinguishing between orthographically marked and unmarked pauses, optional and mandatory pauses, and reasonable and impossible pauses.

An orthographically marked pause is a pause that is signalled in a text by means of a punctuation sign; any other pause that cannot be related to a textual sign is an orthographically unmarked pause. In this study, we will try to explain and predict the appearance and location of orthographically unmarked pauses. While being aware of the simplification that this implies, we assume that punctuation signs are associated to a pause.

A pause is considered to be mandatory if the speaker is forced to fragment the sentence, while it is considered to be optional if different speakers could locate the pause in different places in the same sentence.

Finally, we say that a pause is impossible if no Spanish speaker would make such a pause in a neutral reading. On the other hand, if a pause is acceptable to a listener, we are dealing with a reasonable pause.

To achieve a better understanding of these distinctions, it is worth looking at a sentence such as (3)

(3) *Las silenciosas pausas entre las estaciones dejaron de ser vividas como una suspensión del sentido y ya no fueron vistas como una momentánea parálisis de la norma ni como una gran crisis o relativización.*
Silent pauses between seasons were no longer perceived as an interruption of sense and they were no longer seen as a momentary paralysis of norms, or as a great crisis or as a relativization.

A speaker has read this sentence with the pauses marked in (4)

(4) *Las silenciosas pausas entre las estaciones dejaron de ser vividas como una suspensión del sentido $*[4] *y ya no fueron vistas como una momentánea parálisis de la norma $ ni como una gran crisis o relativización.*

It is obvious that mandatory fragmentation must occur in this sentence for the sake of maximum comprehension on the part of the listener. Our speaker has made two pauses, but in fact there is at least one other possible place to locate a reasonable pause: that is, before the verb *dejaron*. On the contrary, a pause before *entre* will generate an unacceptable result.

2.3 Constraints guiding pause location

The analysis of a corpus of read text in Spanish is the source of the description of the prosodic and syntactic factors that guides the pause location in texts (cf. Marín *et al.* 1996). We summarize below the generalizations found in the empirical study which are the basis for the formal model.

The length of the sentence, measured in terms of the number of SGs, determines the obligatory appearance of a pause. This prosodic constraint can be summarized as follows: in a neutral text, at a normal speech rate, at least seven SGs are required to insert a pause, while the existence of ten or more groups requires the segmentation of the sentence. As a consequence, the pause is optional in a sentence of between seven and nine SGs.

There is also a prosodic explanation of the location of the pause: in general, pauses tend to appear in the middle of a sentence. This fact can be related to the tendency of speakers to balance the length of the resulting phonic groups (cf. Nespor and Vogel 1983).

It is proposed here that the CSG is a unit that can explain the syntactic factors constraining the location of pauses. It has been found that the type of CSG favours or blocks the appearance of a pause before it. Thus, it is possible to establish a hierarchy of CSGs, as follows: ccg > vg > cg > gg > clg > adg > pg > qg > ptg > ig > ng > ag.

However, the CSG hierarchy is not enough to prevent the impossible pauses. Consider, for example, sequence (5)

(5) [...] *Juan y Pedro dijeron* [...].
John and Peter said.

According to the hierarchy above, a pause will have to appear before *y Pedro.* However, our linguistic competence indicates that this pause is not acceptable: if a pause were to appear in this sentence, it should appear before *dijeron.* In order to solve such cases, a battery of syntactic restriction rules interacts with the hierarchy of CSG. Going back to (5), a rule forbidding the appearance of a pause between two successive nouns is necessary.

3 A formal description

In this section we undertake a formal description of the concepts and methodology outlined in the preceding section. Our aim here is to give a simple description, using the basic elements of set theory, suitable for use in a system running in real time.

3.1 Concepts

A text **T** is any n-tuple where if $\mathbf{w} \in \mathbf{T}$ then **w** is a Spanish word (token) or a punctuation sign. The set of Spanish words is a primitive in the system.

In any n-tuple, the position of an element **w** is defined as the order number that this element has in its n-tuple. So, in the text ⟨**de, la, casa**⟩, **la** has position number two. Evidently, the same word type can appear as different tokens in the same text. In this case, every token has its own position. In the text ⟨**de, la, casa, de, mi, padre**⟩, there are two different token appearances of word-type 'de': the first of them has position number one and the other position number four.

tag is a categorial function if and only if, for every $\mathbf{x} \in \mathbf{T}$, where **T** is a text, **tag**(**x**) = **c**, where $\mathbf{c} \in$ **Cat**, a finite set that contains all the categories in which Spanish words are divided for the purposes of our study and nothing else: **Cat** cannot be the empty set.

For example, let us consider **Cat** = {**noun, verb, adjective, adverb, quantifier, preposition, punctuation-sign**}. Then, our function **tag**, applied to all the elements of ⟨**de, la, casa**⟩, will give us **tag(de)** = **preposition**, **tag(la)** = **quantifier**, **tag(casa)** = **noun**. Depending on the elements that form **Cat**, we will have different types of functions, with possibly different images for every word type.

If we make some changes to our original **Cat** set and develop **Cat'** = {**noun, verb, adjective, adverb, quantifier, de-type-preposition, non-de-type-preposition, punctuation-sign**}, then our new **Cat'** will give us **tag(de)** = **de-type-preposition**. Thus the system is not restricted to an a priori closed group of categories, but rather it offers the possibility of adding, extracting and modifying categories as the study goes along.

Obviously, the function is not sensitive to the position of the element in the utterance, so, using **Cat** as the base set, in the utterance ⟨**de, la, casa, de, mi, padre**⟩ both **de** in position one and in position four have the same image, that is, **preposition**, and their different positions have no effect on the result.

Leaving aside the formal aspect, a tagger would be responsible for implementing the function **tag** in a computer application.

st is the stress function when, for every $\mathbf{w} \in$ T, **st**(**x**) = **s**, where $\mathbf{s} \in$ {**stressed, unstressed**}. It is interesting to observe that, contrary to **tag**, **st** is fixed, because stressed and unstressed are basic categories we do not plan to alter; instead, we merely accept phonetic evidence. The **st** function can be implemented by means of a database combining phonetic and lexical information to decide whether a word is stressed or not.

As already stated, our system aims to detect orthographically unmarked pauses, once the orthographically marked ones have been assigned. This implies that the main algorithm is applied not to the whole text, but to utterances, that is, fragments of the text separated by punctuation signs. The formal definition of utterance is as follows. An utterance **U** is obtained from a text **T**, and **U** is an m-tuple where a) for every **w1**, **w2** ∈ **U** if **w1**'s position in **U** is n and **w2**'s position in **U** is n+1, then **w1**, **w2** ∈ **T**, **w1**'s position in **T** is m and **w2**'s position in **T** is m+1; b) the first element of **U** is either: 1) the first element of **T**; or 2) the next element in **T** after an element **w** ∈ **T** such that **tag(w)** = **punctuation-sign**; c) the last element of **U** is either: 1) the last element of **T**; or 2) the previous element in **T** before an element **w** ∈ **T** such that **tag(w)** = **punctuation-sign**; d) for every **w** ∈ U, **tag(w)** ≠ **punctuation-sign**.

We can say that an m-tuple **ftu** is a fragmentation of a text **T** in utterances if and only if: a) **p** ∈ **ftu** then **p** is an utterance obtained from **T**; b) for every **w** ∈ **T** such that **Cat(w)** ≠ **punctuation-sign** there is a **p** ∈ **ftu** such that **w** ∈ **p** and **p** is unique.

A categorial stress group **CSG** from an utterance **U** is an n-tuple, where every element **x** ∈ **CSG** has the form ⟨**w, cat,** s⟩, where **w** ∈ **U**, **Cat** = **tag(w)** and **s** = **st(w)** and a) if a **CSG** has n elements, then the element with position number n is a 3-tuple ⟨**w, cat,** s⟩, such that **s** = **stressed** and if ⟨**w', cat',** s'⟩ ∈ **CSG** and ⟨**w', cat',** s'⟩'s position < n, then **s'** = **unstressed**; b) if ⟨**w, cat,** s⟩ ∈ **CSG**, ⟨**w, cat,** s⟩'s position in **CSG** is n, ⟨**y,cat',s'**⟩ ∈ **CSG** and ⟨**y,cat',s'**⟩'s position in **CSG** is n+1, then **w** ∈ **U**, **w**'s position in **U** is m, **y** ∈ **U** and **y**'s position in **U** is m+1; c) **CSG** ≠ ∅.

3.2 Formal description of the algorithm

3.2.1 Generating categorial stress groups

We will define **group** as a function that for every utterance **U** with m elements gives an n-tuple **TCSG**, where m ≥ n and every element **w** ∈ **TCGS** is a **CSG** obtained from the utterance **U** and a) for every **w1** ∈ **U** there is one and only one **CSG** ∈ **TCSG** such that ⟨**w1, tag(w1), st(w1)**⟩ ∈ **CSG**; b) for every **w1, w2** ∈ **U** such that **w1** position is n and **w2** position is n+1 then either 1) there is one **CSG** such that ⟨**w1, tag(w1), st(w1)**⟩ ∈ **CGS**, ⟨**w2, tag(w2), st(w2)**⟩ ∈ **CGS** and if ⟨**w1, tag(w1), st(w1)**⟩ position is m, then ⟨**w2, tag(w2), st(w2)**⟩ is m+1; or 2) there are **CSG1, CSG2** ∈ TCGS such that **CSG1** position is **x** and **CSG2** is x+1 and the last element of **CSG1** is ⟨**w1**, **tag**(**w1**), **st**(**w1**)⟩ and the first element of **CSG2** is ⟨**w2**, **tag**(**w2**), **st**(**w2**)⟩.

Not every utterance **U** can be an argument for **group**. The necessary and sufficient condition for it is that the last word of the utterance be stressed. Observe that, if the last word is not stressed, then no matter how the former words are packed into CSGs, this last word cannot form part of a CSG because there are by definition no further elements after the last one. This last word of the utterance should be the end of a CSG, but according to point a) in the definition of CSG (cf. §3.1) the last element of a CSG must be stressed. Since we assumed that the last element was unstressed, this poses a contradiction, and **U** cannot be divided into CSGs.

3.2.2 Modeling the prosodic constraints

The first prosodic constraint can be translated as follows: in a text, the more SGs there are, the more likely it is that a pause is needed. We can assign this criterion by means of presenting an interval of SGs where the pause is possible. Here is the function pause-type: **pt** is a function that goes from **N** to **typause**, where **typause** is a set whose members are **typause** = {**non-existent**, **optional**, **mandatory**}. Integers from 1 to 6 have **non-existent** as image, integers from 7 to 9 have **optional** as image, and integers greater than 9 have **mandatory** as image.

The other prosodic constraint states that in a sentence, the more centered the pause, the better. We model it with a function that takes an utterance and erases the first and last three SGs in it. Formally **cut** is a function that takes an utterance **U1** of length m and produces another utterance **cut**(**U1**) = **U2** where **U2** length is m-6 and: a) **U2** is a subsequence of **U1**, that is, **U1** is like a text from which **U2** has been obtained; b) if **pt**(**U1**) = **non-existent** then **cut**(**U1**) = **U1**. If this is not the case, then: c) the first element of **U2** is **w**, where **w** ∈ **U1** and **w** position is 4; d) the last element of **U2** is **w2**, where **w2** ∈ **U1** and **w2** position is m-3.

3.2.3 Modeling the syntactic constraints

A syntactic constraint stipulates which categories are more likely to have a pause; formally, the function **catco** is used to model this constraint.

The function **catco** has two arguments, both belonging to **Cat**, which represent the head and the modifier. It has a natural number as image, which indicates the probability of a CSG with the first category of **catco** as head and the second as the modifier with a pause before. When the head and the modifier coincide we simply repeat the category. Extensionally, **catco** can be defined as follows **catco**(cc,v) = 1; **catco**(cc,n) = 2; **catco**(v,v) = 3; **catco**(c,v) = 4; **catco**(g,g) = 5; **catco**(cl,v) = 6; **catco**(ad,ad) = 7; **catco**(p,n) = 8; **catco**(p,v) = 9; **catco**(p,a) = 10; ...

These probability assignations were obtained by the authors in an empirical study described in Marín *et al.* 1996. Other combinations are in principle possible but only very occasionally present pauses, so they have associated an 0, indicating that no pause can be found.

There are in fact two different **catco**, because optional and mandatory pauses have different probabilities in the assignation of pauses. So, we use **catco2** to determine the most likely place for a pause to appear in a sentence that has an optional pause and **catco1** to calculate the probability of pause in mandatory pause sentences. These functions are alike, except that some of the items are not considered, and therefore assigned numerical probabilities differ.

3.2.4 Restriction rules

As mentioned above (cf. §2.3), the hierarchy of CSG types is not sufficient to prevent some impossible pauses. In these cases, a battery of restriction rules has been defined. Formally, the restriction rules are governed by the function **rest**: **rest** is a function that assigns a 'yes' if there is no restriction between two **CSG** types to have a pause and 'no' if the pause is inadmissible: **rest** (⟨Cat,Cat⟩,⟨Cat,Cat⟩) → **yes, no.** We present rest extensionally: **rest**(⟨cc,v⟩,⟨n,n⟩) = **yes**; **rest**(⟨v,v⟩,⟨cc,n⟩) = **yes**; **rest**(⟨n,n⟩,⟨v,v⟩) = **yes**; **rest**(⟨a,a⟩,⟨cc,a⟩) = **no**; **rest**(⟨ad,ad⟩,⟨v,v⟩) = **no** ...

3.2.5 A model for locating pauses in a text

Our algorithm takes a text and returns an n-tuple where this text is divided into utterances; there should be no pause within these utterances, although there should be a pause between each of them. First, the system takes the text and applies **Cat** and **st** to every word of it. Then, the text is divided into utterances, obtaining an **ftu** of the text with every utterance in it. The next step is to segment every utterance into CSGs. Afterwards, with the help of **pt** the system decides whether or not a pause is needed for each utterance. If there is no pause, the task is complete.

However, if there is a mandatory or optional pause, the second prosodic constraint is applied and **cut** is activated. Once the new utterance is obtained, the syntactic constraint is applied by means of **catco**. The possible place for a pause is checked using rest to make sure that it is really suitable. If it is not, another position is searched for using **catco**, and examined with **rest** until a satisfactory place to insert a pause is found. In the case of an optional pause, no other position is searched for. Once this is done, the remaining utterances are checked with **pt** until every utterance has been successfully divided into pauses.

4 Evaluating the methodology

The formal procedure, able to capture the empirical facts, has been implemented in Edinburgh Standard Prolog. The program designed to assign pauses in unrestricted texts contains a set of rules and a database with the words labeled with their lexical category. The text is read from an ASCII format and the output is another ASCII document which duplicates the text, but which markes all the mandatory and reasonable pauses the system computes.

Let us now consider how the program will work on a fragment of text, by means of the following two examples

(6) *Trabajaba en Barcelona.*
He/she worked in Barcelona.

(7) *Su módulo de tres cuerpos y la acertada resolución espacial están a la altura de cualquier modelo europeo y son superiores a los americanos.*
Its three-story module and its successful spatial resolution are comparable to any European model and are superior to the American ones.

The sentence in (6) has two SGs, so it is too short to contain a pause. Since a pause cannot appear if the sentence has less than seven SGs, the program will not break the sentence.

However, the sentence in (7) has fourteen SGs, so according to the first prosodic constraint, a pause will be obligatory. Regarding the location of the pause, it has been mentioned above that pauses tend to appear in the center of a sentence.

This is implemented by removing the first and the last three SGs in an utterance, as shown when comparing (8a) with (8b)

(8) a. *[Su módulo] [de tres] [cuerpos] [y la acertada] [resolución] [espacial] [están] [a la altura] [de cualquier] [modelo] [europeo] [y son] [superiores] [a los americanos]*
b. *[y la acertada] [resolución] [espacial] [están] [a la altura] [de cualquier] [modelo] [europeo]*

The most central place would be between the CSGs *a la altura* and *de cualquier*. However, these two CSGs maintain a strong syntactic dependence, while there is less syntactic cohesion between *espacial* and *están*. This is represented by the hierarchy of CSGs implemented with the function **catco1**: it is preferable to insert the pause before a [vg] rather than before a [pg]. Therefore, the program will locate the pause before [*están*]. After the first pause is located, we have two new utterances

(9) a. *Su módulo de tres cuerpos y la acertada resolución espacial*
b. están a la altura de cualquier modelo europeo y son superiores a los americanos.

The first one is only six CSGs long, so it cannot be segmented. The second one is eight CSGs long, so it may have an optional pause. The location of the pause is determined by the hierarchy of CSGs and solved by **catco2**. Once **catco2** is loaded, we find a place where an optional pause is suitable, namely between *europeo* and *y son*, that is before a cc(v). The final result would be as follows

(10) *Su módulo de tres cuerpos y la acertada resolución espacial $ están a la altura de cualquier modelo europeo $ y son superiores a los americanos.*

If we compare this segmentation with another performed by a speaker, the obligatory pauses are found to coincide and it is only in the domain of optionality that divergences are found.

5 Conclusions

In this paper, a formal description of a syntactico-prosodic analysis for unrestricted text has been presented. The central unit in the analysis is the

CSG, an SG which is syntactically labeled; in other words, a prosodic unit which carries syntactic information. This unit has proved to be useful in a system for automatically assigning pauses in texts.

The empirical facts have been formalized and implemented in a system. This syntactico-prosodic system can assign all the mandatory pauses a text needs, and also generate some optional pauses that are always reasonable according to our definition above, the final result being an acceptable assignation of pauses. The formal model avoids syntactic recursion, which makes it possible to have a program of greater computational simplicity, speed and effectiveness. This is especially important in such applications as TTS systems, where all transformations have to be performed in real time.

Notes

1. We would like to thank Sergio Balari for his valuable comments. R. Marín's work was partially supported by a grant from Generalitat de Catalunya (AP-LP/95-2704).
2. For a more detailed discussion of stressed and unstressed words in Spanish, see Navarro Tomás 1925.
3. We use "quantifier" in its broad sense, including categories such as determiners, demonstratives, possessives, ...
4. Throughout the article, we will use the sign '$' to represent a pause.

References

Bachenko, J. and Fitzpatrick. E. 1990. "A computational grammar of discourse-neutral prosodic phrasing in English". *Computational Linguistics* 16(3): 155–170.

Dechert, H. W. and Raupach, M. (eds). 1980. *Temporal Variables in Speech.* The Hague: Mouton.

Emerard, F., Mortamet, L. and Cozannet, A. 1992. "Prosodic processing in a text-to-speech synthesis system using a database and learning procedures". In G. Bailly and C. Benoit (eds), *Talking Machines: Theories, Models and Designs.* Amsterdam: Elsevier Science Publishers, 225–254.

Frenkenberger, S., Schnabel, B., Alissali, M. and Kommenda, M. 1994. "Prosodic parsing based on parsing of minimal syntactic structures". *Proceedings of The Second ESCA/IEEE Workshop on Speech Synthesis.* New Paltz, 143–146.

Gee, J. P. and Grosjean, F. 1983. "Performance Structures: A Psycholinguistic and Linguistic Appraisal". *Cognitive Psychology* 15: 459–466.

Hirschberg, J. and Prieto, P. 1996. "Training intonational phrasing rules automatically for English and Spanish text-to-speech". *Speech Communication* 18(3): 283–292.

Hirschberg, J. 1991. "Using text analysis to predict intonational boundaries". *Proceedings of the Second European Conference on Speech Communication and Technology.* Genova.

Marín, R., Aguilar, L. and Casacuberta, D. 1996. "El grupo acentual categorizado como unidad de análisis sintáctico-prosódico". In C. Martín–Vide (ed), *Lenguajes Naturales y Lenguajes Formales XII.* PPU: Barcelona, 487–494.

Navarro Tomás, T. 1925. "Palabras sin acento". *Revista de Filología Española* XII(4): 335–375.

Nespor, M. and Vogel, I. 1983. "Prosodic Structure above the Word". In A. Cutler and R. D. Ladd (eds), *Prosody. Models and Measurements.* Heidelberg: Springer Verlag, 123–140.

Nooteboom, S. G., Brokx, J. P. L. and de Rooij, J. J. 1978. "Contributions of prosody to speech perception". In W. J. M. Levelt and G. G. Flores d'Arcais (eds), *Studies in the Perception of Language.* Chichester: John Wiley, 75–107.

Ostendorf, M. and Veilleux, N. 1994. "A Hierarchical Stochastic Model for Automatic Prediction of Prosodic Boundary location". *Computational Linguistics* 20(1): 27–54.

Pierrehumbert, P. 1980. *The Phonology and Phonetics of English Intonation.* PhD Thesis, MIT.

On Some Fundamental Concepts of Mathematical Linguistics: Means and Functional Domains

Zygmunt Frajzyngier
Jan Mycielski

University of Colorado

Abstract

We propose an explanatory model of the structure of natural languages and of FOL (first-order logic). The fundamental elements of this model are the concepts of functional domains and of coding means. Within each functional domain there may be subdomains. The elements within each domain are encoded by various means. For natural language we illustrate the model on the domain of the unaffected object. For first-order logic we illustrate the model on the domain of expressions denoting mathematical objects and on the domain of truth-value expressions.

Outline of basic concepts

We would like to introduce two concepts which we believe to be useful in the description of both natural language and the language of first-order logic (FOL). These concepts are means of coding and functional domains.

In natural languages, the basic means of coding are lexical, and grammatical. Lexical means include derivational morphology. Grammatical means include configuration, nominal and verbal inflection, serial verb constructions, adpositions, complementizers and subordinators, prosody, phonological changes at the phrase internal-positions and phrasal boundaries, and possibly a few others. These means of coding can be combined with one another. The means of coding assure the principle of well-formedness, namely, that every element of an utterance must have a transparent role. Transparency is assured either by the inherent lexical properties or by the means of coding. The inherent lexical properties include the predicate for verbs, the argument for nouns, and the modifier of an argument for adjectives. The inventory of morphemes in languages can thus be divided into those elements whose role in an utterance is determined by their inherent properties, and those whose primary function is to code the role of other elements.

Functional domains are implicitly accepted in most theoretical frameworks and are described in modern grammars of individual languages. When linguists talk about aspectual systems or tense systems, they are in fact talking about functional domains. A number of contemporary syntactic theories do not distinguish between functional domains and means of coding. The lack of such distinction results in confusion, which prevents the understanding of the structure of language. The categories AUX, COMP, INFL, CASE, used at various times in the GB tradition, represent a lack of distinction between means and functions. Other examples of confusion between means and functions are evident in discussions of pronouns and of agreement, or AGR, as if they represent functional domains. Heine 1993 explicitly postulates the notion of 'semantic domain' but acknowledges difficulties in defining this concept. A clear understanding of the notion of functional domains and a clear distinction between the means of encoding and the functional domains allow for a better understanding of the structure of language and of the synchronic and diachronic processes that operate in language (cf. Frajzyngier 1995).

We propose that functional domains in natural languages are definable in two independent ways:

(a) A domain D is a class of mutually exclusive types of expressions constructed by a set of specific means of coding $M(D)$.

(b) The types of expressions within the domain D have a specific pragmatic or semantic function in common.

(c) A domain D is a class of types of expression with a certain set of meanings D^* such that D^* is disjoint with E^* for any domain $E \neq D$ of the same language.

We propose that the core of the description of a grammar of a language L should consist of at least three components:

(1) A list of functional domains $D_1, D_2, \ldots$, defined by means of the sets of meanings $(D_1)^*, (D_2)^*, \ldots$;

(2) Alternative descriptions of $D_1, D_2, \ldots$, by the system of means $M(D_1)$, $M(D_2), \ldots$ of coding used for $D_1, D_2, \ldots$;

(3) The means of construction of expressions composed of expressions belonging to different domains of L.

For a given functional domain, various systems interact to form subdomains. A functional domain may include other functional domains, which either form a nesting system or are disjoint. The description of the smallest functional domain must include a statement of what larger functional domains it is part. Figure 1 illustrates potential interrelationships of subdomains within a functional domain:

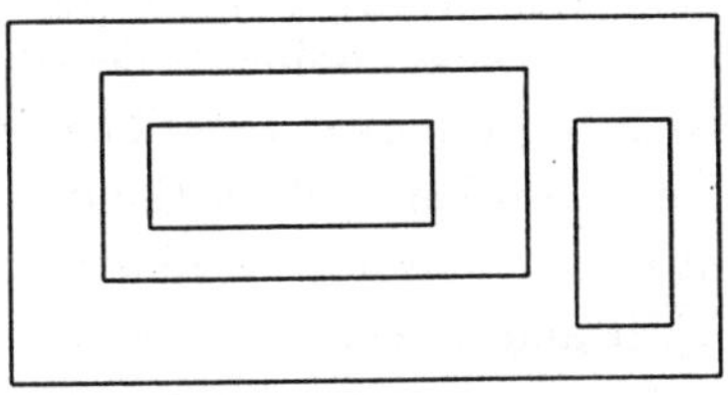

Figure 1. Configuration of subdomains within a functional domain

Scope of the paper

In the present paper we provide a number of examples of domains $D_1, D_2, \ldots$ for several natural languages L and for FOL and their characteristics of types (1) and (2). We show that the system of semantic distinctions

$(D_1)^*, (D_2)^*, \ldots$ depends on the system of means $M(D_1), M(D_2), \ldots$. We propose that for natural languages and for FOL the list of domains and subdomains within each domain depends on the grammatical means available in a particular language.

Natural language illustration

The domain of grammatical relations

For natural languages we selected one broad domain: that of relationship between verb and arguments ('grammatical relations'). This domain contains subdomains. Grammatical relations present a number of issues that continue to be controversial in contemporary linguistic theories.

The domain of grammatical relations may be coded by configuration, case marking on nouns, coding on the verb, adpositions, and various combinations of these means. For the purpose of illustration we narrow our scope even further, and focus on the relationship between the unmarked argument in nominative–accusative languages, 'subject'; and the second argument, often referred to as 'object'. (At this stage we make no claim as to how these notions are to be represented in the grammar, or even whether the notions of subject and object have any universal validity.)

By virtue of the different means of coding deployed to mark subject and object, we consider them to be different functional domains. These two functional domains and several others within the domains of grammatical relations are independent of one another, as illustrated below in Figure 2 (only the domains of subject and object are illustrated).

Nominative–accusative languages may differ in their semantic relationships between the category subject and the verb and also in their semantic relationships between the category object and the verb.

In some nominative–accusative languages the default semantic value of the subject is a feature control, viz., the subject encodes the argument that controls the verb. In many languages the default feature of the object is affectedness, viz., without any additional markers the object represents the argument affected by the verb: It undergoes a change as a result of the action of the verb. Nominative–accusative languages also vary in the availability of additional functional domains with respect to subject and object. The existence of the functional domains is a piece of evidence for the default relationships that hold between the verb and subject and object in those languages.

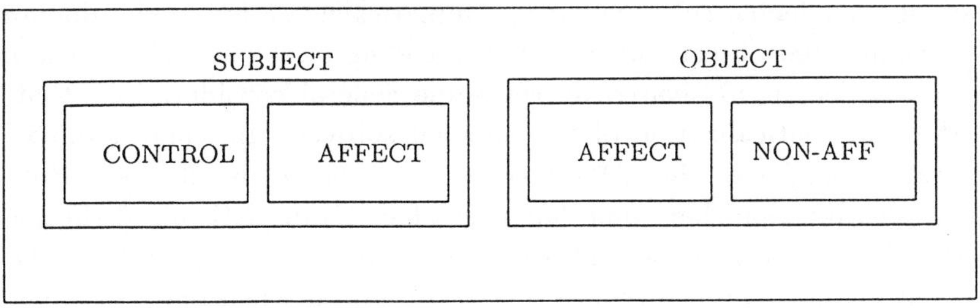

Figure 2. A fragment of a domain of grammatical relations

Domain of affected subject

The existence of the universal category 'subject' is a controversial issue in itself (cf. Mithun 1991, Shibatani 1991, Dryer 1996). It is possible that in various languages 'subjects' may have different functions, semantic ones in some languages and discourse functions in others. There is a subtype of nominative–accusative languages where the default function of the subject of an unmarked transitive verb is [+ controller] and [-affected]. Given these default properties of the unmarked subject, it is quite reasonable to expect that a speaker may wish to indicate that the subject is affected. We propose the following hypothesis: Some nominative–accusative languages may have grammaticalized means to encode the affectedness of the subject of a transitive or an intransitive verb. The functional domain of the affectedness of the subject may be coded by several means, depending on whether the event is coded as a state or a process or as a permanent versus temporary state (Frajzyngier 1978, 1982, Jaggar 1988, Lichtenberk 1994). For a full discussion of the affected subject we refer readers to Frajzyngier (1997). In what follows we concentrate on the domains of the unaffected object.

Domain of non-affected object

We propose here that languages, like their grammaticalization of the domain of the affected subject, have grammaticalized a functional domain of the non-affected object. Moreover, the coding of the domain of the non-affected object is motivated by the same general considerations that led to the grammaticalization of the affected subject. In some nominative–accusative languages the default value of the object is affected. But one might also imagine that some languages have grammaticalized the means to encode and that the second argument, contrary to expectations, is not affected, or not completely affected. And indeed when one examines the manner in which grammatical relations are encoded, one finds that there are several means deployed by languages to encode the object. In the rest of this section we will show that some of these means encode the non-affected object. More specifically we discuss here three means to encode the non-affectedness of the object: case marking on nouns, inflectional marking on verbs, and adpositions. Again, as in the case of the affected subject coding this discussion provides the main evidence for the default semantic relationship between the verb and the object.

Coding the non-affected or not completely affected object by case

In inflectional nominative–accusative languages the default marker of the object is the accusative case. We claim it to be the default marker because it occurs in affirmative indicative clauses, e.g.:

(1) zrobił chałę to prawda,
make:PERF:PAST:3M:SG sloppy job:ACC DEM truth
ale jest to chała aż ostentacyjna,
but be:PRES:3SG DEM sloppy job:NOM even ostentatious
'it is true that he made a mess of the job, but it is too ostentatious' (Sources)

The genitive case is deployed to mark the partial affectedness of the object:

(2) ojciec nabrał wody w usta
father take:Perf:Past:3MSG water:GEN in mouth
'father was silent' (lit. father took water into his mouth) (Sources)

(3) forsy ma jak lodu
money:GEN have:PRES:3SG how ice:GEN
'he is loaded' (lit. he has as much money as there is ice) (Sources)

Cf.

(4) ma forsę
have:PRES:3SG money:ACC
'he/she has money'

The systematic evidence for the function of the genitive as coding not-complete affectedness is provided by the fact that it may not be used with the perfective form of verbs that encode complete affectedness of the object, e.g.:

(5) Pan chciałby tu zaprowadzić nowe porządki
sir want:HYP here introduce:PERF:INF new:ACC order:AC
'you would like to introduce here a new order'

Cf.

(6) *pan chciałby tu zaprowadzić nowych porządków
sir want:HYP here introduce:PERF:INF new:GEN order:GEN
'you would like to introduce here a new order'

The genitive is also the case that marks the unaffected object. The most important evidence for this function of the genitive case is the fact that the genitive rather than accusative case is used in all negative clauses, where the object cannot be affected, e.g.:

(7) nie puścimy płazem tego wybryku
NEG release DEM:M:GEN prank:GEN
'we will not let this prank go unpunished' (Sources)

(8) nie ma dla mnie wyjścia
NEG have:PRES:3SG for 1SG:ACC exit:GEN
'there is no way out for me' (Sources)

(9) nie psuj naszego sukcesu ...
NEG spoil:IMPER our:GEN success:GEN
'do not spoil our success' (Sources)

(10) ... nie mam zamiaru tym
NEG have:PRES:1SG intention:GEN DEM:M:INSTR
pana obciążać
sir charge:INF
'I have no intention to charge you with this' (Sources)

The genitive is used to encode the subject of the negative existential clause, as in the following sentence where the same noun occurs as the subject of the affirmative and negative existential clause:

(11) chluba jest i chluby nie ma
pride:NOM be:3SG CONJ pride:GEN NEG have:3M
'There is pride, and there is no price' (Sources)

Coding of unaffected object through verbal inflection

Many Bantu languages have applicative affixes, which according to traditional analyses are used when the action is performed for the benefit of somebody. This function is partially supported by the data, e.g.:

(12) Jóni a-ná-(wá)-bvin-ir-a á-na
John$_i$ he$_i$-PAST-dance-APPL-INDIC children
'John danced for the children' (Trithart 1979:7)

(13) Jóni a-ná-wá-i)-ph-er-a á-na n-khúku
John$_i$ he$_i$-PAST-them$_j$/it$_k$-kill-APPL-INDIC children$_j$ chicken$_k$
'John killed a chicken for the children' (Trithart 1979:7)

But the applicative marker does not always occur in clauses with beneficiary. More specifically, it does not occur if the beneficiary is made the subject of the clause. In such a case, the verb has a passive rather than an applicative marker. This indicates that the applicative marker has a different function from the one indicating that the action was done for the benefit of somebody:

(14) á-na a-ná-(wá)-phik-ir-ídw-a ndí Cátherine
children$_i$ they$_i$-PAST-them$_i$-cook-for-PASS-INDIC by Catherine
'the children were cooked for (by Catherine)' (Trithart 1979:14)

Instead of the traditional approach, we propose that the applicative affix indicates that the noun phrase that directly follows the verb, i.e. the noun phrase that occupies the position of the object, is not in fact the affected argument, e.g. the argument undergoing a change as a result of the action of the verb. The first two examples from Chichewa fully support our hypothesis, because the noun phrase following the verb is interpreted as beneficiary. This interpretation is a result of computing the applicative affix, the meaning of the verb, and the properties of other noun phrases in the clause.

The most important piece of evidence for the proposed hypothesis is the fact that the applicative affix must be used whenever the verb is followed by an argument other than the affected object. Thus, if there is no instrumental preposition preceding the noun phrase and the noun phrase directly follows the verb, the applicative affix is obligatory. This affix, combined with the meaning of the verb and the properties of the noun phrases involved, gives an instrumental reading for the noun phrase:

(15) Jóni a-ma-(li)-;o,-ir-a khasu
John$_i$ he$_i$-HABIT-it$_j$-farm-APPL-INDIC hoe$_j$
'John cultivates with a hoe' (Trithart 1979:9)

If the noun phrase is preceded by the instrumental preposition, the applicative affix is optional, because the preposition indicates that the following noun phrase is not the affected object:

(16) Jóni a-ma-(*li)-lim-(ir)-a ndí khasu
John$_i$ he$_i$-HABIT-it$_j$-farm-APPL-INDIC with hoe$_j$
'John farms with a hoe' (Trithart 1979:8)

Coding of unaffected object through adpositions

A number of languages have grammaticalized adpositions to code the unaffected object. Thus in French, the partitive object, i.e. the object that is only partially affected, is marked by the preposition de, which otherwise has a genitive function, e.g.:

(17) je buvais de bonne bière
'I used to drink good beer' (Grevisse 1991:914)

(17) Si j'avais sous la main une bonne plume, de la bonne encre et du bon papier
'If I had a good pen, some good ink and good paper handy' (Grevisse 1991:914, from Gide)

The indefinite object of the negative clause, i.e. an argument that is not affected, is also marked by the preposition de, e.g.:

(19) Il y a un enfant
'there is a child'

(20) Il n'y a pas d'enfant
'there is no child' (Grevisse 1991:915)

(21) Vous ne m'avez jamais fait de peine
'You never caused me any trouble' (Grevisse 1991:914, from Proust)

If a language has grammaticalized means to code the unaffected object, such means are deployed with the verbs that take only unaffected complements. Thus, the following examples from Polish where the second argument must be encoded by the genitive case must be translated into English by the preposition, whose functions, not by chance, overlap with the functions of the genitive in Polish:

(22) boję się mamy
be afraid:PRES:1SG REFL mother:GEN
'I am afraid of my mother' (Sources)

(23) pierwszej łzy przeraziłeś się
first:F:GEN tear:GEN frighten:PERF:PAST:2M:SG REFL
'you became frightened at the first tear' (Sources)

Thus in languages which have several means of coding the second argument, such as preposition or nominal inflection, whether the second argument is affected or not affected can be coded by the grammatical means. In Polish, the second argument, both in negative clauses and in affirmative clauses with verbs that do not affect the argument, is coded by a genitive case marker. In clauses in which the second argument is affected, it is coded by the accusative case marker.

Illustration from first-order logic

An example of a simple language is FOL (first-order logic), the universal formal language of mathematical logic, which permits one to express all mathematics. We are able to define all the domains of FOL. For the most common versions of FOL there are only two domains D_1 and D_2, namely D_1 is the domain of terms, and D_2 is the domain of truth-valued formulas. In some versions of FOL, D_1 splits into several domains called sorts (e.g. in the theory of linear spaces or in various axiomatic systems of analysis when there are several sorts of object denoted by appropriate variables and terms).

The purpose of this section is to describe FOL from a new point of view, the result of attempts by the second author to avoid the actual infinity that is present in the classical semantics of mathematical theories. This naturally led him to the use of Hilbert's ε-symbols and a description of mathematical logic that distinguishes two domains of this language:

D_1 the domain of expressions denoting mathematical objects.
D_2 the domain of truth-valued expressions.

In the applications of mathematical logic, which at this point in time are still of a theoretical nature (since we have not developed a practical calculus ratiotinator as imagined by Leibniz), the domain D_1 of names of objects splits in various ways into smaller domains, such as the domain of groups, rings, topological spaces, functions, etc. But in this paper we shall not introduce this subdivision. We introduce only the most general domains D_1 and D_2 defined above.

In mathematics we often use expressions such as $x^2 = y$, $x(y+z) = xy+yz$ or $x \in y$ without claiming that they are true. When reading such expressions we may have thoughts of the following kind: x and y are general elements of a ring and we recognize $x^2 = y$ as an atom in Boolean algebra, so that in our calculus of thoughts $x^2 = y$ can be an argument of Boolean operations. Likewise $s(y+z) = xy$ and $x \in y$ are atoms (in the first, x and y are general elements of a ring and in the second, x and y are general sets). Thus such expressions are significant on their own; they represent useful thoughts (and not only truth valued functions over appropriate universes of x's and y's). In fact such universes are imagined but not all their elements are imagined and hence these functions exist only in some potential sense. On the other hand, the Boolean atoms above are actually constructed. Then we construct more complex expressions, for example $\neg A \to B$, where A and B are atoms (i.e., atomic formulas).

Expressions in D_1 and D_2 will be terms of an appropriate algebraic language. (The description will be rather involved since both D_1 and D_2 are needed to define any one of them.) Both D_1 and D_2 will be algebras of terms. We recall that terms are built from certain basic expressions (such as variables or constants) by compositions using function symbols.

In our description of logic we have:

$x_1, x_2, \cdots$ variables in D_1;
$p, q, r, \ldots$ variables in D_2;
$F_1, F_2, \ldots$ function symbols with finitely many argument places from D_1 to D_1;
$=$ a binary function symbol from D_1 to D_2;
$1, \neg, \to$, which are: a constant in D_2 (the truth value), a unary function symbol (negation) and a binary function symbol (implication) both from D_2 to D_2;

$R_1, R_2, \ldots$ function symbols with finitely many argument places from D_1 to D_2;
$\equiv$ a binary relation symbol;
ε an operator that can be applied to any variable x_i and any term φ in D_2 to produce a new term in D_1 of the form $\varepsilon x_i \varphi$.

In the usual parlance of mathematical logic, $x_1, x_2, \ldots$ are called individual variables; $p, q, r, \ldots$ are called propositional variables; F_1, F_2 are called function symbols; R_1, R_2 are called relation symbols but in our treatment they are functions; $1, \neg, \rightarrow$ are called truth, negation, and implication respectively; $\equiv$ is called logical equivalence; ε is called Hilbert's ε-symbol.

We assume that the reader is familiar with the significance of all but the last of these symbols, namely that of ε which will be explained below. Notice, however, that in our language every declarative sentence has the form $\varphi \equiv \psi$ or $\varphi \equiv 1$. where φ and ψ are terms in D_2. Here our convention differs from the traditional language of mathematics in that $\equiv$ is the only relation symbol. If we want to declare not$(\varphi \equiv \psi)$ we can express it in the form $\varphi \equiv \neg\psi$. If we want to declare that $\varphi \equiv \psi$ implies $\xi \equiv \zeta$ we can state it is the form $((\varphi \leftrightarrow \psi) \rightarrow (\xi \leftrightarrow \zeta)) \equiv 1$, where $\alpha \leftrightarrow \beta$ is an abbreviation of $(\alpha \rightarrow \beta) \wedge (\beta \rightarrow \alpha)$, and $\gamma \wedge \delta$ is an abbreviation of $\neg(\gamma \rightarrow \neg\delta)$.

Now, the role of the operator ε is the following: We can write a term of the form $\varepsilon x_i \varphi$ which denotes the general object satisfying the condition φ as long as such an object is conceivable; thus $\varepsilon x_i \varphi$ denotes a general object (like the variable x_i) restricted to the set of objects x_i satisfying $\varphi(x_i) \equiv 1$. Thus

A_1 $[\varphi(x_i) \rightarrow \varphi(\varepsilon x_i \varphi)] \equiv 1;$

is an axiom of logic. [For completeness we list the remaining axioms of logic:

A_2 $[(p \rightarrow q) \rightarrow ((q \rightarrow r) \rightarrow (p \rightarrow r))] \equiv 1;$

A_3 $(p \rightarrow ((\neg p) \rightarrow q)) \equiv 1;$

A_4 $(((\neg p) \rightarrow p) \rightarrow p) \equiv 1;$

A_5 $(1 \rightarrow p) \equiv p.$]

Every mathematical statement can be expressed by a term of D_2. For example, $\exists\, x_i \varphi(x_i)$ can be expressed by $\varphi(\varepsilon x_i \varphi)$ and $\forall\, x_i \varphi(x_i)$ can be expressed by $\neg\exists\, x_i \neg\varphi(x_i)$. [Thus of course $\forall\, x_i \varphi(x_i) \equiv \varphi(\varepsilon x_i \neg\varphi) i$]
And if we want to construct the name of such and such a mathematical object (of appropriate generality) we form an appropriate term in D_1.

In mathematical practice a great number of terms are formed in D_1 and D_2. Many axioms, definitions and theorems are stated and proved i.e.

expressions of the form $\varphi \equiv \psi$ where φ and ψ are in D_2. The rules of proof are those of *two-sorted equational logic* which will be stated below.

Thus, assuming that the reader is familiar with the usual syntax of FOL (first-order logic), the means of construction $M(D_1)$ and $M(D_2)$ of the terms of D_1 and D_2 are clear. But notice that other means are also possible. For example, in the most common expositions of FOL there is no mention of Hilbert's ε; only the quantifiers $\exists$ and $\forall$ are introduced. But this sweeps under the rug the actual way mathematics is developed; indeed in every significant step of this development new terms are born and the uses of ε represent this process. Another advantage of the formal account of mathematics as defined above is that it simplifies the rules of logic. Indeed, A_1–A_5 are simpler than the usual rules (this was envisioned by Hilbert (1925)). Now, the rules of deduction are the rules of equational logic (formulated by G. Birkhoff (1935)), namely, the following four rules:

$\sigma \equiv \sigma$;

$\sigma \equiv \tau$ yields $\tau \equiv \sigma$;

$\sigma \equiv \tau$ and $\tau \equiv \theta$ yields $\sigma \equiv \theta$;

$\sigma(x) \equiv \tau(x)$ and $\xi \equiv \zeta$ yields $\sigma(\xi) \equiv \tau(\zeta)$, for any terms ξ and ζ such that $\sigma(\xi)$ and $\tau(\zeta)$ are well formed.

Now we turn to the semantic functions of $D1$ and $D2$. To explain them (to a reader familiar with the elements of model theory) it suffices to define the models of the axioms A1–A5. These models are algebraic structures of the form:

$$\langle A, B; f_i, =, r_j, 1, \neg, \rightarrow, \varepsilon \rangle_{i \in I, j \in J}$$

where $\langle B; 1, \neg, \rightarrow \rangle$ is a Boolean algebra $f_i : A^{m(i)} \rightarrow A$, $=: A^2 \rightarrow B$, $r_j : A^{n(j)} \rightarrow B$, and ε is an operator defined on term-definable functions $r : A^n \rightarrow B$ such that the following equation holds:

$$(r(x_i) \rightarrow r(\varepsilon x_i \neg r)) \equiv 1.$$

We shall not list the axioms concerning the function of $=$. They are given in Mycielski 1995. Thus A is the universe of individual objects denoted by the terms of D_1 and B the universe of truth valued objects denoted by the terms of D_2.

We think that the above description of FOL shows an important aspect of this language, namely its algebraic or equational nature. This also allows a constructive interpretation of mathematics (which is quite hidden if one accepts quantifiers as primitives, i.e., undefined symbols, rather than symbols defined by means of the ε-operator). This issue is discussed in Mycielski 1992 and 1995.

Comparison between the structure of FOL and natural languages

Some of the similarities and some of the differences between natural languages and the language of FOL are as follows: With respect to means, the two types of languages are similar in that they both have a list of elementary symbols, namely lexical items in natural languages and terms in the above version of FOL. They also have some means of encoding, more specifically configuration and changes in the basic elements in natural languages; order and Hilbert's ε expessions in our version of FOL.

An interesting difference between natural languages and FOL is in the functional domain of truth. In many (but not all) natural languages truth is the default value of the indicative clause (cf. Frajzyngier 1985, 1987). In our version of FOL truth is encoded through equations of the form $\varphi \equiv 1$. In natural language the functional domain involving truth also contains such subdomains as doubt in truth and the sources and types of knowledge involved. (Cf. papers in Chafe and Nichols 1986).

Notes

1. *Zygmunt Frajzyngier's work on this paper was supported by a grant from the National Science Foundation.

Abbreviations

(only less common abbreviations are listed)

ACC	Accusative	AFFECT	Affected
APPL	Applicative	CONJ	Conjunction

DAT	Dative	DEF	Definite
DEM	Demonstrative	F	Feminine
FUT	Future	GEN	Genitive
HABIT	Habitual	HYP	Hypothetical
INDIC	Indicative	INF	Infinitive
INSTR	Instrumental	LOC	Locative
M	Masculine	NEG	Negative
NOM	Nominative	PERF	Perfective
PL	Plural	QUANT	Quantifier
REL	Relative	SG	Singular
SUBJ	Subjunctive		

References

Anderson, J.M. 1994. "Case". Asher and Simpson 1994, vol. 2, 447–453.

Asher, R.E. and Simpson J.M.Y. (eds), 1994. *The Encyclopedia of Language and Linguistics.* Oxford: Pergamon Press.

Birkhoff, G. 1935. "On the structure of abstract algebras". *Proceedings of the Cambridge Philosophical Society* 31, 433–454.

Chafe, W. and Nichols, J. (eds), 1986 *Evidentiality: The Linguistic Coding of Epistemology.* Norwood, N. J.: Ablex.

Dryer, M.S. 1996. "Grammatical relations in Kutenai (Ktunaxa)". In H.C. Wolfart (ed) *Voices of Rupert's Land*, Winnipeg.

Frajzyngier, Z. 1978. "An analysis of BE passive". *Lingua* 46, 133–156.

Frajzyngier, Z. 1982. "Indefinite agent, impersonal, and passive: A functional approach". *Lingua* 58, 267–290.

Frajzyngier, Z. 1985. "Truth and the indicative sentence". *Studies in Language* 9 (2), 243-254.

Frajzyngier, Z. 1987. "Truth and the compositionality principle: A reply to Palmer". *Studies in Language* 11 (1), 211–217.

Frajzyngier, Z. 1993. *A Grammar of Mupun*, Berlin, Reimer.

Frajzyngier, Z. 1995. "Functional theory of complementizers". In Joan Bybee and Suzanne Fleischman (eds), *Modality in Grammar and Discourse.* Amsterdam & Philadelphia: John Benjamins, 473–502.

Frajzyngier, Z. 1997. "System interactional approach to reflexives". Paper read at the International Symposium on Reflexives and Reciprocals. Boulder, Colorado. Ms.

Frajzyngier, Z. In press. "Pronouns and agreement: Systems interaction in the coding of reference". In Hans Benis, Pierre Pica and Johan Rooryck (eds), *Atomism and Binding*, Dordrecht: Foris.

Givón, T. 1990. *Syntax. A Functional-Typological Introduction*, Amsterdam: Benjamins.

Grevisse, M. 1991. *Douziéme édition refondue par André Goosse. Le bon usage.* Paris: Duculot.

Heine, B. 1993 *Auxiliaries*. Oxford: Oxford University Press.

Hilbert, D. 1977 (1925). "On the infinite". In Jean van Heijenoort (ed), *From Frege to Goedel. A Source Book in Mathematical Logic* 1879–1931. Cambridge, Ma. London: Harvard University Press, 367–392.

Jaggar, Ph.J. 1988. "Affected-subject ('Grade 7') verbs in Hausa: What are they and where do they come from?" In Masayoshi Shibatani (ed), *Passive and Voice*. Amsterdam/Philadelphia: Benjamins.

Kurcz, I., Lewicki, A., Sambor, J., Szafran, K., and Woronczak, J., 1990. *Slownik frekwencyjny polszczyzny wspólczesnej*. Kraków: Polska Akademia Nauk, Instytut Jezyka Polskiego.

Lichtenberk, F. 1994. "Reflexives and reciprocals". Asher and Simpson 1994, v. 7. 3504–3509.

Mithun, M. 1991. "The role of motivation in the emergence of grammatical categories: The grammaticalization of subjects". Traugott & Heine 1991, v. 2, 159–184.

Mycielski, J. 1992. "Quantifier-free versions of first-order logic and their psychological significance". *Journal of Philosophical Logic* 21, 125–247.

Mycielski, J. 1995. "Equational treatment of first-order logic". *Algebra Universalis* 33,. 26–39.

van der Pose, L. 1986. *The Lost World of the Kalahari*. New York: Harcourt Brace & Co.

Shibatani, M. 1991. "Grammaticization of topic into subject". Traugott and Heine 1991, v. 2, 93–134.

Trithart, L. 1979. "Topicality: An alternative to the relational view of Bantu passive". *Studies in African Linguistics* 10 (1), 1–30.

A Model of Personal Pronouns

Manfred Kudlek

Hamburg University

Abstract

An approach to a precise mathematical model for the description of personal pronouns in natural languages is presented in this paper, such that the category of personal pronouns can be seen as one of several universal categories in natural languages.

The first step is the description of a communication situation with normally one speaker (first person), several listeners, the audience (second persons), and also several other persons or things (third persons), and the definition of a mathematical personal pronoun.

The second step is the encoding of this situation by a word or several words over some alphabet. Normally, such an encoding is not unique and may depend on the communication situation. There may exist several encodings for the same mathematical personal pronoun, e.g. possessive pronouns and forms for different cases, and one expression may also encode several mathematical personal pronouns.

The third step is a presentation of certain relations between mathematical personal pronouns, describing actions with several participants, and their encoding.

The basic communication model

A normal situation of communication among people includes a single speaker and not a choir (first person), an audience consisting of one or several listeners (second persons), and a group of persons or things spoken about (third persons). Usually, the speaker receives information about the audience and other persons or things by seeing them, and sends information to the audience. This situation can be described in the following simple communication model using sets for the different participants in the communication process

1 sender (speaker, 1st person)	$\{s\}$
several receivers (audience, 2nd persons)	R
several others (thirds, 3rd persons)	T

with a 1-way communication channel for receiving visual information by s about R and T, represented by a visibility relation σ, and another 1-way audio communication channel for sending information from s to R, represented by a relation $\tau = \{s\} \times R$.

$\sigma \subseteq R \times \{s\} \cup T \times (\{s\} \cup R)$

with $R \times \{s\} \subseteq \sigma$

In a more general situation not all members of T can be seen by s, thus causing a partition of T into 2 disjoint sets T_0 (not seen by s) and T_1 (seen by s).

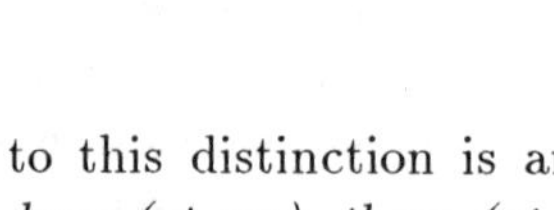

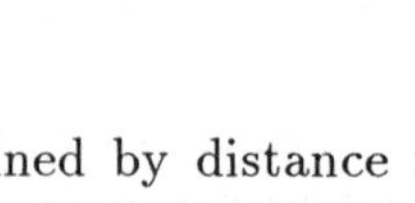

Related to this distinction is another one, defined by distance from the speaker: *here (at me), there (at you), over there (at them), further away.*

In a still more general situation R can also receive visual information about T, thus partitioning T into 4 disjoint sets. This can be described by

$$T_{00} = \{t \in T \mid \neg(t,s) \in \sigma \wedge \neg\exists r \in R : (t,r) \in \sigma\}$$
$$T_{01} = \{t \in T \mid \neg(t,s) \in \sigma \wedge \exists r \in R : (t,r) \in \sigma\}$$
$$T_{10} = \{t \in T \mid (t,s) \in \sigma \wedge \neg\exists r \in R : (t,r) \in \sigma\}$$
$$T_{11} = \{t \in T \mid (t,s) \in \sigma \wedge \exists r \in R : (t,r) \in \sigma\}$$

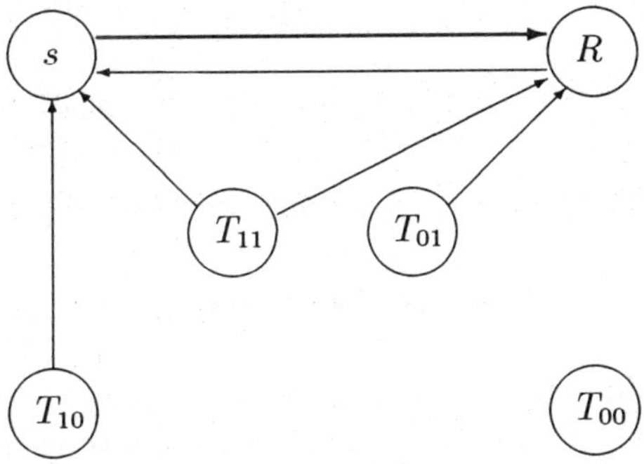

A **mathematical personal pronoun** can now be defined simply as some subset

$P \subseteq \{s\} \cup R \cup T.$

The visibility relation will give s information for the encoding of the mathematical personal pronouns. In a strict sense, s also has to receive information about the subset of T seen by all $r \in R$. But for simplicity this will be neglected in this context.

Features of mathematical personal pronouns

In many natural languages the elements of $\{s\} \cup R \cup T$ have a number of features, e.g. *(animate, inanimate)*, *(female, male, neuter)*, or degrees of social rank. In some natural languages several such features are present. The features can be modelled at best by finite sets $C_i, 1 \leq i \leq k$. The elements of such sets are usually called **classes**, and for simplicity they can just be enumerated from 1 to m_i

$C_i = \{1, \cdots, m_i\}.$

The properties of elements $p \in \{s\} \cup R \cup T$ are given by feature functions f_i which may be assumed to be surjective

$f_i : \{s\} \cup R \cup T \rightarrow C_i, 1 \leq i \leq k.$

Mathematically, all k features may be combined into one by considering the Cartesian product

$C = C_1 \times \cdots \times C_k$ with elements $(j_1, \cdots, j_k)$.

For linguistic reasons, however, only the model with several features will be presented. Some examples of such features are

$C = \{1\}$	no distinction by gender or social rank (Chinese)
$C = \{1, 2\}$	$\{female, male\}$ (Arabic)
	$\{animate, inanimate\}$
$C = \{1, 2, 3\}$	$\{female, male, neuter\}$ (German)
$C = \{1, 2, 3, 4, 5, 6\}$	6 classes (Swahili)

The feature functions introduced, however, are not sufficient for a description of the features of an entire mathematical personal pronoun P. Therefore, the definition has to be generalized. This can be done by generalizing the f_i from single elements $p \in \{s\} \cup R \cup T$ to subsets

$F_i : 2^{\{s\} \cup R \cup T} \rightarrow C_i$

with several possibilities to generalize from one element to a subset, e.g.

$F_i(P) = min\{f_i(p) \mid p \in P\}$ or

$F_i(P) = max\{f_i(p) \mid p \in P\}$.

Cardinality

The mathematical personal pronoun P introduced so far allows an arbitrary number of different possibilities. In natural languages, however, these are put into a few categories (or mathematical equivalence classes) only, usually defined by **number (cardinality)**, the most common ones being *singular, dual, (trial), plural.* Normally, only the following distinctions between such cardinalities are important, with the number of equivalence classes (see below) given in the 3rd column

≥ 1	no distinction	3
$(1, > 1)$	singular, plural	9
$(1, 2, > 2)$	singular, dual, plural	14
$(1, 2, 3, > 3)$	singular, dual, trial, plural	21

Possible mathematical personal pronouns depending on their cardinalities will be considered below. To simplify the notation, r, t will be written for $p \in R$, $p \in T$, respectively.

Singular

In this case there are only 3 possibilities, given in the following list with some English encoding and a short notation in the 1st column

s	$\{s\}$	I
r	$\{r\}$	you
t	$\{t\}$	he/she/it

Dual

There are 5 possibilities in the case of dual, 4 of them distinguished in a number of Amerindian languages. The 1st column gives a short notation again. Inclusive and exclusive relate to the addressee.

sr	$\{s, r\}$	we both inclusive	rr	$\{r, r'\}$	you both
st	$\{s, t\}$	we both exclusive	rt	$\{r, t\}$	both you and he
			tt	$\{t, t'\}$	they

Trial

In this case, rather rare in natural languages, the following pronouns are possible

$\{s, t, t'\}$	we excl.	$\{r, r', r''\}$	you
$\{s, r, t\}$	we all	$\{r, r', t\}$	you all
$\{s, r, r'\}$	we incl.	$\{r, t, t'\}$	you all
		$\{t, t', t''\}$	they

Plural

For simplicity only the case of > 2 with 6 equivalence classes will be presented. A short notation is given in the 1st, and special situations in the 5th column.

sT	$s \in P, P \cap R = \emptyset, P \cap T \neq \emptyset$	we excl.	$P = \{s\} \cup T$
sR	$s \in P, P \cap R \neq \emptyset, P \cap T = \emptyset$	we incl.	$P = \{s\} \cup R$
sRT	$s \in P, P \cap R \neq \emptyset, P \cap T \neq \emptyset$	we all	$P = \{s\} \cup R \cup T$
R	$s \notin P, P \cap R \neq \emptyset, P \cap T = \emptyset$	you	$P = R$
RT	$s \notin P, P \cap R \neq \emptyset, P \cap T \neq \emptyset$	you all	$P = R \cup T$
T	$s \notin P, P \cap R = \emptyset, P \cap T \neq \emptyset$	they	$P = T$

In natural languages there is usually no distinction between RT or R, and between sRT and sR.

Encoding of mathematical personal pronouns

A mathematical personal pronoun defined in the previous sections, or more precisely, its equivalence classes according to cardinality, is mapped onto one word or several words over some alphabet V, or onto a finite set of such words. This encoding may depend on several relations based on features of the different participants in the communication, and on syntactical or semantic categories.

In the simplest case the encoding is a function
$c : \{s\} \cup R \cup T \to V^*$ or $c : \{s\} \cup R \cup T \to 2^{V^*}$

In the general case the encoding c may depend on the communication situation, or more precisely on the features of the different participants in the communication. This means that several such encodings depend on $f(s)$, $F(R)$, and $F(T)$, giving functions $c_{(f(s),F(R),F(T))}$.

Furthermore, the encoding may depend on syntactical or even semantic categories i, like cases. This gives functions $c_{(f(s),F(R),F(T)),i}$.

In the simplest situation the encoding is independent of such features and categories, giving a function c.

The first example is from *Mixe* (Hoogshagen and Halloran de Hoogshagen 1993), a language spoken in Southern Mexico.

s	uch	sR	uchajt
		sT	uchajcxy
r	miich	R,RT	miichajcxy
t_{10}, t_{11}, t_{01}	yı'	T_{10}, T_{11}, T_{01}	yı'ajcx
t_{00}	je'	T_{00}	je'ajcx

The following example is from Classical *Arabic* giving the encodings of pronouns as prefixes and suffixes of verbs in the indicative imperfect tense. In this case the feature set is $C = \{1, 2\}$ (denoting $\{male, female\}$), with $F(P) = min\{f(p) \mid p \in P\}$, and with short notations for singular, dual, and plural.

Sing.	f(p)	$c(P)$	Dual	F(P)	$c(P)$	Plur.	F(P)	$c(P)$
t	1	y - u	tt	1	y - āni	T	1	y - ūna
	2	t - u		2	t - āni		2	y - na
r	1	t - u	rr,rt	≤ 2	t - āni	R,RT	1	t - ūna
	2	t - īna					2	t - na
s	≤ 2	' - u				sR,sT,sRT	≤ 2	n - u

The third example is from *Potowatomi*, an Algonquian language, and presents the possessive pronouns, again as prefixes and suffixes. There is no distinction of gender.

Sing.	$c(P)$	Plur.	$c(P)$
r	k -	R,RT	k - wa
s	n -	sR,sRT	k - nan
		sT	n - nan
t	w -	T	w - wa

The encoding is achieved by the following algorithm for prefixes (pref) and suffixes (suff)

The feature set is $C = \{1, 2, 3\}$ for *male, female, neuter*

Begin
If $P \cap R \neq \emptyset$ then pref $= k$
else if $s \in P$ then pref $= n$ else pref $= w$
if $card(P) > 1$ then
if $s \in P$ then suff $= nan$ else suff $= wa$
End.

Example: *n-čiman-nan = our (excl.) canoe.*

The fourth example is from *Samoan* (Marsack 1962).

s	a'u, 'ou	st	māua, ma	sT	tatou
		sr	tāua, ta	sR,sRT	matou
r	'oe, e	rr	oulua, lua	R,RT	outou
t	ia	tt	laua, la	T	latou

Another example is from *Huave* (Stairs Kreger and Scharfe de Stairs 1981), a language spoken in Southern Mexico. The table presents the subject forms.

s	xique	sT	xicona
r	ique	R,RT	icona
t	nej	sRT	icootsa
sR	icora	T	nejiw

The next example is from *German* and presents different encodings c_i for mathematical pronouns according to linguistic case (nominative, dative, accusative), possessive, and (additional) verbal suffix.

P	Nom.	Dat.	Acc.	Poss.	Suff.
s, $f(s) \leq 3$	ich	mir	mich	mein	
r, $f(r) \leq 3$	du	dir	dich	dein	st
t, $f(t) = 1$	er	ihm	ihn	sein	t
2	sie	ihr	sie	ihr	t
3	es	ihm	es	sein	t
sR,ST,sRT	wir	uns	uns	unser	n
R,RT	ihr	euch	euch	euer	t
T	sie	ihnen	sie	ihr	n

In a more complex case the encoding may depend on the feature of the speaker, giving a function $c_{f(s)}$. This can be found in the incomplete example from Classical *Mixtec* .

	r				t			
	man	boy	woman	girl	man	boy	woman	girl
man	dzi				ye	dacu		
boy			do			dacu		
woman			dzi		dzu	dzuq		
girl							yco	yco

Other possibilities are $c_{F(R)}$, $c_{(f(s),F(R))}$, which are important for languages with several social ranks.

Theoretically, also $c_{F(T)}$, $c_{(f(s),F(T))}$, and $c_{(f(s),F(R),F(T))}$ are possible.

To illustrate this, a simple theoretical example is presented. In this example there is only one feature $\{male, female, nonhuman\}$, abbreviated by $\{m, f, n\}$. The encoding of P depends on $f(s)$, $F(R)$, and $F(T)$. F is defined by

$$F(P) = \begin{array}{ll} m & \text{if } \exists p \in P : f(p) = m \\ f & \text{if } \neg\exists p \in P : f(p) = m \wedge \exists p \in P : f(p) = f \\ n & \text{if } \neg\exists p \in P : f(p) = m \wedge \neg\exists p \in P : f(p) = f \\ & \quad \wedge\exists p \in P : f(p) = n \end{array}$$

with $f(s) \in \{m, f\}$ and $F(R) \in \{m, f\}$.

This gives 4 functions $c_{(m,m)}$, $c_{(m,f)}$, $c_{(f,m)}$, and $c_{(f,f)}$ which have to be used for the encoding in the corresponding situations.

Relations between personal pronouns

In the previous sections only isolated pronouns have been considered, either as mathematical objects or as encodings. There are, however, also relations between personal pronouns, ranging in arity from 1 to some n. This relations are important for verbs with their participants in actions. Verbs or verb forms with 1 participant are usually called (not in the mathematical but in the linguitic sense) **intransitive**, those with 2 **transitive** (also **reflexive** in some situations). To intransitive verb forms belong also **passive** forms. Most natural languages have special encodings for these situations. There exist also natural languages with special encodings for verb forms with 3 or even 4 participants.

Mathematically, these are just relations on the Cartesian products $R_k \subseteq (\{s\} \cup R \cup T\})^k$ with elements $(P_1, \cdots, P_k)$.

Unary relations

Unary relations ($k = 1$) are just the mathematical personal pronouns themselves. In natural languages they are realized for instance as **subjects** in 1-referent actions (active or passive), or possessors.

Binary relations

Binary relations $R_2 \subseteq (\{s\} \cup R \cup T)^2$ are common for most natural languages describing for instance 2-referent actions.

The first component P_1 is called **subject**, the second one P_2 **object** in a binary relation.

The relations can be classified in the following way:

$P_1 \cap P_2 = \emptyset$	transitive
$P_1 \cap P_2 \neq \emptyset \wedge P_1 = P_2$	pure reflexive
$P_1 \cap P_2 \neq \emptyset \wedge P_1 \neq P_2 \wedge P_1 \subset P_2$	reflexive
$P_1 \cap P_2 \neq \emptyset \wedge P_1 \neq P_2 \wedge P_2 \subset P_1$	reflexive
$P_1 \cap P_2 \neq \emptyset \wedge P_1 \not\subset P_2 \wedge P_2 \not\subset P_1$	(incomparable)

This yields, with the short notation introduced in section 4, the following possibilities for transitive actions (only singular and plural):

	s	r	t
s		(s, r)	(s, t)
r	(r, s)	(r, r')	(r, t)
t	(t, s)	(t, r)	(t, t')
sT		(sT, r)	(sT, t')
sR		(sR, r')	(sR, t)
sRT		(sRT, r')	(sRT, t')
R	(R, s)	(R, r')	(R, t)
RT	(RT, s)	(RT, r')	(RT, t')
T	(T, s)	(T, r)	(T, t')

	sT	sR	sRT	R	RT	T
s				(s, R)	(s, RT)	(s, T)
r	(r, sT)	(r, sR')	$(r, sR'T)$	(r, R')	$(r, R'T)$	(r, T)
t	(t, sT')	(t, sR)	(t, sRT')	(t, R)	(t, RT')	(t, T')
sT				(sT, R)	(sT, RT')	(sT, T')
sR				(sR, R')	$(sR, R'T)$	(sR, T)
sRT				(sRT, R')	$(sRT, R'T')$	(sRT, T')
R	(R, sT)	(R, sR')	$(R, sR'T)$	(R, R')	$(R, R'T)$	(R, T)
RT	(RT, sT')	(RT, sR')	$(RT, sR'T')$	(RT, R')	$(RT, R'T')$	(RT, T')
T	(T, sT')	(T, sR)	(T, sRT')	(T, R)	(T, RT')	(T, T')

where r', t', R', or T' indicate that in the corresponding pronouns either $t' \notin P_j$ $(j = 1, 2)$, $P_1 \cap P_2 \cap T = \emptyset$, $r' \notin P_j$ $(j = 1, 2)$, or $P_1 \cap P_2 \cap R = \emptyset$.

The distinction of different subsets of the addressed group R is rather theoretical, however.

Ternary relations

As there are too many possibilities for characterizing ternary relations only **transitive** ones will be introduced. R_3 is called such if

$P_1 \cap P_2 = P_1 \cap P_3 = P_2 \cap P_3 = \emptyset$.

With only singular and plural, excluding different subsets of R, the following triples are possible:

(s, r, t)	(s, r, T)	(s, R, t)	(s, R, T)	(s, t, t')	(s, t, T')	(s, T, t')	(s, T, T')
(r, t, t')	(r, t, T')	(r, T, t')	(r, T, T')	(R, t, t')	(R, t, T')	(R, T, t')	(R, T, T')
(t, t', t'')	(t, t', T'')	(t, T', t'')	(t, T', T'')	(T, t', t'')	(T, t', T'')	(T, T', t'')	(T, T', T'')

An example in English with 3 participants is:

You give *me her* book.

Encoding of binary relations

There exist many possibilities for the encoding of binary relations between mathematical personal pronouns. Only some will be considered.

In the simplest case the encoding of the mathematical personal pronouns is unique, and it is also used for the encoding of personal pronouns in binary relations, yielding

$c(P_1, P_2) = (c(P_1), c(P_2))$.

Combined with a verb V, either isolated or affixed, this gives the possibilities (all permutations)

$c(P_1) - c(P_2) - V$, $c(P_1) - V - c(P_2)$, $V - c(P_1) - c(P_2)$, $c(P_2) - c(P_1) - V$, $c(P_2) - V - c(P_1)$, and $V - c(P_2) - c(P_1)$.

Reflexive forms can also be encoded by using some special word ρ yielding $c(P) - \rho - V$ and its permutations.

In the next case the encoding of binary relations is related to the encoding of unary relations. Here there exist 2 encodings of unary relations, c and c'.

They can be also used to encode the subject in active and inactive (passive) actions with 1 participant.

If the active participant of 1-participant actions is encoded by $c(P)$ (for **nominative**) and the participants of 2-participant actions are encoded by $(c(P_1), c'(P_2))$, this situation is called a **nominative-accusative** structure.

If the active participant of 1-participant actions is encoded by $c(P)$ (for **nominative**) and the participants of 2-participant actions are encoded by $(c'(P_1), c(P_2))$, this situation is called a **nominative-ergative** structure.

There is also the possibility that two encodings c and c' are used for 1-participant actions (active and passive for instance), and the 2-participant actions are encoded again by $(c(P_1), c'(P_2))$ or $(c'(P_1), c(P_2))$.

An example for a natural language with a nominative-accusative structure is German, encoding the subject $c(P_1)$ in nominative, and the object $c'(P_2)$ in accusative:

$c(P_1) - V$ and $c(P_1) - V - c'(P_2)$.

An example for a natural language with a nominative-ergative structure is *Quiché* (Ximénez 1701), a language spoken in Guatemala. In this language the personal pronouns are encoded by prefixes:

Sing.	$c(P)$	$c'(P)$	Plur.	$c(P)$	$c'(P)$
s	nu, v	i, in	sR, sRT, sT	qa, q	oh
r	a, av	at	R, RT	i, iv	iš
t	u, r	∅	T	ke, k	e

where the second variants have to be used before vowels.

1-participants forms (active or passive) are $c(P) - V$, and 2-participant (transitive) forms are $c'(P_2) - c(P_1) - V$. (k is the present tense prefix).

Example: *keloq'on* = *they love*, *kiloq'oš* = *I am loved*, *katnuloq'oh* = *I love you.*

Some natural languages use an entirely different encoding of binary relations. The following example is from *Potowatomi* (Hockett 1966) again.

The encoding starts with the question which kind of participants is present in the action : R, s, and T? (in this order), marked by prefixes k, n, and w, respectively. The next fact to be encoded is the direction of the action, namely $s \to R$, $R \to s$, $s \to T$, $T \to s$, $R \to T$, $T \to R$, $T \to T'$, and $T' \to T$, where T' stands for more distant participants. This is encoded by suffixes *un*, *uy*, *a*, *uk*, *a*, *uk*, *a*, and *uko*, respectively. Finally, the cardinality of the entire group $G = P_1 \cup P_2$ of participants has to be encoded asking $card(G) = 2$, $card(G) > 2$? (in this order). In the second case further questions, $s \in G$, $R \subseteq G$, $T \subseteq G$? are put (in this order), encoded by suffixes *mun*, *nan* for s, *wa* for R, and *wa*, *k* for T, respectively.

All forms are presented in the following double table:

	r	R,RT	sR,sRT
r			
R,RT			
sR,sRT			
s	k - un	k - un-um	
sT	k - un-mun	k - un-mun	
t	k - uk	k - uk-wa	k - uk-nan
T	k - uko-k	k - uk-wa-k	k - uk-nan-uk

	s	sT	t	T
r	k - ∅	k - uy-mun	k - a	k - a-k
R,RT	k - um	k - uy-mun	k - a-wa	k - a-wa-k
sR,sRT			k - a-mun	k - a-mun
s			n - a	n - a-k
sT			n - a-mun	n - a-mun
t	n - uk	n - uk-nan	w - a-n	(w - a-n)
			w uko-n	(w - uko-n)
T	n - uko-k	n - uk-nan-uk	w - a-wa-n	(w - a-wa-n)
			w - uk-wa-n	(w - uk-wa-n)

Example: *n-wapm-uk-nan-uk = they see us (excl.)*, *k-wapm-a-mun = we (incl.) see him.*

The next example is from *Quechua* (Hartmann 1985), the second official language of Peru. The personal pronouns can be encoded by suffixes being used for 1-participant forms:

Sing.	$c(P)$	Plur.	$c(P)$
s	-ni	sT	-niku
r	-nki	sR,(sRT)	-nchik
t	-n	R,(RT)	-nkichik
		T	-nku

Some, but not all, 2-participant relations can be encoded by suffixes indicating the direction of the action, and by suffixes for participants. The directions $s \to R$, $R \to T$, $T \to s$, and $T \to R$ are encoded by the suffixes *yki*, *wan*, *wan*, and *su*, respectively. All possible forms are given in the following table.

	s	*st*	*sR*	*r*	*R*	*t*	*T*
s				-yki	-yki-chik		
sT				-yki-ku			
sR							
r	-wan-ki	-wan-kiku					
R	-wan-kichik						
t	-wan	-wan-ku	-wan-chik	-sun-ki	-sun-kichik		
T							

Example: *pukllaniku = we (excl.) are playing, qayasunkichik = he is calling you.*

Another complex example is from (Chafe 1967), an Iroquois language. This language has forms for *singular, dual* and *plural.* The following three tables present the 1-participant and 2-participant forms.

	S	O		S	O		S	O
s	ke	'ake	st	'akhni	'ọkhni	sT	'akwa	'ọkwa
			sr	hni	'ọkhni	sR,sRT	twa	'ọkwa
r	se	sa	rr,rt	sni	sni	R,RT	swa	swa
t_m	ha	ho	tt_m	hni	hoti	T_m	hati	hoti
t_f	ye	ko	tt	khni	'oti	T	wati	'oti
t_n	ka	'o						

	s	st	sT	sr	sR,sRT
s					
st					
sT					
sr					
sR,sRT					
r	ske	skhni	skwa		
rr,rt	skhni	skhni	skwa		
R,RT	skwa	skwa	skwa		
t_m	hake	shọkhni	shọkwa	shọkhni	shọkwa
t_f	'ọke	'ọkhi	'ọkhi	'ọkhi	'ọkhi
tt,T	hoke	'okhi	'ọkhi	'ọkhi	'ọkhi

	r	rr,rt	R,RT	t_m	t_f	tt,T	$T_{\overline{m}}$	t_n
s	ko	khni	kwa	he	khe	khe		
st	khni	khni	kwa	shakhni	'akhi	'akhi		
sT	kwa	kwa	kwa	shakwa	'akhi	'akhi		
sr				shehni	'ethi	'ethi		
sR,sRT				shetwa	'ethi	'ethi		
r				hehse	she	she		
rr,rt				shesni	'etsi	'etsi		
rT,RT				sheswa	'etsi	'etsi		
t_m	ya	shesni	sheswa	họwọ	shako	hakọ		
t_f	'esa	'etsi	'etsi	họwọ		họwọti	kọwọti	
tt,T	hosa	'etsi	'etsi	họwọ	shakoti	họwọti	kọwọti	
t_n								kọwọ

Here, $S, O, t_m, t_f, t_n, tt_m, T_m, T_{\overline{m}}$ denote *subject, object* in 1-participant forms, 3rd person *male, female, neuter* singular, 3rd person *male* dual, *male* plural, and 3rd person *non-male* plural, respectively.

In an extreme case all (P_1, P_2) may be encoded differently.

References

Bloomfield, L. 1962. *The Menomini Language.* Newhaven and London: Yale Univ. Press.

Chafe, W. L. 1967. *Seneca Morphology and Dictionary.* Washington: Smithsonian Press.

Hartmann, R. (ed). 1985. *'rimaykullayki'.* Berlin: Reimer.

Hockett, C. F. 1966. *What Algonquian is really like.* IJAL vol. 32, no. 1, 59–73.

Hoogshagen Noordsy, Searle and Halloran de Hoogshagen, Hilda. 1993. *Diccionario Mixe de Coatlán.* México: ILV, Serie Vocabularios y Diccionarios Indígenas 32.

Marsack, C. C. 1962. *Teach Yourself Samoan.* London: The English University Press.

Reyes, Antonio de los, 1593. *Arte en Lengua Mixteca.* México.

Stairs Kreger, Glenn Albert and Scharfe de Stairs, Emily Florence. 1981. *Diccionario Huave de San Mateo del Mar.* México: ILV, Serie Vocabularios y Diccionarios Indígenas 24.

Ximénez, Fray Francisco. 1701. *Arte de las Tres Lenguas Cakchiquel, Quiché y Tzutujil.* Guatemala.

A Mathematical Model for the Post-Creole Continuum in Hawaii

Shinya Matsunami

University of Hawaii

Introduction

Hawaiian Creole English and Post-Creole Continuum

The Hawaiian islands were originally inhabited by native Hawaiian people until the arrival of the first westerners in the late 18th Century. In the late 19th Century, sugar cultivation became a major industry, and many people emigrated from China, Japan, the Philippines, and other countries to work in the sugar fields. The immigrant workers and native Hawaiians started to communicate by using a pidgin English, which developed later into Hawaiian Creole English. In 1959, Hawaii became the 50th state of the United States. Today, Hawaii's major industry is tourism, receiving 7 million visitors annually from all over the world. Despite this tremendous internationalization and Americanization, people raised in Hawaii still retain many creole features in their English. It is said that Hawaiian Creole English has been changing toward a variety of English which is spoken on the mainland U.S.A. (= Standard English or SE, hereafter). Of the local people of Hawaii raised in the creole English community, some show stronger creole accents than others. Moreover, an individual can often switch between more creole-accented speech and less creole-accented speech, depending on the environment. Day (1972) suggests that the language situation in Hawaii is undergoing 'decreolization' from the 'basilect', Hawaiian Creole (HC, hereafter)[1], towards the 'acrolect', standard English (SE), creating a 'post-creole continuum'. 'Decreolization' is defined in Day as the process that the system changes gradually over time and acquires many of the same features which are in a more prestigious system. Decreolization occurs in post-creole speech communities, in which there is no sharp distinction between the creole and the superordinate language. According to Day, decreolization is a change from below, which occurs during the language acquisition process. After analyzing the speech data of many informants, Day concludes that the Hawaiian Post-Creole Continuum (HPCC, hereafter) consists of a number of 'overlapping lects'. The goal of the present study is the mathematical formalization of HPCC based on the data described in Day.

Day's account

Day suggests that there is a gradual acquisition of SE features in the use of the copula in a certain fixed order by various HPCC speakers. The first major area of the copula use is that of the predicate copula 'is' (and its variation) in the four environments shown in (1).

(1) Example HPCC sentences with 'is' in the four predicate environments

- Before a noun phrase (_ NP):	*His name is Eki.*
- Before a predicate adjective (_ PA):	*The boy is different.*
- Before a locative (_ Loc):	*My bed is against the door.*
- Before a progressive (_ Ving):	*We was playing basketball.*
	'We were playing basketball.'[2]

Day's data show that the use of 'is' gradually starts in the environment 'before a noun phrase' (_ NP), followed by the environments 'before a predicate adjective' (_ PA), 'before a locative' (_ Loc), and 'before a progressive' (_ Ving). In (2), I arranged 'is' in the four different environments by using the implication symbol ($A \supset B$ means that the use of 'is' in environment A implies the use of 'is' in environment B). A speaker who uses 'is' before a progressive (_ Ving) at least sometimes uses 'is' before a locative (_ Loc), but not vice versa. In the same way, a speaker who uses 'is' before a locative also uses 'is' before a predicate adjective (_ PA) at least sometimes. And a speaker who uses 'is' before a predicate adjective uses 'is' before a noun phrase (_ NP) at least sometimes. No speaker, however, uses the copula 'is' always in all of these environments. That is, the zero use of 'is' (ϕ)[3], is also implied by any other use of 'is'. Thus, when a speaker at least sometimes uses 'is' in one environment, it is predictable that he/she uses 'is' in all the other environments to its right in (2). The leftmost usage in the environment '_ Ving' is most acrolectal. In basilectal speech, on the other hand, the zero usage occurs.

(2) _ Ving $\supset$ _ Loc $\supset$ _ PA $\supset$ _ NP $\supset$ ϕ

Day gives two other major areas of copula use, which also show implicational orders. One of them is the use of copula 'ste'. 'Ste' is a special copula in HPCC, which is used in the two environments: 'before a locative' (_ Loc) and 'before a progressive' (_ Ving). Some example sentences with 'ste' are shown in (3).

(3) Examples of HPCC sentences with 'ste' in the two environments
- Before a locative (_ Loc):
  He ste Maui. 'He is in Maui.'
- Before a progressive (_ Ving):
  She ste running. 'She is running.'

'Ste' also alternates with the zero usage (ϕ). The implicational relation of the use of 'ste' in these three environments is shown in (4).

(4) _ Ving $\supset$ _ Loc $\supset$ ϕ

The last major area of the copula use is that of the existential 'get', which alternates with its acrolectal equivalent, 'there (+BE)'[4]. Some examples with the both forms are given in (5).

(5) Example HPCC sentences with 'get' and 'there'
- (Get) *Over here get ledge.* 'Over here, there is a ledge.'
- (There) *There is a banyan tree.*

This case is somewhat different from the uses of 'is' and 'ste'. 'Get' and 'there (+BE)' occur in the same syntactic environment. In addition, there is no case of zero use: the speakers always use 'get' or 'there (+BE)'. Otherwise, there is an implicational relation between the occurrence of the two forms (as in the use of 'is' and 'ste'), as shown in (6). The use of 'there (+BE)' by a speaker implies the use of 'get' by the same speaker. Also, the form 'there (+BE)' occurs less frequently than 'get'. Thus, 'there' is a more acrolectal expression than 'get'.

(6) there (+BE) $\supset$ get

Finally, Day examines the number and the types of the lects (code systems) to be generated by the three rule systems: i.e. the uses of 'is', 'ste', and 'get-there'. These rule systems provide five, three, and two possible lects, respectively, as given in (7).

(7) a) Lects generated by the 'is' rule system
1) the lect which never uses 'is'
2) the lect which uses 'is' in '_ NP'
3) the lect which uses 'is' in '_ NP' and '_ PA'
4) the lect which uses 'is' in '_ NP', '_ PA', and '_ Loc'
5) the lect which uses 'is' in '_ NP', '_ PA', '_ Loc', and '_ Ving'

b) Lects generated by the 'ste' rule system
1) the lect which never uses 'ste'
2) the lect which uses 'ste' in '_ Loc'
3) the lect which uses 'ste' in '_ Loc', and '_ Ving'

c) Lects generated by the 'get-there' rule system
1) the lect which uses 'get'
2) the lect which uses 'get' and/or 'there'

Thus, so far as these three systems are concerned, there will be 30 logically possible (super-)lects: i.e. $5 \times 3 \times 2 = 30$. For example, a speaker may have the most basilectal lect in which he/she never uses 'is' and 'ste', and uses only 'get' (the combination of a-1, b-1, and c-1 in (7)). The most acrolectal lect, which is the combination of a-5, b-3, and c-2, uses 'is' and 'ste' in all the respective environments, and uses both 'get' and 'there'. Day actually found 15 of the 30 possible lects in speech samples from 23 subjects. These three rule systems are of course a part of the overall system of HPCC, and it can be inferred that there is a great number of such rule systems involved in HPCC, creating a great variety of lects. Day concludes that there are numerous 'overlapping' systems (lects) in HPCC. Decreolization can be seen in the gradual acquisition of the SE features by various HPCC speakers.

A mathematical model for HPCC lects

The formalization of each rule system

Day recognizes a rule as a 'rule system', which comprises the stipulation for the fundamental function (such as 'insert a copula') as well as the all environmental restrictions for the application. For example, the 'is' rule system is one rule consisting of the common stipulation, 'insert a copula in the following environments', followed by the environment specifications such as 1) before a noun phrase, 2) before a predicate adjective, etc. Thus, the implicational scale as given in (2) is characterized as a series of the syntactic environments contained in one rule. In my model, on the other hand, the application in each syntactic environment is treated as the application of an independent rule unit. I refer to such a rule as a primitive rule (PR, hereafter), a set of which collectively constitutes the larger rule unit, i.e. the rule system. For example, the PR which generates 'is' before a noun phrase contains the basic information of the 'is' rule as well as the environmental specification 'assign a copula between the subject noun phrase and the predicate noun phrase of a sentence'.[5] The PR which generates 'is' before a predicate adjective stipulates: 'assign a copula between the subject noun phrase and the predicate adjective phrase of a sentence.' Each of these is an independent rule unit while both PRs are members of the 'is' rule system.[6]

The 'is' rule system

The 'is' rule in SE discussed in Day applies to all the four environments: i.e. _ NP, _ PA, _ Loc, and _ Ving. In HPCC lects, however, the 'is' is not always present, but occurs more frequently before a noun phrase (_ NP), and progressively less frequently in the environments to the left in (2). In my analysis, on the other hand, there will be four PRs in HPCC lects: a PR which generates 'is' before a noun phrase, a PR which generates 'is' before a predicate adjective, a PR which generates 'is' before a locative, and a PR which generates 'is' before a progressive. I will refer these four PRs as a, b, c, and d, respectively. These PRs can also be put into the same implicational order as (2). Following Day's suggestion that decreolization is "a change from below, which occurs during the language acquisition process," PR a is acquired by the HPCC speakers earlier than PRs b and c, and PR d is acquired latest. If we assume that a feature which is acquired later is more difficult/complicated, it is also the case that PR a is least difficult, followed by progressively more difficult PRs b, c, and d. Thus, the relation of the four PRs can be represented with '$<$' ('is less difficult than'), as shown in (8). This '$<$' relation is irreflexive, asymmetric, and transitive. The four PRs are in strict linear order.

(8) $a < b < c < d$ where: a = PR for _ NP
b = PR for _ PA
c = PR for _ Loc
d = PR for _ Ving

As discussed in (7a) above, there are five possible lects to be generated by these four PRs. These lects can be represented as the sets of the PRs as shown in (9).

(9) Lect 1 — ϕ
Lect 2 — $\{a\}$
Lect 3 — $\{a, b\}$
Lect 4 — $\{a, b, c\}$
Lect 5 — $\{a, b, c, d\}$

Any lect in (9) except lect 5 is a proper subset of a more difficult lect. I regard a PR as an obligatory rule; i.e. it must be applied always whenever the lect containing it is used. Thus, ϕ and a PR never conflict in application. The lects in (9) are in the relation 'is a subset of', as shown in (10).

(10) Lect $1 \subseteq 2 \subseteq 3 \subseteq 4 \subseteq 5$

The subset relation is reflexive, antisymmetric, and transitive. Also, the lects in (10) are linearly ordered, since the lects are connected by '$\subseteq$'. This relation can be interpreted as 'is less difficult than or as difficult as'. In the present analysis, a HPCC speaker who uses 'is' at least sometimes before a predicate adjective (_ PA) uses at least lect 3 (it can be lect 4 or 5 as they contain PR *b*) as well as all the other less difficult lects (at least, lects 1 and 2) in his/her competence. By some unknown mechanism, the speaker switches from one lect to another among these three. All PRs in the lects are obligatory rules. Thus, the deletion of the present SE copula in the speech of a HPCC speaker, who also uses 'is' sometimes, is explained as 'lect- switching', in this case, either lect 3 or 2 to lect 1. (Day, on the other hand, simply analyzed the same speaker as having one single lect, with which he/she uses 'is' at least sometimes before a predicate adjective.) The present model also explains Day's finding that the frequency of the occurrence of 'is' in the most difficult environment (_ Ving) is very low in his data, while that in the least difficult environment (_ NP) is generally high. It is analyzed in the present model that the speakers who have lect 5 (which contains PR *d* in their competence) also have all the other less difficult lects as subsets (which do not contain PR *d*). If the speakers switch lects randomly, the frequency of the use of PR *d* will naturally be least and the use of PR *a* will be most. The use of 'is' in these environments increases until it achieves 100 % of frequency in all the environments, that is, until when the HPCC lects merge into SE. In this case, only lect 5 is used always. This may be described as the gradual replacement of less difficult lects by more difficult lects as the decreolization proceeds. One might suppose that, before decreolization started (when HC and SE were spoken in two separate communities), there was no SE copula in HC, and lect 1 was used 100 % of the time. In the early stage of decreolization, some speakers acquired PR *a* and started to switch from lect 1 to lect 2 sometimes. While acquiring more difficult PRs (b, c, d) and getting more familiar with each lect through switching among these lects, the use of 'is' in the environment _ NP increased drastically because all the lects except lect 1 have PR *a*. At some stage, the use of 'is' in the environment _ NP finally reaches 100 % in frequency. This shift can be captured as the abandonment of lect 1 from the basilectal end (within the 'is' rule domain) of HPCC, and lect 2 takes its place. Then, in the next stage, the use of 'is' in the next more difficult environment (_ PA) becomes 100% in frequency. This means that lect 3 takes the place of lect 2 as the basilectal end lect, and lect 2 is discarded from HPCC. The replacement of the basilectal end lect by a more acrolectal lect continues until when lect 5 replaces lect 4. Then, there will be no basilect-acrolect difference in HPCC and the decreolization process ends (in this case, only within the 'is' rule system).

The 'ste' rule system

Another copula form 'ste' occurs in two environments in HPCC lects: i.e. 'before a locative' (_ Loc) and 'before a progressive' (_ Ving). There are also cases when 'ste' is absent in these environments. In the same way as in the 'is' rule system, the PRs in the 'ste' rule system are in strict linear order relation, 'is less difficult than' ($<$), as shown in (11).

(11) $e < f$ where: e = PR for _ Loc
f = PR for _ Ving

There will be three possible lects, as given in (7b). I label the lects in (7b) as 1', 2', and 3', respectively, starting from the least difficult one. These lects can be represented as the sets of the PRs, as given in (12).

(12) Lcct 1' — ϕ
Lect 2' — $\{e\}$
Lect 3' — $\{e, f\}$

In the same way as in (10), these lects are linearly ordered by the 'is a subset of' relation ($\subseteq$), as shown in (13).

(13) Lect 1' $\subseteq$ Lect 2' $\subseteq$ Lect 3'

The 'get-there' rule system

The use of the existential copula 'get' is a basilectal feature in this system, which is gradually to be replaced by more acrolectal 'there' or 'there + BE'. The two PRs are in the 'is less difficult than' relation ($<$), as given in (14).

(14) $g < h$ where: g = PR for the use of 'get'
h = PR for the use of 'there'

This rule system is different from the other two rule systems since there are no lects which don't use 'get' or 'there (+BE)' at all. There will be two possible lects, as indicated in (7c) in the previous section. The one is the lect which uses 'get' only, and the other the one which uses 'get' and/or 'there'. When we analyze the possible lects as the sets of the PRs in (14), however, an unusual result emerges. (15) presents the two sets made of the two PRs just in the same manner as in the 'is' and 'ste' rule systems.

(15) Lect 1" — $\{g\}$
Lect 2" — $\{g, h\}$

The problem is that the two PRs apply to the same environment. Thus, in lect 2", the two rules must conflict with each other in their application. However, only the difference between the two PRs is that they use different morphemes (either 'get' or 'there'). There is a property of their relationship which we cannot ignore; i.e. a speaker who uses 'there' also has the ability to use 'get', but not vice versa. Eventually, (15) can be treated in the same way as the other rule systems by clearly stipulating the function of PR h as mainly to replace the form 'get' assigned by PR g with the form 'there (+BE)'. Thus, as given in (16), the subset relation ($\subseteq$) also holds between the two lects.

(16) Lect 1" $\subseteq$ Lect 2"

This analysis is somewhat different from that of Day, who suggested that the two lects generated by the 'get-there' rule system are one in which the speakers use only 'get', and the other in which the speakers use both 'get' and 'there'. In the latter lect, 'get' and 'there' alternate. According to the present analysis as given in (15) and (16), the second lect with PR h describes the speech with 'there'. The alternation between the two forms occurs as a result of switching between lects 1" and 2".

The lects generated by plural rule systems

Next, we should look at the number and types of possible lects generated by the three rule systems combined. First, I will discuss the lects generated by the two of the three rule systems, viz. the 'is' and 'ste' rule systems. Then, I will discuss the case when all three rule systems are involved.

The lects generated by the 'is' and 'ste' rule systems

As mentioned above, the number of lects generated by the PRs of the 'is' rule system is five. The number of lects generated by the PRs of the 'ste' rule system is three. Therefore, the number of possible lects generated by the combination of these two rule systems is $5 \times 3 = 15$. In (17), the possible lects are shown as the super-sets (which are labeled with capital letters, A through O) of the lects from the two rule systems. The sets in (17) are not ordered pairs, but, for the convenience of discussion, the first member in the symbol { } represents a lect from the 'is' rule system, and the second member a lect from the 'ste' rule system.

(17)

	Lects of the 'is' rule system				
	1	2	3	4	5
Lects of 1'	A {1, 1'} ⇒	B {2, 1'} ⇒	C {3, 1'} ⇒	D {4, 1'} ⇒	E {5, 1'}
	⇓	⇓	⇓	⇓	⇓
the 'ste' 2'	F {1, 2'} ⇒	G {2, 2'} ⇒	H {3, 2'} ⇒	I {4, 2'} ⇒	J {5, 2'}
	⇓	⇓	⇓	⇓	⇓
rule sys. 3'	K {1, 3'} ⇒	L {2, 3'} ⇒	M {3, 3'} ⇒	N {4, 3'} ⇒	O {5, 3'}

When we look at these 15 lects from a set-theoretic perspective, there is a subset relation ($\subseteq$) between the lects within each row and each column. That is, in (17), all lects in each row are different only by the first member, and all lects in each column are different only by the second member. Since the first members come from the 'is' rule system and the second members from the 'ste' rule system, the lects in each row or column are in linear order as in each rule system (see (10), (13), and (16)). For the convenience of discussion, the subset relation ($\subseteq$) between the lects in (17) are represented by the symbol '⇓' (for the vertical relation) and '⇒' (for the horizontal relation). Since each lect in (17) is a set of lects from each rule system, the relation is reflexive as a set is a subset of itself. There is the same '$\subseteq$' relation between the lects over the columns and rows, as long as the two lects are related by the arrows transitively. This transitive relation must be only in certain directions. That is, to trace from a less difficult lect to a more difficult lect, we must follow the arrows from the tail to the head. To trace from a more difficult lect to a less difficult lect, we must follow the arrows from the head to the tail. As long as the lects are traced this way, we can always go through the lects which are 'comparable' to one another with the subset relation. On the other hand some lects in (17) are not comparable. Two lects are incomparable in terms of the ' $\subseteq$' relation, when the one lect contains lects (or PRs) x and q as its members, and the other lect contains lects (or PRs) y and p, where x and y belong to one rule system and p and q belong to another rule system, and $x < y$, and $p < q$. In (17), any two lects which are on the diagonal line running across the upper right through the lower left are incomparable. They have more than one arrow between them pointing opposite directions (e.g. one is from the head to the tail and another is from the tail to the head). Thus, some examples of pairs of incomparable lects in (17) are, B { 2, 1'} vs. F { 1, 2'}, B { 2, 1'} vs. K { 1, 3'}, I { 4, 2'} vs. M { 3, 3'}, E { 5, 1'} vs. M { 3, 3'}, etc. The relation among the lects in (17) is also antisymmetric, since each lect is distinct from each other while it is a subset of itself (reflexive). Each lect is distinct because the comparable lects differ from each other in having one or two different sub-lect(s) as the member(s). The lower-level lects generated within each rule system differ from each other in having one or more different PR(s) while all the PRs are in the strict linear order relation. Thus the total set of lects, A - O, in (17) are partially ordered as their relation fulfills the conditions of reflexivity, antisymmetry, and transitivity. Since (17) has incomparable elements, the lects are in nonlinear order. Moreover, (17) is a lattice as any pair of elements have the least upper bound and the greatest lower bound. For example, any comparable pair of distinct lects has its more difficult member as the least upper bound, and its less difficult member as the greatest lower bound (e.g. $G \vee M = M$, $D \wedge O = D$, etc.). Also, the least upper bound or the greatest lower bound of a single set is itself (e.g. $O \vee O = O$, $O \wedge O = O$). Any pair of the incomparable lects has both the least upper bound and the greatest lower bound on the diagonal line between them running from the upper left to the lower right (e.g. $H \vee L = M$, $D \vee M = N$, $E \wedge I = D$, $C \wedge K = A$, etc.). Lects A (the least difficult lect) and O (the most difficult lect) are the lower bound and upper bound of the whole lattice structure, respectively.

The lects to be generated by the three rule systems

By combining different lects from the three rule systems (the 'is', 'ste', and 'get- there' rule systems), there will be $5 \times 3 \times 2 = 30$ lects. That is, we think about the case when the 'get-there' rule system is added to the analysis of the other two rule systems discussed in the previous section. In (14), I assigned the names, *g* and *h*, to the PRs of the 'get-there' rule system. Also, I used the labels, lects 1" and 2", in (15) for the possible lects to be generated by this rule system. We can make such sets of the (super-)lects by adding lect 1" to each set of the 15 lects in (17), and adding lect 2" to each set of the 15 lects in (17), thus having two different sets of 15 lects. Suppose we name these two sets as S1 and S2. S1 and S2 are isomorphic lattices. There are also relations among the lects between S1 and S2. For example, lect A' in S1 is a subset of lect A" in S2 because they differ only in the presence of lect 1" in A' and lect 2" in A", and 1" ⊆ 2" whereas the other members are the same. In the same way, any lect X' in S1 has its counterpart X" in S2, and these two lects differ only in one member such that 1" ∈ X', 2" ∈ X", where 1" ⊆ 2". Thus, X' ⊆ X". Suppose lects X' and Y' are the lects in S1, and their counterparts X" and Y" are in S2. Since each of them is a set, and a set is a subset of itself, there is a reflexive relation among them. There is also antisymmetric relation among them as every lect is distinct from another except from itself. The antisymmetric relation also exists between X' and X" as well as Y' and Y" since these lects are distinct from one another but all related by the same subset relation. Among these four lects, there is a transitive relation: X' ⊆ Y' and Y' ⊆ Y", then X' ⊆ Y"; also X' ⊆ X" and X" ⊆ Y", then X' ⊆ Y". Each of the four lects is also related with some other lects outside by the same relation. For example, W' ⊆ X' (both are in S1), and X" ⊆ Z" (both are in S2), then W' ⊆ Z". Moreover, there are always the greatest lower bound and the least upper bound for any pair of the lects among the four lects, X', Y', X", and Y", such as X' ∨ X" = X", Y' ∨ X" = Y", Y' ∧ X" = X', etc. Therefore, the structure between S1 and S2 is also a lattice with the same '⊆ ' relation. Thus, the whole structure is a lattice. Lect A' is the least difficult lect since every member of A' is the least difficult lect in each rule system. On the other hand, lect O" is the most difficult lect since every member of O" is the most difficult lect in each rule system. Thus, lects A' and O" are the lower bound and the upper bound of the whole system, respectively. Day identified 15 of the possible 30 lects in his empirical data: B', C', E', F', H', I', J', L', M', and M' out of 15 lects (A' - O') in S1, and D", E", H", J", and N" out of 15 lects (A" - O") in S2. It seems that they are allocated rather evenly in the lattice. If we look at more speakers of HPCC lects in terms of the three rule systems in future research, it is probable that we will encounter the other lect types in the lattice.

Lects generated by more than three rule systems

When we consider the number, types and relations of the lects generated by more than three rule systems, the same method used so far can be repeated. For instance, suppose there is a fourth rule system with two PRs, t and u, in the 'is less difficult than' relation, $t < u$. This generates three possible lects, i ($= \phi$), ii ($= \{t\}$), and iii ($= \{t, u\}$), in the implicational relation, iii $\supset$ ii $\supset$ i. We create a lattice of the sets each of which comprises four members, by adding each one of the new lects, i, ii, or iii, to the whole lattice structure of S1 and S2 combined (= S3, hereafter). The outcome structure comprises the three isomorphic lattice sets of S3, which can be named P, Q, and R, respectively. And, i $\in$ P, ii $\in$ Q, and iii $\in$ R. When there is lect Y as a member of P (i $\in$ Y $\in$ P), it differs from Y' of Q (where Y $\subset$ Y') only in having lect i while Y' has lect ii. And a member Y' of Q differs from Y" (where Y' $\subset$ Y") of R only in having lect ii while Y" has lect iii. Thus, all the members of R are one step more difficult than those in Q, which are one step more difficult than those in P. This relationship among P, Q, and R was generated by the relation of the lects, i $\subseteq$ ii $\subseteq$ iii of the fourth rule system. Thus, in this whole system, any lect in P has the '$\subseteq$' relation with some lect(s) in Q, and any lect in Q has the same relation with some lect(s) in R. Therefore, the relation structure between the three lattices P, Q, and R are also a lattice with the same $\subseteq$ relations. If the fourth rule system generates four lects, there will be four isomorphic sets of S3 such as P, Q, R, and S. Or, if there is a fifth rule system, which generates five lects, we must have five isomorphic sets of the set generated by the four rule systems. Each of the five sets is a lattice with the same $\subseteq$ relation, which is one step more difficult than another except the least difficult set. And the structure relating the five lattice sets will always be a lattice with the same $\subseteq$ relation. Therefore, the whole structure will always be a lattice. Then, no matter how many rules will be involved in generating the lects in HPCC, it is possible to see the relation of a lect to the whole system in a lattice, i.e. how close the lect is to the acrolect or how apart the lect is from the basilect. Also, it is possible to see the relative distance between any two lects in the system.[7]

Notes

1. Day uses the term HC with the reservation that it does not necessarily refer to an attested variety of speech but to a collection of non-SE features.
2. Throughout this paper, the SE gloss will be provided only when the given HPCC sentence differs structurally from the SE counterpart.
3. The examples of zero use of 'is' are:

(_ NP)	This the first time that ...	'This is the first time that ...'
(_ PA)	George different.	'George is different.'
(_ Loc)	My bed by the door.	'My bed is by the door.'
(_ Ving)	I not joking.	'I am not joking.'

4. The form 'there' sometimes occurs with the succeeding copula but sometimes does not.
5. This concept is of course expressed differently in different grammatical theories.
6. The discussion here is limited to syntactic rules. However, PRs presumably describe other levels of language such as phonology, morphology, semantics, etc. The present mathematical model treats all the rules simply as undifferentiated grammatical rules of the language.
7. As discussed earlier, the speaker switches among the lects in his/her competence. A time goes by, the basilectal lect will be discarded from one's competence or from the HPCC community. When a least difficult lect within a single rule system such as lect 1 (with the zero use of 'is') in the 'is' rule system is replaced by a more difficult one such as lect 2 (with the use of 'is' in _ NP), all the lects which have lect 1 as the member must be abandoned. Then, the whole lattiice system will be re-formulated with the renewed rule system (in this case, the new 'is' rule system generating four lects instead of five).

References

Day, R. R. 1972. *Patterns of Variation in Copula and Tense in the Hawaiian Post-Creole Continuum.* Doctoral dissertation, University of Hawaii, Honolulu, Hawaii. (The content of this dissertation is also discussed in: Romaine, S. 1988. Pidgin & Creole Languages. New York: Longman.)

Intaxis: a Syntactical Model of Intonation

Francisco Javier Sánchez González[a]
Jose Luis Caramés Casal[b]

[a] *Consejo Superior de Investigaciones Científicas*
[b] *Universidad Complutense de Madrid*

Abstract

In this paper a *syntactic intonation model (SIM)* is presented. Although intended for present day Spanish, we believe its conclusions and procedures are easily generalizable for other languages, once their particular tone rules have been specified. Since we intended to remain in the syntactical area, we attempted to avoid other contributions to the intonation curve such as pragmatical (mood, modality), morphological, semantic and phonetic information. But all these linguistic levels have shown themselves to be interconnected with each other and with the syntactical level; we have therefore limited –where possible– the generality of our model to neutral assertive sentences with only three syntactical levels: Sentence, Theme–Rheme Syntagma (constituent) and *syntagmatic word (SW)*. Each one of these levels is represented by intonational *layers*, which, once added together, produce the full sentence intonation. With these boundaries, the model is able to intone automatically a written text, and to provide a foreign speaker with a key to intone a *syntactically well ordered (SWO)* text. To assess the goodness of this syntactical ordering, the concept is first defined, and then a theorem that states that any syntactical tree can be SWO is proved. From the SIM a practical punctuation based model (PBM) is derived, using also three punctuation signs: Full Stop, Theme–Rheme Comma and No-Comma (absence of comma). Since syntax is structure on the abstract level, and intonation is structure on the realisation level, we shall reflect the *signifiant/signifié* duality, and call this intonational syntaxis *Intaxis*. The basic three-level models (SIM and PBM) are afterwards generalized for multi-sentence, multi-level, multi-mood and multi-lingual texts.

Introduction

Spanish intonation has received wide attention but the general approach has been mostly descriptive, as can be seen in (Alarcos Llorach 1971), (Fernández 1986), (Navarro Tomás 1974) and (Quilis 1981). The huge complexity of speech intonation seems to have prevented the appearance of simple and systematic models, with the exception of mood prosodemes (asseveration, question and order), which are fairly well typified, perhaps due to their easy perceptibility (see Bergé and Sánchez 1995 for this aspect). Other phenomena, perceived more unconsciously, have been overlooked (in the past and even to this day) by scholars who make exclusive use of their hearing. To this end, measuring devices (when wisely used) have proved to be very useful to detect subtle shades of intonation. We have developed and made extensive use of these tools in this and previous studies, eg. (Sánchez 1977, 1979, 1995, 1996) and (Bergé and Sánchez 1995).

English intonation, on the other hand, has been well described through definitions, models and notation by (Bolinger 1972), (O'Connor 1973), (Crys tal 1975), (Lyons 1982), (Roelof de Pijper 1983) and (Halliday 1988). More formal approaches have also been presented, specially for the syntactical domain, in (García Calvo 1979, 1983) –for Spanish–; (Pierrehumbert 1981), (Selkirk 1984), (Kaisse 1985) and (mainly for metrics) (Liberman 1975) –for English–; (Vaissière 1974) –for French. (Laver 1994) makes a comparative study of several languages in which similar behaviour can be detected, even for tone-languages. All these studies, by linguists, phoneticians, acousticians and electronic engineers, show the extreme importance of pitch and intonation to separate, construct and express, in speech.

Our initial purpose has been to formalize, where possible, a *SIM*, that is, a *syntactic intonation model*, as well as a synthetic mechanism for intoning sentences which adds the contributions of each syntactical level to obtain a global realistic image of *natural intonation* –the one accepted and understood by the average competent listener. This is useful for understanding how syntax is represented by intonation, i.e., how intonation is syntax, and to feed a speech synthetizer with an intonational model in order to read correctly a written text. Let us call this tonal structure Intaxis . In written text, punctuation constitutes the main source of information on syntactical structure, marking, almost formally, how the lexical chain must be grouped in superior units, until sentence level is reached. But punctuation is vague: commas are arbitrarily used, semicolons do not have a definite status, etc. Moreover, punctuation has a double function, in syntax and mood, as we shall see.

Semantics influences intonation as well. First with the accent or stress, which belongs to the word, more intimately in Spanish, as in '*pal'eto*'/'rustic'– '*palet'o*'/'overcoat', but also to a certain degree in English, as in 'pr'esent–pres'ent'. In Spanish, the accent is a phoneme which permits meaning to be opposed in phonetically similar chains. Thus the meaningful words, stored in the Lexicon of each language, already influence intonation. Following (García Calvo 1979), we call Syntagmatic Word (SW) a meaningful word (like nouns, pronouns, verbs, adjectives, indefinite articles) joined with preceding (proclithic-like) or following (enclithic-like) meaningless word(s) (like definite articles, prepositions, conjunctions, and similar particles), called indices. The SW are basic for our models: they are the lowest syntactical units, as we will see. Second, any sentence, since it offers knowledge about the *World (Reality)*, acquires a certain meaningful entity: it becomes a new idea, a new semantic item. Phrases such as *'Caballo de Troya'*/'Trojan horse', *'Polvorones de Astorga'*/'Astorga sweets', are near to constituting new words. Here syntax semantizes itself.

This bring us to morphology. We see both disciplines as logic (arbitrary) segmentation in a continuous process of agglutination and fusion, as Figure 1 shows, for the constituent *'Estados Unidos'* / 'United States'. Intonation closely follows this process, with the absorption of one accent by another, the previous pair of SW becoming only one SW, because of the loss of importance of one accent (') with respect to the other (').

The assembled pieces may have an equal or a different nature: SW-SW (*'parabrisas'*/ 'stops+winds', *'correcalles'*/ 'run + streets'); index-SW (*'Del-*

monte'/ 'of+the+mount', *'Alcazar'*/ 'the+castle'); or index-index (*'asimismo'*/ 'so+same', *'encima'*/ 'in+top'). The accent will usually fall on the second word with equal nature constituents, and on the meaninful word when unequal. Even no accent might be assigned to these new words (*'porque'*/ 'for+that').

This process can be prolonged upwards, enlarging the strict concept of syntax (i.e., word relations within a sentence) or defining new concepts (text, paragraph, subject, etc.; see the last paragraphs of this paper).

Of course, speech intonation needs a time interval to be uttered and understood. But no special temporal phenomena such as syllables, metrics and rhythm seem to us to be relevant for intonation and syntax: we consider them to be related to the act and technique of communication, here even artistic speech, such as in poetry and theatre. We treat these matters elsewhere, in (Sánchez 1995) and in (Sánchez and Puyá 1996); for structured metrics, see (Liberman 1975) and (Selkirk 1984).

Let us consider Pragmatics *environment, context, empractics, implication, supposition, etc* as everything that helps the speaker and hearer to find a sense in the sentence as a communication act (Alcaraz Varó 1990; Buhler 1985; Bustos 1986). Thus all the words that *point to*, such as deixis, anaphora and cataphora, belong to it. The sentence mood (Downing and Locke 1992) is also included, since, in conversation, the same string of words can be used for different purposes: to ask, to order, to exclaim, to affirm. The theme-rheme question ('theme-proper', in (Firbas 1992, quoting Svoboda) is syntactic because of its repercussion on sentence construction but, since this implies a former conversation which constitutes the context of the present one, it is also pragmatic; in the same way as a full stop is as much a sentence conclusion mark as an enunciative sentence indicator, the comma is both a syntagma separator and (often) a theme marker.

Indeed the comma performs a great variety of functions, which extend from the optional comma, to that of boundary marker to paratactic sentences, sintagma (group and phrase complexes), etc. We think it useful to begin separating these functions as their intonation contour, in all probability, varies: rising in the pair {Th, Rh} (theme, rheme), and falling in the inverted pair {Rh, Th}, as is usual in Spanish: *'/Juán/, se vá \.'*/ 'John, is leaving' vs *'/Se vá \, Juán \ .'* / 'He is leaving, John'.

The preceding paragraphs show that, besides pure syntactical intonational elements, we must include in our model other syntax-related linguistic elements.

Word order

Spanish

Spanish presents great freedom in word order: *'Juan vendrá mañana'*/'John will come tomorrow' can be also uttered *'Mañana vendrá Juan'*, *'Mañana Juan vendrá'*, *'Juan mañana vendrá'*, *'Vendrá Juan mañana'* and *'Vendrá mañana Juan'*, despite some slight differences in meaning and style. But this freedom must not break the syntactic coherence of the sentence. To settle this point, let us state a theorem about good word ordering before presenting our model of intonation. We assume an already parsed sentence, in the usual inverted-tree pattern as shown in Figure 2. The only difference is that we will consider as terminal, those branches corresponding to the SW of the sentence, which, as we saw, are the real syntactic words in the sentence –in the figure, branches with two subindices.

Theorem. *Any tree (partially ordered set) can be SWO at least once.*

We consider a tree SWO when:

1- It has a *good ordering* (there is a first element);

2- It has a *total ordering* (any element has a precedent, except the first);

3- Between any two final branches (SW), there is no other coming from a Common Node higher than their *Lower Common Node (LCN)*: R121 cannot be between R111 and R112 because the Common Node of the three, R1, is higher than the LCN of the pair,

Proof. Let us prove it with an ordering rule, an algorithm: we climb to the first node and place all the SWs belonging to a branch (which therefore becomes the first, R1) before any SW belonging to the other branches of the same node; we choose another branch as second, R2, and place its SWs before any other SW belonging to the rest of the unused branches of this node. And so on, until all these branches have been used and numbered. R1, R2,.., Rn.

Let us go down to the first node in R1, and repeat the previous method, until we obtain the secondary branches R11, R12,..., R1n. We repeat this for all the other branches of similar level, obtaining R21, R22,.., R2n;...; and Rm1, Rm2,.., Rmn. With this algorithm, any SW in a branch (i.e., R22), precedes any other SW in any other branch with a greater first subindex (i.e., R31).

We continue this process with all the tree nodes until we arrive at the terminal branches (the SW of the sentence). And we find that the text is SWO: any SW precedes (let '>>' symbolize *precedes*) another

Rijk...lmn >> Ri'j'k'..l'm'

if the first non equal homologue index (it will be 'k-k', if 'i=i'; 'j=j'; 'k/=k') in both terminal branches is minor for the first SW (k<k'). For instance, R1245 >> R1261, because 4<6. This is also valid for branches of unequal length: R1245 >> R126, should R126 be terminal.

The SWO ordered set (for a binary tree) is, therefore:

R11..11, R11..12, R11..21, R11..22, ..., R12..11, R12..12,..., R21..121, R21..21,...,R22..22

For instance, the lines in an Aleixandre poem ('*La Tierra', Sombra del Paraíso*):

"...*/ acaso la corteza pudo un día, / de la tierra, sentirte, humano /*..."
"... perchance the crust one day, of Earth, did feel you, human ..."

are not SWO because two close SW, *'la corteza'* and *'de la tierra'* form a hyperbaton, the normal syntactical order being something like:

{*humano*}{*acaso [(la corteza) (de la tierra)] [(pudo)(sentirte)] [(un día)]]* }

Therefore, *'humano, acaso la corteza de la tierra pudo sentirte un día'* is a SWO sentence, as well as '*acaso un día pudo sentirte la corteza de la tierra, humano'* and some others.

Models

Intonational grammars

Intonational grammars are those pitch contours that give life to syntactical categories and that in turn form a syntax which we believe, and this is our proposal, corresponds exactly to syntax in the narrow sense. It is a bijective structural relation which binds both pitch and syntax and constitutes therefore an isomorphism. The bond is natural if we maintain as other linguists do that syntax is realized through intonation: *"l'intonation fait la phrase"*. Syntax **is** intonation, although not *all* the intonation comes from it, of course. Let us look for the intonation units that mirror syntactic units and will became the elements of our intonational grammars.

The observation of a natural utterance (Figure 3) permits the decomposition of its intonational shape into several syntactically related contributions. In the figure, we see the pitch estimation (F0 contour) for the sentence *'La mamá de Manolo no sabía sumar'*/ 'Manolo's mamma did not know how to add up', whose phonetic realisation is entirely voiced but for the 's':

[lamam'aðeman'olon'osaß'iasum'ar]

We can find roughly three syntactic levels, and three corresponding contours can be attached to each level, in such a way that the point-to-point addition of all these curves reproduces the original– as we proceed in the Fourier analysis and synthesis of an analytical function.

The stretches of contours are assembled by inclusion in a similar fashion to those stretches that link syntactic categories; in other SWs sentence contour extends over all phrase constituents and phrase contours over the phrase's constituent SW as seen in the figure. In (written) text, starting from punctuation, the sentence curve acts over all the sentence (words between two full stops); the thematic clause curve acts over the clause's words (those between commas or between full stop and comma). The SW curve acts over the SW's words (those between '⊘'s, *comma absence*), between ⊘ and comma, and so on: we find a SW between any combination pair of the signs (., ⊘).

The peak of contour level 0, SW, coincides in time with the stress of its corresponding head (lexical) word and the curve shows the tonic prominence of the corresponding syllable and vowel.

These curves have a phonological character, and not merely, a descriptive, although useful, one: a change in punctuation brings a change in intonation and hence a change of sentence meaning and sense; again, "Intonation makes the sentence".

We shall exclude the many varied pragmatic and expressive prosodies that escape for the moment any attempt at coding, (if it is at all possible, because any spoken sentence is also an act, an event). To utter a sentence is to affirm its proposition, should it have no other purpose. We retain, therefore, only those syntactic contours that correspond to sentences uttered without any intention, connotation, context, modality or truth values, without any connection with the *real world* (we insist, if that is at all possible). As neutral sentence mood we will use the asseverative, using full stops as sentence boundary, commas as syntagma delimiters and comma absence as boundaries between SWs. Only three syntactical levels will thus be considered: Sentence, Syntagma and SW. No quantity and intensity are used.

We limit our model to spoken Spanish (Castilian), in its educated variety (university, radio and TV), but, as we said before, we believe its validity to extend to other Spanish and Western languages (see the *Multi-lingual* paragraph).

SIM syntactical levels

We adopt three basic intactic (syntactic-intonational) levels, as can be seen in Figure 4. The tonal contribution of all syntactical units are added, point to point: thus a word will receive the contribution of all the units to which it belongs: in a sentence such as *'El perro, come carne de vaca'*/ 'The dog eats cow's meat', the word *'perro'* will therefore receive three syntactical contributions: those of the sentence, the theme, and the SW (Figure 5). The higher pitch in the SW coincides with the accent of the SW word-nucleus. Since the sum of several straight lines is a straight, we always find a straight as the tonal variation between one accent and a contiguous punctuation sign, as the lower pitch line of the figure shows. So we find:

A PBM: Punctuation based model of SIM

From an SWO written text, a Tonal Text (TT) is derived: it is defined as a succession of pairs (a s), preceded by an initial s:

$$TT = s \oplus (\oplus_n (a\ s)) \qquad a \in A = \{\text{'}\ Ra\} \qquad s \in S = \{\varnothing\ .\}$$

where $\oplus$ means concatenate, $\oplus_n$, n-multiple concatenation (n, natural number), 'a' is either an Accentuation Rule (Ra) or a graphical sign (') which means (tonal) accentuation; s is any of the normal punctuation signs (.,) complemented with an absence sign,$\varnothing$, omitted in plain writing. Ra are idiomatic (last syllable in French, any in Spanish), and so is the graphical accent, present in Spanish and a few more languages. The intonation of this TT will be made with tonal variations belonging to set I = { / \ } (rising or falling tones). The intonation curve will be: $E = \oplus_{2n}\ i$, a succession of tonal intervals, interspersed in the TT chain in the way: [s i s i s i a i s i a i s]. For instance, the former sentence: '*El perro, come...*', with the intonational structure: '*./{/[(el_p/'e\rro)]/,\[[(c/'o \me)][(c/'a\rne)(de_v/'a \ca)]]/\}\.*' gives the TT shown in Figure 6.

Practical Implementation of PBM

The described models have been implemented in the computer to assess thoir perceptual validity. Any Spanish text (in a computer file or manually entered) is converted into two strings: one phonetical, by means of a set of rules for its alphabetical-phonetical transcription; the other composed of blanks (no event), accents ('), commas (,), full stops (.) and no-commas ($\varnothing$).

These punctuation signs have been taken, either from the text itself (commas, full stops, Spanish graphical accents) or derived from a set of rules on Spanish accent (which can fall on any syllable, as is known). The program, *SETS32* (Sánchez and Becerra 1991), can then concatenate phonetic stretches corresponding to the phonetic string obtained from the text, assigning the whole signal a melody derived from the punctuation string by adding together the tonal contributions of each syntactical level suggested by these punctuation signs, as formalized above.

We have found the absolute and relative degrees of falling and rising curves –straights in our case– very important. Our choices have been: ** -7 semitones (a *fifth*, 3:2 ratio) between beginning and end of sentence falling curve (compensated with +7 semitones from the sentence end till the beginning of the next one). ** +7 semitones between the theme-rheme comma peak and the extremes (theme beginning and rheme end). ** +3 semitones in the accent peak of a SW.

Let us see some melodic contours assigned to the sentence used above: *'La mamá de Manolo no sabía sumar'.* They depend on the particular syntactic structure of the sentence(s), which in turn has been derived from the punctuation signs embedded in the text. Two cases are shown in Figures 7 and 8: one sentence without theme-rheme; and a two-sentence utterance, the first with a theme-rheme and the second without (full stop after *'no'*).

Generalisations of SIM and PBM

Pitch contour simplifications

Straight segments have been selected to join low and high points in intonation curves due to the simplicity of conception and computation. But naturally other curves can be selected, probably with a closer approximation to the natural intonation. The main improvements that we foresee are an initial rise in the onset of the sentence curve, and an additional segment in the SW curve for those with 3 or more syllables (eg. : ' \ / \ '), which improves the naturalness by emphasizing the accent place.

Other prosodic traits

In our model, only pitch/tone has been used as the perceptive trait that realizes syntax: indeed it is the most important, and is sufficient to express the finest shades in all the linguistic levels mentioned above. However, other features also contribute to the naturalness, and therefore to the effectiveness, of the pitch melody.

The main additional trait is quantity, which is useful in (at least) two ways. The first is the trait itself used as marker or emphasizer: any speech segment becomes prominent when lengthened. For example, accents improve their perceptibility. The second function of quantity is related to pitch: complex movements need time to be produced and perceived. For instance, neighbouring pitch phenomena such as stress and full stop only complete their realisation by allowing vowel pitch rise and fall according to the prosodic circumstances. Let us take the pair of sentences ' No! Stop!'. At least three stages can be found for each vowel: rise to the accent peak, accent, fall from the accent and/sentence, as the diagram in Figure 9 shows. Pauses, as well as useful separators, are in a way similar to quantity: as void intervals, they take their attributes from the previous events, thus prolonging them.

Intensity enhances syntactical and phonetic situations, as in the accent – stress. This trait is concomitant with pitch, and therefore, the sentence begins with more energy than at the end (indeed, vowels at the end of a final sentence are often unvoiced, as a result of this gradual fading).

Timbre can also be used in accents, making their peak vowels clearer (that is, more distinct from the neutral vowel, *schwa*) than the unaccented.

Multi-level below the sentence's

The simple three-level structure described previously can be generalized to several syntactic levels, always between the extremes, S and SW. Each new level will be suggested by an additional comma, which will mark both the peak intonation and the boundary between a new theme-rheme construction. These new levels complicate the sentence by offering many possibilities for their relative positions. Indeed each comma must be ascribed to one of the levels, the number of different organizations growing geometrically with the number of levels: the maximum number of syntactical structures is the number of permutations of the indices that ascribe each comma to a particular level, Pn = n !, which gives the pairs (n, Pn): (1,1); (2,3); (3,6), (4,24).

To actually find one of these structures, one must choose the comma with the highest level (below the sentence's); afterwards one of the remaining commas in each half must be chosen as the highest, and so on in each new division, until all have been ascribed an order. For this purpose a simple extended punctuation can be used, by repeating the usual sign as many times as its level order. A text such as *'Mi mamá, alegremente, gastaba mucho. La mamá de Manolo, no, sabía sumar.'* /'My mamma, wildly, spent a lot. Manolo's mamma, no, she knew how to add up.' could thus be punctuated as '.. *Mi mamá, alegremente,, gastaba mucho. La mamá de Manolo, no,, sabía sumar..'* where two levels of commas and full stops have been used, showing a richer syntactic content than that of normal punctuation.

The implementation of these structures in our SIM will use any previous parsing information on the sentence. But, in the absence of that parsing, one canonical order must be selected in our alternative PBM: our choice has been to consider the last as the highest in the hierarchy, in the whole sentence and in each of its parts as well. This technique will consider the last portion (text between the last comma and the final full stop) as the rheme of the whole sentence, RH0; the penultimate as the rheme, RH1, of the first theme, TH0, and so on. Correlatively, the first portion will be the first theme RHn of the lower division. Thus, we rediscover a punctuation-based syntactical tree.

Multi-sentence level

A higher level than sentence seems to be necessary. The speech equivalent to the written paragraph uses at least two intactical full stops: the intermediate and the final, which are differentiated by using a stronger fall for the last one (with an optional pause). This intactical paragraph is intoned in our model with an additional falling curve (straight in our implementation) that covers all the spoken paragraph. Of course, the longer the paragraph, the slighter the fall (otherwise several octaves would be necessary), and the more perceptually difficult it is to grasp this slight fall. But the situation is equally difficult to decode in human speech.

Multi-mood

In the preceding paragraphs, only declarative sentences, coupled with falling pitch contours, were considered. But well-known pitch curves for different moods (questions, imperatives,...) can be used instead, substituting the appropriate contour, while maintaining the rest of the contributions unaltered, according to our layer concept. Some problems, however are expected to arise. One of them is the placing of the turning points of these more complex curves. The easy straight fall of the asseverative sentence becomes bent for other moods, and their turning points have to be placed into the temporal scope of the sentence, which could require a syllabic analysis of the utterance, a task avoided so far in our unextended SIM and PBM.

Multi-lingual

Despite the fact that our SIM has been developped for Castilian Spanish, we believe its validity to expand over other Peninsular languages (Catalan, Basque, Gallician) and others in our linguistic and cultural vicinity. Indeed, sentence gradual falling, peaked accents and theme tonal emphasis are constant in these languages, as can easily be perceived by the ear or measured with electronic and/or mechanical devices. Therefore our SIM could be applied to those languages as well, after some language-dependent adjustments –such as the degrees of falls and rises for each level, canonical form for each contour, and so on.

Another task should be to adapt the freer Spanish order, which we mentioned in the Word Order paragraphs, to other more restrictive languages, such as English.

Multi-punctuation

So far, only commas, no-commas and full stops have been used. Indeed they are the fundamental signs, which represent, despite their ambiguity, the main grammatical structural units. Other punctuation signs however can easily be added to our models, SIM and PBM: first, the mood signs (see 4.5) and functions (in pairs for Spanish): '¿ ?', '¡ !'. After the pairs '()' and '– –', parentheses and inserted clauses, are marked by a change of pitch register. No less important are the colon (:) with a surprising almost equal intonation to that of the full stop, and the semicolon, with an imprecise status close to a light full stop. For the latter we can count up to three conclusive signs: final and intermediate full stops and semicolons. For intonation of these signs, see (Sánchez 1996). We have already seen the use of multiple comma and full stop, in the Multi-level... paragraph.

Multi-pragmatical

Pragmatics, even when mood has been excluded, is so rich and unexpected that no attempt has been made so far in this study to include its contribution. We do not know even if this contribution can be considered as a layer to be added to the others (as a cover or coat) as we did with the syntactical layers. Immediate work is being carried out into this interesting area, which lacks delimitation in its scope, description and typification of its intonational behaviours, and classifications of its functions.

Conclusions

A syntactical model for intonation, *SIM,* has been described, showing how each syntactical level adds its own contribution to global intonation. Although intonation is a wide subject, a practical model of SIM, *PBM*, has been applied with satisfactory results: our listeners have understood correctly the different meanings of each syntactical tree attributed to the same text (word + punctuation).

The main concept of SIM is the *Layer*, a pitch (F0) function that covers all the speech segment corresponding to the text included in the syntactical division. SIM constitutes a (syntactically) global approach to sentence intonation, which, despite its difficulties (some of them mentioned above) we consider successful. It provides useful results, such as an improved theoretical knowledge of intonation and syntax –*Intaxis*–, some interesting applications in Foreign Language Learning, in Actors' training, and a tool in Automatic Speech Synthesis.

Figures

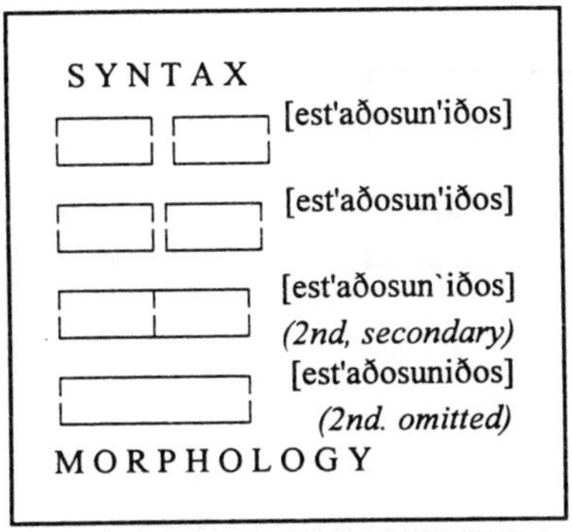

Figure 1. From syntax to morphology

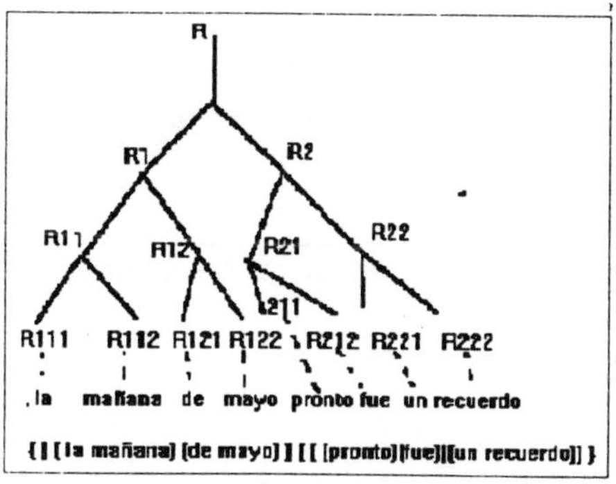

Figure 2. 'La mañana de mayo pronto fue un recuerdo' / 'That May morning was soon a memory'. *The sentence is SWO.*

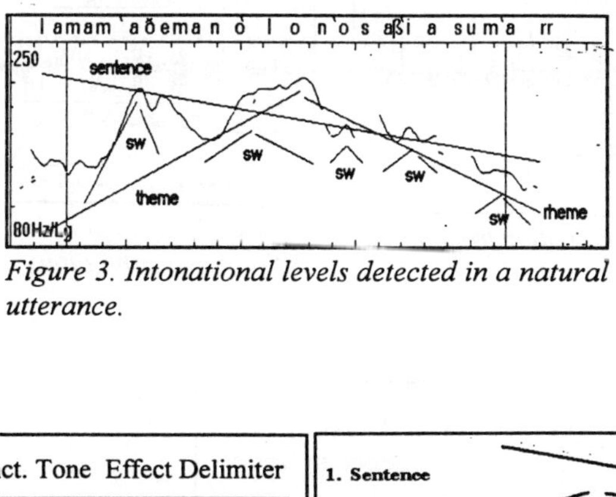

Figure 3. Intonational levels detected in a natural utterance.

Synt.Unit	Punct.	Tone	Effect	Delimiter
Sentence:	.	\	Fall	{}
Theme-Rheme:	,	/\	Rise-Fall	[ ]
Syntag.Word:	°	/\	Rise-Fall	( )

Figure 4. Intonational levels detected in a natural utterance.

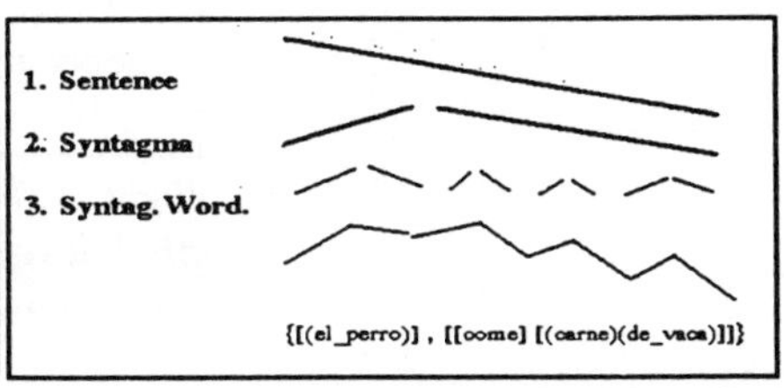

Figure 5. Intonational units added up to find the pitch line.

Figures

```
 El perro come carne de vaca.
.    '     o '   o '    o    '  .
S    A     S A   S A    S    A  S
```

Figure 6. Tonal text of a sentence.

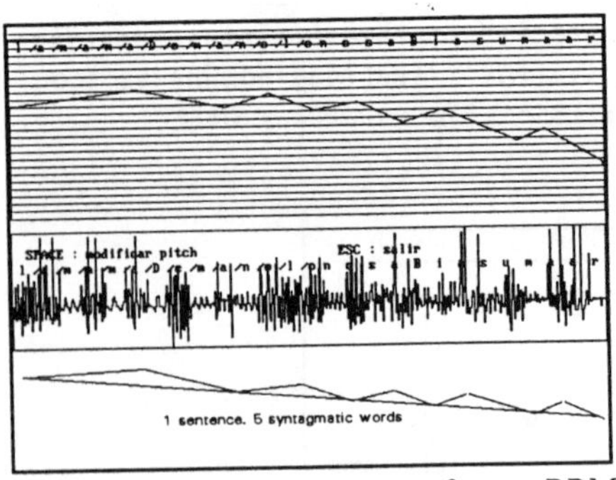

Figure 7. Synthetic intonation from a PBM of a simple sentence.

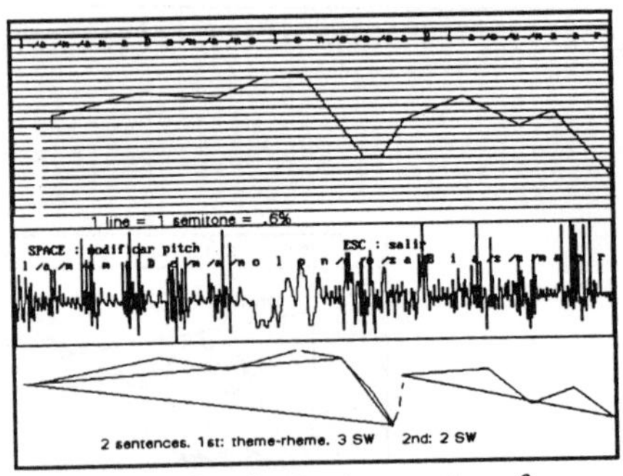

Figure 8. Synthetic intonation from a PBM of two contiguous sentences.

```
  /'\\  /'\\
 nooo.stooop
```

Figure 9. Multiple pitch levels on a single vowel

References

Alarcos Llorach, E. 1971. *Fonología Española.* Madrid: Gredos.

Alcaraz Varó, E. 1990. *Tres Paradigmas de la Investigación Lingüística.* Alcoy: Marfil.

Bergé, H. and Sánchez, F.J. 1995. "Percepción tonal consciente e inconsciente en el habla". In *Actas Congreso AESLA 95* Castellón: Aesla.

Bolinger, D. (ed). 1972. *Intonation.* London: Penguin.

Buhler, K. 1985. *Teoría del Lenguaje.* Madrid: Alianza.

Bustos, E. 1986. *Pragmática del Español.* Madrid: UNED.

Crystal, D. 1975. *The English tone of Voice.* London: Arnold.

Downing, A. and Locke, Ph. 1992. *A University Course in English Grammar.* London: Prentice Hall.

Fernández Ramírez, S. 1986. *Gramática Española 2. Los sonidos* in Polo, J. (ed). Madrid: Arco.

Firbas, J. 1992. *Functional Sentence Perspective in Written and Spoken Communication.* Cambridge: Cambridge University Press: 80.

García Calvo, A. 1979. *Del Lenguaje.* Madrid: Lucina.

García Calvo, A. 1983. *De la Construcción (Del Lenguaje II).* Madrid: Lucina.

Halliday, M.A.K. 1988. *An Introduction to Functional Grammar.* London: Arnold.

Kaisse, E.M. 1985. *Connected Speech. The Interaction of Syntax and Phonology.* Orlando, Fl: Academic Press.

Laver, J. 1994. *Principles of Phonetics.* Cambridge: Cambridge University Press.

Liberman, M. 1975. *The intonational system of English.* Ph.D. Thesis. M.I.T. (distributed by Indiana Linguistic Club).

Lyons, J. 1982. *Language and Linguistics.* Cambridge: Cambridge University Press.

Navarro Tomás, T. 1974. *Manual de Entonación Española.* Madrid: Guadarrama.

O'Connor, J.D. 1973. *Phonetics.* Harmonsdworth: Penguin.

Pierrehumbert, J. 1981. "Synthesizing intonation". Journal of the Acoustical Society of America. 70(4). Oct.

Quilis, A. 1981. *Fonética Acústica de la Lengua Española.* Madrid: Gredos.

Roelof de Pijper, J. 1983. *Modelling British Intonation.* Dordrecht: Foris / Cinnaminson.

Sánchez, F. J. 1977. "Application of Dissimilarity and Aperiodicity Functions to Pitch Extraction and Voiced- Unvoiced Decision". Proceedings 9th International Congress of Acoustics, Madrid: ICA.

Sánchez, F.J. 1979. *Tratamiento de Señales Pseudoperiódicas.* Ph.D. Thesis Universidad Politécnica de Madrid: Escuela Técnica Superior de Ingenieros Industriales.

Sánchez, F.J. 1995. "Teoría preliminar de la sílaba". In Martín Vide, C. (ed). *Lenguajes Naturales y Lenguajes Formales, XI.* Barcelona: Promociones y Publicaciones Universitarias: 569-578.

Sánchez, F.J. 1996. "En busca de una interválica musical subyacente en la palabra". In Martín Vide, C. (ed). *Lenguajes Naturales y Lenguajes Formales XII.* . Barcelona: Promociones y Publicaciones Universitarias: 539-546.

Sánchez, F.J. and Becerra, N. 1991. "Síntesis de habla por concatenación alofónica" *Memoria Interna.* Madrid: Laboratorio Tratamiento de Palabra y Música, IEC-C.S.I.C.: 2-88.

Sánchez, F.J. and Bergé, H. 1993. "Hacia una implementación computacional de una Semántica Multicontextual". In Martín Vide, C. (ed). *Lenguajes Naturales y Lenguajes Formales, IX.* Barcelona: Promociones y Publicaciones Universitarias.

Sánchez, F.J. and Puyâ, M. 1996. "Human and machinal recitation model for accentual (Spanish) and quantitative (Persian) metrics". *Proceedings of the International Conference and Exhibition of Multi-lingual Computing, 1996.* Cambridge: Cambridge University Press: 8.1.1-8.1.10.

Selkirk, E. 1984. *Phonology and Syntax: The Relation between Sound and Structure.*Cambridge, Mass.: MIT Press.

Vaissière, J. 1974. "Fréquence fondamentale des phrases déclaratives en français ". *5émes Journées d'Etude.* Orsay: Groupe Communication Parlée: 58.

An Information-Based Treatment of Punctuation in Discourse Representation Theory

Bilge Say
Varol Akman

Bilkent University

Abstract

Punctuation has so far attracted attention within the linguistics community mostly from a syntactic perspective. In this paper, we give a preliminary account of the information-based aspects of punctuation, drawing our points from assorted, naturally-occurring sentences. We present our formal models of these sentences and the semantic contributions of punctuation marks. Our formalism is a simplified analogue of an extension—due to Nicholas Asher —of Discourse Representation Theory.

Introduction

Punctuation marks have not been studied much by linguists apart from the prescriptive angle, until recently. Similarly, most Natural Language Processing (NLP) systems do not take punctuation marks into account (except for the period and the spacing). Some linguistic works have attempted to produce systematic characterizations of punctuation marks descriptively. Levinson (Levinson 1985) emphasizes the distinction between the orthographic sentence and the grammatical one, and also explains how punctuation marks bind entities according to their informational links. Meyer (Meyer 1987) gives a classification of punctuation marks (in American usage) according to their functions and studies the realization of these functions. Nunberg (Nunberg 1990) shows how punctuation is a linguistic system on its own and devises a "text-grammar" for this purpose, using mechanisms of lexical grammars.

Based on Nunberg's seminal work, several researchers have tried to integrate punctuation marks into their NLP systems, frequently using a syntactic point of departure (Briscoe 1996; Jones 1997; White 1995) . Osborne (Osborne 1996) has shown the improvement—in a combined model-based and data-driven grammar learning approach—obtained as a result of using knowledge of punctuation to enhance the grammar, although his assumption of punctuation marks of all kinds attaching to maximal projection phrases is too strong. Kettunen (Kettunen 1996) has underlined the need for syntactic and semantic contexts in high-level "typographical spell checking" in his somewhat prescriptive study.

The overall, long-term goal of our research in punctuation is to contribute toward the construction of a systematic and principled theory of punctuation and human information processing vis-à-vis punctuation marks. More specifically, we want to add to the existing useful works a formal characterization—formulated in a contemporary semantic theory (Kamp and Reyle 1993) —of the information that punctuation contributes to the discourse, semantically and pragmatically, within or above the grammatical sentence level.[1]

Punctuation and discourse representation theory

Punctuation marks play various roles in natural language texts. They can have a morphological role such as in *anti-feminist*, a delimiting role such as in *Jones, my brother, came yesterday*, or a separating role such as in *two bottles of wine, three cans of beer*. They can also have distinguishing roles such as usage of capital letters for proper names. These roles sometimes

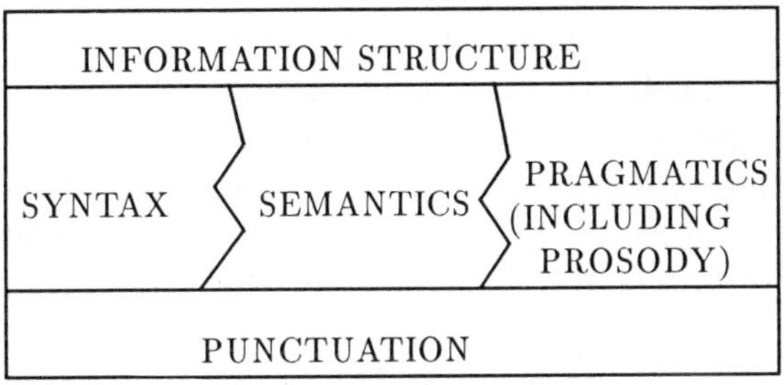

Figure 1: *Effects of punctuation to information structure*

serve to resolve ambiguities, e.g., *new, regular time for Tai-Chi classes* versus *new regular time for Tai-Chi classes.* If our intended meaning is to announce classes with a fixed schedule, the second description would be ambiguous. As in the last example, some of the roles of punctuation may have semantic roots. Our claim is that punctuation may even change the analysis of discourse. In fact, various punctuation marks operate above the sentence level, connecting independent clauses that can function as stand-alone sentences. In addition, these connections can deliver special effects such as "elaboration" (Mann and Thompson 1987) .

Vallduví's (Vallduví 1992) treatment of *information packaging* may be used to explain, in a rather abstract sense, various effects of punctuation marks (cf. Figure 1). By information packaging, he means the non-truth-conditional meaning of a sentence and how the latter is brought about. Information is defined as the propositional content which constitutes a contribution of knowledge to a reader's knowledge store. Vallduví gives the following simple example (Vallduví 1992, 2):

(1a) He hates broccoli.

(1b) Broccoli he hates.

Sentences (1a) and (1b) are clearly truth-conditionally equivalent but they say what they claim about *he* (a particular male) in different ways. Vallduví devises a scheme that could account for such differences in information packaging. He cautions that the way information packaging is realized linguistically (i.e., by means of intonation, syntax, or morphology) may differ from language to language. Following a common trend in the punctuation research community, we concentrate on the structural punctuation marks and take the combined effects of syntactic, semantic, and (to a certain extent) pragmatic uses in order to explain the value punctuation marks add to the information structure of a sentence. By *structural*, we mean those marks that act on units not larger than the orthographic sentence (thus no paragraphs) and not smaller than the word (thus no hyphens or apostrophes).[2]

While Vallduví's framework is very instructive, a more suitable and precisely defined medium to realize our goal is the *Discourse Representation Theory* (DRT) (Kamp and Reyle 1993) . This is a formal proposal to integrate the current approaches to discourse in a fully-fledged semantic theory. The aim of DRT has been stated as providing a systematic specification of the truth conditions of a given multi-sentential discourse (or text). To be able to do this, representational devices called *Discourse Representation Structures* (DRSs) are incrementally built while the discourse is interpreted in a top-down fashion.

As a somewhat superficial example of the "discourse effects" of punctuation, consider

(2a) Jane, and Joe and Sue write books on England. If her books are best-sellers then they are going to be jealous.

(2b) Jane and Joe, and Sue write books on England. If her books are best-sellers then they are going to be jealous.

In both fragments, the exact position of the comma alone controls the proper resolution of pronominal anaphora. Suitable "triggering configurations" (Kamp and Reyle 1993) will lead to different structures within DRT: in (2a) we have *her* attached to Jane and *they* to Joe and Sue, whereas in (2b) we have *her* attached to Sue and *they* to Jane and Joe. This difference can be handled with plain DRSs—enriched with temporal and aspectual information, when necessary—as shown in Figure 2.

As for the effects of restrictive and nonrestrictive clauses, example (3a) below implies that Sam has a cat that once belonged to Fred whereas (3b) implies that Sam has a cat but there is no information as to whether it once belonged to Fred (both sentences taken from (McCawley 1981, 103)). This semantic distinction can be dealt with straightforwardly with plain DRSs (cf. Figure 3).[3]

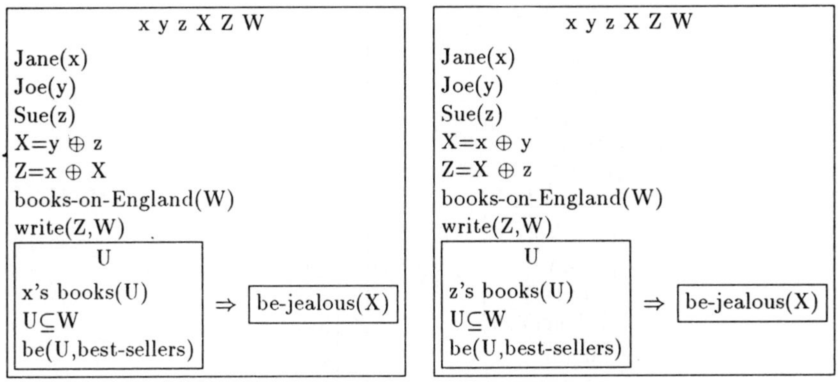

Figure 2: *DRSs for (2a) and (2b), respectively*

(3a) Tom has two cats that once belonged to Fred, and Sam has one.

(3b) Tom has two cats, which once belonged to Fred, and Sam has one.

Asher's extension and its adaptation to modeling punctuation

The simple examples in the preceding section give a taste of DRT capturing some semantic effects of punctuation. Still, more involved requirements for modeling punctuation effects are not readily expressible in standard DRT, and we have to define additional constructs. Several such constructs are provided by Asher (Asher 1993) within another theory he develops for analyzing abstract entity anaphora in discourse. According to Asher, the structure and the segmentation of discourse may help to determine the antecedents of abstract anaphoric references. To see an example of what is meant by "abstract," consider the following paragraph (excerpted from (Asher 1993, 346)):

(4) The Ashers were predictably short of groceries the day of the party. Nicholas Asher went out to get some, got lost and arrived back only after the party had ended. Because of this, the committee made sure that the Ashers never gave a party for the Society again.

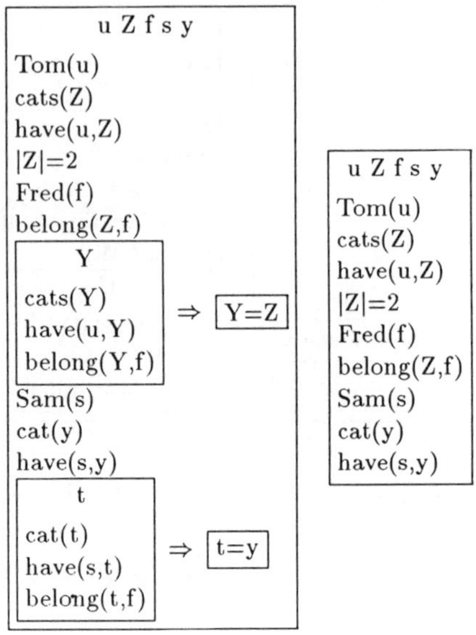

Figure 3: *DRSs for (3a) and (3b), respectively*

Here, *this* anaphorically picks up a certain sum of events. Just which events are available for anaphoric reference is a result of the discourse structure. The basic entities at this stage are called the *Segmented* DRSs (SDRSs) . They are imposed on the logical structure created by the DRSs by associating the DRSs with discourse relations, which act as conditions for SDRSs. Asher takes, by default, each basic constituent of an SDRS to correspond to a sentence ended by a full-stop; this can clearly be overridden by clauses or longer stretches of text where required. When the SDRS structure is updated, the constituents are revised for possible anaphora resolution, and the truth condition changes. An important rule is that the coherence of the discourse must be maintained as new constituents are attached.

Asher uses a subset of relations from the *Rhetorical Structure Theory* (RST) (Mann and Thompson 1987) and some other discourse structure theories for his purposes. He divides the relations he uses in his theory of SDRSs into two (viz. rhetorical and coherence relations) according to how they relate sentences and contribute to the truth conditions. More importantly (at least for our aims), he also classifies the relations according to whether they affect the hierarchical structure of the text. *Summary* and *topic* are examples of such structural relations that dominate other constituents. Also important are the relations *parallel* and *contrast*, which involve pairing structurally similar objects according to whether they are semantically similar or dissimilar, respectively.

Asher's theory of SDRSs has been very influential on our work. In a way, we had to incorporate intra-sentential punctuation phenomena to his theory. (His theory obviously deals with inter-sentential discourse phenomena.) While the exact definitions of the relations used in our punctuation-oriented study may be found in (Say 1995), the following illustrative examples may offer a glimpse of this study.

In example (5) (taken from (Meyer 1986, 81)), the sentence-final dash indicates a *result* of the previously accumulated eventualities and does not directly represent a parenthetical occurrence. The state expressed after the dash follows from the subsentences before it. The resulting SDRS is given in Figure 4.[4]

(5) She had cried, she had implored, she had been miserable at this refusal, and finally he had relented—and now how happy she was, how expectant!

In contrast to the previous sentence, example (6) below (adapted from (Ehrlich 1992, 80)) also has a sentence-final dash which does indicate a parenthetical. As a solution to this under-determination problem, we may need to resort to heuristics, founded on corpus analysis of punctuation mark usage, because rules alone do not suffice to determine the effect of the dash. The relevant SDRS for (6) is also depicted in Figure 4.

(6) Now, I tell you the entire story—but first you have another cup of coffee.

In examples (7) (taken from (Meyer 1986, 83)) and (8) (taken from (Ehrlich 1992, 81)), the parenthetical remarks clarify the parts of a plural discourse referent (*a variety of environmental supports* and *the problem*, respectively). These remarks are important for the discourse when such a clarification is sought by the reader. The relevant SDRSs are shown in Figures 5 and 6, respectively.

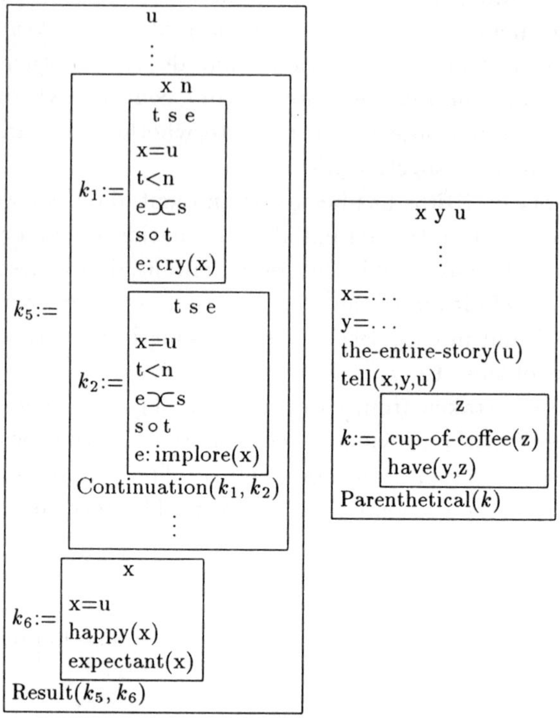

Figure 4: *SDRSs for (5) and (6) [some details omitted]*

(7) Simultaneously, a variety of environmental supports—a calm but not too motherly homemaker, referral for temporary economic aid, intelligent use of nursing care, accompaniment to the well-baby clinic for medical advice on the twin's feeding problem—combined to prevent further development of predictable pathological mechanisms.

(8) The problems—unemployment and inflation—perplex economists and mystify the public.

In example (9) (taken from (Dawkins 1995, 537)), the comma coincides with an intonation group boundary to indicate focus. We understand that John has been unable to go to school for a year; therefore *today* is a special

X y t n e
a-variety-of-environmental-supports(X)

k:= [Y u r v z
calm-but-not-too-motherly-homemaker(u)
referral-for-temporary-economic-aid(r)
intelligent-use-of-nursing-care(v)
accompaniment-to-the-clinic(z)
$Y=u \oplus r \oplus v \oplus z$
$X=Y$]

Parenthetical(k)
$t<n$
$e \subseteq t$
further-development-of-predictable-pathological-mechanisms(y)
e: combine-to-prevent(X,y)

Figure 5: *SDRS for (7)*

day. Neither a plain DRS nor an SDRS can show such an information structure: we simply have to introduce a new construct. The *focus* relation can be used to this end, as Figure 7 illustrates.

(9) Today, John went to school. He had been hospitalized for a year.

We can now consider semantically contributing instances of semicolons and colons. In example (10) (taken from (Quirk et al. 1972, 1065)), there is a *contrast* between the first text-clause and the second text-clause. It is clear that we run into the problem of under-determination once again. The proposed SDRS is displayed in Figure 7, where the sign $\sum$ is employed as a means to build the sets of leaders (*those who lead*) and followers (*those who follow*).

(10) Those who lead must be considerate; those who follow must be responsive.

In example (11a) (taken from (Quirk et al. 1972, 1068)), a text-phrase constitutes a DRS of its own and serves as an *explanation*. Apart from this, both (11a) and (11b) (also taken from (Quirk et al. 1972, 1068)) can be straightforwardly processed in our given framework. The relevant SDRSs would be as shown in Figure 8.

X Y W	
problems(X)	
k:=	x y Z unemployment(x) inflation(y) Z=x⊕y X=Z
Parenthetical(k)	
economists(Y)	
perplex(X,Y)	
the-public(W)	
mystify(X,W)	

Figure 6: *SDRS for (8)*

(11a) There remained one thing he desired above all else: a country cottage.

(11b) In one respect, government policy has been firmly decided; there will be no conscription.

Finally, the reader is invited to consider (12) (taken from (Levinson 1985, 134))

(12a) Margaret and Gregory met in 1932, falling in love in a fever of conversation and theory-building on the shores of Sepik River in New Guinea, where Margaret had come to work with Reo Fortune, her second husband.

(12b) Margaret and Gregory met in 1932, falling in love in a fever of conversation and theory-building on the shores of Sepik River in New Guinea. Margaret had come there to work with Reo Fortune, her second husband.

(12c) Margaret and Gregory met in 1932, falling in love in a fever of conversation and theory-building on the shores of Sepik River in New Guinea; Margaret had come there to work with Reo Fortune, her second husband.

In (12a), there is considerable irony which is taken out in (12b), and restored to some degree in (12c). Paragraphs (12b) and (12c) have different

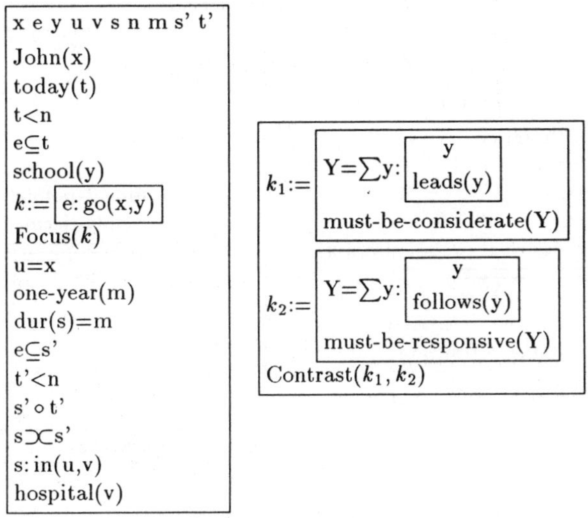

Figure 7: *SDRSs for (9) and (10)*

interpretations, which are construed in the SDRSs in Figure 9.

Conclusion

Information cues provided by punctuation marks should be valuable to NLP systems if captured carefully and adequately. Our ongoing work is directed towards classifying the (especially semantic) uses of punctuation with respect to various available resources such as the Wall Street Journal (ACL/DCI 1991) and the SUSANNE corpus (Sampson 1995). At the same time, keeping the interactions with syntax in mind, a system of semantic rules that takes into account the characterization of punctuation marks is being written, extending earlier works by Briscoe (Briscoe 1994) and Lee (Lee 1995). Alvey Natural Language Tools Grammar (Grover et al. 1993), a GPSG- style unification grammar with an event-based and unscoped compositional semantics expressed in λ-calculus, is being used in this endeavor. A computational framework for extracting the informational cues from actual punctuation practice is planned to be the concrete outcome of this

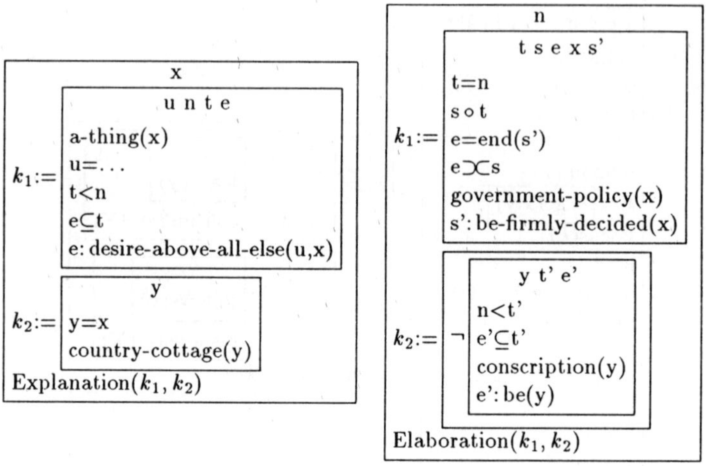

Figure 8: *SDRSs for (11a) and (11b)*

work.

Acknowledgments

The first author is grateful to the Scientific and Technical Research Council of Turkey (program code: BAYG/NATO-A2) for financial aid, and Dr. Ted Briscoe for his willingness to accommodate her during a visit in Fall '96 to the Computer Lab., Cambridge University, Cambridge, UK. Finally, our heartfelt thanks to Dr. Carlos Martín-Vide for moral support.

Notes

1. The reader is referred to (Say 1995) for a detailed review of punctuation. Other recent papers of our group which may also be useful include (Bayraktar et al. 1996; Say and Akman 1996b; Say and Akman 1996a) .
2. This definition is borrowed from Meyer (Meyer 1986, 80).
3. For a detailed analysis of the role of comma in various types of coordinate compounds, the reader is referred to (Min 1996). A corpus-based study of the semantic functions of comma is reported in (Bayraktar et al. 1996).

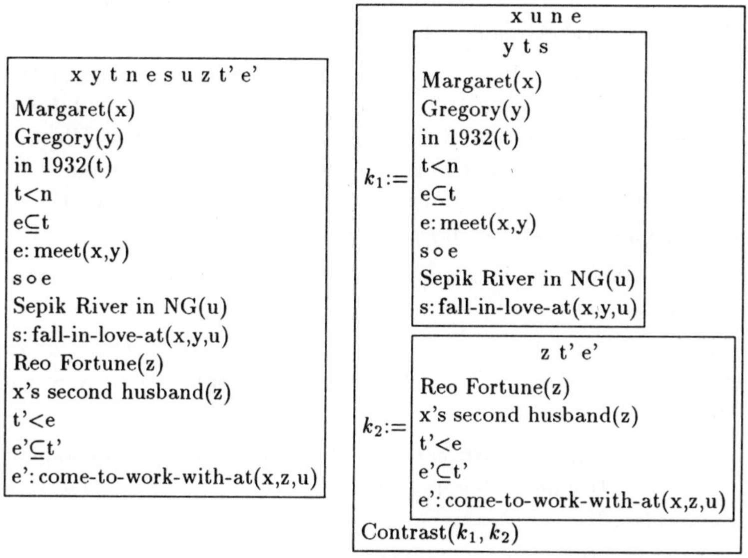

Figure 9: *DRS and SDRS for (12b) and (12c)*

4. In this figure and the others in the sequel, the reader may ignore the special symbols appearing in the DRS boxes, when their meaning is not obvious from the context. Thus, only a general understanding of the inner details of the SDRSs is required.

References

ACL/DCI. 1991. Association for Computational Linguistics Data Collection Initiative, CD-ROM 1. Information available from Linguistic Data Consortium on the WWW: http://www.ldc.upenn.edu

Asher, N. 1993. *Reference to Abstract Objects in Discourse.* Dordrecht, Netherlands: Kluwer Academic Publishers.

Bayraktar, M., Akman, V. and Say, B. 1996. "Analysis of English punctuation: the special case of comma". Manuscript, Dept. of Computer Engineering and Information Science, Bilkent University, Ankara, Turkey. Submitted for publication.

Briscoe, T. 1994. "Parsing (with) punctuation". Technical report, Rank Xerox Research Centre, Grenoble, France.

Briscoe, T. 1996. "The syntax and semantics of punctuation and its use in interpretation". In *Punctuation in Computational Linguistics*, UCSC, Santa Cruz, CA. SIGPARSE 1996 (Post Conference Workshop of ACL96), 1–8. Available from Human Communication Research Center (University of Edinburgh) on the WWW: http://www.cogsci.ed.ac.uk/hcrc/publications/wp-2.html.

Dawkins, J. 1995. "Teaching punctuation as a rhetorical tool". *College Composition and Communication* 46(4): 533–548.

Ehrlich, E.H. 1992. *Schaum's Outline of Theory and Problems of Punctuation, Capitalization, and Spelling*. Schaum's Outline Series. New York, NY: McGraw-Hill Book Co.

Grover, C., Carroll, J. and Briscoe, T. 1993. "The Alvey natural language tools grammar". Technical Report 284, Computer Lab., Cambridge University, Cambridge, UK.

Jones, B. 1997. "What's the point? A (computational) theory of punctuation". Ph.D. thesis, Centre for Cognitive Science, University of Edinburgh, Edinburgh, UK.

Kamp, H. and Reyle, U. 1993. *From Discourse to Logic: Introduction to Modeltheoretic Semantics of Natural Language, Formal Logic and Discourse Representation Theory.* Dordrecht, Netherlands: Kluwer Academic Publishers.

Kettunen, K. 1996. "Low-level typographical spell checking: a proposal". *Computers and the Humanities* 30(1): 77–84.

Lee, S. 1995. "A syntax and semantics for text grammar". Master's thesis, Engineering Dept., Cambridge University, Cambridge, UK.

Levinson, J.P. 1985. "Punctuation and the orthographic sentence: a linguistic analysis". Ph.D. thesis, City University of New York, New York, NY.

Mann, W.C. and Thompson, S.A. 1987. "Rhetorical structure theory: a theory of text organization". Technical Report RS-87-190, USC Information Sciences Institute, Marina Del Rey, CA.

McCawley, J.D. 1981. "The syntax and semantics of English relative clauses". *Lingua* 53: 99–149.

Meyer, Ch.F. 1986. "Punctuation practice in the Brown corpus". *ICAME Newsletter*, 80–95.

Meyer, Ch.F. 1987. *A Linguistic Study of American Punctuation.* New York, NY: Peter Lang Publishing Co.

Min, Y.G. 1996. "Role of punctuation in disambiguation of coordinate compounds". In *Punctuation in Computational Linguistics*, UCSC, Santa Cruz, CA. SIGPARSE 1996 (Post Conference Workshop of ACL96), 33–40. Available from Human Communication Research Center (University of Edinburgh) on the WWW:
http://www.cogsci.ed.ac.uk/hcrc/publications/wp-2.html.

Nunberg, G. 1990. *The Linguistics of Punctuation.* Number 18 in CSLI Lecture Notes. Center for the Study of Language and Information, Stanford, CA: CSLI Publications.

Osborne, M. 1996. "Can punctuation help learning?". In S. Wermter, E. Riloff, and G. Scheler (eds), *Connectionist, Statistical, and Symbolic Approaches to Learning for Natural Language Processing*, Lecture Notes in Artificial Intelligence, Number 1040. Berlin: Springer-Verlag, 399–412.

Quirk, R., Greenbaum, S., Leech, G., and Svartvik, J. 1972. *A Grammar of Contemporary English.* Harlow, Essex, UK: Longman.

Sampson, G. 1995. *English for the Computer: The SUSANNE Corpus and Analytic Scheme.* Oxford, UK: Oxford University Press.

Say, B. 1995. "An information-based approach to punctuation". Doctoral Proposal, Dept. of Computer Engineering and Information Science, Bilkent University, Ankara, Turkey. Available on the WWW: http://www.cs.bilkent.edu.tr/~say/bilge.html.

Say, B. and Akman, V. 1996a. "Current approaches to punctuation in computational linguistics". Manuscript, Dept. of Computer Engineering and Information Science, Bilkent University, Ankara, Turkey. Submitted for publication.

Say, B. and Akman, V. 1996b. "Information-based aspects of punctuation". In *Punctuation in Computational Linguistics*, UCSC, Santa Cruz, CA. SIGPARSE 1996 (Post Conference Workshop of ACL96), 49–56. Available from Human Communication Research Center (University of Edinburgh) on the WWW: http://www.cogsci.ed.ac.uk/hcrc/publications/wp-2.html.

Vallduví, E. 1992. *The Informational Component.* New York, NY: Garland Publishing.

White, M. 1995. "Presenting punctuation". In *Proceedings of the Fifth European Workshop on Natural Language Generation*, Leiden, The Netherlands, 107–125.

Author Index

(Boldface numbers send to bibliographical references)

Subject Index

In the series LINGUISTIC AND LITERARY STUDIES IN EASTERN EUROPE the following volumes have been published. As of 1996 the series is continued under the new title STUDIES IN FUNCTIONAL AND STRUCTURAL LINGUISTICS, beginning with volume 43.

1. ODMARK, John (ed.): *LANGUAGE, LITERATURE & MEANING.* I: *Problems of Literary Theory*. Amsterdam, 1979.
2. ibid. II: *Current Trends in Literary Research.* Amsterdam, 1980.
3. BAUR, Rupprecht S., et al.: *RESÜMIERENDE AUSWAHLBIBLIOGRAPHIE ZUR NEUEREN SOWJETISCHEN SPRACHLEHRFORSCHUNG (gesteuerter Fremdsprachenerwerb).* Amsterdam, 1980.
4. KIEFER, Férenc (ed.): *HUNGARIAN GENERAL LINGUISTICS.* Amsterdam, 1982.
5. ZIMA, Peter V. (ed.): *SEMIOTICS AND DIALECTICS: Ideology and the Text.* Amsterdam, 1981.
6. FIZER, John: *Psychologism and Psychoaesthetics: A Historical and Critical View of Their Relations.* Amsterdam, 1981.
7. SMITH, Barry (ed.): *STRUCTURE AND GESTALT: Philosophy and literature in Austria-Hungary and her successor states.* Amsterdam, 1981.
8. STEINER, P., M. ČERVENKA & R. VROON (eds): *THE STRUCTURE OF THE LITERARY PROCESS: Studies dedicated to the Memory of Felix Vodička.* Amsterdam, 1982.
9. *PRAGUE STUDIES IN MATHEMATICAL LINGUISTICS*, vol. 7. Amsterdam, 1981.
10. SCHMID, Herta & Aloysius Van KESTEREN (eds): *SEMIOTICS OF DRAMA AND THEATRE.* Amsterdam, 1985.
11. BOJTÁR, Endre: *SLAVIC STRUCTURALISM IN LITERARY SCIENCE.* Transl. from the Hungarian. Amsterdam, 1985.
12. VACHEK, J. (ed.): *PRAGUIANA: Some Basic and Less Known Aspects of the Prague Linguistic School.* Amsterdam, 1983.
13. MEL'ČUK, Igor A. & Nikolaj V. PERTSOV: *SURFACE SYNTAX OF ENGLISH: a Formal Model within the Meaning-Text Framework.* Amsterdam, 1987.
14. ŠVEJCER, A.D.: *CONTEMPORARY SOCIOLINGUISTICS.* Amsterdam, 1986.
15. ŠVEJCER, A.D. & L.B. NIKOL'SKIJ: *INTRODUCTION TO SOCIOLINGUISTICS.* Amsterdam, 1986.
16. SGALL, Petr (ed.): *CONTRIBUTIONS TO FUNCTIONAL SYNTAX, SEMANTICS, AND LANGUAGE COMPREHENSION.* Amsterdam, 1984.
17. *PRAGUE STUDIES IN MATHEMATICAL LINGUISTICS.* Volume 8. Amsterdam, 1983.
18. SHCHEGLOV, Yu & A. ZHOLKOVSKY: *POETICS OF EXPRESSIVENESS: A Theory and Application.* Amsterdam, 1987.
19. MEY, Jacob (ed.): *LANGUAGE AND DISCOURSE: TEST AND PROTEST. A Festschrift for Petr Sgall.* Amsterdam, 1986.
20. DIRVEN, R. & W. FRIED (eds): *FUNCTIONALISM IN LINGUISTICS.* Amsterdam, 1987.
21. ANDRÁS, Laszlo & Zoltán KOVECSES (comps): *HUNGARIAN-ENGLISH SLANG DICTIONARY.* Taken from the program.

22. *PRAGUE STUDIES IN MATHEMATICAL LINGUISTICS*. Volume 9. Amsterdam, 1987.
23. CHLOUPEK, Jan and Jĭrí NEKVAPIL (eds): *READER IN CZECH SOCIOLINGUISTICS*. Amsterdam, 1987.
24. VOLEK, Bronislava: *EMOTIVE SIGNS IN LANGUAGE AND SEMANTIC FUNCTIONING OF DERIVED NOUNS IN RUSSIAN*. Amsterdam, 1987.
25. BUSZKOWSKI, W., W. MARCISZEWSKI & J. van BENTHEM (eds): *CATEGORIAL GRAMMAR*. Amsterdam/Philadelphia, 1988.
26. RADOVANOVIĆ, Milorad (ed.): *YUGOSLAV GENERAL LINGUISTICS*. Amsterdam/Philadelphia, 1989.
27. TOBIN, Yishai (ed.): *THE PRAGUE SCHOOL AND ITS LEGACY*. Amsterdam/ Philadelphia, 1988.
28. TOMASZCZYK, Jerzy and Barbara LEWANDOWSKA-TOMASZCZYK (eds): *MEANING AND LEXICOGRAPHY*. Amsterdam/Philadelphia, 1990.
29. PETERSON, Ronald E.: *A HISTORY OF RUSSIAN SYMBOLISM*. Amsterdam/Philadelphia. 1993.
30. FISIAK, Jacek (ed.): *FURTHER INSIGHTS INTO CONTRASTIVE ANALYSIS*. Amsterdam/Philadelphia, 1990.
31. RANCOUR-LAFERRIERE, Daniel (ed.): *RUSSIAN LITERATURE AND PSYCHOANALYSIS*. Amsterdam/Philadelphia, 1989.
32. MILOSAVLJEVIC, Petar (ed.): *YUGOSLAV LITERARY-THEORETICAL THOUGHT*. Amsterdam/Philadelphia. n.y.p.
33. WRÓBEL, Janusz: *LANGUAGE AND SCHIZOPHRENIA*. Amsterdam/Philadelphia, 1989.
34. *PRAGUE STUDIES IN MATHEMATICAL LINGUISTICS*. Volume 10. Amsterdam/ Philadelphia, 1990.
35. BONDARKO, Alexander V.: *FUNCTIONAL GRAMMAR. A FIELD APPROACH*. Amsterdam/Philadelphia, 1991.
36. CHLOUPEK, Jan and Jĭrí NEKVAPIL: *STUDIES IN FUNCTIONAL STYLISTICS*. Amsterdam/Philadelphia, 1993.
37. TESITELOVA, Marie: *QUANTITATIVE LINGUISTICS*. Amsterdam/Philadelphia, 1992.
38. FISIAK, Jacek and Stanisław PUPPEL (eds): *PHONOLOGICAL INVESTIGATIONS*. Amsterdam/Philadelphia, 1992.
39. SGALL, Peter, Jĭrí HRONEK, Alexander STICH and Ján HORECKÝ. *VARIATION IN LANGUAGE, Code Switching in Czech as a Challenge for Sociolinguistics*. Amsterdam/Philadelphia, 1992.
40. LUELSDORFF, Philip A. (ed.): *PRAGUIANA 1945-1990*. Amsterdam/Phildelphia. 1994.
41. LUELSDORFF, Philip A. (ed.): *THE PRAGUE SCHOOL OF STRUCTURAL AND FUNCTIONAL LINGUISTICS*. Amsterdam/Philadelphia. 1994.
42. ČMEJRKOVA, Světla and František ŠTÍCHA (eds): *THE SYNTAX OF SENTENCE AND TEXT, A Festschrift for František Daneš*. Amsterdam/Philadelphia. 1994.
43. ANDREWS, Edna and Yishai TOBIN: *TOWARD A CALCULUS OF MEANING. Studies in markedness, distinctive features and deixis*. Amsterdam/Philadelphia. 1996.

44. JESSEN, Michael: *Phonetics and Phonology of Tense and Lax Obstruents in German.* n.y.p.
45. MARTÍN-VIDE, Carlos (ed.): *Mathematical and Computational Analysis of Natural Language. Selected papers from the 2nd International Conference on Mathematical Linguistics (ICML '96), Tarragona, 1996.* 1998.
46. ŠTEKAUER, Pavol: *An Onomasiological Theory of English Word-formation.* n.y.p.